T0298322

Heterodox views on economics and the economy of the global society

Heterodox views on economics and the economy of the global society

edited by:
G. Meijer
W.J.M. Heijman
J.A.C. van Ophem
B.H.J. Verstegen

Mansholt publication series - Volume 1

Wageningen Academic
P u b l i s h e r s

ISBN-10: 90-76998-96-5
ISBN-13: 978-90-76998-96-1

ISSN 1871-9309

First published, 2006

Wageningen Academic Publishers
The Netherlands, 2006

Mansholt Publication Series

The Mansholt Publication Series (MPS) contains peer-reviewed textbooks, conference proceedings and thematic publications focussing on social changes and control processes in rural areas and (agri)food chains, and the institutional contexts in which these changes and processes take place. MPS provides a platform for researchers and educators who would like to increase the quality, status and (international) exposure of their teaching materials or of their research output.

MPS is supported by the Mansholt Graduate School which also appoints the members of the editorial board responsible for the quality and content of the overall series. MPS is published and marketed internationally by Wageningen Academic Publishers.

The Mansholt Publication Series editors are:

Contents

Economic paradigms and theories

Population and society

Corporate issues

Environment

Preface

Gerrit Meijer
ISINI President 2003-2005

It was at the History of Economics Conference in Fairfax (1985) that I first met Anghel Rugina. I presented a paper founded on the third chapter of my dissertation on the History of Neoliberalism in Several Countries (1987a). It turned out that he knew the Freiburg School and in particular Walter Eucken very well. He took his doctor's degree at the University of Freiburg on his thesis *Geldordnungen und Geldtypen* (Monetary Orders and Money Types) in 1949.

Later on he invited me for a conference of the Association of Social Economics in 1986 at Toronto. The paper I presented on History of Neoliberalism: Affinity to some Developments in Economics in Germany, was included in the Festschrift in Honour of Anghel N. Rugina (1987b). This gave a common ground to our friendship in the world of ideas.

In his work there are two important lines of thinking which interested me at that time. First his monetary theory. I paid attention to this in my last mentioned paper. Second it is the idea of *Quinta Methodica* that he defends in the footsteps of Schmoller and Eucken. This idea is at the background of the International Society for Intercommunication of New Ideas (ISINI), that he founded in 1988 in Boston, and of which he was the first president, and is now at the age of 93 the honorary president. *Quinta Methodica* means that economic science has five different, yet interrelated, subdivisions: economic history; economic theory; economic ethics; economic policy and history of economic thought.

In 1987 Rugina visited the Netherlands. First he met Tinbergen in Rotterdam. Then he and his wife Irene (Aurelia) were our guests in Bussum for a few days. From there we brought them to Jaap en Meta Krabbe in Wageningen. Via Freiburg (Hayek), St Gallen (Dopfer) and Paris (Henri Guitton) they travelled back to Boston. After this trip and these consultations Rugina founded ISINI. Tinbergen and Hayek both Noble Laureates in economics became honorary fellows from the beginning, in this way showing their sympathy with the initiative. It shows also the broad concept and vision of ISINI.

Since the foundation global international meetings were held in Paris, France (1990); Athens, Greece (1992); Boston, Mass., U.S.A. (1995); Maastricht, The Netherlands (1997); Mexico City, Mexico (1999); Miami, Florida, U.S.A. (2001); Lille, France (2003), and again in the Netherlands in 2005, this time in Wageningen. This shows that ISINI is steadily moving forwards and that it has answered challenges and taken advantage of opportunities since it was founded.

The purpose of the Society is according to article 2 of the Statutes threefold:

a. To foster and support the discovery and dissemination of new ideas in particular in economics and other social sciences and to arrange for their testing (logical and /or empirical) in the realm of various possible social, economic and political systems, as far as analysis can go.

b. To initiate and cultivate a contact and consultation not only among economists, sociologists and political scientists but also between social and natural scientists including men of arts and letters.

c. To study systematically (using both theoretical and practical reason) the application of new ideas to problems of the real world of today and tomorrow in various existing social regimes and considering the diverse levels of development and historical circumstances.

Also we read in article 5 of the Statutes that the Society has (ideally) seven sections:

Section 1. History and Statistics.

Section 2. Theory, New Concepts, Principles, Interpretations and Explanations (Positive Science).

Section 3. Ethics, What Ought to Be, General Stable Equilibrium (Normative Science).

Section 4. Policy Matters or How to achieve a certain given goal without creating other problems. This Section is for those who have the skill, inclination and background to test both theoretical and practical ideas for consistency and efficiency in terms of the ultimate values of a free, just and stable society. These are what may be called "scientific", tested policies.

Section 5. Doctrines, History of Thought.

Section 6. Arts and Humanities.

Section 7. General supporter of the society in any other way.

The first five sections reflect the *Quinta Methodica.*

The papers presented at the conferences were originally published in the International Journal of New Ideas. A Journal of Interdisciplinary Approaches, that was published during four years (1992-1995). Since the Maastricht-conference (1997) the papers and proceedings of the conferences were published in book- or electronic form. The papers for the Eighth ISINI Conference are all at the website. This website will be a means of communication between us at least until the Ninth ISINI Conference to be held next year in Romania.

This volume contains revised papers that were presented at the Eighth ISINI Conference in Wageningen. It is wholly in the strain of thought of Rugina (and the Statutes and Bylaws formulated by him) that we had two special invited speakers on the institutional and cultural aspects of human society, Backhaus and Klamer respectively. More about these lectures will be written in the Introduction of the Editors to this volume. I am grateful to the Mansholt Graduate School (MGS) for supplying the resources for the keynote speech of Backhaus. His keynote speech is also published as the sixth Mansholt Lecture of the MGS.

In this preface I also think a few words on the future of ISINI can not be omitted. Thinking about this has to start at the background of the original purpose, organisation, and methods how to reach them in the Statutes and Bylaws when ISINI was founded in 1988. At August 23, 1997, at the General Assembly in Maastricht, a motion of Rugina was accepted, which again clearly stated the purpose and vision of ISINI, and for that reason is cited here in full:

'Every professional organisation is striving to have something new, some new ideas or practice in its own field, but the vision of ISINI transcends this usual common purpose. ISINI has a new message. Its very existence finds justification in the motto 'In searching for new ideas, new better concepts, new better theories and new better interpretations of past and/or present ideas'. Of course we are in favour of an open dialogue, not only with other already established directions: mainstream economics, social economics, institutional economics, evolutionary economics, etc., but also in addition with other fields, first the other sisters in social sciences and also with natural sciences. But ultimately, our motto remains as a new message. Its roots are in methodology of science and in analysis. The final dream is a methodological unification of all sciences. Indeed, if economics pretends to be a science than it must have a common denominator - of course retaining and keeping its individual character - with all other sciences, i.e. the rest of our sisters in the fast field of studying human societies of today and other times, together with the study of Mother Nature, i.e. natural sciences. This is the first final dream in analysis: the methodological unification of all sciences. The second final dream, actually an continuation of the first one, namely in practice, in application of methodology of science, is to show consistently and systematically how to realise and to maintain in the real world the great ideal of all nations, of all races, that is of humanity: the dream of a Free, Just and Stable Economy and Society. With this new message ISINI was officially founded in the fall of 1988 and registered as a non-profit institution in Boston, MA, USA.' (Meijer et al., 2000: xiii).

I further refer in this respect to the preface to this volume written by my successor Liviu Drugus. In this contribution to the book he pleas *'for using new ideas and especially transdisciplinary approaches in unifying the too many so called 'sciences'- as a matter of fact narrower and narrower slides of knowledge with the peak when a super-specialist knows all about almost nothing. ISINI is considered as an excellent laboratory of developing research units generating unified science'.*

In this contribution he also mentions that for that purpose he intends to organise sessions that pay special attention to this theme in the conference in Romania in the second half of August, 2007. We are still far away from having achieved its ideals. A lot of work has been done, and there is still much work to do. In this context I refer to the comprehensive work of A. Rugina, especially to his Prolegomena (Rugina, 1998). In this work the fundamental thoughts of the founder of ISINI are explained.

Gerrit Meijer

I wish to express my thanks to all the people who contributed to the conference with papers and by attendance. Moreover I thank the Economics of Consumers and Households Group of Wageningen University for facilities offered in the organisation of the conference.

I am also in debt to those who assisted me during my presidency, the organisation of the conference and the editing of this book. More in particular I have to mention the invaluable support of my daughter drs. Ymkje van 't Riet-Meijer since I became president in 2003.

References

Meijer, G., 1987a. The History of Neo-Liberalism: A General View and Development in Several Countries. Rivista Internazionale di Scienze Economiche e Commerciali 7, 577-591.

Meijer, G., 1987b. The History of Neoliberalism: Affinity to Some Developments in Economics in Germany. Essays in Honour of Anghel Rugina. Part II. International Journal of Social Economics 14, 142-155.

Meijer, G., W.J.M. Heijman, J.A.C. Van Ophem and B.H.J. Verstegen (eds.), 2000. The Maastricht ISINI Papers, Volume I. Shaker, Maastricht.

Rugina, A.N., 1949. Geldordnung und Geldtypen: Fundamente für eine allgemeine Geld- und Wirtschaftstheorie. (Monetary Orders and Money types). Kohlhammer, Stuttgart/Köln.

Rugina, A.N., 1998. Prolegomena to any Future Study in Economics, Finance and Other Social Sciences: The Road to a Third Revolution in Economic, Financial, Social, Ethical, Logical and Political Thinking. International Journal of Social Economics 25, 1-388.

ISINI - the inter- and transdisciplinary project of a great thinker: Anghel Rugina

Liviu Drugus
George Bacovia University, The Management Faculty, Bacau, Romania; ldrugus@ugb.ro
President of ISINI for 2005-2007

1. Introduction

In the eighties, I was very keen interested in interdisciplinary and even transdisciplinary approaches not only in Economics but in Social Sciences. The reason was my doctoral dissertation on American radical economic thinking just because many of its representatives were using interdisciplinary approaches.

Although, in 1990, in Paris, I already presented my End-Means Methodology (EMMY) as a transdisciplinary and integrative approach in Social Sciences, some of my later developments were influenced and encouraged by the large vision of the Ruginian way of thinking I have met only then and there. Just in Paris I have added to my previous binom (end & means) a third term (the third included, or "*tertium datur*") which was "the level of adequacy between ends and means". So, from Iasi to Paris I came with a binom, but from Paris to Iasi I came back with a trinom, which proved to be very useful later in my research and in understanding the new ideas of Anghel Rugina.

I mention this just to show that from its very beginnings ISINI and its meetings contributed a lot to generating new ideas, not only in my work, but also in that of other members. The encouragement given by Anghel Rugina to my research was of great importance and I discovered later that we have two (slightly) different theories, but a common thinking

2. ISINI in a nutshell

The International Society for Intercommunication of New Ideas (ISINI) was founded in 1988. The founder and promoter of this scientific organisation is Anghel N. Rugina (born in 1913, May 24, in Romania), Professor Emeritus of the Northeastern University at Boston.

The first conference was held in Paris, France in August 1990, under his moderation. After 15 years, at the Eighth Conference in Wageningen, The Netherlands in August 2005 the discussions were also highly stimulated by him. I mention his presence not only from my sincere respect for a world famous Romanian born scholar, but for his *Quinta Methodica* and for his methodological courage to break old barriers, frontiers and brakes for the advance of social and economic knowledge. A very impressive scientific work was done. Just for giving some examples I mention here Rugina (1993, 1998, 2000a, b).

It is important to stress here that ISINI's roots are - in conformity with its Bylaws (ISINI, 1988) and the motto taken from the Motion of Prof Anghel Rugina (Rugina, 2000c) - "In searching for new ideas, new better concepts, new better theories and new better interpretations of past and/or present theories". In order to attain such results it is necessary to develop the "methodology of science" just because "final dream is a methodological unification of all sciences". And another our dream is a practical one, *i.e.* "to show consistently and systematically how to realise and to maintain in the real world the great ideal of all nations, of all races, that is of Humanity: the dream of a Free, Just and Stable Economy and Society".

As a matter of fact, ISINI is not only an economic nor a financial studies organisation. It is meant to stimulate the dialogue and methodological borrowings into and onto different disciplines that are linked with human development. Health management, financial management, sociological investigations, ideological analysis, teleology, political marketing, cognitive science, psychology of cognition, history of economic, political and ethical doctrines, and methodological developments - to mention only some of the areas of the scientific dialogue - were presented at the eight world conferences, most of them in Europe and North America (USA and Mexico). As a free organisation meant to facilitate dialogue and intercultural communication ISINI contributed a lot to economic reform in former European countries with totalitarian regimes and also to some scientific developments.

ISINI is as open as possible to the new scientific trends that have already made serious changes both in research and in curriculum. The importance given to the ethical aspects in all human sciences (humanistics) is the very result of these new inter- and trans-disciplinary research. I take the advantage of having the possibility to address myself to people keen interested by research development (*i.e.* new ideas) to present here a concrete example of trans-disciplinary approach I launched over 30 years ago: End Means Methodology (EMMY). EMMY suggests that it is not very useful and rational to study separately and to be specialised only in one of the three fundamental humanistic disciplines (Economics, Politics or Ethics). I think that only a simultaneous study of all three disciplines, in an inter- and trans-disciplinary approach may generate a holistic and integrative behaviour of people. More than that I shall make a parallel between trends and realities in research activities on the one hand and the trends and realities in economic, political and social realities on the other hand.

3. Management theory (EMMY) - as a triadic, transdisciplinary, teleologic, post-modern, holistic and synthetic way of human thinking and doing. Management as a Doxa-Praxis continuum

Many of the managerial aspects may be better understood by the political-economical-ethical continuum, and managerial strategies are well developed only by taking into account a fabric of cognitivistic, psychological, sociological, anthropological, juridical, strategical, ecological and of many other human dimensions disciplines. Management is, par excellence, the case of inter- and transdisciplinary approach. As a mater of fact, management is not a simple scientific discipline or a concrete specialised practice, but a long chain of different information, rules and principles from a lot of different disciplines. Management is more than the total sum of all disciplines studying the human behaviour. Management could be a serious basis for integrating all the so called Social Sciences at least at methodological level. Management is about establishing ends/goals for individuals or organisations, choosing the right means for attaining them and fitting and matching all the time (permanently) proposed means with selected means. Instead of teaching separately hundreds of hours of (micro/macro/mondo) Economics to our students, followed then by other many hours of Ethics or of Political science it is better to introduce in the curriculum the transdisciplinary approach called now Management (I call it EMMY - End-Means Methodology).

In EMMY there are explained and used the basics of fundamental human dimensions: the political one (*i.e.* establishing and fulfilling ends in function of existing means); the economic human dimension (*i.e.* the means combination and their consumption for attaining certain ends); and the ethical human behaviour (*i.e.* how people is considering the "good" use of means to specific ends and establishing ends in function of existing or future attracted means). I suggest that this extremely simple description of politic, economic and ethic fields is to be taught at grammar school, a bit more developed to high and higher school and of course, at master degrees any development could be made but only in the same triadic structure. Of course all these explanations should be associated with facts of life (from household and family, from school and shops, from sport and movies *etc.*). The final result would be a better understanding of the three fields - at every level of education - in comparison with that obtained after reading the big textbooks that are boring most of the students. And a final remark: EMMY was better receipted in USA than in Europe. At least in the last years in American newspapers and even in scientific and philosophical journals I found a real "endmeansmania", but not in a very developed mood. As a member of the Editorial Board of the Romanian Journal of Bioethics, but also as a simple contributor with articles to this journal I promoted, in many articles, at least three main new ideas: 1) transdisciplinarity, 2) the essential identity between Management and Ethics and 3) the ethical dimension is inculcated both in Politics and Economics, so no Political Economics is to be taught without the ethical dimension.

4. What is transdisciplinarity?

There are more perceptions and views on transdisciplinarity. Far from being contradictory I do consider them as complementary and creating a broader vision on transdisciplinarity. One of the pillars of transdisciplinarity is the logic of the third included (also called "the logic of the included middle", or "*tertium datur*". Worth to mention here that "trans" means "three"). This means that this kind of logic suggests that if there are two antagonistic dimensions ("to be" and "not to be", A and nonA, *etc.*) there should be another dimension to link and to combine them as a bridge of communication (Lat. *comunicatio-onis* = to put things together, to consider them as a common ownership). In my mind, the most complex and well known example of transdisciplinarity is the Holy Trinity: every two persons of the Holy Trinity are transcended and bridged by the third one (the third person is included as a bridge between the other two persons). The easiest example (for our understanding) of bridging and uniting the two other persons is the Holy Spirit, as a bridge between the God Father and the God Son (Jesus Christ). Or, using the existential triad described by the Russian born physicist Ilya Prigogine[1] as "Substance-Energy-Information", we may describe the three persons of the Holy Trinity as follows: The God Father is Information, The God Son is Substance and the Holy Spirit is Energy. So, it is simple to imagine that in every piece of cosmic existence the energy is keeping together the information and substance. Of course, this is only to offer an example of transdisciplinarity. Another example is that of Ethics viewed (at least by me...) as a third middle between Politics and Economics (See, at large Drugus, 1995, 2003).

Of course there are similar or complementary explanations of transdisciplinary approach. Basarab Nicolescu from the Centre International de Recherches et d'Etudes Transdisciplinaires (CIRET, Paris) said: *"As the prefix "trans" indicates, transdisciplinarity concerns that which is at once between the disciplines, across the different disciplines, and beyond all discipline. Its goal is the understanding of the present world, of which one of the imperatives is the unity of knowledge."* (See, Nicolescu, website). I applied this definition to the Holy Trinity and...it works! God - as a three-unity of information, substance and energy - is beyond, across and between the three persons.

In explaining how transdisciplinarity works, Nicolescu (website) uses *"Disciplinary research concerns, at most, one and the same level of Reality; moreover, in most cases, it only concerns fragments of one level of Reality. On the contrary, transdisciplinarity concerns the dynamics engendered by action of several levels of Reality at once".* The "levels of Reality"; so, I do agree with Nicolescu's vision on transdisciplinarity. It is very helpful and explanatory. Of course, it is possible to find other applications of Nicolescu's definition and explanation of transdisciplinarity as it is very possible to find out new or at least a bit different explanations of the (relatively) new approach.

I try to go further with Nicolescu's definition and to offer another example of multiple levels of Reality, with three of them as fundamental ones (national-monodisciplinary, federal-pluridisciplinary, international-interdisciplinary and transnational-transdisciplinary) from the so called Social Sciences It is simply to observe that the disciplinary approach

---

[1] Nobel Prize winner 1974 and a honorary member of ISINI. In our tridimensional space, it is clear that the fundamental cosmic existence is structured as Substance-Energy-Information. Of course other less fundamental structures may be imagined or discovered. The Christian religion (even other religions and beliefs) stated a tri(u)nitary God, as our existence is triadic and trialectic. This is not a Christian propaganda, but only a (possible) example... I do consider that a isomorphic construction based on religion, philosophy and (natural) science is possible and this could be reported in future ISINI conferences.

was contemporary with the time of formation of nation states (Machiavelli's time and all following modern times), that interdisciplinary approach was contemporary with the development of international relations and the transnational approach was/is contemporary with the transnational relations and integrative processes. This congruence is very useful to demonstrate the objectivity of the transdisciplinary approach in a world of fusions, integrations and globalising of all our activities. It is worth to mention here that there is a close link between the ideological options of scholars fond of one or the other of the three scientific and political (ideological) trends. So, the "disciplinarists" are very close to ethnicist, tribalist and nationalistic political (ideological) visions. The "interdisciplinarists" are much closer to "internationalist" movements - that ones that are preserving and protecting nations but recognise the necessity of foreign exchanges and of a vivid exchange of new ideas.

This is also the case with ISINI from its beginnings. ISINI is an international organisation for exchanging of new ideas. Of course, the transdisciplinary trend was present even at the Paris ISINI Conference. There is a clear temporal and contextual connection between transnationalisation processes and the transdisciplinary approach, just because the postmodern times are characterised by mixing up and melting things, ideas and energies in order to obtain something new with bigger utility or usefulness. The transnationalisation of business is part of the globalisation process.

The transdisciplinary approach is not simply a combination of disciplinary, multidisciplinarity and interdisciplinarity approaches, but something much more and with richer results than the former disciplines could offer. As in any human action the results are the best measure of its efficiency. So, transdisciplinarists are asked to prove by results the opportunity, necessity and utility of their approach. In my opinion, Rugina's research is a good example of a transdisciplinary approach, even if it was not defined and described as such. Needless to say that the transdisciplinarists are not a homogenous group, that there are many visions and definitions on transdisciplinarity: some of them are doing transdisciplinary research without defining it with this name, others are putting as an immediate objective generating of a unified science (or better said, unified knowledge where spirituality, art, philosophy, technology and classical science will merge and form a unified body), and finally some other researchers are working to prepare a common background for the neuronal and cognitive basis of creativity and innovation. For Nicolescu "The three pillars of transdisciplinarity - levels of Reality, the logic of the included middle, and complexity - determine the methodology of transdisciplinary research". It is worth to note that "the logic of the included middle" (or "the logic of the third included") is an innovative contribution of Stephan Lupasco (Lupascu, 2000), another Romanian born French philosopher.

For transdisciplinarian thinkers there may be considered as very good and interesting forerunners the Dada movement (founder is considered to be the Romanain Jewish born thinker and poet known under his literary pseudonim Tristan Tzara - former Samy Rosenstock) and especially the well known American economist Nicholas Georgescu-

Roegen (born in Constantza, Romania in 1906) which had revolutionary ideas in resources management, entropy law and ecological principles. He is the founder of Bioeconomics. In my opinion, it is possible to speak about the Romanian school of non-orthodox (I mean innovative and integrative approaches to) social and economic thinking. Some of them could be listed here: Tristan Tzara, Stefan Lupascu, Anghel N. Rugina, Nicholas Georgescu-Roegen, Basarab Nicolescu, Radu J. Bogdan (Prof. Radu Bogdan is a Romanian born scholar who is teaching philosophy and is directing the cognitive science program at Tulane University, New Orleans, USA), Traian Dinorel Stanciulescu (see Stanciulescu, 2005) and so on. The last one is still in Romania but is very highly appreciated abroad. One mention is, still, necessary: all of them flourished only in European and/or American scientific free contexts.

It is quite necessary to underline the fact that I do not think there are "old" and "new" scholars, "good" and "bad" ones, or that there is "correct" or "incorrect" thinking. I do believe that altogether all research methods are useful and necessary at least for explanatory and descriptive reasons. So, it is specific to transdisciplinary vision to accept all older or newer methods, mixed up in different new ways in order to obtain new results. It is not opposed or antagonistic to disciplinary or interdisciplinary approaches, but complementary to them.

5. ISINI and the transdisciplinary approach

I am proposing here that ISINI should become an important player in the struggle for implementing the new way of thinking and of doing research. In this respect I propose to sign protocols of cooperation with as many as possible organisations and institutions open to or dedicated to transdisciplinary research. I will mention some of them: CIRET, UNESCO and the University of UN in Tokyo, ISSEI, SPACE, CEEMAN and of course there are a lot of other organisations or university departments promoting inter- and transdisciplinarity. Just because ISINI may be an organisation with good results in transdisciplinary approach I'll include a special session at the 9th ISINI Conference to be organised in Romania at the last week of August 2007. Please put this date in your agenda and try to enter dialogue with me (ldrugus@ugb.ro) and with other people or organisations interested in transdisciplinary methods before coming to Romania. A call for papers will be addressed to all of you this summer.

At the meeting of the SPACE Committee on research (called ERA) from Edinburgh (October 2005) I proposed that some introductory lessons on research in general and on transdisciplinarity in particular should be taught at licence degree but especially at master degree. More than that, I do consider that Managerial Continuous Education (Long Life Learning) should comprise some workshops on research, on transdisciplinarity and on unified methodologies for humanistics.

References

Drugus, L., 1995. The Scope of the Economic, the Politic and the Ethic. What is, at last, studying the Political Economics? Economica (Chisinau, Republic of Moldova) 3: 35-51.

Drugus, L., 2003. Ethics is Political Economics. Moral behaviour is good management. Revista Romana de Bioetica 1: 45-54.

ISINI, 1988. Bylaws of The International Society for Intercommunication of New Ideas, Inc., Boston, Massachussets, November 1988.

Lupascu, S., 2000. Principiul antagonismului si logica energiei. Prolegomene la o stiinta a contradictiei. S. Lupascu (Ed.), Iasi. This is the Romanian version of Lupascu's book "Le principe d'antagonisme et la logique de l'energie. Prolegomenes a une science de la contradiction", Herman et Co, Paris, 1951.

Nicolescu, B., website. The Transdisciplinary Evolution of the University - Condition for Sustainable Development. http://nicol.club.fr/ciret/bulletin/b12/c8htm

Rugina, A.N., 1993. Principia Oeconomica. Academiei Romane, Bucuresti, 433 pp. (translation in Romanian of the "Principia Oeconomica. New and Old Foundations of Economic Analysis").

Rugina, A.N., 1998. Prolegomena to any Future Study in Economics, Finance and other Social Sciences. The Road to a Third Revolution in Economics, Financial, Social, Ethical, Logical and Political Thinking. International Journal of Social Sciences 25, nr 5.

Rugina, A.N., 2000a. Prolegomena 2: To any Future Study in Integrated Logic and a more Comprehensive Methodology for the Unification of all Sciences, Natural and Social. An Orientation Table for Economics and any other Science and its Application in Theory and Practice. International Journal of Social Economics 27, nr 5-6.

Rugina, A.N., 2000b. The Concept of Social and Economic Justice: why we are not successful in analysis and practice? Rivista Internazionale di Scienze Economiche e Commerciali (International Review of Economics and Business) XLVII, nr 2, June, CEDAM, Milan.

Rugina, A.N., 2000c. Purpose, Vision of ISINI: Motion of Prof Dr Anghel N. Rugina, Honorary President addressed to 4th ISINI Conference in Maastricht, 23 August, 1997. In: G. Meijer, W.J.M. Heijman, J.A.C. van Ophem, B.H.J. Versteegen (eds.), The Maastricht ISINI papers, Volume 1. Shaker, Maastricht.

Stanciulescu, D.T., 2005. Signs of Light. A Biophysic Approach to Human (Meta)Physical Fundamentals. Cristal Concept & WDO Printing House, Geneve, third edition.

Introduction

This volume includes two keynote lectures, and a selection of the papers originally written for the Eighth International Conference organised by the International Society for Intercommunication of New Ideas (ISINI), August 24-27, 2005 in Wageningen, The Netherlands.

The ISINI exists to promote international communication of new ideas and to foster interdisciplinary research on problems of today. All contributions have been subjected to professional reviewing and editing.

As the title above indicates, this volume deals with two primary issues:
1. Heterodox views on economics.
2. The economy of the global society.

The volume predominantly consists of heterodox contributions, which generally deviate from traditional neo-classical analysis in the sense that they integrate theories and evidence from other social sciences or, in some cases, simply reject the restricted type of analysis of societal phenomena common in mainstream economic theory and focus on the problems of today.

Clear examples of the latter are found in the contributions of the keynote speakers Backhaus and Klamer or in the contribution of Houmanidis on Rugina's orientation table. Contributions covering similar material can be found in the sections on population and society, corporate issues and, to a lesser extent, environmental issues.

Further discussions include genotype selection, voices and income distribution in market capitalism, the relation between non-traditional family types and changing life cycles, price perception and consumer demand, ethical egoism, public/private ownership issues and tradable permits from an evolutionary perspective.

Other contributions focus on the economy of the global society. The earth is rapidly becoming a global economy and, perhaps to a lesser extent, a global society. Consequently local and regional subsystems are becoming increasingly interdependent in the face of a range of common challenges - from poverty and employment to trade regulation and environmental responsibility.

This editorial presents a brief overview of the volume, arranged in six categories: keynote lectures; economic paradigms and economic theories; population and society; corporate issues; environment, and international relations.

Gerrit Meijer, Wim Heijman, Johan van Ophem and Bernard Verstegen

1. Keynote lectures

Backhaus's keynote lecture discusses the interdisciplinary sciences of the state as a research paradigm. The lecture has five parts:

In Part 1 Backhaus explains the concept of state sciences ('Staatswissenschaften'), tracing their history and development from the seventeenth century, especially in Germany, until the beginning of the last century. Subsequently he addresses the factors of decomposition in the Twentieth Century and identifies the difficulties in bringing together the decomposed parts. In part four he makes the link to ISINI, a research program focussing on international communication and interdisciplinary research on problems of today. In Part 5 policy areas are defined where the sciences of state can furnish an effective research paradigm with respect to a range of social issues, including the aging of society, education, health, security, cultural heritage and religion.

The topic of *Klamer's* keynote lecture is the economics of culture. He explains that economics is 'thinking in values'. Goods are like values, in that they represent social and sometimes cultural values. The striving towards the good, therefore, is the striving to gain (common) goods and hence the realising of values. This makes for a different economics - an economics more like the moral science that Aristotle and Adam Smith had in mind.

2. Economic paradigms and theories

This section opens with a discussion by *Houmanidis* on Anghel Rugina's contribution to economic science, particularly his proposal for a money-commodity. Houmanidis examines Rugina's orientation table and his thoughts on how to achieve steady equilibrium. He further compares Rugina's model with that of Leon Walras. Rugina refers to the different kinds of disequilibrium due to the 'anti-numeraire', monetised money. In his orientation table he presents seven models. The first (M1) refers to a 100% equilibrium and the last (M7) to a model of 100% disequilibrium. Rugina also takes into account the corresponding institutional and social framework. In doing so, he develops a more complete model than Walras did. Houmanidis adds his theory of cost dependence to complete the model of Rugina. Finally he criticises the proposal for a money-commodity gold, which is defended by Rugina as an international numeraire. Gold stocks, according to Houmanidis, are insufficient to cover the needs for it, in the event of an international gold standard.

The focus of *Meijer's* contribution is money, freedom and order in the European Union. The introduction of the Euro and the working of the European Central Bank are discussed at the background of the general problems of the role of money, the monetary system and monetary policy in a free society. The historical background, the objectives and the consequences of the political decisions in this field of policy of the European Union are explored. The paper concentrates on the consequences for freedom and order of this monetary institutional system and policy and on possibly better alternatives for the future. In this respect he discusses free banking and international commodity money.

The contribution of *Smatrakalev* addresses the interplay between taxes and elections. In democratic societies people are both taxpayers and voters, which makes it very important that in every voter should speak the taxpayer's language and *vice versa*. The paper explores this dualism in human nature, and how the taxpayer influences the voter. Elections generally influence taxes in three ways - tax legislation, tax rates and tax burden. Each of these concerns the development stage of a society. The foreseen tax harmonisation in the European Union didn't happen for electoral reasons. Referring to Bulgaria as a case in point *Smatrakalev* asserts that in Eastern Europe, fear of the past is replaced by fear of taxation.

In his paper *Tarrit* discusses Analytical Marxism, a term first coined by Gerald A. Cohen in defending historical materialism on the basis of analytical philosophy and of logical positivism. This school of thought presented itself as an attempt to renew Marxism with non-Marxist methodological tools. John Roemer extended it in reconstructing Marxian economics with neoclassical tools and Jon Elster generalised it in interpreting Marxism with methodological individualism and rational choice theory. *Tarrit* further addresses the assumption that Analytical Marxism turned Marxism into an opposing ideology.

3. Population and society

This part subjects a number of issues to analysis. In his consequentialist approach, *Moroz* analyses the benefits that potential parents can enjoy when they have the possibility to choose the genotype of their children. He demonstrates that there is no relationship between the genetic variability of a population and its survival capability. Hence it is impossible to anticipate the benefits that result from the choice of a genotype.

Macarov tackles another societal problem. His paper calls for new methods of caring for the world's tens of millions of orphans. All current efforts to ameliorate the condition of orphans focus on small-group, family-like settings. There is, however, no empirical evidence that this focus is more efficacious than that of large orphans homes or children's villages, encompassing hundreds - and sometimes thousands - of children. An exploration of possible alternatives to current efforts, including large-scale methods of housing and caring for orphans, is urgently required. He discusses the comparative costs of such activities and the steps necessary to achieve such child-care.

According to *Powers*, efforts to bolster market capitalism seem to reduce poverty in some countries and aggravate it in others. Even if market adjustment produces generally beneficial outcomes in countries with relatively low levels of inequality, the 'invisible hand of the market' may produce maladjustments when levels of inequality are high. The reason is that extreme disparities in disposable income leave many people without appreciable voice in the market place. Disparities of that kind can hamper the processes that might otherwise produce socially rational market adjustment. The central premise of Powers' arguments is that people without disposable income are essentially voiceless in the marketplace, so their needs are likely to go unmet even when market adjustment occurs.

Until recently, the dominant family type, the nuclear family (husband, wife and their own children) followed a traditional life cycle. Nowadays, most modern-industrialised countries have entered an era of new biographic models. People have a wide choice in selecting their own life course menu. By means of a typology of family types *De Hoog & Van Ophem* explore the consequences of changing life cycles and the emergence of non-traditional family types and lifestyles in particular. They discuss the implications of lower fertility and higher divorce rates.

Referring to Dutch data for the period of 1996-2005, *Antonides, Heijman & Schouten* analyse the types of expenditures that influence consumer perception of inflation. They conclude that neither the introduction of the Euro nor the aggregate consumer price index have significantly influenced perceived inflation. However, prices of transportation, appliances and food have had a positive effect, whereas hotels and clothing have clearly had a negative effect on perceived inflation.

In the last contribution of the part on Population and Society, *Nentjes* proposes a reform by entitling every citizen with a fixed budget for lifetime consumption in the domain of social policy and by delegating the decisions on how to spend the budget to the budget holder. This system replaces the current one, in which welfare states citizens have entitlements to a variety of social services provided for free or a price far below cost, such as education, health care, social security and housing. Every citizen benefits, but in their present organisation the social services also have major deficiencies such as lack of choice, incentives encouraging over-consumption and X-inefficiency.

4. Corporate issues

One of the major topics in the contemporary economics and business literature is the question of public or private ownership. Generally, it is argued that private ownership of organisations is to be preferred unless the organisation supplies products or services with characteristics of common goods. However, it is becoming more and more apparent that there are problems with the functioning of the private sector economy as well as the public sector economy. Both aspects are to be considered if a comparison private/public ownership is discussed. Private ownership of an organisation may dysfunction because of a number of reasons. The system of voting by shareholders may cause problems with respect to the reliability of the information available to shareholders or their capacity to digest this information. It may lead us to consider other forms of coping with the complexity of corporate governance.

Van den Burg proposes the establishment of proxy voting institutions with an intermediate role between shareholders and firms. According to Van den Burg such voting institutions would have a disciplining role on managers of firms. On a still more fundamental level the role of 'trust' and 'mistrust' can be discussed. In the recent wave of breakdowns in corporate governance it became common knowledge that it would be foolish to trust corporate financial behaviour. In spite of all initiatives building gigantic frameworks of promoting regulations, huge problems exist.

Furuyama describes the known Enron case in this perspective. He records the developments of Enron through the years and the extreme way in which information was furnished to external stakeholders. Furuyama concludes that there is an important role to play for business ethics, in particular ethical egoism, in high-trust societies like the US.

Given the functional and dysfunctional aspects of private and public ownership we could monitor the actual transfer of organisations from mutual ownership to private ownership. That would generate empirical research with respect to the problems that actually occur in such a process. *Shiwakoti* looks at the demutualisation of building societies in the UK. What were the specific arguments in favour of demutualisation of building societies and are these arguments valid in concrete cases, when looking in retrospect? Shiwakoti's paper provides a mixed answer to these questions.

The Website is a space which offers the firm the possibility of presenting financial and non-financial information as well as mandatory and standardised information already published in traditional media. *Trabelsi* shows in his paper that the inadequate methodologies and theories employed in measuring the Internet's specific contribution to financial reporting leaves us with very little knowledge on the question. Prompted by this observation and by the fact that this research topic is relatively unexplored, he proposes avenues for gaining a better understanding of the ins and outs of the Internet's incremental contribution to the process of financial reporting.

5. Environment

Evolutionary economics has carved out a niche of its own in economics, especially in the area of environmental economics. In this respect *Woerdman & De Vries* oppose the opinion of the evolutionists Rammel and Van der Bergh that the solution to a large number of environmental problems, preferred by mainstream economists, *i.e.* tradable permits, is not superior to an evolutionary perspective. They argue that tradable permits are also efficient from a long-term evolutionary point of view.

Krozer contributes on the estimation of emission reduction cost functions. Emission reduction generates costs. Because of the limited availability of adequate data, estimation of these costs is a complex task. Krozer develops a way to estimate accurate cost functions for a number of abatement options. Another part of environmental economics deals with the consequences of free trade for the environment.

The article written by *Ivanova, Angeles & Martinez* analyses the policies adopted by the APEC regarding trade and environment with respect to the three Latin American members Mexico, Chile, and Peru. The central argument of their paper is that regional economic integration must be complemented by the creation of regional frameworks for environmental management. In this way, trade and environmental policies can mutually reinforce each other.

The consequences of international environmental standards for foreign trade are the topic of the article by *Wysokińska*. She reviews the literature related to the theory of the relationship between foreign trade and environmental issues (Multilateral Environmental Agreements). Results from a survey among 286 Polish enterprises confirm the pro-ecological emphasis of restructuring efforts in transition economies, particularly when combined with the significant increase in their foreign trade in environmental goods and services.

Nentjes & Shybayev discuss a game theoretic verification of economic theory's postulate of Pareto-efficient international conventions on pollution reduction. With respect to the Second Sulphur Protocol (SSP) they find that the SSP is potentially Pareto-efficient.

6. International relations

In international trade the issue of Free Trade Agreements (FTA) is a topical one. *Sakhornrad* discusses the Thai trade policy with respect to the bilateral free trade agreement with three partners - Japan, the United States, and China, after 1997. By investigating the trade and investment structure (including the protection structure) of these three bilateral FTA partners with respect to Thailand utilising selected international trade indices, the FTA's bilateral approach could be explained by both economic and political factors. The results suggest that the Thai government should reassess its priorities in light of the economic and social considerations.

In his contribution *Leelawath* concentrates on the social welfare effects and urban employment of Free Trade Agreements (FTA). He shows by means of formal analysis that FTA may cause an increase of urban employment and welfare. Trade creation is welfare-improving, only if the elasticity of return to scale in the manufacturing sector is at least as much as that of the agricultural sector. Under the same condition, trade diversion is more likely to cause an increase in social welfare than otherwise would be the case.

In his survey of the literature *Visser* starts first to analyse the theoretical pros and cons of outward Foreign Direct Investment (FDI). The empirical evidence generally suggests a positive effect of FDI, in particular on exports. Outward FDI has been negatively correlated with domestic investment in general. Furthermore, FDI leads to a shift from lower-skilled to higher-skilled jobs. The impact of FDI on technology in the home country is ultimately quite diffuse and hard to establish. Whatever the result, without outward FDI a country would generally not be better off. What counts is an environment conducive to Schumpeterian 'new combinations'.

In developing countries financial sector reforms have a considerable impact on daily life. In his contribution *Adebiyi* analyses by means of a vector autoregressive model the monetary policy transmission mechanism in Nigeria. He concludes that since the monetary reforms of 1986 monetary policy has a higher impact on the economy. In addition, he advises to take the exchange rate as an alternative monetary policy instrument.

In concluding we, the editors, would like to thank all those who contributed to this volume. We are especially indebted to those who assisted in its production - Annelies Coppelmans, Ymkje van 't Riet-Meijer, and Margaret van Wissen.

Gerrit Meijer
Wim Heijman
Johan van Ophem
Bernard Verstegen

Keynote speakers

The Sciences of State as a Research Paradigm

Jürgen Backhaus
Krupp-Stiftungsprofessur für Finanzwissenschaft und Finanzsoziologie, Staatswissenschaftliche Fakultät, Universität Erfurt, Nordhäuser Straße 63, 99089 Erfurt, Germany. juergen. backhaus@uni-erfurt.de

Avant Propos: In Honour of Sicco Leendert Mansholt (1908 - 1995)

It is certainly a pleasure to accept this honour to deliver the Mansholt Lecture[1]. I think we should not really harbour mixed feelings about Sicco Mansholt. Keep in mind that when the common agricultural policy was conceived, agriculture looked very different from what it is now. I recently took a trip to Northern Germany. There is a village where my grandmother operated a farm during the war. The farm absorbed lots of refugees and people. First refugees from Hamburg, which had, of course, been bombed twice with duly conceived bombing raids that involved first positioning light bombs, then fire bombs and explosive bombs thereafter, thereby setting off a fire storm (Groehler, 1990), and then the many refugees who came from the East. It was amazing how many people such a farm could absorb. This was a village that had six, at that time considered large, farms. You must conceive several hundred people on each of these farms, all being fed and all being put to work on these farms. Today, there is actually only one operator in that village, and he is also farming two other villages. So, you can witness an enormous structural change due to the Common Agricultural Policy (in short: CAP). The CAP should be seen in dynamic terms aimed at achieving deep structural change.

Our British friends always say that the CAP is just an obstacle, a hindrance to the operation of free markets. I beg to disagree. After more than a century of protected agriculture in Europe, free markets first had to be brought about. Markets tend not to invent themselves. Today, we have almost reached the point of global markets in agriculture. The CAP may be a hindrance and obsolete now, and its days may be counted, but the amount of structural change it has brought about is rather stunning and should be credited to the person who conceived of how to actually bring it about.

Now, these introductory remarks were impromptu, this is not the matter of the talk itself, but it could very well have been. Sicco Mansholt's CAP would be a very interesting case study in institution building, the central topic of the Sciences of State. In fact, it even serves as an example of building institutions that are set up in such a way as Friedrich List (1983 [1837]; compare Backhaus, 1992) would always suggest: building an institution that carries

---

[1] Sicco Leendert Mansholt started out as the Dutch Secretary of Agriculture (1945-58), moved on to become European Commissioner of Agriculture (1958-72), and crowned his career with the Presidency of the European Commission (1972). Compare Mansholt (2001).

the germs of its own dissolution once it has attained its purpose, and so, in this sense, perhaps Sicco Mansholt was actually a very interesting figure. He may not have intended all of the results that he brought about, but that is typically the case in all areas of policy that we can observe, and certainly in successful policy. Many of the fruits that we can reap are not intended, but come about by way of fortuitous circumstances, from which we can learn. On the basis of this learning (for the interpretation of economic policy as a process of learning compare Pelikan and Wegner, 2003) we can repeat and emphasise in our policy design those fortuitous circumstances that tend to bring about the desired results.

1. Introduction: The Sciences of State as a research paradigm

The lecture has five parts. I first strive to explain what we actually have to understand by the Sciences of State, then I decompose this in part two, and explain in part three what the difficulties are in bringing about the co-operation among the decomposed parts. Part four builds a bridge to the International Society for Intercommunication of New Ideas (ISINI), a research programme in itself. Finally, policy areas are identified, where the Sciences of State can bear rich fruit, not just as an educational tool, but in particular as a research paradigm. That is an ambitious order, hopefully fitting the occasion and the purpose of this lecture.

2. Part I: Describing the Sciences of State[2]

The Sciences of State came about at a time when Germany was really in a very difficult situation, and by the way, the Netherlands too. This was towards the end of what is called the Eighty Years' War in the Netherlands and the Thirty Years' War in Germany. The pivot was that the war could not be won by any of the warring parties, but this had become obvious only after twenty-two years of warfare. Around 1640, the Elector of Saxony had already made a peace offer promising large demobilisation payments. One of the Swedish colonels, one of the princes of the House of Saxony, simply decommissioned, went home to Saxony, and asked his brothers, there were altogether seven of them, for his share in the Duchy. He received his share, which was the area around Gotha, a very small and insignificant town at that time, and started to build from scratch a Duchy which was conceived to be a model state. His name was Ernest I of Saxony-Gotha, called "the Pious". He proceeded to marry his cousin, who was the heiress of the Duchy of Altenburg. Her father was an avid collector of books, and so was Ernest. Hence, one of the biggest libraries that still exists in Germany was assembled in a very large castle, which had only protective purposes. It was appropriately called the *Friedenstein* (Rock of Peace), and a very utilitarian residence was built around this castle, which you can still visit today. There was no military value in the whole matter during the First and Second World War.

---

[2] Compare the special issue: Veit Ludwig von Seckendorff (1626-1692), Anonymous (2005).

This Duke, Ernest I of Saxony, had no resources in the way of mining yields, had no access to any waterways, was not even near any commercial crossroads, and did not have custom fees of any significance. Hence, he lacked all the prerequisites for a successful Mercantilist political programme. He conceived the idea that the only realistic source of revenue was the education of his people. He went about this in terms of actually educating a class of civil servants, and foremost a person whose name was Veit Ludwig von Seckendorff.

To Veit Ludwig von Seckendorff we owe two major contributions, both in lengthy book form. The significance of the twin work - and how the two belong together - will appear in due course. The first is a book, the title of which we can roughly translate as The German Principality[3]. The first version of it appeared in 1665. This is a book of about a thousand pages with a very deep index. It goes all the way from *Ablass* (indulgence) - the sale of indulgencies by the Catholic Church which caused Luther's Reformation - to *Zuchthaus* (penitentiary), from A to Z. The book was going to be the essential handbook in each chancellery of the up to twenty dozen states that had come about as a consequence of the threefold Treaty of Münster, Osnabrück and Münster in 1648[4]. We have to visualise a continent with a large number of states in its centre, operating within the newly re-created framework of the Holy Roman Empire, yet intensely competing with each other (Backhaus and Wagner, 1987). At the periphery, though, there were larger, contiguous maritime states such as Spain, Portugal, France, Britain, Sweden, and Turkey, which followed different (with the exception of Turkey) Mercantilist policies.

Hence, there were competing states and that meant that they had to focus their policies on development. This is an extremely important thing to note that the whole outlook of the state was on fostering development because, as you know, essentially the peace treaty system was very effective in establishing the peace. There were conflicts to be sure, but the peace treaty system was very effective in subduing them rather substantially. By the way, Saxony Gotha and Altenburg did not even maintain an army. They never did and were able to keep intact due to skilful diplomacy, until the Duchy perished and was joined with Coburg so

---

[3] Seckendorff, Veit Ludwig von. Teutscher Fürsten Stat. (German State of Princes). New edition. Two volumes. Glashütten/Taunus: Detlev Auvermann. 1976. Reprint of the third corrected edition of 1665.

[4] The first treaty was concluded on January 30, 1648, between Spain and the Dutch Republic. It is a very short treaty, essentially espousing the state doctrine of Johannes Althusius (1603). Having conceded independence to the Dutch Republic, the Spanish Crown could turn to France, which prompted the negotiations of Münster concluded on October, 23rd. This is a very complicated treaty, involving territorial concessions to France. Compare Six (1942 reprint). Simultaneously, the negotiations with the Swedish proceeded in Osnabrueck and were concluded on the same day. This treaty only partly reproduces the second treaty of Münster and, although it involves territorial concessions to the Swedish, accomplishes this without ceding imperial lands. In addition, a large demobilization payment to the Swedish was agreed on and paid. The English translation of the treaty in Toynbee's Collection is not reliable, since it does not acknowledge the difference between the two treaties of October 23rd.

as to become Saxony-Coburg and Gotha as it was then called, but this was simply because they had died out.

The next step after having established this book, The German Principality, which was supposed to become the handbook for the instruction of the chancellor of any German state, was to translate it into political action, in all fields of policy, from A to Z. Other principalities followed suit. The states were indeed following these precepts, for there was no systematic education. This changed, when Christian Wolff (1754, reprint 1980) suggested a complete system of political economy in his *Natur- und Völkerrecht*, (The Law of Nations), which today has become extremely important again in the Court at The Hague, because he also discusses human atrocities in war. In this part, in this Law of Nations, there is a whole segment which is essentially an outline of political economy in the context of a law of nations. This is important to understand. The outline of political economy has its roots in the context of the law of nations. Here, you essentially have the germs of what later became Political Economy, but it took another person to work it out.

In either December 1750 or January 1751, Johann Heinrich Gottlob von Justi gave two lectures upon excepting his dual appointment at Vienna, the appointment on the one hand as professor of rhetoric at the Academy of Knights, that was going to be the institution where knights, typically destitute nobility, were supposed to be trained for the civil service; and on the other as the Director of Mines, because their hope always was that there was going to be some kind of revenue through mining. So, he got this dual appointment, and gave these two lectures, the theoretical lecture is about twenty pages long, and is interesting, because here he took the precepts of Wolff, of course without ever acknowledging where he got them from, which was the custom of the time. You only see where he got it when he disagrees with Wolff, but it is very clear. He worked out what Wolff had suggested and came up with a systematic treatment of sciences that he called cameralism. This is because, as I have pointed out, Seckendorff wrote his German Principality for the use of the chancellors. This is different from Machiavelli's *Principe*; that was for the use of the prince. Seckendorff's encyclopaedic book was for the use of the chancellors, and the chancellor, of course, works in the chambers of the prince, and that is why this science was called cameralism. It is the science that the people who are the principal administrators of the prince, need and rely upon. Justi distinguished between two parts of this science. It was on the one hand cameralism proper, that is essentially everything that the State can do in order to establish markets, and secondly the idea of what we today would call public administration. He called it *Policeywissenschaft*, police science, which is not the traffic police that we mean today, but rather regulation. The State essentially has the particular purpose, on the one hand, first of all to establish a market, and bring about preconditions of what needs to be done; the other part is to regulate these markets. To take a simple example: health. On the one hand, the purpose is to have a sufficient number of well-educated and responsible doctors in the principality, so you have to encourage them to come in, which in particular means to break local monopolies. In particular in the health industry at that time, there was a plethora of local monopolies. Therefore, the point was to break down traditional barriers, for instance, doctors may be admitted only if they graduate from particular universities or something like that, hence, a liberal policy of granting practicing licences. That is the cameralist part, but then there was also the aspect of regulating the health industry in order to make sure that you did not have quacks operating out there. Essentially, very often the idea is to encourage self-regulation. So, this was the structure of the first scientific approach. The books appeared in the middle of the eighteenth century, in 1750, 1751 and 1752. He had one book every year, because he was also living off his books. As a matter of fact, he had one book every half year. For each Leipzig book fair, they have documented so far, he had a book, and not necessarily a new and original one. There is a lot of recycling of material.

At about the same time, in 1727 - that is not at the same time, but actually a generation earlier, but without having this scientific treatment that I was just dealing with - two chairs in what we later called political economy, in cameralism, were established by Frederick William I, in Frankfurt/Oder and in Halle/Saale. This is important to know, because the first chair in political economy in Britain was established exactly 99 years later in 1826 at Oxford with Nassau Senior as the first appointee. I mention this not because of the priority, but because the two approaches are markedly different. As you have noticed, the cameralist approach grew out of Wolff's Law of Nations. In Britain, the approach to political economy grew out of the question that Adam Smith had raised, trying to inquire about the Causes and the Nature of the Wealth of Nations. That is a very different approach. It is not true that Adam Smith does not see a very important role for the State in economic development. It is, of course, true that the Dutch translation does not originally include book five, where this is discussed, but it is absolutely true that Smith never said that the State has no function. He was only very critical of particular enterprises that the State was entertaining, for instance he has a ridiculing discussion of the practice of the City of Hamburg to run pharmacies. He said, these senators should have something better to do and he thought, of course, that they should trade. The reason why they ran pharmacies was, of course, very obvious (at least to them and their citizens). It was not in the first place to make money, but it was because a port city was always very much in danger of having contagious diseases coming into the harbour. For that reason, the senators were interested in doing health management themselves, as a first order of business.

To be sure, the first important date here was 1727, when the Sciences of State were established as a set of two chairs. Then, about a generation later, we had the first textbook treatments. The next thing that really happens in terms of the question of the research paradigm of the Sciences of State is the issue of what was considered the Social Question. LaSalle had put it as the Social Question: rapid industrialisation meant that traditional institutions, in which the risks of life of people were somehow cushioned, were no longer available. The primary insurance system was the farm. I mentioned this in my introductory remarks. That farm was no longer available. Wolff calls it the house. Once young people, in order to be able to marry, had left the villages and joined the industrial workforce in the cities, something awful could befall them. They could loose their ability to work, they might have orphans without support, there would be widows without support and also people due to their age unable to support themselves. So, these were risks that today would be considered insurable, but they were not insurable then, because there was no capital market that could support a private market-based insurance system. Therefore, the founders of the *Verein für Socialpolitik* (Backhaus, 1994), who were thoroughly trained in the Sciences of State, designed a concept of dealing with these risks and that accomplishment was pretty much finished by 1890. Not included was unemployment insurance. This was the bone of contention between the Emperor with his Easter Messages, William II and his Chancellor, then Prince Bismarck, later Duke. The bone of contention was whether unemployment insurance could be included. The Emperor very much wanted the risk of unemployment to be insured. Bismarck insisted that this was not possible at the present stage of how, from the point of view of commercial policy (Rieß, 1997), industrial progress could be supported. Keep in mind; there were recurrent economic deep crises at the time, in German called *Gründerkrisen*. This meant launching new enterprises on a large scale, then there would be a bubble resulting in lots of bankruptcies, and that was something that you could not really insure against. Hence, the risk remained with what Schmoller would then call the new social institutions[5], those risks that I have just mentioned.

This essentially was the primary accomplishment of the new Sciences of State, but there is more. The civil code is also an accomplishment of the scientists of state. A commission was set up in the late seventies, a couple of years after the foundation of the *Reich* in 1871, to study the possibility of a German code. There were more than one hundred and twenty different legal regimes in Germany at the time, with twenty-five states, and that, of course, is not really conducive to market integration and economic development: hence, the notion of introducing a common civil code. There were civil codes already in force. Of course, we know the Code Napoleon, 1804. Frederick II of Prussia already had one, but that was written in French. Hence, it was not readily accessible to the commoners. There was another one in German, in the Kingdom of Saxony, but now, there should be a comprehensive one and indeed, a draft was put forth in the early nineties. At this point, Schmoller organised great opposition against this on the basis of legal empirical research. He pointed out that the draft was essentially deductive law, totally alien to economic practice, therefore not really worth it. The draft was completely reworked on the basis of empirical legal research done by social scientists trained in economics, but also in law. The enabling act was passed in 1896 in the summer in order to become effective on the first of January of 1900.

That was, as far as I can see, the last really major accomplishment of the people who worked in the tradition of the Sciences of State. Then something happened that we should take note of. The German sociological association is founded a couple of years later, followed

---

[5] See Schmoller (1923). In particular chapter 7 on work contract and work environment (pp. 294-367), and chapter 8 on new social institutions and welfare legislation (pp. 367-481).

by such associations in the United States. The University of Chicago is founded with the express purpose of launching sociology as a science of social engineering in order to solve social problems. That was the mission. A disintegration of the Sciences of State occurs. This brings me to point II.

3. Part II: The decomposition of the Sciences of State

The disintegration of the Sciences of State was not originally intended. First comes sociology, and the leading people in sociology, we think of scholars like Max Weber, Alfred Weber, Werner Sombart, or Georg Simmel. All made important contributions to economics, and at first just thought that economics had become more specialised. They felt a separate science of sociology was important next to economics in order to not loose sight of the whole picture. Difficulties between economics on the one hand, and law on the other began to emerge. The last big integrator was, of course, the person who had fought the battle over the civil code with Schmoller, Otto (later von) Gierke, and that was won actually by Gierke's writing, a very important commentary on the code. The code was then read through the commentary, and that was how the empirical part came into it.

In the first decade of the twentieth century follows the inception of another new science: and that is business economics, or business administration. You had important schools, called Schools of Commerce, for instance in Leipzig, in Vienna, in Berlin, and later in Rotterdam. It was certainly important to have such a science, but this development also laid the foundation for the disintegration of the Sciences of State. Those who started the approach to business economics (or "administration" (sic!)) were economists by training, bona fide economists, and they would never have thought of leaving that framework of discourse, but there was a development that occurred later - I shall explain it in a moment - that led to the separation of the two economic disciplines.

4. Part III: The difficulties of integration

Later, there were schools of public administration with their own disciplinary approaches, and after the Second World War also political science, and later policy sciences. Policy sciences are also interesting. For the re-integration of what used to be the Science of State, the programme of the Kennedy School of Government is an almost perfect example. These are sciences which again try to pick up the notion of integration. This is again an approach going back to the original concept of the Sciences of State. By the way, the most recent development is a discipline called communication studies. We have entire schools of communication and they are very successful. Again, their curriculum consists of an amalgam of different social sciences. The difficulties in bringing all these separate disciplines together lie in that each of the disciplines will develop its own culture, its own research focus, and its own methods of communicating research. They will typically also have their own standards of excellence, and these are very much tied to that very discipline. For instance, in law it is not important to publish in international journals. In economics, this is absolutely necessary. In economics, a particular type of empirical research is extremely important. It must be quantitative, which means that qualitative research has very much travelled into the discipline of sociology. Public administration, again, has totally different standards of excellence and so, it is very difficult to hold a faculty or research group together, emphasising the Sciences of State, because each of the component parts has different standards of excellence and there is no common denominator. This means, necessarily, since the meeting of standards of excellence is also tied with resources in terms of rewards that you have constitutionally established (*i.e.* because the organisation is constituted this way), centrifugal tendencies, when you put the Sciences of State together in the form that I have just described, as separate, individual disciplines.

5. Part IV: The connection to ISINI

Let me just say a word about the International Society for Intercommunication of New Ideas (ISINI). As I understand, these new ideas need not necessarily be new, but they may very well have been forgotten. The emphasis on intercommunication points to a difficulty with disciplinary research paradigms, *viz.* there is no check whether the areas between the disciplines remain researched. Each of them originally has a tendency to narrow its scope and then to narrow the allowable methods, those that are supposed to be excellent. Both of these tendencies result in the possibility that vast areas of knowledge not only do not get researched and produced, but also get lost. Knowledge that used to be available gets lost, because it is no longer taught in required courses or at least in elected ones. And if they are not taught, there is no preparation, and then there are no textbooks for it, and ultimately in time this knowledge becomes forgotten.

In addition, there was the language shift. Much of this work in the Sciences of State was originally published in German, also in French; English came in a little later as the major language of communication. Certainly, it became dominant after the Second World War and this means that there is a lot of knowledge that remains unknown and has the very strong chance of being forgotten. Hence, I think this is a particularly opportune time to ask for the intercommunication of ideas that may look very new, but can actually have been hidden in knowledge that was hitherto known.

6. Part V: A research programme of the State Sciences

I now come to the fifth point, the question: Where are the major areas to apply this research paradigm to? The first that comes to mind is a phenomenon that we are confronted with and is actually a very happy phenomenon, but we are not very well equipped to deal with: the *ageing* of society. Of course it is great if people live longer and can be productive for longer, but it also means that we have to provide for institutions in which this can take place and in which this can happen in a productive way. This is not a question of actuarial insurance mathematics, as which it very often is dressed up. It is also very much a question of understanding the sociology of the workplace; the law that governs the workplace and how to make it economically attractive to keep people employed, because, currently, this is not the case. Hence, age certainly is something that will really require a common effort of scholars in the Sciences of State as a problem very much akin to the social problem[6] in the nineteenth century.

Second, as far as I can see, is the issue of *education*. Education has very much been taken over, in particular higher education, by the State. This is also true for the United States, and here we have a debate in which even the President of the United States is immersing himself into the question what is supposed to be taught in schools. In his case, the question of evolution is paramount, and the President insists that both sides of the coin should be taught. However, there can be no question, there is only one scientific approach in this case, and there are no two sides of the coin. This is not a coin; it is a totally different issue. I mention this only because there is a limit to the possibility that the State can be helpful in this area. We have to come up with concepts that allow the institutions of higher education to have streams of revenue without having the strings attached that necessarily come, if the schools - or any purpose that the State may accomplish - are funded through tax finance. But we cannot do as the princes, for example Phillip the landgrave of Hesse, in the time of the Reformation did, that we simply take over the monastery and give it to Marburg University. They still have a major portion of their finances from the proceeds of this wonderful monastery. We are not in the time of the Reformation and great changes of property rights; today this is not an approach open to us. A more gradual approach should be taken, but Phillip the founder of the University of Marburg at least understood the basics of the issue. He did not want to intervene with the operation of the university. He was just interested in having a strong university and that should very much be our approach as well.

Health is a third issue where the State becomes increasingly involved, and not necessarily with good results. Even in the United States, the involvement is substantial, the lure to get involved in a democratic state is very tempting and the results are not particularly appealing. This again is the result of the fact that the issue is now essentially the subject of a very narrow discipline, health economics, which came about essentially when the British health system was created and the British needed people who could run this system, side by side with doctors. So, the Warwick School in Britain was founded, and they turned out these health administrators. However, health administrators perceive the issue of health in a very peculiar way: in the way that it is presented to them, as an administrative problem. Rather, health is a societal problem, which should be looked at from all sides of the Sciences of State.

Security is yet another case. The traditional ways of maintaining security may not be particularly effective. Everybody who has recently travelled in the United States in airports

---

[6] See Backhaus, J. forthcoming: The Social Question, Journal of Economic Studies.

is made keenly aware of this. What the Federal Authorities have organised there is patently ineffective and very costly. Our unwillingness to go beyond disciplinary lines is really costing us a lot of resources. Our knowledge of how to deal with security issues is limited and not well geared to the task of the security issues that we are facing today. We always had pirates, operating in particular seas, and that was a nuisance which could be dealt with by sending in a couple of battleships with the Marine, but the issue of pirates, which we still have today, can be dealt with. That is not the difficulty. Currently, the difficulty is global terrorism, and that requires a totally different understanding of what makes these network organisations tick.

Finally, the *cultural heritage*, which also includes religion, deserves our attention. We have to understand what motivates people to operate in a society, not only in organisations, in firms, in government agencies, in schools, in the military, but what motivates them in terms of the cultural heritage. We have to maintain the cultural heritage, which means we have to teach it, but we also have to have enough resources for the museums and for the collections. We have to make sure that the electronic revolution does not bring about the idea that we can throw away the books, and part of this is, of course, also religion. Religion is part of the cultural heritage, whether you want it or not, and a debate about the question whether there should be division between Church and State does not answer the question of how we deal with our religious heritage. The latter is not the same issue as the division between Church and State, because religion motivates people and it is therefore something we have to understand in terms of a mover in economics, in organisations, in the outcome of elections, in the motivation of court opinions, and in what is happening in the parliaments.

So, my lecture gives you at least five areas in which I think the Sciences of State provide a very interesting area to test that research paradigm.

References

Althusius, J., 1995, [1603]. Politica. F.S. Carney (Ed. and Transl.), Indianapolis, Liberty Fund.

Anonymous, 2005. Veit Ludwig von Seckendorff (1626-1692), European Journal of Law and Economics. Issue 19.3 (special issue), May 2005.

Backhaus, J., 1992. Friedrich List and the Political Economy of Protective Tariffs. In: S. Todd Lowry (ed.), Perspectives on the History of Economic Thought VII, Cheltenham: Edward Elgar Publishing Limited, pp. 142-156.

Backhaus, J., 1994. The German Economic Tradition: from Cameralism to the Verein für Socialpolitik. M. Albertone and A. Masoero (Ed.). Political Economy and National Realities. Torino. Fondazione Luigi Einaudi, pp. 329-356.

Backhaus, J. and R.E. Wagner, 1987. The Cameralists: A Public Choice Perspective. Public Choice 53, pp. 3-20.

Groehler, O., 1990. Bombenkrieg gegen Deutschland. Berlin: Akademie-Verlag.

List, F., 1983,. [1837]. The Natural System of Political Economy. W.O. Henderson (ed. and transl.), London: Frank Cass.

Mansholt, 2001, Brockhaus, Leipzig/Mannheim: F.A. Brockhaus, Vol. 14, pp. 178.

Pelikan, P. and G. Wegner (eds.), 2003. The Evolutionary Analysis of Economic Policy. Cheltenham, UK: Edward Elgar. Series: New Horizons in Institutional and Evolutionary Economics.

Rieß, R., 1997. Worker Security and Prussian Bureaucracy: A Meeting in the Prussian Ministry of Commerce. Essays on Social Security and Taxation.: J. Backhaus (Ed.), Marburg: Metropolis, pp. 143-171.

Schmoller, G. 1923. Grundriß der Allgemeinen Volkswirtschaftslehre [Principles of Economics]. Two volumes. (Blueprint I and II). Munich, Leipzig: Duncker & Humblot.

Six, F.A, 1942 (reprint). Der Westfälische Friede von 1648. (Westphalian Peace of 1648). Bremen: Faksimile-Verlag.

Von Seckendorff, V.L., 1976, [1665]. Teutscher Fürsten Stat. (German Principality). New edition. Reprint of the third corrected edition of 1665. Two volumes. Glashütten/Taunus: Detlev Auvermann.

Wolff, C., 1980, [1754 Halle]. Grundsätze des Natur- und Völkerrechts. (Principles of Natural Law and the Law of Nations). Collected Works, 1. Division, German Writings, Vol. 19. Reprint. M. Thomann. (Ed.). Hildesheim, New York: Olms.

Economics of culture

Arjo Klamer
Erasmus University, Erasmus School of Economics, Department of Economics of Art and Culture, PO Box 1738, 3000 DR Rotterdam, The Netherlands

1. Thinking in terms of values

Thank you for the honour to be able to give a lecture here for you in this conference. I feel always somewhat uncomfortable in lecturing because as a scholarly community we are used to share our insights in seminars, at least that should be the objective. So I will be most pleased if you will interrupt.

I now remember my very first presentation at an International Conference of the History of Economic Thought Society at Duke University. I shared the panel with an economist named Rugina, who at that time was known to be out of the mainstream and hard to place. I could not make a great deal of sense of what he was saying at the time. I could not place it in the training that I had received here at the University of Amsterdam in econometrics and at Duke. But throughout the years I have come to recognise that his way of thinking is actually close in many ways to the line of thinking that I have pursued myself.

Having the floor I take the liberty to take you on an excursion in a terrain that I have been exploring myself over the last few years in the hope that it means something to you, although I fear, seeing the papers that have been presented at this conference, that there is a good chance that we will miss each other, and that I will be talking about things that are of no interest to you. But I have to take my chances.

Economics is taking a strange turn these days. Last year the Clark medal went to Steven Levitt who this year published the book Freakonomics, written together with Stephen J. Dubner and dealing with all kind of issues that are hard to connect with economics such as the relation between abortion and crime. The greatest contribution to the decrease in crime he argues is not stronger penalties for crime, higher prison sentences and the like, but the more liberal abortion laws. Because of those potential criminals are being aborted. At least so Levitt argues. An economist's point? He has also interesting studies about what goal keepers should do facing a penalty. It's hard to see what such topics have to do with the big economic issues of today and what the economics is in his analysis. Even so, his work seems to be appealing to mainstream economists, It's fun as, one economist commented this morning in a column. Whether it is important is another matter. I prefer to deal with more important issues.

Let us take a really important issue. My wife and I wanted to go out. We have some small children as well as an older son. So we asked him to baby-sit. We asked him a long time in advance. He agreed. One day before our day out, it was a Wednesday, my son suddenly came to tell me "sorry I cannot do it tomorrow because the neighbours called and I can baby-sit there." What followed was a major discussion in the household. One of us proposed to forbid him to do this. He agreed to baby-sit at this house and he should stick to his promises. The other argued that if we hold him to his promise he never would promise to baby-sit again. So we never can make any appointment with him. It was suggested we pay him. But if we pay him then he will ask to be paid any time he baby-sits. It became a big row. Doors were slammed. What to do? In the end we reached a typically Dutch compromise: he went to the neighbours and arranged a girlfriend to baby-sit with us. So we ended up paying but not to our son.

All this I am telling you in order to illustrate that culture matters and that value matters. I like to start with everyday cases in the hope to drive the point home but you can also see the role of culture and values when it comes to issues like how to pay for health care-through the government or through the market or through other means?-, or how to pay for the arts - a topic that occupies me given my chair here in the Netherlands. I would like to convince you that these issues are important, and that a great deal of economic science as it has been developed over the last hundred years is of not great use to approach such issues. I say so with some pain in my heart because like Rugina I belonged to the Tinbergen School. Being a good Dutchman I was moved by Tinbergen to study econometrics; it was he who introduced me to what I would now call a modernist way of looking at the world. A modernist way of looking at the world means being inspired by the physics model, by the idea that a mathematical model of the world can capture the essential characteristics of that world, and shows us how to tinker with that world. Governments, after all, can influence the outcomes of the system by changing one variable or another. I took up the study of economics in order to contribute to the cure of poverty, unemployment and inequality in pace with Tinbergen. I was no exception. Many young economists were as idealistic as Tinbergen was at the time.

We have all seen what followed. Economic thinking became more and more technical and abstract and this led to what I just have called freakonomics. The thinking remains within the mainstream but the original faith in the objectives of modernist economics has been lost. We do not believe anymore that we can solve the problems of the world with our models.

So we're struggling to figure out what economics is good for if it does not generate the instruments to conduct policy. My proposal is, along the lines of what Rugina is arguing, to take our history seriously and realise that we don't all think new thoughts all the time, but stand on the shoulders of others. Going back to Aristotle or to Adam Smith, the moral philosopher, who dedicated one book to the subject of economics, we learn to think about what is good, about what contributes to a good society. Adam Smith, for example, argues that specialisation, a division of labour can contribute to a good society if it coincides with market transactions. In such a society we cannot appeal to the love and generosity of our brothers and sisters - "brothers" was his word; we cannot appeal to the friendship of all as he says in chapter 2, but we have to appeal to the self love of the butcher, brewer or the baker. Not that he thought that that is good from a moral philosophical point of view, but such action is the prudent thing to do in civil society where you are in need of the help of numerous others even though friendship would be preferable from his moral point of view. Smith had a moral point of view. Also Keynes saw economics as a moral science, or as a science that has to instruct us what to do, like how to finance health care or whether I should pay my son to baby-sit.

I would like to revive that notion of economics as a moral science, as a science that gives us a guideline on how to behave by means of systematic investigation. Should we privatise health care, is that better? Should we bring in the markets in the cultural sector? Should we pay more attention to the functioning of cultural capital in cities and organisations? Should we pay each other for service we render each other? Should we pay each other in a situation like this or should we stick to the communal interactions that we are used to enter with colleagues? After all, I'm not being paid for giving this lecture. Other arrangements are conceivable. We could pay for lectures given or maybe because of the scarcity of attention these days the lecturer should pay the audience for listening. And because I'm very much in need for supportive comments I will pay you for those as well. So anyone who makes an interesting comment gets, well let's negotiate about the price. Do I pay you before or after? As you can imagine the moment of payment could make a great deal of difference. But think it through and what difference would that make if I were to pay you and how we're going to determine what the price is and what is a valuable contribution? I just bring this in to make you realise how relevant a change in our interactions and transactions can be. If we all agree that what happens here is valuable and we're economists then we know that what's valuable has a price. So why not price it? Well, we immediately sense that that's not the way to do things.

I think we already have a contractual relation. You feed us by talking to us and we appreciate it. So that's what you provide and in turn we provide you with attention. Only if there is no equilibrium, some additional payment may be done.

I would like to argue that it makes a critical difference whether money comes in or not. When the money comes in explicitly we would move into another sphere of values, Let me try to show you what I mean. I want to depict for you a cultural economic perspective or, to give it another label, a neo-Aristotelian approach to economics. This perspective makes us write culture large and goes further than the practice of bringing in culture as a variable in economic models.

Culture, and I will define it better in a moment, is as you know not a concept that appears in economic textbooks. I challenge you to find the concept mentioned in any standard textbook. In certain circles culture gets recognised as an explanatory factor. Two years ago I was at a conference at the World Bank dedicated to the role of culture in developing economies. The belief is settling in that culture matters. Most well known is the Max Weber argument that Protestantism accounts for the rise of capitalism and market economies in Northern Europe. The challenge is now to show how for example Japanese culture can account for the success as well as for the failures of the Japanese economy. Anyhow, culture is here used as an explanation. But culture is not just an explanatory variable. I would like to turn things around.

Take the argument concerning the emerging importance of creative industries and the role that the government is supposed to take stimulating the development of these industries. The argument here is that culture is important for the economy and that the government should get involved in the promotion of creative industries in order to promote economic growth. I rather would reverse the order of the argument, arguing that the economy, the economics of the creative industries for example, serve the goal of furthering cultural causes.

The cue for this reversal of the chain of causation comes from old Greek thinkers, although you can find traces of that way of thinking throughout the ages. These Greek philosophers maintained that our life is about striving towards the good. The idea is that you and I are striving to realise the good, whatever the good is. Posing the issue this way is to problematise the self-interest that economists are wont to stress. What constitutes that self-interest? Is it in your interest to increase your wealth, to seek ever more profit and income? Maybe the pursuit of profit cost you a few friendships, or even a family along the way. Maybe you have to engage in suspicious transactions or deal with suspicious characters. The purpose, so we keep telling each other, is to pursue maximum happiness. That is what this is all about: happiness. That defines our self-interest. If that is so, we are in trouble. The reason is that although we in the Western world are becoming ever more richer, we don't seem to get happier as Bruno Frey and Slater have shown. On the contrary, all kinds of findings point at a decrease in happiness. Something is wrong. Either something is wrong in what we do or in what we think. I opt for the latter. There's something wrong in what we think. I suggest that we need to rethink what it is that we are after in order to account for the increasing level of unhappiness in a country like this.

My proposal is the following. Inspired by a neo-Aristotelian perspective, I stress the importance of values when I try to understand the behaviour not only of people but also of organisations and countries. I first distinguish economic values and economic capital. Economic values are the ones that we think so much about, that we measure so well; they are represented by income, wealth, and profit. Economic capital is then the power to generate economic values, something we can measure quite well too. Human capital is part of economic capital in the sense that economic capital enables us to generate income.

Economic values are nothing more and nothing less than means to generate other values. I don't have to tell an economist that we don't earn an income or that we generate wealth for the sake of earning income or for the sake of generating wealth. You earn an income to generate various goods or values, most important of all social values. Let me elaborate. If we assume, like Aristotle already did, that we are foremost social beings, it would follow that the realisation of social values is the major source of our feeling well. What I mean by such values are the values that we share with other human beings in certain settings. In a setting like this the social value can be collegiality. It most likely will have a major influence on how you are feeling about yourself right now. Other social values are solidarity and conviviality; they tell us how well we interact with each other, what our feelings are and what the quality of the feelings for our fellow human beings is. Within organisations social values show in the passion and motivation of workers. Responsibility is another social value. I would argue that a great deal what we do, including the buying and eating of ice-cream or buying a house or going on vacation, has the purpose of generating social values. There are other values of course, but I would stress the importance of social values, or social capital, that is, the power to generate social values. The problem with these concepts is that they appear very hard to measure.

Social values are important for the economy. The quality of the relations among people attests to the strength of the society, or the organisation for which they work. You will probably function better in a faculty that gets along with each other than in a department with lots of bickering and fighting. You benefit a great deal from having supportive colleagues and it causes a great deal of anxiety and trouble in your life when you don't have them. Likewise, you do better with having good friends, a good family, a good country, and an identity. So you could say that a great deal of our life and a great deal of what we do economically is directed at the generation, realisation and sustenance of social values. When you buy a car, you don't just buy a vehicle that gets you from a to b at a pretty good speed, safe and well, but you also buy yourself into a social group. A red Ferrari gives you another social standing than if you were to drive a Toyota. When you drive a BMW you distinguish yourself from someone who drives a Peugeot or a Rovers. It's not that these machines are all that different, but you and I connect meanings to them. And so there are meanings connected to them when you drive them. People are willing to pay a great deal extra to acquire such meanings. As a matter of fact, an important part of the economy is geared towards the generation of these meanings that provide and add to social values.

In addition to social values people strive to realise cultural values in their lives, organisations, cities and countries. Social values are important, but we humans distinguish ourselves in the sense that we also need, you can call this whatever you please, but let's call it inspiration. You and I need getting inspired so now and then, and in order to have that experience we act quite irrationally at times. Like paying too much money for a painting, or going to expensive concerts, or building very expensive churches and temples. And we do that because we're striving for some cultural values; we invest in our cultural capitals so to say. We do that as individuals, we do that as organisations, we do that as countries, we do that as cities, we do that on all levels. Small towns spend an extraordinary amount of money to erect some construction that has no other purpose than to represent something beautiful, something ecstatic, something strange. Indians built totem poles, Buddhists build temples, Christians build churches, now we build high rise buildings to celebrate financial institutions, we do all kind of things, just to generate that what we call cultural values.

Accordingly, people strive towards the good, and to accomplish their goal realise and sustain social as well as cultural values. They seek to establish relationships as well as moments of inspiration. As a consequence we spend time listening to music, walking in nature, and devoting ourselves to one religion or another, or search for the truth.

To the objection that these values can not be measured, let me evoke the joke that travels so well among economists. It is about a drunken man who is asked what he is looking at under the lamppost. He answers "my keys" and to the question why he is looking under the lamppost "this is where the light shines." Likewise we keep on focussing on economic measures whereas the answers may rather be found in the realm where we do not or cannot measure. If social and cultural values are important, we should not ignore them because we have no measurements for them. After all, hundred years ago we had no measures for economic growth, unemployment and inflation either. The development of good measures will take time.

2. Common goods

Let me offer an additional notion with which we may be able to probe the darkness. It concerns another category of goods. In economic reasoning we tend to think of two types of goods: public goods and private goods. Private goods you can buy on the market, collective goods or public goods you cannot buy. They have to be provided by the government, basically. But with this division economists ignore the most important genre of goods for our striving. I would call them common goods. These are goods that you cannot own yourself, so they're not private.

They are not public, no they are owned by a certain group of people and exclude others from its use. A good example is friendship. Friendship is good, you benefit from having a good friend. It's good for all kind of things. It's also an economic good in a sense that you have to make an effort to gain friends. Friends don't come like that, I mean you have to spend time, attention, money to gain friends. Friendship also has the curious feature that when you make use of it, you may actually strengthen the friendship. But although a friendship is so important, you cannot own it yourself, even though you say that's my friend. You can gain friends, you can loose them, but you cannot buy and sell them. I cannot offer you extra friends of mine for whom I do not have the time right now.

The same is true for a family. If you have a nice family, a warm family if I were to visit you and I'm overwhelmed by the warmth of your family, you clearly benefit. You get a lot of love, attention and appreciation from your family members; you have a nice place to go to. You obviously have made a great effort to have such a family. Families don't come like that as I discovered myself. You have to sacrifice things in order to have a good family life. That is family: you cannot sell it, it is not from you, it is not yours, it is something that you share with the other members of the family. It is what you have in common. But others outside the family including myself are not part of it. We don't co-own that, we are excluded from it. Therefore you have fences in the front door, you exclude others from sharing this warmth and this love in your own family. It's a common good.

And so you can go on. Collegiality and a nice college you share with your colleagues as a common good. Relationships in general are a common good. The same you could say of culture, for culture is a common good as well. Having strong social and cultural values means that you have those in common with others. Common goods make up a culture. Culture, in turn, is that what you share with a distinct group of people and in which you distinguish yourself from other people. So the Dutch share a culture, excluding or at least distinguishing themselves from others. In that sense that they are different from others. When you are Dutch you can say that is my culture. If you're not Dutch you are outsider and it will take a great effort to become part of it and to call that culture your own. Some believe it is almost impossible to do so. The same applies of course for Ghanese culture or Japanese culture or wherever you are from. All those cultures are something that you can call yours and exclude others. Cultures can be nice, can be not so nice, they're different, but it is a common good and for all purposes it turns out that it is important that we have it.

3. Concluding remarks

Surely, this exploration of the role that values play in our actions and the importance of common goods has been preliminary. We still have a long way to go along this route before it will pay off. But the first results are already noticeable. For example, the notion of the common goods appears to put the problem of altruistic behaviour aside. The problem has haunted the science of economics as altruistic behaviour contradicts the economic assumption of the self-interestedness of individual agents. But now we understand that altruistic behaviour is nothing but behaviour directed at one common good or another. Artists appear to sacrifice a great deal for their art but what they gain is the common good of the artistic community. We scientists sacrifice income and family time in order to be able to share the common good that is the scientific community.

Goods in the sense that I am using the notion here, are like values. A relationship is a good, and as such represents social and sometimes cultural values. The striving towards the good, therefore, is the striving to gain (common) goods and with those the realising of values. It makes for a different economics, for an economics that is more like the moral science that Aristotle and Adam Smith had in mind and to which Keynes had hoped to contribute. We are only contributing to this honourable tradition.

Economic paradigms and theories

Some aspects of professor Anghel Rugina's proposal to a money-commodity

Lazaros Th. Houmanidis
Professor Emeritus, Dept. of Economics, University of Piraeus, Piraeus, Greece

Abstract

The above mentioned paper concerns to the contribution of Professor Anghel Rugina and includes an orientation table on the achievement of steady equilibrium. The paper also includes a comparison between the model of Walras and the model of Rugina who refers to the different kinds of disequilibrium because of the anti-numeraire, monetised money. At this point Rugina presents to us the models M1, M2, M3, M4, M5, M6, M7. The first of them (M1) refers to a 100% equilibrium and the last (M7) to a model of 100% disequilibrium. In the as above paper the author also takes into account the corresponding institutional and social framework (R1, R2, R3, R4, R5, R6, R7) that Professor Rugina proposes so as to obtain a more complete model than that of Léon Walras. The author combines his own theory of cost dependence which coincides with Rugina's models from 0% to 100% cost of dependence (models 1 to 7). He also does not omit to mention the difficulties for a money commodity gold, as the stock of gold is not enough to cover the needs for it.

JEL classification: B0

Keywords: equilibrium models, Rugina's orientation table, steady and monetary equilibrium, simple and expanded reproduction, Walras

1. Classics and equilibrium

For Adam Smith (1723-1790) the leader of the Classical School, price is directly determined by supply and demand. The price is proportional to demand and inversely proportional to supply. Supply and demand determine the price, and the latter determines supply and demand.

The French Smithean Jean Baptiste Say (1767-1832) devised the law of *loi des débouches*, implying that supply creates its own demand. Say argued, that under free competition, the incomes generated are used to purchase the products offered in the market, thus leading to economic equilibrium without unemployment. The mere creation of a product immediately opens a vent for another product, offsetting the whole amount of such value (Say, 1972 [1803]). Once a new good is produced, income accrues to the factors of production; the latter do not have to use this income for purchasing their own output but can be used for another good. Thus, any overproduction of a good would be offset by the underproduction of another good (Pen, 1965) and total output would be absorbed by aggregate demand. As Say explains, *if some products are in super abundance, this happens because other products are scarce* (Say, 1972: 142). In his view, the liberal system has therefore exhibited an undisturbed harmony, governed by the law of self-interest, as pointed out by Adam Smith. Any malfunctioning of this economic system would be automatically remedied by the "invisible hand", which accompanies free competition and corrects any disturbance of the system.

In the light of Smith's philosophical view that individuals are motivated by their own interests and sacrifice less to achieve more, this behaviour is beneficial to the society, too. Added together, the behaviour of every individual member of a nation would lead that nation to progress, as they would deliver maximum benefit at minimum cost.

This overall bright picture of the liberal economic system was marred by the pessimistic views of its long-term evolution, as expressed by the classical economists Thomas Robert Malthus (1766-1834) and David Ricardo (1772-1823). The former argued that human populations tended to grow at a geometric progress, while foodstuffs grow at an arithmetic rate. This was Malthus's law of population. Building on this law, Ricardo formulated his well-known theory of land rent, postulating that, as a result of the continuous growth of population, cultivation expands to less and less fertile land, so that through the various stages of cultivation the price of the product adjusts to the price of the least fertile land - marginal land - for the benefit of inter-marginal land. Thus, at some point of time, productivity would decrease, resulting to the absorption of the diminishing profits and wages by land rent.

It is not my intention to discuss Ricardo's theory of rent here, which would be certainly beyond the scope of this article. Nevertheless, I could argue, at a first approach, that the marginal land could also offer a rent, since the growth of population would exert upward pressure on the price of the product of the marginal land, causing it to rise above cost, but not as much as to cultivate another land.

This gloomy outlook of the system and the miserable conditions of workers during the industrial revolution (1760-1830) nourished the ideas of the opponents of liberalism, *i.e.* socialists and the most ruthless critic of the capitalist system, Karl Marx.

We have already mentioned the economic equilibrium according to Adam Smith. However, the law of supply and demand explains changes in prices, but not economic value. In this respect, Smith retained the distinction between natural price (cost) and market value (price) and provided a cost-based explanation of value. Marx also adhered an objective consideration of value.

2. Marx and disequilibrium

According to Marx (1818-1883), only labour is productive, and only labour-force as a commodity creates value and surplus-value (the latter notion was also captured by Hodgskin, Thompson and Sismondi). Surplus value is appropriated by the owner of the means of production and is defined as the yield from the exploitation of labour force, which as a commodity is underpaid, *i.e.* it is purchased at below its value. Surplus value is the reason for social conflict, *i.e.* class struggle, as well as for economic disequilibrium. It enables the capitalist entrepreneur to accumulate capital and the worker to accumulate unpaid sweat, depending on his contribution. In addition, under these conditions, as a result of competition, between the employed and the unemployed in the labour market and between capitalists, the means of production replace more and more units of labour, ultimately leading to a fall in the average rate of profit (surplus value in relation to total capital, *i.e.* capital invested in means of production plus capital invested in labour). Thus, according to Marx, the fall of the average of profit in the long run will ultimately bring the capitalist system to its inevitable end (Marx, 1968: Vol. III, Ch. IX).

3. From Classical to Austrian thought

Admittedly, the Classical School has not answered some fundamental questions, in fact asked by its own major proponents, such as Malthus, who recognised that the under-consumption implied by the law of population would tend to cause for humanity a gloomy economic future. From his own point of view, Ricardo observed that the continuous diminishing productivity would increasingly lead to a decline in profit-induced capital accumulation, hence a decline in investment, at the expense of also the workers themselves.

Another question still waiting for an answer refers to the phenomenon of value. Smith did observe the paradox of water, which is so useful, yet in most cases has no exchange value, but refrained from a further investigation into the matter. This venture was undertaken in about 1870 by an Austrian, Carl Menger (1840-1921), a Frenchman, Léon Walras (1834-1910), and an Englishman, Stanley Jevons (1835-1882), all of whom introduced utility into the unit of quantity to formulate the theory of marginal utility. By Menger's "lowest importance of use", Walras's "intensity of the last want satisfied" or "scarcity" and Jevons's "final degree of utility", economic phenomena are no longer examined objectively, as by Smith and his followers (Malthus, Ricardo, Senior, J. St. Mill) and Marx, but subjectively/psychologically.

The above subjective authors, like the Classics, are also based on the assumption that individuals are motivated by their own interests within an economy of free competition and on the concept of a timeless automatic static equilibrium, barely touching the phenomenon of monopoly.

4. Walras and economic equilibrium

Walras, the leader of the School of Lausanne, or Mathematical School or School of Economic Equilibrium, explored the equality between effective demand and effective supply of every good or service, which also gives the economic equilibrium. This equilibrium tends to be restored within free perfect competition in a system that comprises the equilibrium of exchanges without frictions and every kind of monopoly.

Demand and supply according to Walras act on each other, each economic factor trying to achieve the greater satisfaction through the least effort. Each product has one and only one price, the same happens with services *i.e.* soil, labour, capital. The rendered services are formed into products by the auctioneer-entrepreneur who is standing between the two separate markets of goods and services. The sellers of the services come into bargaining with the entrepreneur who demands them for his production of goods. The current price in the arena of the market in which the price equalises the bargaining between sellers and buyers, and equalises these two counter-balancing forces. The cutting of the two curves of demand and supply is the point where rarity, intensity of the last want satisfied and cost coincide. At this point there is no dynamic profit and equilibrium; the supply exceeds the demand, the prices fall and *visa versa*. The equalisation between the two separate markets (products and services) forms the general equilibrium-money in the market without causing any disequilibrium.

At this point Walras (1924 [1874]) examines two cases: a) money-commodity and b) fiduciary money (credit money).

If, says Walras, we have money-commodity, *i.e.* gold, silver or anything else that can also be used as money (Q_a), of which one part (Q'_a) circulates as commodity and the other part as money (Q''_a), the quantity Q''_a has a price Pa in terms of another commodity and desired cash balances (*encaisse desirée*) are denoted by H, then:

$$Q''_a P_a = H \qquad \text{(Eq. 1)}$$

If cash balances decline, then the general level of prices will rise accordingly. If both the total quantity of money and cash balances decrease, prices will fall proportionally. The next step for Walras is to argue that if the desired cash balances are equal to the quantity of money, we have equilibrium in production, capitalisation and circulation. This, according to Walras, implies that money is governed by the fundamental principle that value rises with an increase in utility and falls with an increase in quantity. Taking also the use of credit money (F) (drafts, banknotes, *etc.*) into account, Equation 1 takes the following form:

$$(Q''_a + F) P_a = H \qquad \text{(Eq. 2)}$$

Equation 2 represents monetary disequilibrium. This is so because both entrepreneurs and banks do not put in circulation the same quantity of capital in proportion to the quantity money in circulation so that cash balances can remain constant and the quantity of money and price can change accordingly. Therefore, it is only Equation 1 that shows that the stock of money will be equal to cash balances and equilibrium would be achieved by the stabilisation of prices.

5. Rugina's contribution to economic equilibrium

As is the case with all equilibrium economists, Professor Rugina's thinking can be traced back to Walras. However, Rugina has moved further beyond Walras, as he has moved further and further in each of his Prolegomena.

Equation 1 of Walras coincides with Model M1 in Rugina's Orientation Table (see Annex) according to which we have constant economic equilibrium with money-commodity 100% and anti-numeraire 0% (credit money and monetisation of credit).

Turning from Equation 1 to Equation 2 that includes credit money, we have, according to Walras, disequilibrium. According to Anghel Rugina, however, this marks the beginning of Models M2 to M7 (see Annex), *i.e.* of increasing disequilibrium up to 100%, with 100% monopoly and 100% anti-numeraire, which is according to Anghel Rugina "the paper money plus the monetised bank credit". Numeraire is the instrument which helps to obtain stable measurement of marginal utilities (Rugina, 2001).

Anghel Rugina also goes beyond Walras by his function of unified knowledge, *i.e.* S = f (A, P), where S is the practical solution of any economic problem, A the all existing utilities at the actual conditions of disequilibrium and P the future potential possibilities under the optimal conditions of general steady equilibrium. If we are to reach the desirable solution of moving from A to P, we have to implement, as Rugina claims, a monetary policy of 100% money-commodity, accompanied by 0% anti-numeraire and 100% free competition, *i.e.* 0% monopoly. Thus, we are told by Rugina, we avoid disequilibrium that goes hand in hand with unemployment.

In my view, however, under free competition it is impossible to avoid monopoly (as free competition can ultimately lead to monopoly) but only in free competition we can obtain economic equilibrium. Thus we must restrict monopoly to less than 5% of minor deviations from equilibrium. I believe that with a favourable institutional framework we can achieve a 100% free competition. At this point Rugina contributed to add an institutional factor R in his models M1 to M7 (see Annex).

I would like to herein mention my theory of the dependence cost or dependence cost effect (Houmanidis, 1957: in French 1994, Chap. IX). This cost is psychological and refers to a factor of production (factor A) on another factor (factor B) that is remunerated by factor A for services provided by B to A. The higher the reward paid by factor A to factor B, the lower the cost of B's dependence on A. Conversely, the higher the reward paid by A to B, the lower the cost of A's dependence on B. Therefore, in accordance with my theory of the cost of dependence it will tend to rise as we move from M1 to M7 (in accordance with the Orientation Table of Rugina). Thus in model M1 the cost of dependence should be zero at M7 its highest point 100% of dependence.

As already mentioned, Rugina draws heavily on Walras. However, he moves further, realising that Walras's model lacks the institutional factor, which is represented by R in Rugina's Orientation Table.

Model M1 coincides, according to Rugina, with Marx's circuit of simple reproduction of capital, C (commodity) - M (money) - C: simple circulation of commodities "money that is money only". Models M2 to M7 coincide with the Marxian circuit of expanded reproduction, which starts from a money-capital and ends at surplus value, *i.e.* M (money-capital) - C (commodity) - M' (surplus value). Thus in, the circuit of expanded reproduction, money (unconverted money and credit money) is not only a medium of exchange but also capital, which buys labour force for the owner of the capital to exploit - according to Marx - and thus earn surplus value. This is the case, as Rugina points out, of what Schumpeter calls "capitalist function of money" (Rugina, 1975).

6. Concluding remarks

The first circuit of Marx develops normally and indicates balanced growth (Rugina, 1975), while profit is achieved normally through successful combinations of factors of production *i.e.* contribution of the entrepreneur. The second circuit shows buoyant profits with a different form of circulation (Marx, 1968 [1868]; Rugina, 1975).

Under the second system of expanded reproduction, remuneration is not appropriately allocated across the factors of production, and indebtedness to banks causes excess saving, in excess of normal capital formation. This leads to forced saving through inflation, as well as to an inevitable decrease in incomes at the expense of consumers (Schumpeter, 1955 [1911]; Rugina, 1975; Houmanidis, 1999). Forced saving is a consequence of anti-numeraire which coincides with a disequilibrium and irrational economy.

Rugina added in the Walrasian formula the factor R (institutional and cultural framework) in order to achieve a steady equilibrium which is included in his Orientation Table and which he analyses by exposing his political, institutional and moral ideas.

Rugina added also for the most efficient economic policy the natural parameter that is connected with money commodity. For this reason Rugina considers the Euro as money which would create disequilibria.

The point here concerns to the fact whether there are reserves of gold or silver to adopt a money-commodity currency. I must say that Gustav Cassel (1927, [1918]) from his point of view proved that the reserves of gold do not correspond to the need for it.

I have nothing else to discuss herein about the Orientation Table of Anghel Rugina. A lot could be probably said on this subject, but this cannot be done in the narrow limits of an article. Still, the work of the Romanian-American scholar does not end here. He conceives a set of philosophical, economic, social, political and moral ideas within a new economic system, which should be studied and appreciated as an outstanding contribution to economics.

Acknowledgements

I would like to thank Gerrit Meijer and the other editors for their fruitful comments. I would also like to thank my granddaughter Athanasia Megremi for her assistance in the final form of the article.

References

Cassel, G., 1927 [1918]. The Theory of Social Economy. Augustus Kelly, New York.
Houmanidis, L., 1994 [1957]. The Theory of Wages, from the Classics until Today (in Greek), preface by Amintore Fanfani. French translation Le Solaire Ouvrier depuis les Classiques jusqu'a nos jours, ed. Synchroni Ekdotiki, Athens.
Houmanidis, L., 1999. History of Economic Theories (in Greek). Synchroni Ekdotiki, Athens.
Marx, K., 1968. Capital. Vol. III. Public Publishers, Moscow.
Pen, J., 1965. Modern Economics. Penguin Books, London.
Rugina, A.N., 1975. A Monetary Dialogue with Karl Marx, its significance for both capitalist and socialist countries. East European Quarterly III, No 3 and No 4.
Rugina, A.N., 2001. Prolegomena 3. Fundamentals to any Present and Future Economic, Monetary, Financial and Social Stabilization Plans. International Journal of Social Economics 28, No. 1-2.
Say, J.B., 1972 [1803]. Traité d' Economie Politique. Levy, Paris.
Schumpeter, J.A., 1955 [originally in German 1911]. The Theory of Economic Development. Oxford University Press, New York- Oxford.
Walras, L., 1924 [1874]. Elements d' Economie Politique Pure. R. Pichon - R. Durant, Lausanne.

Annex: Rugina's Orientation Table for economics and finance (Rugina, 2001)

Models

M_1 = A system of 100 percent (Co+Nu) + R_1
This is the Walrasian model of general stable equilibrium at its limit of perfection and in its more complete form. It is immune to anomalies, relativity uncertainty. This is the "economics of pure and perfect competition" (certainty).

M_2 = A system of 95 percent (Co + Nu) + 5 percent (Mo + anti-Nu) + R_2
This approximates to the model that Quesnay, Adam Smith and other classical thinkers up to Marshall inclusive, have used in their analysis. It may be called the "economics of classical laws" with minor deviations. This is the area of weak minor disequilibria.

M_3 = A system of 65 percent (Co + Nu) + 35 percent (Mo + anti-Nu) + R_3
This is a mixed economy where equilibrium elements still prevail but relativity begins to play a important role. It belongs to the "economics of simple relativity" or relativity I. This is the area of strong minor disequilibria.

M_4 = A system of 50 percent (Co + Nu) + 50 percent (Mo + anti-Nu) + R_4
This particular combination represents a mixed economy of static nature and hidden stagnation. It is the true model that Keynes improperly called "equilibrium with unemployment". Actually it is the domain of the "economics of unstable equilibrium": in his dynamic analysis Keynes left out the limit 50:50 and dealt with the "economics of relativity" in general terms. Modern capitalism moved up and down around Model M_4 or between Models M_3 and M_5 and thus Keynes' observation of "involuntary unemployment" was correct empirically and analytically. This is the area of weak disequilibria.

M_5 = A system of 35 percent (Co + Nu) + 65 percent (Mo + anti-Nu) + R_5
This is a mixed economy where disequilibrium elements prevail. Below this line the business cycle becomes unmanageable. It is the domain of what may be called the "economics of compound relativity II". This is the area of strong major disequilibria.

M_6 = A system of 5 percent (Co + Nu) + 95 percent (Mo + anti-Nu) + R_6
This is the model of a decaying mixed capitalist economy in a country where a Marxist or fascist revolution succeeded in overthrowing the old system and instituted a brand new socialist or fascist regime. It is the domain of the "economics of compound relativity III" or more explicitly, the "economics of a centrally planned and controlled economy and society".

M_7 = A system of 100 percent (Mo + anti-Nu) + R_7
This is the limiting Marxian model of total revolution, disequilibrium and uncertainty, which requires a government of absolute powers to hold an unstable system together. It is the domain of the "economics of pure and perfect state monopoly" (uncertainty).

Money, freedom and order in the European Union

Gerrit Meijer

Maastricht University, Faculty of Economics and Business Administration, Larixlaan 3, 1231 BL Loosdrecht, The Netherlands. g.meijer@hetnet.nl

Abstract

The introduction of the Euro and the working of the European Central Bank are discussed at the background of the general problems of the role of money, the monetary system and monetary policy in a free society. The historical background, the objectives and the consequences of the political decisions in this field of policy of the European Union are explored. The paper concentrates on the consequences for freedom and order of this monetary institutional set-up and policy and on possibly better alternatives for the future. In this respect free banking and international money commodity is discussed.

JEL classification: B1, B2, E5, E42, F33

Keywords: money, monetary policy, European Central Bank, monetary system, free banking

1. Introduction

In this paper the introduction of the Euro and the working of the European Central Bank are discussed at the background of the general problems of the role of money, the monetary system and monetary policy in a free society. Money in a free society has an international and a national aspect. It serves as a medium of exchange and as a medium of account. It makes a nation- and worldwide division of labour and therefore the combination of freedom and the great society possible.

The historical background, the objectives and the consequences of the political decisions in this field of policy of the European Union are explored. The paper concentrates on the consequences for freedom and order of this monetary institutional set-up and policy and on possibly better alternatives for the future. In this respect free banking and international money commodity is discussed.

These problems are discussed as much and as far as possible in six sections with the corresponding subjects: Money, Freedom and the State; The International Monetary Constitution; The National Monetary Constitution I; The National Monetary Constitution II; Monetary Problems of Today in the European Union I; Monetary Problems of Today in the European Union II. Moreover a few concluding remarks will be made.

2. Money, freedom, and the state

To answer the questions 'What is money?' and 'What is the relation between money and the state?' we will pay attention to the discussion around 1900 between Menger and Knapp.

From these two authors, Menger is well-known as the founder of the Austrian School of Economics. He wrote an article on money in 1892 as a contribution to the discussions on the Austro-Hungarian monetary constitution. Knapp is a member of the German Historical School who published his book *Die staatliche Theorie des Geldes* in 1905.

The answer to the first question: 'What is money?' depends on what people accept and use as money. This differs according to circumstances of time and place. This is also the case with regard to the Euro. Although in most cases the fiat of the state comes after, in the case of the Euro it came before the introduction. It is artificial, constructivist money. In this way the spontaneous order is corrupted. The future of this money unit depends on the acceptance of it in Europe (in the countries were it is legal tender) and internationally (as an international reserve; there it competes with other international currencies like the dollar, the yen, the pound sterling, the Swiss franc, *etc.*). Most important in this respect is trust.

In the long run forced money can not work. Trust depends in this case on the organisation and management of the European monetary system. This point is discussed further in sections 5 and 6.

With regard to the other question it can be concluded that the difference of opinion between Knapp (1905) and Menger (1892), in which the first stated that money was a creation of the state and the latter that money had its origin in convention was not an absolute one. According to Howard S. Ellis (1934), who extensively wrote on the Menger-Knapp discussion, Knapp did not write and contend that the state determined the value but only the validity of money (acceptance as legal tender).

The state can mismanage money as well as reform the monetary system. Examples are the German hyperinflation after World War I and the German monetary reform (1948) after World War II. Menger was aware of the fact that the state defined in modern times what the money unit is, *etc.* Knapp knew from history that money as an institution was a result of human action, not of human design.

Although the state not always defined what money is at all times and places (especially not in prehistory) and later on not for all kinds of money (due to the problem of defining what money is) it usually did. However it were always people that in the end decided what money is, in spite of what the state had decided. The state is providing a service: seigniorage. People can refuse it. In the short run the state can dispose. In the long run the people disposes.

3. The international monetary constitution

First special attention will be given to the concepts of order (in German *Ordnung*) and constitution (in German *Verfassung*). They are used in the meaning given to them by Walter Eucken (1952; see also Meijer, 1988, 1994). According to Eucken the economic process can either be co-ordinated by prices via the competitive market (the market order or competitive order) or subordinated via a central plan (the centrally administered economy).

The market order (competitive order) has six constitutive principles: A stable monetary system, private property, free entry and exit, freedom of contract, full accountability, constancy of policy. Therefore a framework of law has to be provided by the participants in the economic process and government. These provisions are *e.g.* the monetary constitution (*Geldverfassung*), and the constitution for private property (*Eigentumsverfassung*). He also distinguishes an economic constitution (*Wirtschaftsverfassung*) and a state constitution (*Staatsverfassung*), being respectively the framework of law for the economic and the political process.

In the following the problems around international money (standards) are discussed on the basis of three texts written by F.A. Lutz (1954, on flexible exchange rates), J. Rueff (1960, on the gold exchange standard), and F.A. Hayek (1943, on the commodity reserve standard).

F.A. Lutz (1901-1975) was born in Germany and belonged to the Freiburg School of which Walter Eucken (1891-1950) was the head. He was professor at Princeton and Zürich. With regard to the question free and fixed exchange rates he was in favour of free (flexible) exchange rates. The decisive argument for this was that fixed exchange rates only worked well in case of flexible wages and prices and that these did not exist in reality because of monopolistic and oligopolistic markets for labour and goods and services. Moreover governments followed full employment (not the avoidance of inflation: stable money) as the primary policy goal.

This means resignation for economic and political power concentrations. Maybe not in the sense that he did not want to destroy them by competition and labour market policy, but in the sense of accepting them for the time being as facts. There anyhow exists a tension with the position of the Freiburg School (to attack all kinds of concentrations of economic and political power (including amongst others abuse of power by labour unions, entrepreneurs or political parties, or combinations of them), and especially Eucken (1952; see also Meijer 1988, 1994), who was in favour of fixed exchange rates, 100% money and the commodity reserve standard. This is less pronounced in the case of Friedman (1953), who writes in favour of flexible exchange rates at almost the same time not against the background of Germany (or more general Europe) but against the background of the United States. In the United States the competition policy and labour market policy were more strict against abuse of power of entrepreneurs and trade unions.

In this case the overriding purpose for Lutz is to reach full convertibility in international moneys, and as a consequence free movement of goods, and of the production factors labour and capital. This would mean free international trade and international competition, which would increase competition in and between countries and erode positions of concentrated power. When the price and wage system is inflexible in case of fixed exchange rates a policy of deflation would have to be followed which would mean an increase of unemployment, which in the existing economic and political circumstances will not be an acceptable policy for unions and government, *i.e.* 'politically impossible'.

The French economist Rueff (1960), and adviser to General De Gaulle, points out the danger for the West of the gold exchange standard, and therefore of the then existing System of Bretton Woods. He wants to go back to the gold standard and to increase (double) the gold price. Although the System of Bretton Woods was left by the United States some years later, there was no return to the gold standard. The United States preferred the system of flexible exchange rates. The reasons are similar to the arguments in favour of flexible exchange rates and against fixed exchange rates. It was thought to be 'politically impossible'. The question can be raised whether it would be possible to restore some kind of an international monetary standard, *e.g.* an improved gold standard (a.o. Rugina, 1949; for a summary of his ideas see Meijer, 1987), the commodity reserve standard, or still other possible standards (like the silver or the oil-standard).

Hayek (1943) thinks the commodity reserve standard has some advantages compared to the gold standard, because it is not based on one commodity. The system however is very intricate and complicated compared to the gold standard.

4. The national monetary constitution I

In this section the role of the state in relation to the national monetary system is the central problem. With regard to the rules for monetary policy special attention is paid to the discussion on neutral money. J.S. Mill (1865) wrote: *"There cannot, in short, be intrinsically a more insignificant thing, in the economy of society, than money; ... it only exerts a distinct and independent influence of its own when it gets out of order."* There does not exist an essential difference between a monetary and a non-monetary order. Lutz (1969) and De Jong (1973) discuss several interpretations of this concept, especially those of Wicksell (the price level has to be stable), Hayek (M resp. MV has to be constant), and Johan G. Koopmans (hoarding plus money destruction has to be equal to dishoarding plus money creation, or: net pure demand for money has to be zero). De Jong points out that neutral money means monetary equilibrium.

Hayek criticises the use of the price level as a guideline for monetary policy. When this is done technical progress, and the cost- and price reduction that is its consequence, is not taken into account. He sees in the monetary policy that followed the rule that the price level had to be stable, the main cause of the Great Depression.

Formally the MV approach is the same as the Keynesian C+I approach. There is however a difference about the causalities. Friedman is a correction of the Keynesian approach (Meijer, 1988). He shows in his econometric work that the marginal and average consumption quote are constant and not declining by increase of income. There is not a liquidity trap. There are always enough investment opportunities. From his monetary research it follows that the velocity of money is relatively constant. Therefore it follows according to Friedman that the relation between M and P.Yr is important for monetary and budget policy. Friedman (1953) bases his money growth rule on this.

In the later discussions of Patinkin (1965) and Gurley and Shaw (1960) conditions are formulated for neutrality of money. Money does not have a disturbing influence on the economic process when certain conditions with regard to the organisation of the economic process (economic order) are fulfilled. In this way conditions for neutral money which were implicit in the work of the pioneers in this field were made explicit.

Related to this discussion was the discussion on rules versus authorities. For this discussion the publications of Henry C. Simons (1948 [1936]), who lived from 1899-1946, and Hayek (1972 [1960]) are important. Have monetary authorities to be bound by law to certain rules for monetary policy, or is it to be left to their discretion? The argument they think is decisive is that the economic subjects for making their plans need to know what the policy will be. In relation to this point, discussions on 100% money and independence of the Central Bank started.

With regard to the first point, those in favour of 100% money think only then the Central Bank can control the money supply (inclusive credit creation by banks). In the debates between the monetary schools in the nineteenth century (see next section) this was an important point. Both questions become central in the following sections.

5. The national monetary constitution II

Some other proposals and opinions on the solution of the problem of freedom and order with relation to money, especially the free banking proposal/denationalisation of money go back to the discussions in the nineteenth century between the currency school, the banking school and the free banking school. In 1844 the Peel Act, which followed the ideas of the Currency School, came into force, and was the outcome of the political struggle between these three schools. For a summary of that discussion I refer to A.J. Schwartz (2003) and Yeager in his Preface to the reprint of the book of Vera C. Smith (1990, XIII-XXVI). Vera C. Smith (1912-1976) was married to F.A. Lutz, and wrote her book as a dissertation under the direction of F.A. Hayek at the London School of Economics (1936).

In the discussions two problems were in the centre. The first was whether there ought to exist one independent (that means private, and independent from the government) banknote emission bank (Central Bank) or that there ought to be free banking (competition between private banknote emission banks). The latter was related to 'normal' banking, *e.g.* credit creation.

History shows that several solutions were found in practice. In the nineteenth century, before the Peel Act came into being, discussions took place at the background of financial history in the two centuries before.

For Smith (1936, reprint 1990) and her followers (*e.g.* Hayek 1976; Selgin (1988); White (1984);Yeager (1990, 1997)) the history of money and banking was extended by the period after the introduction of the Peel Act. The influence of the Central Bank(s) increased. However they became also more dependent on government and in several countries they became nationalised. Also it turned out that private banks were able to create money by credit creation, which was the origin of the business fluctuations (business cycle). To fight this the Central Bank had the possibility to use the monetary instruments for trying to achieve 'neutral money'. This is by discount policy, open market policy and policy with relation to reserve ratio's. This led especially in the thirties to discussions on norms for monetary policy (the neutral money discussion), on rules versus authorities, and on the independency of the Central Bank).

In the time after the enacting of the Peel Act the deficiencies of this act were clearly understood by *e.g.* Bagehot (1873) but he saw it as politically impossible to change the system fundamentally. He was satisfied by pointing out these deficiencies, and warned against them. He proposed improvements within the system.

As a more fundamental proposal of change the 100% proposal has to be referred to. Also important is in this connection the proposal of an improved gold standard and of the commodity reserve standard.

In recent times the proposals for free banking and denationalisation of money have been worked out basing on the experience with and the theory of free banking. Free banking or denationalisation of money does not mean that the state has no role with regard to money and the organisation of money and banking. In this field government, just like in all other fields of economic life, has to create and enforce an economic order (rules on free entry, contract, liability, competition *etc.*). Often it is also tried to combine this system with the proposals of 100% money and the commodity reserve standard. With respect to the last proposal it has to be kept in mind that it is very complex and intricate, and needs discretionary (international) government interference.

In case competition is imperfect between non-homogenous moneys, transaction costs would be high in case of free banking (Pellanda, 2003). Other problems indicated in the above mentioned literature are how we can recognise good money, and how the problem of runs can be handled. Why should people have distrust in the state and not in private business? How to control the producers of money and trust? Is this done better with public money or with competition in moneys?

In this connection the historical record of free banking is favourable, especially the historical example of free banking in Scotland. It did work, with only one failure in 100 years. There was no tendency to monopoly. It was a fractional reserve system. In fact it was a clearance system with a daily check on over-issue. The London Pound was the numéraire. The pound was issued in London on a 100% gold base.

6. Monetary problems of today in the European Union I

In the sections 5 and 6 the monetary problems of today in the European Union will get attention. What is the historical background, and what are the objectives and consequences of the political decisions with regard to money? Furthermore it will be tried to answer the question: What are the consequences for freedom and order? The purpose is to give information and evaluation as regards to the economic, juridical and political aspects. In the following this will be summarised (See Amtenbrink (1999), Pollard (2003), Zilioli and Selmayr (2000)).

6.1. Background

The original purpose of the European Economic Community (Treaty of Rome, 1958) was to create a common market. Recently a common monetary union, a common money unit (the Euro), and a European Central Bank (ECB) were introduced as a supplement to this Treaty.

As a consequence the Euro became legal tender in 2001 instead of the national money units. The national central banks became member banks of the ECB. However the ECB does not issue banknotes. This is done by the member banks. Important are also the Maastricht Criteria which are part of the Maastricht Treaty. They are known as the Stability Pact (later on Stability and Growth Pact). This Stability Pact was meant to support monetary policy by containing moral hazard. Its objective is to discipline governments in budget policy, by forbidding government deficits higher than 3%. The Maastricht Treaty also introduced developments to a political union through the backdoor. It was followed by the Treaty of Amsterdam, and the Treaty of Nice. Later on a Concept for a constitution for the European Union was formulated, but is still not ratified. The Treaty of Rome did not have this objective.

It would have been possible to use the *Deutsche Mark* (DM) as a common unit, but this was not feasible, more particular for emotional/psychological reasons. The monetary system in Germany after World War II had shown that it was relatively stable, although its working diminished since the German unification. By founding the ECB it was tried to change the existing monetary constitution while keeping the monetary system of Germany as heart of the system. However where the DBB (*Deutsche Bundesbank*) followed a modified Friedman rule, the ECB has more discretionary power.

6.2. Objectives of monetary policy

The norm for monetary policy is a stable price level. In fact this is supposed to mean that the price level is allowed to increase no more than 2%. This is a dangerous objective. It is inflationary. The Stability Pact is inconsistent with an independent monetary policy. The European (Political) Union will not allow countries/governments to go bankrupt. The Growth and Stability Pact clearly is not an (unchangeable) constitution, as is shown by its 'enforcement' and 'adaptability' to 'new circumstances'. The independence of the ECB directors is not real. They come from member state banks. There is no consistency between the political and economic order. For that reason no good future is to be expected.

6.3. Consequences for freedom and order

The question whether the Euro does increase freedom has to be answered in the negative. There is less choice in moneys and less competition between moneys. The system increases the power of one central institution with far reaching consequences in particular when mistakes are made. Now we have a monopoly of the ECB. Before, within the European Community, we had competing Central Banks. Also the ECB has more discretionary power, and its policy is less transparent than that of *e.g.* the DBB.

After introduction of the New Monetary System the balance of payments problem within the European Union has disappeared. There is no longer a disciplining function from this kind of policy. Especially, countries lost the instrument of exchange rate policy. There is only an external exchange rate. Governments will try to influence the policy of the ECB, by re-interpreting the monetary rules and the rules for budgetary policy.

There will be different developments of wage levels and employment in different countries. Trade unions are strong in Europe, although different in different countries. Trade unions serve special interests, and are often backed by political parties, who influence national governments. Is the ECB strong enough to follow an independent policy and to resist this pressure? Or will we still live under a labour standard? The consequences of this system will be different for the several countries. This problem of diverging national developments comes to the fore in discussions and critique on the interest rate policy of the ECB. Can the

ECB take effective measures when it has strong regional differentiated effects, *e.g.* in case of a strong rise in interest?

Will the Euro develop as international money? This depends on whether the ECB policy will be trusted in the Euro-area and internationally. How will it work in case of external shocks? We can only wait and see. Its future depends also on the development of the European (political) constitution. The ECB is part of the economic and political order and the economic and political process. Formal independence of the ECB is not enough. The other parts of the economic and political order have to be consistent with the monetary constitution. In the several countries and in the European Union this is not the case.

7. Monetary problems of today in the European Union II

By now the deck is cleared for further discussion on the questions: 'What are the consequences for freedom and order', and 'Are there better alternatives?'

As mentioned the original purpose of the European Economic Community (Treaty of Rome, 1958) was to create a common market. A market order (economy) has as constitutive principles: private property, accountability, free entry, freedom of contract, competition, constancy of policy, a stable monetary system. When we suppose this was the purpose with the recent changes of the monetary institutions, the questions are in how far this is reached, in how far and how these institutions can be improved and whether there are better alternatives. We have not only to criticise what exists, but if possible think of ways of improvement.

The question is what pressures can be exercised to improve its working. Transparency, accountability and democratic influence have to be fostered. The ECB is not as good a construction as the DBB, which followed a strict modified Friedman-rule. The Price Level-objective of the ECB gives more discretion to the ECB relative to the DBB. There were also stricter rules for budget policy (and stricter enforcement of them) in Germany, than are now formulated in the Stability and Growth Pact.

Also important is that there continues to exist competition of European and other currencies for the Euro, especially from the Pound Sterling, the Swiss Franc, and Scandinavian currencies. This will discipline the ECB (Schwartz, 2004).

Furthermore it is important whether there is made a fundamental choice for a competitive economy and free trade, and against the welfare state. This is necessary for disciplining governments (politicians) in their budget policy, and trade unions. This is necessary for giving the Stability Pact a chance to work favourable. The system can be improved upon by bringing in new elements. For example by fostering global free trade and a global monetary system.

Whether or not a political union will follow is an important question, but to discuss the proposal for a future constitution of the European Political Union is not possible within the context of this paper. We have also (except for a few remarks) to give a serious and wise neglect to other international political aspects (Atlantic Community; America and Europe: Friends or Foes?).

The European Treaties are binding on political actors. They are between states. Now we are in a pre-constitutional situation. The European Union is not a confederation, but it is also not clear what it is and what it will be.

A constitution is operative as long as it is accepted by the general public. In EU originally the states are the actors, but this is changing. There is an emerging political system. In the concept of the constitutional tract the EU is an entente of states, but states can opt out to other ententes. Other ententes *e.g.* with the USA are possible.

In the concept of international politics especially in Germany there are changes since the Treaty of 1958 (Rome). The Atlantic Community was then the German option. In Germany this has disappeared in the background since the Maastricht Treaty (and the unification of Germany, and the end of the Cold War). There is need for going back to that conception.

From the beginning in the fifties there were two streams of thinking about the question: What kind of European Community? Will it be an open economy with free entry and exit, a free-trade agreement or a supranational economic union, that means a closed political union. These different approaches still exist. Where is the EU heading to? These different scenarios are still possible outcomes.

8. Concluding remarks

With regard to the monetary organisations in the European Union different positions can be taken. Some of the discussed authors (those that are in favour of free banking) are defending the position that monetary organisations can not/should not be the outcome of rationalist design in a constitution, but of competition. Others (*e.g.* Pellanda (2003) and Schwartz (2004)), fully aware of the many shortcomings of the existing arrangements, are of the opinion that now we have this Bank, we should keep it at least for the time being, and do the best to let it do not to much harm, and where possible to improve its working. They give the Bank credit. One should not compare the DBB *ex post* and ECB *ex ante*.

Different opinions on the subject of Freedom and Order with regard to Money have always existed among people who like to call themselves liberals. The subject is difficult and the observation of Henry C. Simons (1936) is still true: "*The monetary problem stands out today as the great intellectual challenge to the liberal faith*".

The ultimate solution may go in the direction of thinkers like V.C. Smith (1936), Hayek (1976), White (1984), Selgin (1988) and Yeager-Greenfield. Special attention in this connection needs the proposal of Yeager-Greenfield (Yeager, 1997).

On May 29, 2005 and on June 1, 2005 in France and The Netherlands referenda were held in which a constitutional treaty for Europe was rejected. This gives new problems and also possibilities for politicians and people in Europe. It also will have influence on the working and the future of the monetary organisation of the European Union, and the Euro and the ECB. Not all questions and ideas could be treated, let alone be answered in the range of this article. Thinking about theoretical and practicable alternatives is still necessary.

References

Amtenbrink, F., 1999. The European Central Bank - democratically accountable or unrestrained?, Nederlands Juristen Blad: aflevering 2, 72 - 78

Bagehot, W., 1873. Lombard Street. Henry S. King, London.

De Jong, F.J., 1973. Developments in Monetary Theory in the Netherlands. Rotterdam University Press, Rotterdam.

Ellis, H.S., 1934. German Monetary Theory 1905-1933. Harvard University Press, Cambridge, Massachusetts.

Eucken, W., 1952. Grundsätze der Wirtschaftspolitik. Mohr/Siebeck, Tübingen.

Friedman, M., 1953. Essays in Positive Economics. University of Chicago Press, Chicago.

Gurley, J.G. and Shaw, E.S., 1960. Money in a Theory of Finance. The Brookings Institution, Washington.

Hayek, F.A., 1943. A Commodity Reserve Currency. Economic Journal LIII: number 210, 176-184. Reprinted in: Hayek, F.A., 1949. Individualism and Economic Order, Routledge & Kegan Paul, London.

Hayek, F.A., 1972 [1960]. The Constitution of Liberty. Henry Regnery Company, Chicago.

Hayek, F.A., 1976. Denationalisation of Money: An Analysis of the Theory and Practice of Concurrent Currencies. The Institute of Economic Affairs, London.

Knapp, G.F., 1905. Staatliche Theorie des Geldes. Duncker and Humblot, Leipzig.

Lutz, F.A., 1954. The Case for Flexible Exchange Rates. Banca del Lavoro Quarterly Review VII: number 31, 175-185.

Lutz, F.A., 1969. On Neutral Money. E.Streissler *et al.*, Roads to Freedom. Essays in Honour of Friedrich A. von Hayek. Routledge & Kegan Paul, London, pp. 105-116.

Meijer, G., 1987. The History of Neoliberalism: Affinity to some Developments in Economics in Germany. In: Festschrift in Honour of Anghel N. Rugina, Part II, International Journal of Social Economics 14: 142-155.

Meijer, G., 1988. Neoliberalisme. Neoliberalen over economische orde en economische theorie. Van Gorcum, Assen/Maastricht. (Neoliberalism. Neoliberals on economic order and economic theory).

Meijer, G., 1994. The Institutional Basis of Market Economies: Walter Eucken's Contribution to Economics, Journal of Economic Studies 24: number 4.

Menger, C., 1892. On the Origins of Money. Economic Journal 2: 239-255.

Mill, J.S., 1865. Principles of Political Economy. J.W. Parker, London.

Patinkin, D., 1965. Money, Interest, and Prices. Harper & Row, New York.

Pellanda, A., 2003. The Nature and the Value of Money in F. v. Hayek's Theory. The Role of the European Central Bank. In: J.G. Backhaus, W. Heijman, A. Nentjes and J.A.C. Van Ophem (eds.), Economic Policy in an Orderly Framework. Liber Amicorum for Gerrit Meijer. LIT Verlag, Münster, pp. 329-343.

Pollard, P., 2003. A Look Inside Two Central Banks: The European Central Bank and the Federal Reserve. Federal Reserve Bank of St.Louis Review 85: number 1, 11-30.

Rueff, J., 1960. Gold Exchange Standard a Danger to the West, in: Grubel, H.G.,1963. World Monetary Reform: Plans and Issues, Stanford University Press, Stanford, pp.320- 28.

Rugina, A.N, 1949. Geldordnungen und Geldtypen. Fundamente für eine echte allgemeine Geld- und Wirtschaftstheorie. Kohlhammer, Stuttgart/Köln.

Schwartz, A.J., 2003. Banking School, Currency School, Free Banking School. In: J. Eatwell, M. Milgate and P. Newman (eds), The New Palgrave, A Dictionary of Economics, Volume I, 2003. Stockton Press, New York, pp.182-185.

Schwartz, P., 2004, The Euro as Politics. The Institute of Economic Affairs, London.

Selgin, G., 1988. The Theory of Free Banking. Rowman & Littlefield, Totowa, N.J.

Simons, H.C., 1948. Economic Policy for a Free Society. Chicago University Press, Chicago, pp. 160-183. Originally in Journal of Political Economy XLIV (1936): 1-30.

Smith, V.C., 1990 [1936]. The Rationale of Central Banking and the Free Banking Alternative. Liberty Press, Indianapolis. Preface by L.B. Yeager.

White, L.H., 1984, Free Banking in Britain, Cambridge University Press, New York.

Yeager, L.B., 1997. The Fluttering Veil. Essays on Monetary Disequilibrium. Edited and with an Introduction by George Selgin. Liberty Fund Press, Indianapolis.

Zilioli, C and M. Selmayr, 2000. The European Central Bank: An Independent Specialized Organisation of Community Law. Common Market Law Review 37: 591-644.

Another Marxism: a delimitation of Analytical Marxism

Fabien Tarrit
Laboratoire d'Analyse des Mouvements Economiques (CERAS-OMI), Université de Reims Champagne-Ardenne, France. fabien.tarrit@univ-reims.fr

Abstract

Gerald A. Cohen initiated Analytical Marxism in defending historical materialism on the basis of analytical philosophy and of logical positivism. This school of thought presented itself as an attempt to renew Marxism with non-Marxist methodological tools. John Roemer extended it in reconstructing Marxian economics with neoclassical tools and Jon Elster generalised it in interpreting Marxism with methodological individualism and Rational Choice Theory. This paper deals with the assumption that Analytical Marxism turned Marxism into its opposite.

JEL classification: A12, B24, B51

Keywords: historical materialism, analytical philosophy, logical positivism, neoclassical economics, rational choice

1. Introduction

At the end of the seventies, in the English-speaking academic world, two schools of thought claimed themselves to be Marxist or close to Marxism: the "Social Structure of Accumulation" and "Analytical Marxism". For a comparison between the two, you may look at Dumasy and Rasselet (1999). The Social Structure of Accumulation, with Gordon, Bowles (who also participated in studies of Analytical Marxism), Kotz, Edwards and Reich can be partly associated with the French Regulation School, and it is in keeping with the core tradition of radical economics, in so far as they use Marxist tools for an analysis of contemporary capitalism.

From this tradition, Analytical Marxism kept the interest in Marxism. However this school, under the initiative of Gerald A. Cohen, deals with Marxism with a different logic: it mainly does not use Marx's theory in order to study capitalism, but it studies Marx's theory itself. This paper focuses upon Analytical Marxism for epistemological reasons and because those studies, that deal with all the humanities (economics, sociology, history, philosophy, political science), were widespread and submitted to intense debates and arguments. It is noteworthy that this school was born on the eve of a period marked both by a relatively strong revival of conservatism, especially in the United States and in Great Britain, and by a loss of influence of Marxism.

Although it offers a relatively strong diversity, Analytical Marxism derives its own unity not only from its subject, Marx's theory, but also from its use of traditional academic methods that are not from Marx. It conceives Marxism mainly as a set of cognitive tools, enabling the setting up of a research program with multiple entries, with no specific methodological foundation, and this leads to many internal debates. The object of Analytical Marxism is to determine the core and the periphery of the Marxist research program, in order to *"reconstruct fragments of Marxism which can be salvaged as a social science"* (Lock, 1990: 131, personal translation).

The present paper aims to assess Analytical Marxism with regard to its own objective to reconstruct, recycle, reconceptualise, rejuvenate, restrict, rethink, make sense of Marxism, verbs which have all been used in Analytical Marxist literature. We will try and clarify what Marxism can evolve into, when combined with epistemological tools that are traditionally presented as contradictory to it, and we will speculate upon the impact of such a perspective on the future of Marxist analysis. So we first present the methodological foundations of Analytical Marxism set by Cohen, then we display the way the school was constituted, and finally we deal with the two most accomplished authors of that methodological turn, namely John Roemer and Jon Elster.

2. Cohen's interpretation of historical materialism: the methodological foundations of Analytical Marxism

Departing from dialectical materialism, Cohen set the foundations for a Marxism without a specific method. He studied historical materialism with tools of analytical philosophy and of logical positivism. He attempted to renew the way of thinking about Marxism. Within the Marxian theoretical corpus, he extracted the theory of history, on which he made a conceptual and analytical work. He did not judge the validity of historical materialism in comparison with real history, but on its conceptual consistency. In the traditional analytical way, he precisely defined the elements that constitute the theory beforehand, namely productive forces and relations of production, and then, as a logical positivist, he articulated them with theses, namely the Development Thesis and the Primacy Thesis.

2.1. Isolating the concepts: the hallmark of analytical philosophy

Before stating how the theory is structured, Cohen defined the concepts that appear within the Preface to the Contribution to the Critique of Political Economy (Marx, 1971), from which the central ones are considered to be the productive forces and the relations of production.

He gave a strict definition of the productive forces, in claiming that *"only what contributes materially within and to productive activity as Marx demarcates it counts as a productive force"* (2000: 34). Within the productive forces, he separated the objective dimension - the means of production - from the subjective one - the labour power. Productive forces then correspond to the physical power of the producers and to the level of technology and of qualification, and the development of the productive forces is the growth in productivity. The development of the productive forces is first of all an issue of development of the labour power, since *"this subjective dimension is more important than the objective or means of production dimension; and within the more important dimension the part most capable of development is knowledge"* (1982: 29). For that reason, science is considered as a productive force, and the development of scientific knowledge is central to the development of the productive forces, so that *"in its higher stages the development of the productive forces ... merges with the development of productively useful science"* (2000: 45).

Cohen drew a line between productive forces and relations of production. The relations of production are defined as *"relations of effective power over persons and productive forces, not relations of legal property"* (2000: 63), independently from the productive forces, since *"the economic structure or base ... consists of relations of production only: it does not include the productive forces"* (1982: 29). The distinction between different kinds of relations of production is to be found in the mode of surplus making.

Cohen proposed an approach of society as an articulation between its inner elements, each of them being independently analysed beforehand, like he did with the productive forces and the relations of production. The social relations of production are the form of a given society, the social framework in which some development of the productive forces may occur. The economic structure wears the function of an envelope in which productive forces can develop: *"there are as many types of economic structure as there are any kinds of relation of immediate producers to productive forces"* (2000: 78). Those relations are the foundations of a society, on which a superstructure rises.

2.2. Articulating the theory with theses: the hallmark of logical positivism

Cohen articulated historical materialism with two theses, the Development Thesis - *"the productive forces tend to develop throughout history"* (2000: 134) - and the Primacy Thesis - *"the nature of the production relations of a society is explained by the level of development of its productive forces"* (2000: 134). Productive growth would be a permanent tendency, whereas social forms would be transitional. Social relations of production that exist in a given period constitute the social form which allows the development of the material productive forces, and the Development Thesis is the foundation for the Primacy Thesis, so that the productive forces are the driving force of history. Now let us study the logical structure with which Cohen built the Primacy Thesis.

The latter can be formulated as a deductive-nomological model: the level of development of the productive forces establishes which relations of production allow the development of the productive forces, and those relations of production are as they are because they allow the development of productive forces, then it can be concluded that the level of development of the productive forces explains the nature of the relations of production.

All the same, the infrastructure is primarily explanatory for the superstructure. Therefore the level of development of the productive forces explains the nature of the relations of production, which in turn explains the nature of the superstructure. In Marx's words (1994: 128), "*the amount of productive forces available to men determines social conditions*". Productive forces are the driving force, since their endogenous evolution determines the nature and the transformation of the relations of production.

Then, it can be concluded that the elaboration of historical materialism which was proposed by Cohen keeps original content, but it allows a new form of presentation. Unlike Marx and Hegel, for whom the elements are defined by the relations they have between each other, Cohen previously defined the elementary concepts in order to display their relations. In doing so, he reproduced the foundations of analytical philosophy within the Marxist theory of history, initiating that way Analytical Marxism.

3. A new school of thought

In using the methods of analytical philosophy and of logical positivism for defending historical materialism, Cohen was used as a model for the Analytical Marxists. It is noteworthy that the scope of Analytical Marxism is hardly specific and we will display how it can be considered as a school of thought. We will display first how Analytical Marxism has been known as "Non bullshit" Marxism, and then how it is based on a positivist approach. Finally, we will see how such an approach led to a strong heterogeneity.

3.1. A "Non bullshit" Marxism

Under the influence of Cohen's book, and on the initiative of Elster, Cohen and Roemer, annual meetings were held each September as soon as 1979 until 2000. The 2001 meeting was cancelled because of the 9/11 events and in 2002, the group decided to move to an every-other-year frequency (see Wright, 2004). The group took the name of September Group, and sometimes of Non-Bullshit Marxism Group, referring to the general denial of dialectics by the authors. Pranab Bardhan, Sam Bowles, Robert Brenner, Alan Carling, Joshua Cohen, Andrew Levine, Adam Przeworski, Hillel Steiner, Robert van der Veen, Philippe van Parijs and Erik O. Wright also took part in the September Group. It might be noted that Elster and Przeworski left the group during the nineties. The following authors, even if they did not directly participate in these meetings, can be associated to the topics and methodology that have been under progress: Michael Albert, Robin Hahnel, Stephen Marglin, David Miller, Richard Miller, Geoffroy E.M. de Ste Croix, Michael Wallerstein and Allen Wood.

The expression "Analytical Marxism" was used in seminars by Elster as soon as 1980, and it was first published by Roemer in *Analytical Marxism* (1986). That name was already used before: the school of "Analytico-linguistic Marxism" was constituted in Poland in the fifties (see Skolimowski, 1967; Nowak, 1998) - Analytical Marxism is not directly related to it, but they have in common a separation between scientificity and ethics - and a Japanese school, dealing with mathematical formalisation of Marx's works, is named "Analytical Marxism" too (see Takamasu, 1999).

Analytical philosophy presents itself as a way to break any complex whole up into simple elements, clearing all the redundant ones. Any ambiguous expression is replaced by logical forms. Analytical philosophy has been characterised as an "atomistic revolt against Hegelian holism" (Engel, 1997: 146, personal translation), considered as bullshit. For logical positivism, as Carnap - from the first Vienna circle - claimed, science is supposed to rebuild, with simple logical connexions, the concepts which are used to describe the world. In brief, analytical philosophy breaks complex wholes into their parts, and logical positivism puts them together. Correspondingly, the aim of Analytical Marxism is to *"define a series of abstract concepts.. and then [to] specify the ways in which these concepts can be combined to generate more concrete categories of social forms"* (Wright, 1994: 112).

3.2. A positivist Marxism

"Cohen and his co-thinkers have casually crossed the supposedly impassable border between Marxism and the academic mainstream in philosophy and social theory" (Callinicos, 1989: 3). Marxism is studied as a research program, with a hard core and a protective belt which is tested and modified with the help of analytical philosophy and of logical positivism. Each theoretical part of Marxism is specifically analysed and criticised with the explicit or implicit objective to reconstruct Marxism. Wright displays four elements to specify "what is "Analytical" about Analytical Marxism" (1994, 178):

- "The committment to *conventional scientific norms*" (1994: 181, italics are always in the original):
Marxism is assessed as a positivist social science, and the Analytical Marxists deny the traditional Marxist distinction with the "bourgeois" social science.
- "An emphasis on the importance of *systematic conceptualisation*" (1994: 181):
Analytical Marxism is distinguished on the one hand by a strict definition of the concepts, like Cohen does on productive forces and relations of production, and on the other hand by the analysis of the interaction between the concepts. Complexity is viewed as a combination of simple elements.
- "A concern with a relatively *fine-grained specification of the steps in the theoretical arguments linking concepts*" (1994: 181):
Abstract models are used, with some degree of formalisation. Simplification is used for identifying the central mechanism of a problem, and to clarify some assumptions.

- "The importance accorded to *the intentional action of individuals*" (1994: 182):

Such a feature is normative rather than methodological on the one hand, and it is less consensual on the other hand. Indeed, it would be incorrect to entirely associate Analytical Marxism with methodological individualism, since some advocate it (Elster, 1982; Roemer, 1982; Przeworski, 1984), but some do not (Brenner, 1986; Wright, 1989; Cohen, 1982).

3.3. A theoretical heterogeneity

It is far from obvious that Analytical Marxism is unified in some substantive theories. It rather defines itself by what it does not agree with: Marx's theoretical corpus is judged as unclear and insufficiently refutable. There would be no specific Marxian methodology. Dialectical logic is condemned and replaced with formal logic. The labour theory of value and the law of the tendency of the rate of profit to fall are rejected. It must be noted that only Robert Brenner accepts the labour theory of value.

Marx's theoretical corpus is systematically tested. "*There is probably not a single tenet of classical Marxism which has not been the object of insistent criticism at these meetings*" (Elster, 1985: xiv). Different kinds of studies have been implemented: specific developments in the Marxist theory (Cohen, 2000; Roemer, 1982), empirical applications of Marxist concepts (Wright, 1985; Przeworski, 1985) and reconstructions of what Marx wrote (Elster, 1985; Wright *et al.*, 1992). The core issue is to examine Marx's theory with non Marxist methodological tools, mainly in social science and in philosophy. "*It is hoped that Marxist thought will thereby be freed from the increasingly discredited methods and presuppositions which are still widely regarded as essential to it, and that what is true and important in Marx will be more firmly established*" (Introduction of Studies in Marxism and Social Theory). Studies in Marxist Social Theory (Cambridge University Press) is a collection in which Analytical Marxist books have been published since Elster (1985). This introduction appears on each book of the collection. Analytical Marxism may then be synthesised as an "*attempt... to preserve the classical research program by (a) reconstructing the theory of history along non-Hegelian lines and (b) replacing the classical labour theory of value with contemporary general equilibrium theory*" (Carling, 1997: 770). That is Cohen's and Roemer's work respectively, to which we can add Elster's global approach.

4. Roemer and Elster: from an interpretation to a deconstruction

Under the light of Cohen's epistemology, Roemer and Elster adapted Marxism to orthodox tools, namely neoclassical economics and methodological individualism respectively. Though Analytical Marxism cannot be reduced to these two authors, we will see how they undoubtedly represent the most accomplished part of the reorientation of the Marxian methodological corpus implemented by Analytical Marxism. On the one hand, if Marx's theory can be summarised in a theory of history and a theory of economics, Roemer complements Cohen. On the other hand, Elster collects Marx's work under a methodological individualist interpretation, as a step towards Rational Choice Marxism.

4.1. Roemer: Marxian economics revisited

For Roemer, since Marxian tools are one century old, they do not fit contemporary social science. He judged that any science which does not overcome its own founders is degenerating, and as well as physics forgot Galileo and as contemporary microeconomics is not Smithian, Marxism must live without Marx. For Roemer, Marxism is a question of language, and neoclassical formalisation is the proper language. He acknowledged that his approach is not Marxian, for three reasons: his analysis is not explicitly historical, the concepts that he uses are not explicitly from Marx but they are generalisations of Marx's concepts, and no reference is made to Marx's texts in support of his arguments. We will display then how he deconstructed the labour theory of value and how he transformed the theory of exploitation.

4.1.1. A deconstruction of the labour theory of value

Roemer assessed Marx's labour theory of value from a microeconomic point of view and he intended to reconstruct Marx's conclusions independently from it. Resting upon Morishima (1973) and Steedman (1977), he claimed that, because qualitative differences between different kinds of labour lead to their incommensurability, a labour theory of value is impossible to display. Since he claimed the impossibility of determining value objectively, returning back before the Sraffa debate (Sraffa, 1960), Roemer asserted that the price is determined independently from the value: *"value cannot be defined prior to the operation of the market"* (1981: 203).

Further, he claimed that the assumption of the subsistence wage, which he judged necessary for the labour theory of value to work, is tautological, and he replaced a "special" theory of the subsistence wage by a "general" theory of the "class struggle" wage. *"Once this replacement is made, Marx's implicit motivation for using the labour theory as an exchange theory, at some level of abstraction, dissolves"* (1981, 203). Without subsistence as an objective criterion, he claimed that the issue of exploitation needs a normative justification. Yet, it is noteworthy that such a theory of subsistence wage was severely criticised by Marx when Lassalle proposed it (Marx, 1970).

4.1.2. A transformation of the theory of exploitation

Following Morishima, Roemer built a theory of exploitation independently from the labour theory of value, in treating exploitation as an optimisation process, so that in a subsistence economy, any individual is exploited if he works longer than it is necessary for producing a subsistence amount of goods, and he is an exploiter if he works less than the socially necessary labour time for producing these goods. Then he demonstrated that exploitation exists in capitalism, not directly because of the structure of capitalism, but because the capitalists work less than the socially necessary labour time, whereas workers and peasants work longer than the socially necessary labour time. Exploitation may exist without exchange of labour, without accumulation of wealth, without surplus product, without transfer of surplus value and without class relationship.

The issue of exploitation would rest upon optimisation models. The issue is not an internal relationship between class and exploitation, but a theorem to be proved, the class-exploitation correspondence principle: those who optimise in selling labour force are exploited and those who optimise in hiring labour force are exploiters. Roemer replaced the extraction of surplus labour by property relations, and he claimed that exploitation can logically exist without any exchange of labour. Then he was led to the isomorphism theorem, where the capital market ("the island of credit market") wears the same functions as the labour market ("the island of labour market"). Any agent would be exploiter or exploited in the same way as his fellow on the other island. Exploitation could occur through the exchange of commodities, and classes might exist with a credit market and without a labour market. The only condition is that the coercion is not situated on the point of production, but in the property relations. So the issue of exploitation would not be substantially related to labour and Roemer's conclusion followed as: *"if the exploitation of the worker is an important concept, it is so for normative reasons - because it is indicative of some injustice and not because the exploitability of labour power is the unique source of profits"* (1988: 54).

He also established a correspondence between Cohen's historical materialism and his own theory of exploitation. With the help of game theory, he stated various specifications of the rules of retreat, corresponding to each game, namely to each form of exploitation: the feudal exploitation, the capitalist exploitation and the socialist exploitation. In going from feudal to socialist, a society crosses and removes various forms of exploitation, namely various forms of property relations. *"Each revolutionary transition has the historical task of eliminating its characteristic associated form of exploitation"* (1982: 21).

4.2. Elster: towards a Rational Choice Marxism

Besides Cohen and Roemer, Elster is the third initiator of Analytical Marxism. Whereas Cohen presented a defence of historical materialism, and whereas Roemer elaborated a reconstruction of Marxian economics, Elster developed an uncompromisingly censorious interpretation of all the aspects of Marx's theory, which led to Rational Choice Marxism.

4.2.1. A comprehensive and undialectical approach
In his substantial book (1985) and in some articles (1980, 1982), Elster gave a comprehensive critical reading of Marx's work. Being closely linked with the Anglo-Saxon intellectual tradition that gives primacy to intentional actions, he meticulously tested Marxian methodology, philosophy, economics, theory of history and theory of classes, under the light of methodological individualism. He mainly proceeded allusively: Marx "simply

meant", "clearly has in mind", "believed that" (1985: respectively 249, 261, 425), hence the provocative title of his main book: Making Sense of Marx. Actually, he did not make sense of Marx, but of his own interpretation. Refusing to take Marx's theory as a whole, he broke it up into an economic theory and a theory of history, separated itself into a theory of economic history (the relation between productive forces and relations of production) and a theory of class struggle.

Elster blamed Marxism for Hegelianism, for scientism and for a lack of evidence in his claims. He considered that the main contribution of Marx in the methodology of humanities is the general idea of unintended consequences of intentional actions: *"whether we refer to this method by the terms 'dialectics' and 'social contradictions' is, by comparison, a secondary matter"* (1985: 48). He refused to take Marxist methodology as a whole and he claimed that Marx used various modes of explanation. He judged that some of his works are based upon methodological individualism, especially the theory of crisis stated in Capital, Volume III, and that, on this issue, Marx was anti-teleological. Also he wrote that Marx resorted to functional explanation, particularly in his theory of history, which only aim would be to justify any explanation in function of consequences that would be favourable to the advent of communism. Marx would have been teleological on that issue.

Even though he was clearly more censorious on the classical Marxist theory than Roemer, and than Cohen all the more, Elster equally claimed a legacy of the latter: *"I am sure there are many ideas that I believe to be my own that actually originated with him"* (1985: xv). While Elster and Cohen disagreed on such issues as methodological individualism and functional explanation, they shared the same epistemological background.

4.2.2. Marxism and Rational Choice: an unlikely encounter

Rational Choice Marxism, including Roemer, Elster and Przeworski, intended to make Rational Choice Theory, which is traditionally used for justifying and defending capitalism, a critical weapon against capitalism. Such a methodology has been compared with Marx's: *"what else did Marx do in Capital but subvert the classical political economy of his day by using it to draw anti-capitalist conclusions?"* (Carling, 1990: 107)

Such a Marxism rests upon the assumption that a relatively strong proportion of Marx's works, namely the works of his "maturity", are based upon methodological individualism. So game theory is used in order to analyse the processes of social interaction, with the following postulates: a social state depends on the actions that are chosen by individuals, a social structure does not entirely determine the individual actions. Individuals choose the actions which lead to the best results, and individuals judge other individuals as rational.

Rational Choice Marxism led to relatively important results: it replaced dialectical materialism with methodological individualism and neoclassical economics, it claimed the labour theory of value as unsuited to a theory of exploitation, it asserted that an analysis in terms of relations of production is unsuited to the explanation of class formation, and that the interests of the capitalist class can fit with the interests of the working class. With rational choice analysis, the Analytical Marxists definitely crossed the theoretical border between radical economics and non radical economics in throwing Marx into non radical field, so that Marx's theory seems to have lost his subversive character.

5. Conclusion

Analytical Marxism was initiated by Cohen's defence of historical materialism, in which dialectical materialism was replaced with some analytical reasoning, including functional explanation. It was carried on by Roemer's neoclassical reconstruction of Marxian economics, in postulating that Marxian concepts could be articulated with the assumptions of general equilibrium theory. It was generalised by Elster's use of methodological individualism in all aspects of Marx's theory, leading to Rational Choice Marxism, a kind of Marxism without Marx. Analytical Marxism is not homogeneous but is unified with its research subject, Marx's theory, and its central claim is that its specificity is not methodological but substantial. Having analysed every aspect of Marx's work in the light of non-Marxist methods, they concluded that most of the theory is deficient.

Analytical Marxism, a study of Marx's work by means of non-Marxist methodological tools, reached the conclusion that Marxism is scientifically flawed. Nevertheless, instead of questioning the tools that they used - analytical philosophy, logical positivism, methodological individualism, and general equilibrium - the Analytical Marxists postulated that those tools are efficient and that Marxism is separated from its own method. Since such a premise needs arguments in order to be acknowledged and since these arguments were not developed by the authors, it is still possible to claim that Marxism survived Analytical Marxism, and that the future of Marxism will be without Analytical Marxism.

References

Brenner, R., 1986. The Social Bases of Economic Development. In: J.E. Roemer (Ed.), Analytical Marxism. Cambridge University Press, Cambridge, pp. 23-53.

Callinicos, A. (Ed.), 1989. Marxist Theory. Oxford University Press, London.

Carling, A., 1990. In Defence of Rational Choice: a reply to E.M. Wood. New Left Review 184: 97-109.

Carling, A., 1997. Analytical and Essential Marxism. Political Studies 45: 768-783.

Cohen, G.A., 1982. Functional Explanation, Consequence Explanation and Marxism. Inquiry 25: 27-56.

Cohen, G.A., 2000 [1978]. Karl Marx's Theory of History: a Defence. Expanded Edition. Oxford University Press, London.

Dumasy, J.-P. and G. Rasselet, 1999. Aperçus sur les développements contemporains de la théorie économique marxiste aux Etats-Unis. Revue française d'histoire des idées politiques 9: 77-122.

Elster, J., 1980. Cohen on Marx's theory of history. Political Studies 28: 121-128.

Elster, J., 1982. Marxism, Functionalism and Game Theory: The Case for Methodological Individualism. Theory and Society 11: 453-482.

Elster, J., 1985. Making Sense of Marx. Cambridge University Press, Cambridge.

Engel, P., 1997. La dispute: une introduction à la philosophie analytique. Minuit, Paris.

Lock, G., 1990. Le marxisme analytique entre la philosophie et la science. Actuel Marx 7: 131-138.

Marx, K., 1970 [1875]. Critique of the Gotha Programme. Progress Publishers, Moscow.

Marx, K., 1971 [1859]. A Contribution to the Critique of Political Economy. Lawrence & Wishart, London.

Marx, K., 1994 [1845]. The German Ideology. In: J. O'Malley (Ed.), Marx Early Political Writings. Cambridge University Press, Cambridge, pp. 119-181.

Morishima, M., 1973. Marx's Economics: A Dual Theory of Value and Growth. Cambridge University Press, Cambridge.

Nowak, L., 1998. The Adaptative Interpretation of Historical Materialism: A Survey - On a Contribution to Polish Analytical Marxism. Poznan Studies in the philosophy of the sciences and the humanities 60, 201-236.

Przeworski, A., 1984. Marxism and Rational Choice. Politics and Society 14: 379-409.

Przeworski, A., 1985. Capitalism and Social Democracy. Cambridge University Press, Cambridge.

Roemer, J.E., 1981. Analytical Foundations of Marxian Economic Theory. Cambridge University Press, Cambridge.

Roemer, J.E., 1982. A General Theory of Exploitation and Class. Cambridge University Press, Cambridge.

Roemer, J.E. (Ed.), 1986. Analytical Marxism. Cambridge University Press, Cambridge.

Roemer, J.E., 1988. Free to Lose: An Introduction to Marxist Economic Philosophy. Harvard University Press, Cambridge.

Skolimowski, H., 1967. Polish Analytical Philosophy. Routledge & Kegan, London.

Sraffa, P., 1960. Production of Commodities by Means of Commodities. Cambridge University Press, Cambridge.

Steedman, I., 1977. Marx after Sraffa. New Left Books, London.

Takamasu, A. (Ed.), 1999. Analytical Marxism. Nakanishiya Press, Kyoto.

Wright, E.O., 1985. Classes. Verso, London.

Wright, E.O., 1989. What is Analytical Marxism? Socialist Review 19: 37-56.

Wright, E.O., 1994. Interrogating Inequality: Essays on Class Analysis, Socialism and Marxism. Verso, London.

Wright, E.O., 2004. Grappling with Marxism: an autobiographical reflection. In: S. Turner and A. Sica (Eds.), A Disobedient Generation: '68ers and the Transformation of Social Theory. Sage Publications, London.

Wright, E.O., A. Levine and E. Sober, 1992. Reconstructing Marxism: Essays on Explanation and the Theory of History. Verso, London.

Taxes and elections

Georgi Smatrakalev
Florida Atlantic University, School of Accounting, 111 Las Olas Blvd. Office 547C, Fort Lauderdale, FL 33301, USA. smatraka@fau.edu

Abstract

In the democratic societies people are tax payers and voters. This unity makes it very important that in every voter should speak the taxpayer and *vice versa*. The paper concentrates on this dualism in human nature and figures out how the taxpayer influences the voter. The elections influence usually the taxes in three ways - tax legislation, tax rates and general taxation. These three ways concern the development stage of the society. The foreseen tax harmonisation in the European Union didn't happen for electoral reasons. In Eastern Europe the fear of the past is replaced by the tax fear.

JEL classification: H20, H21, H24, A13, P35

Keywords: taxes, elections, tax rates, rational expectations, direct/indirect taxation

1. Introduction

"...nothing in this world is certain but death and taxes"
Benjamin Franklin

Everyone seems to know this but as one has said "*at least there is one advantage about death; it doesn't get worse every time Congress meets*" and has laid down the junction between taxes and elections. The fight in elections is usually fight for voters through taxes spiced with irrational expectations of the voters.

Humans have so many roles in public life and some of them coincide on different levels. They can govern and be governed; love and be loved; have feelings; feel burdens and levy burdens. In the public choice theory this is the unity of the differences - once in a while the taxpayer becomes a voter and can make a choice of his/her fate how to be taxed. It is only in the era of democracy when these two roles matter. The absolute king doesn't care about the burden of taxation as he won't be changed or not re-elected. In a democracy the issue of taxes has taken one of the major points in all election campaigns. One can hardly find elections around the globe where the issue of taxation is not mentioned. But is it really the choice of the voter that forms his taxpayers' faith?

This theme is so close to every one. The major goal here is to trace how important taxes are in the election campaigns. This will be done through showing what role they are playing for the winner. How the transformation from a totalitarian regime into a democratic society is judged by the role of taxes in the elections. How in different types of democracies, different types of tax issues are sent to the voters. The paper is based on several election campaigns in Bulgaria.

2. How did all this start?

The first correlation between the taxes and the elections can be found long time ago in the Bible (1 Samuel 8)[1]. Related with a request all the elders of Israel gathered and came to Samuel at Ramah, and said to him, *"Behold, you are old and your sons do not walk in your ways; now appoint for us a king to govern us like all the nations."* And Samuel trying to convert them said, *"These will be the ways of the king who will reign over you: he will take your sons and appoint them to his chariots and to be his horsemen, and to run before his chariots; and he will appoint for himself commanders of thousands and commanders of fifties, and some to plow his ground and to reap his harvest, and to make his implements of war and the equipment of his chariots. He will take your daughters to be perfumers and cooks and bakers. He will take the best of your fields and vineyards and olive orchards and give them to his servants. He will take the tenth of your grain and of your vineyards and give it to his officers and to his servants. He will take your menservants and maidservants, and the best of your cattle and your asses, and put them to his work. He will take the tenth of your flocks, and you shall be his slaves. And in that day you will cry out because of your king, whom you have chosen for yourselves; but the Lord will not answer you in that day."* All that Samuel mentioned to the people, to those that want to have a king, were nothing but taxes in kind. So with the establishment of the government comes the necessity to support that government to devote and sacrifice part of everything dear and share it with that government.

In all the totalitarian governments there were no debates. Even were in public life there were no explicit taxes. The kings and counts and pharaohs were gathering different percentages of the product without any possibility for argument or protests. The protests at that time were simple change of the sovereign. Slot the bad king or count and on its place will come a new one but the taxes will be the same. The taxes are as something that is inevitable and people try to live with them. The names of the taxes in centuries are defined according to the social and economic circumstances. In the early centuries in Germany for example paying taxes was related with support from the citizens to the government; so the name *Steuer* which means support. The English duty also has similar meaning and the French *impot* means forced payment.

It is only with the establishment of democracy that taxes started to play an important role in the election process. The democratic development has given the taxpayers the strength

---

[1] http://www.bibleontheweb.com/Bible.asp

of voters. As it comes to taxes it seems that everyone considers him/herself an expert. Even for the past century Goode (1997) reported that the academic analysis of taxation has become more technical, increasingly involving sophisticated mathematics and statistics. For this reason, its language and reasoning have become less and less accessible to those outside academia. Scientists, hoping to influence the policy process, have to think carefully about how to "translate" what they know into what can be convincing and useful for policy. Even those who think carefully about this translation have often been greeted by a dismissive reply that begins, "yes, but in the real world …"

In the real world a tax system needs to be administered and enforced, and some tax systems that look promising on paper fail on these practical grounds.

People, the voters, are more interested in what is left for them after the treasure messes with their income than in the sophisticated models and schemes for lowering the tax burden. They rely more on simple mathematics: Income - tax = what is left for me.

3. How is it in real democracies?

The play between the taxpayers and politicians in fact began after Cromwell in UK and Robespierre in France, after the democratisation of the societies. And since the older democracies have gone their ways it is interesting to analyse the transformation in the emerging market economies. My experience is based on Bulgaria and the transformation there.

The lack of interest in the design of tax policy in the past in almost all communist countries is valid also for Bulgaria. Under state planning, it was physical output that was the subject of policy-making. The financing of government policy through taxation, and the impact on economic incentives through wages and prices received little, if any, attention.

Taxes were implicit and their functions were clearly related with their fiscal function. Taxes were not used as a way to regulate the economic activity, since in the planned economy there was not such necessity. They were a measure for suppressing people's income, since even their fiscal function was lowered. Most of the government expenditures were met by extending subsidies and soft budget financing.

On the elections side, everything was also clear - one party only without competitors. So there was no need for any discussions or any kind of promises. The election activity was 99.99% and the winners were elected with the same percentage.

With the changes in 1989 and the road to market economy and democracy the country was still far away from the public choice theory - taxes and elections. A brief summary of the events and the main players in them is necessary to understand the motives. In the early years it was the fear or will of restoration of the past that motivated the electorate to vote for the Democratic Union[2] or Socialist Party (former communists)[3]. The first democratic elections in 1990 were won by the socialists and then after two unsuccessful governments and "tender" revolution (protests, strikes and interim government) the power was transferred to the Democratic Union in 1991. The weak majority was blocked by the Turkish minority party[4] and again the country was in the hands of the socialists in 1994. This time after real street fights the socialists were thrown out of power in favour of the Democratic Union in 1997. During all this the taxes were not an issue in election campaigns. The fights for power and the fear of restorations were motives for the democrats and empty promises for a bright future were the slogans of the socialists. In fact exactly these empty promises were the reason for their collapse twice. It is obvious that promises do not fill the fridge.

In the election campaign in 2001, for the first time, tax cuts have been mentioned as an issue in the program of the National Movement Simeon II. In 2001 the dipole model of the Bulgarian political life was broken and a new player came on stage - The National Movement Simeon Second. This was a strange creation organised under the rule and the name of the former king of the country and most of the yuppies that had studied in the Western countries (sons or relatives of ex-communists leaders or financed for their education from underground firms also owned by communists). Getting their education in the Western countries, acquiring the major tricks of democracy the yuppies pronounced 0 % corporate tax and drastic lowering of personal income tax. These and some other counterfeit promises secured them majority in the Parliament. So Bulgaria was one of the strangest countries in political life - with a socialist (ex-communist) as a President and a king as a Prime Minister. But the most important thing was that taxes have been introduced to the voter for the first time as a choice. Despite the lower tax literacy in the country and the huge evasion, that throughout the years even has been a government policy, the taxpayers of Bulgaria saw themselves as voters that can change their burden; that can move the scales in their desired way. The country has come nearer to the Western democracies.

One of the first laws, adopted by the first democratic parliament in 1990 was the law on political parties. This law was not doing a good job regulating the property and financing of parties. It took more than a decade and four different parliaments to design the current regulations, which again do not adequately address the issue. What is typical for Bulgaria is a strong ruling class, monopolising all power resources and totally excluding the opposition.

---

[2] Union of the Democratic Forces created 1989 has split several times and in 1997 was elected as United Democratic Forces. (see http://www.sds.bg).

[3] Bulgarian Socialist Party is created from the former Bulgarian Communist Party and has been twice in power. (see http://www.bsp.bg).

[4] In 1990 the Turkish minority in the country formed its own party - the Movement for Rights and Freedoms, which was in the role of balance in the Parliament ever since. (http://www.dps.bg)

And in election campaigns always dominant huge promises are made, which will never be fulfilled.

Taxes are considered in all programs basically in a couple of different ways:

a. Tax legislation
This is the most general approach to taxation in pre-election campaigns. It depends on the tax literacy of the voters - either high or very low. This component is not just a campaign, it is an inevitable part of the political behaviour of the ruling party.

In Bulgarian election campaigns tax legislation was mentioned in fact just as a part of the creation of an European type of legislation in 1997 by the Union of Democratic Forces. After coming to power they did change all the major tax laws from the beginning of 1998. The Personal Income Tax Act changed the for more than fifty years existing act, corresponding to the new realities in the country. The Corporate Income Tax Act replaced the Tax on Corporate Profit elaborated by the socialist government in 1996. The Value Added Tax Act replaced the transition act from 1994 and the Tax Procedure Code replaced several laws for tax administration and tax procedures. All the new legislation was coordinated within the light of the coming negotiations with the EU. Despite all the changes, the tax laws are still very ambiguous. Some of the articles are contradictive to the Tax Procedure Code, others to other laws or even between themselves. This ambiguity implies additional distortion to the investors from home and abroad and lowers the trust in the legislation. Some of the ambiguity was liquidated by abolition of otherwise incentive articles for the investors.

There is no necessity to restrict any good initiative with the notion that all are criminals and will abuse the law. But Bulgaria is not the only country in which good and bad in the legislation are working together.

b. Tax rates
In the euphoria of election campaigns promises for lowering of the tax rates have a positive effect on the voters. This is easy to explain, to accept and will be felt even by the most tax illiterate voter. The game with the rates has its own philosophy in all election campaigns. Everyone promises lowering of the rates of personal, company income tax and in Europe from time to time value added tax. In 2000 The Union of Democratic Forces pronounced its tax strategy for lowering the tax rates - especially of corporate income taxation from 25 % to 10 % in a period of 3 years. On the 2001 elections all the king's men promoted 0% rate for the corporate taxation and 10 % for the personal income tax. Their slogan was immediate and non symbolic reduction of the tax rates. Very similar to the famous "Read my lips. No more new taxes" of President Bush senior in 1992. All that, plus other promises which could difficult be fulfilled, brought the yuppies and the former king to power. But they also created a lot of irrational expectations in the voters. Contrary to the pre-election promises, the new government and the Parliament voted first a lower rate for their own

salaries - reducing the marginal rate with 9 % (from 38 % to 29 %) with the motive that this will create employment and will be an incentive for the high tax bracket taxpayers to invest more. At the same time the lowering of the corporate tax rate and other personal income rates were postponed almost till the next elections in 2005. To secure their positions the ruling party presented changes in the tax laws in the last working day of the Parliament. By this sending the notice to the voters - if we are re-elected we shall start our work where it was stopped by the elections.

At the same time the press is hitting some of the abnormalities in the country that have to be dealt with due to the expected accession in the EU. For example almost the same week when the ruling party sends its messages on lowering income tax rates for personal and corporate income, the requirement from IMF and EU for an increment in property taxes was published also. As one of the Bulgarian newspapers proclaimed: *"The real property taxes will rise right after the elections due to the increment in the base value of the properties and the required reassessment from the IMF memorandum."* This is very typical for the Bulgarian political life. All the necessary price or tax increments are postponed for months or sometimes even a year because of the election campaign, as no one wants to have a lower image in front of the voters.

All relieves and lowering of the rates relate with the lowering of the tax burden in general, although it are not only the rates that compound that burden.

c. Tax burden

From the existence of a tax system costs and burdens of various kinds arise (Sandford *et al.* (1989) and also Allers (1994)). Costs related to the operation of the tax system affect both the private and the public sector. If the public sector is put on the left side of the cost specter several different costs can be examined. The majority are administrative costs that incur in administering an existing tax code, including the enforcement costs as well. They can be regular, arising from the continuing operation of a tax, or "other Exchequer costs" arising from the existence of a lag in tax payment. The latter is strongly related with the personal income taxation because the transfer here is delayed sometimes for a year or more, since most of the businesses are making advance tax payments.

On the right side, where the private sector is, it are mainly compliance costs for meeting the requirements of a given tax structure. Dean (1975) suggests another definition of compliance costs as 'all those extra costs which the entrepreneur must budget for simply in order to comply with tax requirements'. These are the costs that would not have been incurred in the absence of a tax.

Arising from that, temporary costs can be caused by unfamiliarity with a tax and psychic (psychological) costs of the burden of anxiety imposed by the requirement of tax compliance. Johnston (1961) makes a distinction between unavoidable and avoidable costs related with the compliance. The first are those necessarily incurred in order to comply with legal requirements, while the latter are tax planning costs made in order to minimise one's tax bill, or to maximise benefits receipts. He suggests that since firms and individuals change the pattern of their behaviour and activities because of taxation this causes an excess burden (dead weight loss) of taxation.

For both sectors there are commencement costs that are once and for all costs incurred at the inception of a new feature of the tax system. The last costs that are related also with the excess burden of taxation and are affecting both sectors are the social costs, experienced by the community as a whole arisen from the operation of a tax. All these costs are elements of the tax system and are inevitable while making a decision on any market transaction, though some of them are not often an issue in the tax planning.

It is clear that relatively high compliance costs may put the national economy at a competitive disadvantage with the other countries. A comparatively high price level will hamper exports, for example, and high compliance costs may discourage foreign enterprises to invest or set up subsidiaries. In fact sometimes it is not the tax itself that frightens the investors but the high compliance costs and the consequence of them. Especially in the Bulgarian case it is very difficult for any foreign investor to keep up with the changes going in the tax system and this increases his compliance costs all the time, no matter whether he would use professional help or would try to make his own way through them.

All the above mentioned costs together with the tax itself can be examined as a transaction cost in the different market transactions. This puts another view on the taxation. It will not be studied as a transfer from the private to the public sector in exchange for some services or benefits, but it would be simply another cost added in the evaluation of any given market transaction. For example if there is a decision to be made for investment allocation definitely the tax issue will be considered seriously before the legal entity would make any allocation. On the other hand if an employee wants a certain job he definitely should want to know what it is going to cost him - so how much of his income he will share with the government. All these issues are closely related to the tax planning and the transaction costs.

Since the transaction cost is the running cost of an economic system, the cost of effecting an exchange or other economic transaction varies from one economic system to another. It can be stated that the tax itself can be examined as the cost (price) of the income that should be received. Income taxation can be viewed from transaction-costs economics which as Williamson (1995) stated is "an interdisciplinary undertaking that joins economics with aspects of organisation theory and overlaps extensively with contract law. It is the modern counterpart of institutional economics and relies heavily on comparative analysis."

This definition of transaction-cost economics gives opportunity to apply it to the income taxation and reveal another side of tax theory. It could be a good way for combining law and economics on the principle of explanation of legal institutions, procedures, decisions and the like in terms of the economic theories, according to Backhaus (1995).

Usually authors like Hall and Jorgenson (1991) assume that income taxes rest where they are put, and hence the burden is reckoned to lie on the factors of production, and on the other hand that indirect taxes are passed forward and hence the burden is estimated to be on the consumers of the product.

If we divide the costs of doing business in Bulgaria in three categories: (1) costs for entering the business; (2) costs for operating the business; and (3) costs for exiting the business, and look it upon from the transaction-cost economics point of view, it can be stated that income tax regulations fit in as one of the major costs in all three stages. There is an obligatory initial tax registration for the different taxes - income tax, value added tax or excise tax (the latter two are for certain kinds of business only and some restrictions apply). In the third stage one of the actions that should be taken is deregistration which is also a time, nerves and money consuming procedure just as the initial registration.

All kinds of business income should be reported quarterly to the tax authorities and some of the bigger ones monthly by queuing first for purchase of the tax declarations and all the required worksheets and then queuing for delivering the ready forms. This is the usual exercise for the nerves and time of the businessman in Bulgaria. It is evaluated by the Institute for Market Economy that annually the entrepreneurs are loosing between a month and a month and a half business time to comply only with the requirements of the income taxation. All this makes people "risk averse" and erodes the tax moral of the taxpayers.

This also increases the fees paid for the tax consultant and the time spent on the forms. This forced some of the countries with low tax moral and high tax evasion or out of the question of simplicity to introduce a flat tax rate for personal income. This flat tax mania is spreading over Eastern Europe - Russia, Slovakia, Latvia, Estonia, Romania *etc.*, and recently it was mentioned that France also considers to introduce the flat tax rate. In Bulgaria since two years this idea goes around and gains more and more supporters. The Bulgarian case is more radical - it requires a 10% flat tax rate that should cover personal income tax, social security contributions and medical contributions. The flat tax rate replaces in some cases 52-70% of tax rates (10%-28% income tax rate and 42% social security and medical contributions). This may give rise to budgetary problems.

d. Indirect taxes

Consumption taxes are not so often a topic in the election campaigns. The characteristics of these taxes leave them out of the scope but not for long. When all the possibilities in the direct taxation are used then indirect ones come. In Bulgaria the lowering of the value added tax (VAT) rate has been used as a topic in two consecutive election campaigns (1997 and 2001) by different parties. The diversification of the VAT rate is another issue in some of the campaigns as it depends on which groups of special interest the parties want to attract - the newspaper publishers (with promises for 0% rate), the parents with lower rates for kids clothing or retired people with lowering the food stuff rate, *etc.*

4. Conclusion

The elections not only altered the political balance in any Parliament but also the fiscal one too. Generally candidates who had a clear vision of reducing taxes, restraining spending, and making existing tax cuts permanent tended to succeed, while those who muddled their messages often paid the price at the polls. The problem is that the instrumentation for fiscal play with the electorate is limited. Mainly there are three areas for flirting with the voters:

Tax legislation. Usually used either in countries with low tax moral and literacy or in highly developed democracies, where the pocketbook issues weigh heavily on people when they enter voting booths.

Tax rate. One can never be on a wrong side when lowering them. Promising low rates can bring you to the top, but empty promises can't keep you there.

Tax burden. This is ambiguous and relates in people's mind mainly with the rates. Lower rates on broad base are as burdensome as higher rates on narrow base. One of the aspects of burdens is closely related with the compliance costs. The high complexity in filing can drive any investor from otherwise attractive investment.

It is not only necessary to promise changes. You have to implement and enforce them, as usually in four years there are new elections. One of the greatest Bulgarians, Vasil Levski, has written in his note book: "*When you promise something to the people you have to keep your promise, or leave.*" Unfortunately, most of the politicians forget their promises the moment they touch the power, while on the other side people usually have short memories as in the next elections they still believe in fairy tales and promises.

References

Allers, M.A., 1994. Administrative and Compliance Costs of Taxation and Public Transfers in the Netherlands. Wolters-Noordhoff, Groningen.

Backhaus, J.G., 1995. Good Economics, Bad Economics and European Economics. METEOR Research memorandum (University Maastricht).

Dean, P.N., 1975. Some Aspects of Tax Operating Costs with Particular Preference to Personal Taxation in the United Kingdom. University of Bath, London (UK).

Goode, R., 1997. The National Tax Journal in 1948-50 and 1994-1996. National Tax Journal 50, No. 4, 707-18, December 1997, http://ntj.tax.org/

Hall, R.E. and D.W. Jorgenson, 1991. Tax Policy and Investment Behaviour. In: A.B. Atkinson (ed.), Modern Public Finance, Edward Elgar, Cambridge.

Johnston, K.S., 1961. Corporations' Federal Income Tax Compliance Costs. Ohio State University Bureau of Business Research, Monograph No. 10.

Sandford, C.T., M.R. Godwin and P.J.W. Hardwick, 1989. Administrative and Compliance Costs of Taxation. Fiscal publications, Fersfield, UK.

Williamson, O.E., 1995. Transaction Cost Economics: The Governance of Contractual Relations. In: O.E. Williamson and S. Masten (eds.), Transaction Cost Economics, Vol. I, Edward Elgar, Brookfield, Vt.

Population and society

Why prohibit or promote reproductive cloning and genetic engineering? The myth of biodiversity and of genetic hierarchy

David Moroz

Champagne School of Management, Economics Department, 217 Avenue Pierre Brossolette, BP 710, 10 002 Troyes Cedex, France. dmoroz@esc-troyes.fr
Université de Reims Champagne-Ardenne, Laboratoire OMI-EDJ, 57 bis Rue Pierre Taittinger, 51 096 Reims Cedex, France.

Abstract

The aim of this paper is to study the benefits that potential parents can enjoy when they have the possibility to choose the genotype of their children. Our approach is consequentialist and takes account of the radical uncertainty of the natural selection as the geneticist Gould defines it. We demonstrate that there is no relationship between the genetic variability of a population and its survival capability, and that it is impossible to anticipate the benefits that result from the choice of a genotype. To refute our theory on a consequentialist basis therefore necessitates demonstrating the existence of an absolute hierarchy of genotypes.

JEL classification: D8, I1, Q2

Keywords: human genetic pool; radical uncertainty; consequentialism

1. Introduction

The innovations in human genetics can make possible new procreation modes. In the future, the parents could prefer resorting to genetic engineering or cloning rather than sexual reproduction. By these ways, they could choose the genotype (*i.e.* the set of genes) of their children, which is yet not possible in the case of sexual reproduction. The issue is then to determine the nature of the rights of the parents concerning the choice of their children's genes.

Such an issue may appear as a problem of ethics and not of economics. Nevertheless, it is an issue relative to the scarcity and the management of a particular resource, which is the human genetic pool. The management of this resource is problematic because of the radical uncertainty of the natural selection. Indeed, population genetics teaches us that it is impossible to determine *ex ante* if an individual possessing a given genotype will be fitted to the environmental conditions he will meet. Expressed in another way, we cannot know *ex ante* the quality of a given genotype.

On this basis, we demonstrate that it is impossible to define a consequentialist criterion of management of the human genetic pool. We refute notably the theory asserting that the survival capability of a population is an increasing function of its genetic diversity. As a consequence, it is impossible, on a consequentialist basis, to justify the prohibition of procreation technologies other than sexual reproduction.

Our argumentation is constructed in four sections. The first section presents the concept of natural selection. The second section explains the unpredictability of natural selection, and therefore the impossibility to build a hierarchy of genotypes. The third section refutes the existence of a positive relationship between the genetic polymorphism rate of a population and its resilience capability. The fourth section concludes by defining the conditions of refutation of our theory: such a refutation necessitates the conception of a theory that asserts an absolute hierarchy of genotypes.

2. Genetic polymorphism, natural selection and genotype: a presentation of population genetics

The whole set of human genotypes that the human population[1] contains is the human genetic pool (Campbell, 1995: 439). In population genetics, the quality of the genetic pool of a population depends on its polymorphism, *i.e.* its diversity. The genetic polymorphism can be defined as the existence, in the genetic pool of a population, of several different alleles for a same gene (Hartl, 1994: 11; Griffiths *et al.*, 2001: 537-541)[2].

The genetic pool and its polymorphism are the target of the natural selection. According to Darwin's theory, the evolution of populations can be considered as the sorting of individuals by natural selection in populations (Serre, 1998: 150). The natural selection keeps the individuals that are best fitted to the environmental constraints[3], and consequently, they can procreate a greater number of descendants. The effect of natural selection is a differential fecundity of the different genotypes, and so it changes the genetic diversity of populations by increasing the frequency of the best fitted genotypes. While the natural selection is not the only evolutionary pressure[4], it is the only one that has an adaptive function, by accumulating and perpetuating the favoured genotypes in populations.

---

[1] We voluntarily adopt the term "population" and not the term "species" in our argumentation, because of the several definitions of this last one that may create confusions. About this issue, see David and Samadi (2000: 237-247).

[2] More precisely, a polymorph gene is characterized by the fact that its most frequent allele in the population has a frequency that is smaller than 0.95. An allele whose frequency is smaller than 0.05 is said « scarce ». These thresholds are arbitrary and may vary with the authors. See Hartl (1994: 11) and Serre (1998: 28).

[3] We define "environment" as all the elements except the genotype of the individual that can be considered as an input of the phenotype, *i.e.* the set of traits, of the individual.

[4] We can register four evolutionary pressures, *i.e.* four factors that can change the genetic pool of a population: natural selection, mutation, migration, and genetic drift. See Henry and Gouyon (1998).

Three conditions are necessary for natural selection to operate (Griffiths *et al.*, 2001: 536): (1) the variability condition. In a population, there must be a variability of phenotypic characters between individuals, whatever the kind of character (morphologic, physiologic, or behavioural); (2) the heredity condition. The characters on which the natural selection operates must be transmitted from generation to generation, and must possess a genetic component; (3) the selection condition. Some kinds are more efficient than other ones to survive and develop in some given environmental conditions.

To sum up, we can say that the selection can change the genetic structure of a population only if the population presents a variability on which the selection can operate.

The selection results in a differential fecundity of genotypes. This differential fecundity is apprehended through the concept of genetic fitness (Campbell, 1995: 450; Griffiths *et al.*, 2001: 553-555). The genetic fitness is determined on the basis of the relationship that exists between the phenotype of an organism and the environment in which it develops itself. That means that the genetic fitness of a genotype depends on the environment in which it lives (Campbell, 1995: 445; Henry and Gouyon, 1998: 36). As a consequence, if the genetic fitness depends on the environment, no genotype can be said to be unconditionally superior to the others.

The more fitted to its environment the genotype is, the more children the possessors of this genotype procreate, and so the higher the genetic fitness of the genotype is (see Henry and Gouyon, 1998: 33-34). This determination of the genetic fitness of the genotype is deduced from the following axioms of the "synthetic" or "neo-Darwinian" said theory of evolution (Mayr, 1994: xix; see also Ridley, 1997): (1) the hereditary unity is the gene, and not the apparent phenotypic character. In other words, genes are transmitted from generation to generation, not observable characters; (2) the unity on which the selection acts is the individual, through his phenotype. It is not on the gene, but on a set of genes. It means that the environment interacts with the characters of the individual, not with the genes of the individual; (3) the unity that evolves is the population. It is neither the gene, nor the individual; only the genetic pool of the population changes from generation to generation.

Following the second axiom, if the natural selection acts on individuals, then that means that it acts on phenotypes and not on genotypes. The natural selection acts on the global phenotype, which results from the action of several genes and of environmental factors (Hartl, 1994: 114). As a consequence, the selection does not act on some alleles that could be considered favourable or unfavourable. If the selection acts on an individual, possessor of a complex genotype, *i.e.* a combination of interacting alleles, then it is not possible to assert the existence of absolutely favourable or unfavourable alleles (Serre, 1998: 152; Mayr, 1994: 403). The advantage or the cost of possessing a given allele partly depends on the other alleles with which it interacts.

3. Unpredictability of evolution and genetic polymorphism: The quantitative theory of the resilience capability

The evolution of species is characterised by the unpredictability of the modifications of the selection pressure (Gould, 1991, 1996, 1997). Indeed, the natural selection only defines the adaptation of a population to a changing local environment (Gould, 1997: 173). But these changes are unpredictable. That is why we can assert that evolution is an unpredictable and contingent phenomenon (see Gould, 1991:. 311-431 and 1997: 169-181). Our reasoning integrates the radical uncertainty, and it does not seem possible for us to treat this issue by assuming another form of uncertainty, notably a probabilistic form. Indeed, we cannot assume that it is possible to distinguish a set of predictable events and a set of unpredictable events. To adopt such a theory would be equivalent to asserting that we can know *ex ante* the level of our ignorance, which is inconsistent from a logical point of view[5]. As Popper explains, "*if there is such a thing as growing human knowledge, then we cannot anticipate today what we shall know only tomorrow*" (Popper, 1997: vii).

The unpredictability of evolution has two consequences. The first one is that there are no crucial characteristics (Gould, 1991: 409). A phenotypic trait providing a selective advantage at a given date can be a handicap at the following date. The quality of a character is contingent, depending on the modifications of the environment. The second one, which can be deduced from the first one, is that evolution cannot be assimilated to a march towards an inescapable improvement (Gould, 1991, 1997; Hodgson, 1996: 197-213). As a consequence, the greater complexity of organisms like human beings must not be perceived as the ultimate result of evolution.

As a consequence, the unpredictability of evolution prevents us from asserting that an absolute hierarchy of genotypes exists. The genetic fitness of genotypes only depends on environmental conditions, whose changes are unpredictable.

Consequently, determining an optimal mode of management of the human genetic pool (or of any other genetic pool), *i.e.* some optimal rules delimiting the possibility of choice of parents, seems to be illusory. Nevertheless, some authors defend a management mode that seems to be based on what we can call the "quantitative theory of the resilience capability". According to this theory, the resilience capability of a population, *i.e.* its capability to adapt

---

[5] If the scientific research enables the increase of the stock of communal knowledge (Faber and Proops, 1993), this does not imply however that our ignorance about the future can be reduced: asserting the possibility of such a reduction is equivalent to accepting the possibility of dividing the set of future events in a set of predictable events and a set of unpredictable events, and therefore defining the level of our ignorance. Our ignorance about the future is incommensurable. To be less ignorant, in the sense of increasing the stock of knowledge, cannot mean having better information about the future occurrences. Indeed, on the one hand, knowing a greater quantity of possible future scenarios does not inform us about the scenario that will effectively emerge. On the other hand, the conjectures we make are based on theories that cannot be proved to be true.

to environmental changes, is an increasing function of its genetic polymorphism (Ruffié, 1982: 152; Barbier *et al.*, 1995: 26-30; Perrings, 1995). According to one of those authors, Passet (1996: 75-76), "[*a*]*t the level of the population*, if the reserve of genetic variability is diversified enough, there will always be some individuals, in the case of environmental change, who will possess a combination fitted to the new situation and will be able to perpetuate the species" (translated by us; in italics in the original). The proposal of Passet, which seems to be an exposition of the quantitative theory, is a tautology. Indeed, if the genetic pool of a population contains a set of genotypes that are fitted to the prevailing environment, then the population will survive. But there is no relationship between the genetic variability of a population and its resilience capability. The survival of a population does not depend on its genetic variability, but on the set of genotypes it possesses. A population can therefore possess a relatively high genetic polymorphism but not possess the set of genotypes that are necessary to its survival, and inversely. Moreover, if it is impossible to determine a hierarchy of genotypes, then it does not seem possible to construct such a hierarchy for some populations of genotypes. If we cannot know *ex ante* the capability of adaptation of an individual, we cannot evaluate the capability of adaptation of a population of individuals. As a consequence, the theory asserting that the genetic diversity is necessarily beneficial for the survival of the population is not valid. Indeed, it is impossible to define, for a given population, a genetic structure that will ensure its survival. We cannot define the survival probability of a population on the basis of its polymorphism level. The necessary condition for the survival of a population is that its genetic pool possesses the genotype(s) that is (are) fitted to the prevailing environmental conditions. But there is no relationship between the genetic diversity rate of a limited population, *i.e.* with a finite size and the probability to possess the fitted genotype(s).

4. Sexual reproduction, reproductive cloning, and genetic engineering: some unpredictable effects on the resilience capability of the population

Let's assume that the individuals of a population whose size is finite decide to increase the genetic diversity rate of their population by resorting to genetic engineering. The impact of such a decision is limited by the size of the population that is supposed to be finite: the potential parents can only have a finite quantity of children. As a consequence, the genotypes of the next generation have to be chosen, selected by the parents. As we are radically ignorant of the orientation of the natural selection, nothing enables us to assert that the chosen genotypes will ensure the survival of the population. The only thing we can assert is that if the genetic structure of a population is changed, so its evolution is changed. But the effects of such a change on the resilience capability of the population cannot be known *ex ante*.

Following the same argumentation, we can demonstrate, in the case of a population that replaces itself by resorting to sexual reproduction, that an increase of the genetic polymorphism rate may not increase the resilience capability of the population, and may even decrease it. If an increase of the genetic polymorphism rate of a population can have such effects, it is because of an evolutionary pressure other than the natural selection: the genetic drift. The following reasoning is built on the use of the "neutralist" said theory of evolution.

The genetic drift is one of the four evolutionary pressures, with the natural selection, the mutation, and the migration. It contributes to change the structure of the genetic pool of a population from generation to generation. In a finite size population, genes carried by gametes (spermatozoon and ovum) are a sample set of the genes possessed by parents. Consequently, even if there is neither natural selection nor mutation, the frequency of any given type of gene, *i.e.* an allele, will change from generation to generation. The frequency of the allele will randomly fluctuate from generation to generation, without any force making it to come back to its initial level. After a given period, if no evolutionary pressure constrains the frequency of the allele to remain constant, this frequency will fluctuate up to become equal to 0 or 1. Expressed in another way, the allele will be either eliminated or fixed in the genetic pool of the population.

We present now a mathematical formalisation of the phenomenon. The aim of this formalisation is to explain the relationship that exists between the genetic polymorphism rate of a population and the probability for an allele to disappear from the genetic pool of the population. Except for the assumption of a finite size of the population, the exposed model does respect the whole set of hypotheses that constitutes the axiomatic of the Hardy-Weinberg model (Solignac *et al.*, 1995: 105-139): non-overlapping generations, diploid organisms, sexual reproduction, normal meiosis, panmixia mating, no selection, no mutation and no migration.

Let's suppose a population with a finite and constant size N. The vital cycle characteristic of the renewal of generations can be assimilated to the use of a gametic urn (Serre, 1998: 24; Solignac *et al.*, 1995: 111). We suppose that the parents of generation i put their gametes in an urn with the aim of reproduction. Insofar as two gametes, one male and one female, are necessary for procreation, $2N$ withdrawings must be made from the urn at each generation: This is the necessary condition to maintain constant the size of the population from one generation to the following. Let's now suppose a diallelic gene[6], with two possible alleles A_1 and A_2. The frequencies of the alleles in the genetic pool of the population are respectively p_i and q_i, so that $p_i = 1 - q_i$.

The probability to draw the allele A_1 in the gametic urn is equal to its frequency p_i in the population of the generation i. If $2N$ withdrawings are made, the number of alleles A_1 that can be obtained is bounded by a closed interval $[0;2N]$. This number is a random variable X_{i+1}. It refers to the number of alleles A_1 drawn from the urn to produce the generation of

---

[6] In our demonstration, we limit the number of possible alleles for a given gene. Nevertheless, our conclusions remain valid with a greater number of alleles for each gene, and also with a greater number of genes.

individuals $i+1$. The distribution of X_{i+1} obeys a binomial law B(p_i;2N), the expectancy of which is E(X_{i+1})=2Np_i, and the variance $Var(X_{x+1})$=2Np_iq_i=2$Np_i(1-q_i)$. The frequency of the allele A_1 in the population of the new generation $i+1$ is f_{i+1}=X_{i+1}/2N. The distribution of f_{i+1} also obeys a binomial law, the expectancy of which is E(f_{i+1})=p_i, and the variance $Var(f_{i+1})$=$p_i(1-p_i)$/2N. We observe that when N tends towards infinite, $Var(f_i+1)$ is nil: f_{i+1} can only be equal to p_i. On the contrary, the more N decreases, the more $Var(f_i+1)$ increases: f_{i+1} can so get a value that is different from p_i. The variation of f_{i+1} is unpredictable[7]. It only depends on the random sampling. Nevertheless, as we explained it before, there are two situations that will inescapably arise. In the first case, the frequency of the allele A_1 becomes higher than 2N-1/2N, and consequently gets the value 1: the allele A_1 is definitely fixed in the genetic pool of the population, when the allele A_2 is eliminated. In the second case, the frequency of the allele A_1 becomes smaller than 1/2N, and so gets the value 0: this time the allele A_1 is definitely eliminated from the genetic pool, whereas the allele A_2 is fixed.

Let's suppose a population with a finite size, the genetic structure of which presents a relatively high heterozygotic rate, *i.e.* a relatively great diversity of alleles, for one or several genes (Griffiths *et al.*, 2001: 538). The higher this diversity is, the more alleles there are whose frequencies may become nil, or expressed in another way, the bigger the set of alleles is that can be eliminated from the genetic pool. Indeed, all other things being equal, and insofar as the sum of the allelic frequencies is equal to 1 the adding of a new allele in the genetic structure of a population means a decrease of the frequencies of the alleles that are already present in the genetic pool.

Among the different alleles that form the genetic pool of the population, some of them can be said "selectively neutral" (Henry and Gouyon, 1998: 111; Ridley, 1997: 151-155). It means that, compared to other alleles of the same gene, some alleles provide neither an advantage nor a handicap to the genotypes that hold them. These neutral alleles can disappear from the genetic pool, if their frequency is close to . But an allele is not necessarily neutral forever (Hartl, 1994: 172-178). It can be neutral at a given date and provide a selective advantage at a following date.

This reasoning enables us to demonstrate two things. Firstly, in a population that replaces itself by sexual reproduction, a relatively high diversity can be costly for the survival of the species. Some alleles, or genotypes, that could have brought a selective advantage to other generations of individuals, can be eliminated from the genetic pool because their frequency is too low. Secondly, sexual reproduction, and even asexual reproduction, is not necessarily the most efficient technology to ensure the survival of the species. We are however not able to determine the most efficient technology, insofar as we are not able to determine the optimal set of genotypes. As a consequence, we cannot accept the quantitative theory of the

---

[7] The drawing of the generation $i+2$ will be made upon the basis of the new frequency f_{i+1}, still according to a binomial law. We are confronted here with a Markoff process. See Solignac *et al.*. (1995: 159-162).

resilience capability. If such a conclusion is valid for one generation[8], it cannot be for several generations. The conclusion of the static analysis, *i.e.* over the span of one generation, is valid only for one case. Let's suppose two populations each with a finite size, whose genetic pools differ, for one or several genes, by one or more alleles. Expressed in another way, one of the populations holds more alleles. In this case, over the span of one generation, all other things being equal, the higher the polymorphism rate of the population is, the higher its resilience capability is. Let's now suppose two populations, whose genetic pools are strictly different. Even if one of them has a higher polymorphism rate, we cannot affirm that it possesses a greater resilience capability.

This analysis must not lead us to consider the issue of the management of the human genetic pool as only a problem of loss of alleles, of genotypes. The problem is the impossibility to know *ex ante* the set of genotypes that can ensure the survival of the population. If the problem only was to minimise the loss of genotypes, then it could be solved by resorting to reproductive cloning. Let's assume that the cost of cloning the whole human population is nil. The replacement of the population could then be ensured by resorting to cloning exclusively and not to sexual reproduction or genetic engineering. The genetic pool of the population would remain identical from generation to generation. Such a solution cannot however be asserted to be more efficient than the other ones. By resorting to cloning exclusively, one prevents the production of new genotypes that might very well enable the survival of the population.

In fact, the theory we propose is built on the following reasoning: (1) we are radically ignorant of the whole set of environmental conditions prevailing at date $t+1$; (2) as a consequence, we cannot determine the set of genotypes that will enable the population to survive such conditions; (3) we cannot then define how the genetic pool of the population

---

[8] To assert the existence of a necessarily positive relation between the polymorphism rate of a species and its resilience capability, it is necessary to assume that the size of the population is infinite. So let's suppose that, by going from generation i to generation $i+1$, the genetic pool of the population is reduced by v different alleles of one or several genes: if n is the quantity of different alleles that are present in the genetic pool at generation i, the population possesses $n-v$ different alleles at generation $i+1$. As the size of the population is supposed to be infinite, we can assert that its resilience capability decreased. Let's now consider a population whose size is finite. In such a population, whose genetic pool can be changed by genetic drift, we have $v=f(n)$, with $\delta v/\delta n > 0$: all other things being equal, the higher the average heterozygotic rate is, the bigger the quantity of alleles is that may disappear from the genetic pool. The corollary of this proposition is the following: All other things being equal, the probability of the conservation of an allele of a given gene in a finite size population, from one generation to another, is an inverse function of the heterozygotic rate of the population for the considered gene. That is why we can refute the existence of a necessarily positive relation between the polymorphism rate of a population and its resilience capability. If we validated such a theory, we could then determine the optimal rate of polymorphism, which could remain constant or increase over time. But we are radically ignorant of such a rate: Knowing the rate and the nature of the genetic polymorphism of a population does not allow us to know its survival probability.

at date t must be replaced, and we don't know whether the population has to be replaced either by resorting to natural reproduction or cloning or genetic engineering; (4) so we cannot determine whether the genetic pool the population possesses at date t can enable it to be fitted to the environmental conditions prevailing at date $t+1$.

As a consequence, we can neither determine an optimal technology of replacement neither compare the resilience capabilities of different populations. Let's suppose two populations P_1 and P_2. The genetic pool of population P_2 is such that it contains the whole set of genotypes possessed by population P_1 as well as a set of other genotypes that is not possessed by the latter. Over the span of one generation, all other things being equal, population P_2 has an advantage over population P_1 in terms of resilience capability. However, as soon as populations replace themselves at least once, it is not evident that this hierarchy will be maintained: both populations replace themselves on the basis of different genetic pools, and the sets of genotypes obtained after a (some) replacement(s) may be such that population P_1 possesses some fitted genotypes whereas population P_2 does not. If both populations replace themselves by resorting exclusively to cloning, then population P_2 still has, after any given replacement, an advantage over population P_1. However, as we cannot determine the efficiency of a given technology of replacement, we cannot assert that it is beneficial for both these populations to replace themselves by resorting to cloning. As we cannot determine the optimal mode of replacement for any given population, we cannot assert that one of them has the optimal genetic pool that will definitely ensure its survival.

5. Conclusion

The aim of our argumentation is to demonstrate that the quantitative theory of the resilience capability cannot be valid. Because of the unpredictable and contingent character of the evolution, it is impossible to assert a relationship between the genetic polymorphism of a limited population and its resilience capability. In fact, this argumentation can be extended to any consequentialist relationship.

We cannot determine the nature of the relationship that exists between the genetic polymorphism of a population and the set of gains that can be enjoyed by the individuals that form this population[9]. Expressed in another way, we cannot determine the gains, neither explicit nor implicit (see Becker, 1976a), that the individual can enjoy because of having a given genotype and of interacting with some individuals possessing some given genotypes. We can eventually build a theory explaining the nature of some benefits that

---

[9] By this assertion, we refute the part of our Ph.D. thesis that explains the existence of a positive relationship between the genetic polymorphism rate of a population and the gain expectancy of its members. See Moroz (2003: 282-298). The only thing that this theory can explain is a set of advantages that the individuals may enjoy because of the genetic variability of the population to which they belong. Such a theory is however not sufficient to explain that, at the level of the population, the genetic heterogeneity is necessarily better than the genetic homogeneity.

the individuals can enjoy because of their genetic heterogeneity or homogeneity[10]. But we cannot determine, all other things being equal, if two genetically different individuals will enjoy through their life some bigger or smaller gains than those enjoyed by two genetically identical individuals. If the gains enjoyed by the individuals can be explained, they cannot be measured. The problem is not the impossibility of measuring utility, but the unpredictability of the creating capability of individuals. Even if utility could be quantified, we could not determine the gains that could be enjoyed by individuals, because we are unable to expect what they are able to create through their life (see Shackle, 1954, 1967:. 2-11, 1976).

A reasoning whose aim would be to define an optimal genetic structure that would maximise the individual utilities necessitates a particular axiomatic. Indeed, it is necessary to assume that the creating and learning capabilities of the individual are limited or nil, and that his gains depend on his genotype exclusively. But if we are unable to anticipate what an individual can create, then we are unable to define *ex ante* the nature of the relationship between the individual's genotype and his creating capability. As Loasby explains (1991: 37) about structures of production of scientific knowledge, *"[d]ifferent structures may be expected to generate different knowledge. To select a structure is to select - not entirely consciously - what problems can be tackled by what means, and also - [...] - what means will not be employed and what problems will be ignored"*. We have no theory that enables us to assume that such a reasoning cannot be applied to the issue of the genetic structure of a population. Some populations with different genetic pools can adapt differently to a set of environmental changes, and we cannot predict how they can adapt. As a consequence, the members of these populations can enjoy some gains whose nature and level cannot be anticipated.

As it is impossible to determine a hierarchy either of genotypes or of populations of genotypes, then it is impossible to define some optimal rules of population replacement. We cannot neither justify a eugenic politic, nor justify the use or the prohibition of some procreation technologies. Posner (1992: 429-434), when he defends a kind of eugenics, or ourselves (Moroz, 2003: 282-298), when we defend the maximisation of genetic diversity, are wrong. Both of us cannot expect the gains that could be enjoyed by individuals who interact with identical or different congeners. We have no theoretical argument to oppose to the use of reproductive cloning or genetic engineering. We remind that our argumentation is based on a consequentialist approach, and not on a procedural kind of ethics that would favour one or several procreation modes. To refute our argumentation on the same consequentialist basis, it seems necessary to demonstrate that it is possible to build an absolute hierarchy of individuals. It is necessary to demonstrate that an individual produced by cloning or genetic engineering is necessarily less productive (whatever the kind of production) than an individual produced by sexual reproduction, and conversely.

---

[10] Becker (1976b) produced a theory explaining the gains that may enjoy the partners of a couple who share some substitute and complementary traits.

Acknowledgements

The author wishes to thank Pierre van Zyl for improving significantly the English text. Responsibility for any errors or omissions is my own.

References

Barbier, E.B., J.C. Burgess and C. Folke, 1995. Paradise Lost?: The Ecological Economics of Biodiversity. Earthscan Publication Limited, London.

Becker, G.S., 1976a. The Economic Approach to Human Behavior. In: The Economic Approach to Human Behavior, University of Chicago Press, Chicago, pp. 3-14.

Becker, G.S., 1976b. A Theory of Marriage, Part I. In: The Economic Approach to Human Behavior, University of Chicago Press, Chicago, pp. 205-233.

Campbell, N.A. 1995. Biologie. 3ème édition. De Boeck Université, Bruxelles.

David, P. and S. Samadi, 2000. La théorie de l'évolution: une logique pour la biologie. Flammarion, Paris.

Faber, M. and J.L.R. Proops. 1993. Evolution, Time, Production and the Environment. 2ème édition. Springer-Verlag.

Gould, S. J., 1991. La vie est belle: les surprises de l'évolution. Ed. du Seuil, Paris.

Gould, S.J., 1996. Comme les huit doigts de la main: réflexions sur l'histoire naturelle. Ed. du Seuil, Paris.

Gould, S.J. 1997. L'éventail du vivant: le mythe du progrès. Ed. du Seuil, Paris.

Griffiths, A.J.F., W.M. Gelbart, J.H. Miller, *et al.*, 2001. Analyse génétique moderne. De Boeck Université, Paris.

Hartl, D.L., 1994. Génétique des populations. Flammarion, Paris.

Henry, J.P. and P.H. Gouyon, 1998. Précis de génétique des populations. Masson, Paris.

Hodgson, G.M., 1996. Economics and Evolution: Bringing Life Back into Economics. University of Michigan Press, Ann Arbor.

Loasby, B.J., 1991. Equilibrium and evolution: An exploration of connecting principles in economics. Manchester University Press, Manchester.

Mayr, E., 1994. Population, espèces et évolution. Hermann, Paris.

Moroz, D., 2003. La définition de la propriété sur le génome humain: connaissance scientifique, patrimoine génétique humain, et incertitude radicale. Thèse de doctorat en sciences économiques, Université de Reims Champagne-Ardenne.

Passet, R., 1996. L'Economique et Le Vivant. 2ème édition. Economica, Paris.

Perrings, C., 1995. Biodiversity conservation as insurance. In T.M. Swanson (ed.), The economics and ecology of biodiversity decline: The forces driving global change, Cambridge University Press, Cambridge, pp. 71-78.

Perrings, C., K.G. Mäler, C. Folke, C.S. Holling and B.O. Jansson, 1995. Biodiversity Loss: Economic and Ecological issues. Cambridge University Press, Cambridge.

Popper, K.R., 1997 (1st edition: 1957). The Poverty of Historicism. Routledge, London.

Posner, R.A., 1992. Sex and Reason. Harvard University Press, Cambridge.

Ridley, M., 1997. Evolution biologique. De Boeck Université, Paris.

Ruffié, J., 1982. Traité du vivant. Fayard, Paris.

Serre, J.L., 1998. Génétique des populations: modèles de base et applications. Nathan, Paris.

Shackle, G.L.S., 1954. The Complex Nature of Time as a Concept in Economics. Economia Internazionale 7: 743-757.

Shackle, G.L.S., 1967. Décision déterminisme et temps. Dunod, Paris.

Shackle, G.L.S., 1976. Time and Choice. Keynes Lecture in Economics, Proceedings of the British Academy 62: 309-329.

Solignac, M., G. Periquet, D. Anxolabéhère *et al.*, 1995. Génétique et évolution, Tome I: La variation, les gènes dans les populations. Hermann, Paris.

Exploring new methods of helping the world's orphans

David Macarov
Paul Baerwald School of Social Work, Hebrew University, Nayot 8, Jerusalem, 93704 Israel.
davidmacarov@huji.ac.il

Abstract

This paper calls for new methods of caring for the world's tens of millions of orphans. All current efforts to ameliorate the condition of orphans focus on small-group, family-like settings. There is, however, no empirical evidence that this focus is more efficacious than that of large orphans homes or children's villages, encompassing hundreds - and sometimes thousands - of children. An exploration of possible alternatives to current efforts, including large-scale methods of housing and caring for orphans, is urgently required. Previous methods will be examined, the comparative costs of such activities will be outlined, and the steps necessary to achieve such child-care will be discussed.

JEL classification: I31, J13

Keywords: orphans, orphan homes, children's villages, HIV/AIDS

1. Introduction

Continuing rise in the number of AIDS-related orphans throughout the world presents a formidable challenge to all child-centred and humanitarian organisations. In the year 2000 it was predicated that by the year 2010 there would be 44 million orphans, with 68% of them AIDS-related (Porter, 2000). At present, it is estimated that there are fifteen million AIDS-related orphans under the age of fifteen and the number is increasing exponentially. Unless there are startling breakthroughs in health-care in the near future, it is estimated that by 2010 there will be more than an additional ten million AIDS-related orphans. Of these, about half are at present double orphans (that is, with no living parents) and this ratio is expected to triple within the next five to ten years (Africa's Orphaned Generations, 2005). About three quarters of the worldwide population of people living with HIV/AIDS are in sub-Saharan Africa and eighty percent of all the world's children orphaned by HIV/AIDS reside there.

2. Immediate problems

In addition to the enormous current problems of providing food, housing, education and health-care to these children, their social and emotional needs are equally challenging. Since it takes about ten years from HIV infection until death from AIDS, and with global infection rates still rising, *"HIV/AIDS will continue to cause unprecedented suffering among children for at least the next two decades, if not longer."* (Lalor, 2004). Thus, unless conditions change drastically, this generation will produce another generation under the same conditions.

3. Future implications

This has frightening societal implications. We face complete generations growing up without caregivers, role models, protectors, restrainers and social arbiters. Nobody to limit behaviour, to inspire, to give meaning to life, or even just an adult to talk to - which could result in a condition of almost complete anomie. What will be the morals, attitudes, knowledge and activities of millions of people growing up without parents or parental substitutes? The possibilities are almost too frightening to contemplate.

These anomic children (and later adults) are ripe for exploitation by any number of ideologies and entities. Youth gangs are one prospect, since - as has been found in many places - groups can provide emotional support and peer pressure leading to activities beyond the reach of individuals. Many have already been forced into petty crime by their poverty (Porter, 2000), and they may form Mafia-type criminal organisations that will make youth gangs seem like child-play. They may be impressed into, or voluntarily join, military or pseudo-military forces that offer material comfort and social interaction, as has already been the case in some revolts and rebellions in Africa. They might be proselytised by organised religions, or by cult-like movements. Although proselytising as such is the right of religions, the prospect of millions - or tens of millions - new Catholics, Protestants, Mormons, Shiites, Sunnis, or Wahabis in the heart of Africa may be viewed differently by various observers, but that they will represent an entirely new situation is unquestionable. Such proselytising - sometimes accompanied by material aid - has already begun among the tsunami survivors (Rohde, 2005), and there is already fear that this can upset the sometimes tenuous *modus vivendi* arrived at by different religions in some countries *i.e.*, pagans *vis-à-vis* Christians, Christians *vis-à-vis* Moslems, Catholics *vis-à-vis* Protestants, *etc.*

Youngsters in the conditions described might be ripe for movements like that which resulted in Johnstown; or for Satanic groups; or for Mau-Mau-type organisations. There are already 4,000 children in 718 communal settlements in 100 countries affiliated with the "Children of God" movement, which has been charged with child abuse (Goodstein, 2005). What seems certain is that it will be very difficult for these orphans to grow up into moral, polite, altruistic adults, unless their present lives are greatly changed.

4. Current solutions

Traditionally, and particularly in Africa, orphans are taken care of by nuclear family members, by extended families, or even by distant relatives. Supporting and helping such arrangements seems to be the method of choice among many of the organisations active in this area. Unfortunately, foster home and distant relative arrangements are, and increasingly will be, completely inadequate in the face of the overwhelming numbers to be expected. Harber (1999) notes the increasing difficulty of recruiting sufficient black South African adopters. Indeed, the extended family is already, "collapsing under the weight of the HIV/AIDS crisis" *(*Care and Support*, 2004)*.

5. Simulated families

Consequently, another popular method used by organisations seeking to deal with orphans is through simulated families, as in children's villages. This type of facility has a long history. Boys Town, in Nebraska, was opened in 1917 and has now grown to 72 homes throughout the world. SOS-Kinderhof operates 440 children's villages in 173 countries and since it was founded in 1949 has taken care of over three hundred thousand children. Other groups, like the Pestalozzi Children's Village in Trogue, Switzerland, have established group homes. UNESCO has a somewhat similar program operated under the aegis of the International Federation of Educational Committees (FICE), which was founded in 1948, and now operates in twenty-five countries

The philosophy - or, rather, the dictum - of almost all of these organisations is, simply speaking, that small is good. This expresses itself in most cases as an attempt to recreate a nuclear family for the orphan, with pseudo-parents and siblings. Indeed, this is the stated goal of UNICEF operations:

"UNICEF believes that whenever possible, children who are orphaned should remain in their communities to be raised by their extended families. Recognising that family care is far better for children and far less costly than institutionalised care, children who grow up in families also develop better social skills and are psychologically better adjusted than those who grow up in institutions because they receive more affection and attention and develop a better sense of personal identity" (Care and Support, 2004).

In most cases the residents are limited to eight or ten to a house, and the number of houses in a village is likewise limited to ten or less for the same ideological reasons: *"Every SOS 'village' consists of about ten group houses, each with six to eight children and two adults. The goal is to make each village feel like a community, and each home feel like a family"* (SOS, 2005).

6. Is smaller better?

This is a continuation of what was a social work creed for many decades: That any home is better than any institution, or - in the words of former New York mayor LaGuardia - "The worst mother is better than the best institution" (Goodwin, 1994). This axiom is not only the accepted wisdom - it has taken on an almost moral value and become, in effect, a mythology, if not an ideology. This view has become so embedded that "the bias against the orphanage care option dominates the child care profession" (McCall, 1999).

This view seems to be based on a vision of Dickens-like warehousing of children, a view which shows little awareness of the reality of modern institutions.

For example, as long ago as 1927 Makerenko, in Russia, organised a working commune made up of 150 boys and girls aged 13 to 17 years, combining agricultural work with secondary education. This grew to 300 in 1932 and 600 in 1935, and by most reports was successful.

Similarly, even some persons innately opposed to orphan homes view with sympathy Korczak's doomed attempt to take care of hundreds of children in his orphanage - an attempt possibly modelled on the Israeli kibbutz in which he spent six weeks in 1934 (Lifton, 1988).

Nevertheless, the possible positive effects of growing up in a healthy, nurturing environment in an institution seem to be written off in advance, although one former orphan home resident disagrees with this stance, saying: *"Few of us would have entertained adoption, and virtually all of us today shudder at the foster-care option"* (McKenzie, 1994).

And yet, *"No controlled studies exist comparing the effectiveness of orphanages with that of foster care"* (Lachman, 2004). There is almost no research that individualises children in long-term total-care institutions and compares them with those in families, just as it is difficult to locate longitudinal studies of the after-effects of institutionalised childhood. Perusal of the contents of the last five years of issues of Development Psychology, Development Review, Adoption and Fostering, Adoption Quarterly, Attachment and Human Development, and Children and Youth Services Review failed to locate any empirical studies of the effect of institutional versus family environment on child development.

Similarly, a careful examination of published research concludes that, *"There have been almost no studies that rigorously compare outcomes for youth in institutional/group care and foster family care"* (Barth, 2002). The last large-scale survey was conducted about 1929 and no study of such magnitude has been published since (McCall, 1999). Of the scattered research that has been published since that time, McCall (1999) says, *"Oftentimes, the conclusions did not seem justified by the procedures."*

Not only is there no real evidence that institutional living is necessarily bad for children, there are many examples of abuse in foster home placements, as well as corruption and lack of supervision (Kaufman, 2005). As McKenzie (1994) puts it: *"With all the talk about 'family values,' critics must never forget that some families value very little."*

Perhaps the most familiar type of total-care institutional setting in the public mind is the orphan home. Insofar as these are concerned, the most extensive longitudinal study of the outcomes of such childhood are reported by McKenzie (1999). He says: *"Of the (orphan home) boys and girls who graduated from high school in the late 1950s more than 80% now have college and advanced degrees."* Going even further, he conducted two detailed and extensive investigations of orphanage alumni, nine years apart, and found that: *"According to their own reports, the orphanage alumni have outpaced their age counterparts in the general population on a substantial majority of the social and economic measures covered in the study. Also, nine out of ten respondents indicate that they would prefer to have grown up in their orphanages than in foster care."*

In view of the numbers of AIDS-related orphans, there is a pressing need to overcome the idealised image of foster-family and small-group care and to recognise that big is not necessarily bad. With the proper effort, large institutions can offer good developmental care. We must remove the dictum - which has become a virtual firewall - that we must recreate family settings. We must move toward creating very large childcare facilities, rather than continuing to rely on very small group structures. The need is for Herculean, long-term, mass solutions that will at least soften and/or reduce the looming catastrophe.

7. Proposed solutions

This paper outlines the experience of the Israel movement known as Youth Aliyah in absorbing thousands of orphan refugees since the end of World War II, through the medium of relatively large children's villages. The goal, structure, methods, and results of the movement will be discussed in the hope that similar methods can be helpful in the present situation.

8. Youth Aliyah

In 1934, sensing the threat to Jews in Europe, an attempt to rescue the children, at least, by sending them to Palestine, was undertaken. The first group of forty-three children, under the aegis of Henrietta Szold, arrived in Palestine in 1934. The movement was named Youth Aliyah ("Ascent of Youth") and was supported and financed by Hadassah, the Women's Zionist Organisation of America. At the end of the war in Europe, in 1944, the first group of children who had been imprisoned in death camps and survived death marches arrived in Palestine (Gidal, 1957).

The most natural institutions to absorb these children were the kibbutzim (plural of kibbutz) (Macarov, 2001). These voluntary communal villages already had infants' houses, children's houses and youth houses in line with the kibbutz tradition that children should be raised by trained childcare experts. This method, called collective education, was *"unique in that the children live in the children's homes from birth on"* (Yaffe, 2000). However, there was frequent contact with parents in after-work hours and on holidays.

It will be recognised that this was a reversal of the accepted axiom mentioned above concerning families *vis-à-vis* institutions, and the empirical results defied the accepted wisdom. Kibbutz members who grew up in children's and youth houses were no less adjusted and effective within Israeli society than others, and - in fact - often became the leaders in many fields of education, medicine, *etc.* The educational level in the kibbutzim is higher than that in Israel generally, and the same percentage of kibbutz members have an academic degree as does the general population. Twenty percent have post-secondary school certificates, as compared to 12% in the general Jewish population (Yaffe, 2000).

On a more empirical note, a nine-year-long study of the moral development of kibbutz children as compared to children coming from outside the kibbutz found that, *"There were no significant differences in moral-issue choices between kibbutz and non-kibbutz subjects"* in two of the three fields studied. In the remaining field, children from North African parents were more likely to see the father as an authority figure. However, the researchers report that the results might be skewed against the kibbutz subjects, since the instrument used missed: *"The kibbutznicks' (kibbutz members) communal emphasis, social solidarity, and greater emphasis upon collective happiness"* (Snarey *et al.*, 1985). Another study found kibbutz children to exhibit more developed group functioning skills, but less warmth and involvement with peers (Levy-Shiff and Hoffman, 1985).

There has been, of late, a return to children growing up in their parents' homes in the kibbutz, but this was clearly in response to a need expressed by parents, and not by children, nor was it based on perceived outcomes. It was, in fact, a concrete example of the old folk-saying: *"More than the calf wants to suck, the cow wants to suckle."*

In Israel: *"In contrast to most Western countries, which use placements in residential settings only in the most severe cases, in Israel it is the norm. 75,000 (Israeli children) live out of home. Most of them are not considered at risk, and consequently they stay in educational settings"* (Zeria, 2004).

Even the accepted norm that it is better for children to be with their family members than with others has been challenged by research: *"'Kin-caregivers' costs are perceived as a drain on their own emotional resources... In contrast, non-kin foster caregivers appeared to be more focused on the difficulties of the child's behaviour than on feelings of personal distress"* (Timaiaer *et al.*, 2004).

Regardless of the small-group/large-number philosophical and educational argument, it has been made moot by the growing millions of orphans in need of care. The small-home, small-group philosophy is fast becoming a Canute-like response to an overwhelming tide of need.

This is not to denigrate the small children's villages mentioned previously. They are doing a useful service. As the Talmud tells us, *"He who saves a single life is as though he has saved the world,"* and the proposal made here is to supplement, not to supplant, the efforts already being made.

The absorption of small numbers of refugee children was not difficult for the kibbutzim. However, most kibbutzim were themselves small, and the number of children they could deal with was limited. As waves of immigrants continued to arrive, the device of youth villages was necessarily adopted. The six hundred thousand Jews living in Israel at the emergence of the State received and absorbed over two million new immigrants during the first few years. Thus, new, large institutions were needed. The tradition of children and youth living in their own community, with responsibilities, democratic decision-making, and individual choice - as exemplified in the kibbutz children's and youth houses - was extended to the many non-kibbutz children's villages subsequently established.

The largest of the non-kibbutz youth villages was Neurim, with a population of 1,200 children. There seems to have been no educational or physical limits to the expansion of this village, in which the population ebbed and flowed according to need. Housing in youth villages was mostly dormitory style, with fifteen to forty children in each building. There was a central dining room, and various activity rooms. In addition to full-fledged educational programs, activities were centred around agriculture, with a heavy addition of cultural activities. Regardless of age at time of entry, the villages were structured to take care of the children until they could enter into normal Israeli society.

Within the villages there were groupings according to age, and each group had the leadership of educational, recreational, and social teachers and counsellors. There was a heavy use of volunteers - often from Israeli youth movements, and sometimes as a national service provided by the army. In general, the ratio of staff to child was two staff members to about fifteen children (E. Ophir, Director of Youth Aliyah, personal communication, 2004).

The structure of the children's village allowed for as much autonomy as possible on the part of groups, with children's committees, councils and task-forces a prominent feature. Many villages published their own newspapers. Punishment for anti-social behaviour usually took the form of exclusion from certain activities, such as a hike, a visit to a city, *etc.*

In addition to refugee children, Youth Aliyah in its later days began to accept into the villages children who, for many reasons, could not remain at home with their families. These included children from dysfunctional families, victims of parental abuse, children of single parents, and those from homes so poverty-stricken that they could not raise their children properly. According to the present Director of Youth Aliyah, given money, knowledgeable staff and proper supervision, there is no reason why the children's villages pioneered by the organisation could not be expanded considerably (E. Ophir, Director of Youth Aliyah, personal communication, 2004).

It was recognised during the earliest days that success in working with children in such settings could not be based merely upon good will and empathy, but required at least semi-professional training. Consequently, training schools and courses specifically designed to prepare staff for children's village were set-up. The average training course for professional staff was two years, although a myriad of short-courses on specific subjects or problems was continually offered. The prestige of being a Youth Aliyah counsellor was high, and as they organised themselves, they also developed a Code of Ethics to govern their own behaviour in their jobs.

At present, over 300,000 Israelis are graduates of Youth Aliyah villages. There does not seem to be any discrimination or prejudice concerning adults who grew up in youth villages and those who grew up in families. On the contrary, *"The residential villages of Youth Aliyah are very prestigious in Israeli society...some of the leading elites were formed in the residential villages of Youth Aliyah"* (Levy, 2002). It is noteworthy that the present President of Israel - President Katzav - is a Youth Aliyah graduate who grew up in a youth village. Recent studies indicate that 90% of Youth Aliyah students are mainstreamed into regular high schools, with 85% accepted into the Israel Defense Forces (which administers psychological, emotional and other tests to recruits) although preparation for army service was never one of their goals (Levy, 2002).

9. Application to Africa

In comparison with the numbers of children needing help worldwide, the Israel experience may seem minuscule, but the principles and methods outlined above may be helpful. Insofar as timing is concerned, Youth Aliyah has now been active for over seventy years, and given the timeframe of present and future cohorts of AIDS-related orphans, planning and preparation that may take years - even decades - is not only desirable, but absolutely necessary.

9.1. Sponsorship

First and foremost, the efforts to save children in Africa must be African efforts. Others may consult, advise, help, and provide finances, but unless indigenous African organisations undertake to establish children's villages, the effort is almost certainly doomed to failure. Whether these efforts are made by churches, non-governmental organisations, childcare agencies, or governments, only they can fit these ideas into African cultural mores and social needs.

9.2. Staff training

Among the first steps in planning for a widespread program of youth villages is the preparation of staff. Assuming that the necessary teachers as such will have been trained in that discipline, (which will require a massive increase in schools of education) the areas that seem closest to those used by Youth Aliyah leaders are social group work, informal education and child growth and development. Since any of these areas can be full-time long-term subjects, it will be necessary to tease out the parts most needed for the preparation being planned. One precedent for this kind of training may be found in the Hebrew University's Schwartz Program, which was instituted in 1968 to provide directors and senior staff for a planned network of community centers. The program was directed jointly by the schools of social work and education, and after its inception added a specialisation in pre-school development. Another precedent is the course of studies offered by the Youth Aliyah staff training institutions themselves.

There arises a double question: Who will be the teachers, and where will the teachers themselves get trained? Without going into too much detail, it is possible that African schools of social work and education can provide faculty for the initial training of teachers and/or indigenous personnel can be sent for training abroad. There are presently 69 schools of social work in Africa, with twenty of them in South Africa alone (S. Spero, Treasurer, *International Association of Schools of Social Work*, personal communication, 2005). Expansion of these schools and the establishment of new ones - perhaps schools devoted entirely to training staff for children's villages - is indicated.

The subject of teachers and/or youth counsellors relates to another important element, not only as regards staff, but as it affects the children themselves. That is, the importance and difficulty of working with several languages and/or ethnic differences (Chow and Wyatt, 2003).

As has been pointed out, Africa is far from a homogenous entity, and even within one country, or one area, several languages and/or dialects may be spoken (Fratter and Ndagive, 2000). In addition, tribes and clans are an important part of the African tradition, and thus, *"Severing a child legally from the clan would be regarded as depriving a child of his or her birthright"* (Fratter and Ndagive, 2000). Consequently, great care would have to be exercised not to impose a Western pattern on the African community. The goal, ideally, would be to, *"Find ways in which African and Western notions of childcare can be married"* (Harber, 1999).

9.3. Costs

It is difficult to base a cost-estimate of children's villages on the Israeli experience, for all or even part of the target population, given the differences in exchange rates, varying costs of living, rural/urban ratios, *etc.* However, as one possible measure, note that the gross national income per person in Israel is about $16,000. The same factor ranges in sub-Sahara Africa from $3,120 in Gabon to $90 in the Democratic Republic of Congo. The average GNI per capita in fourteen of the African countries under discussion is slightly less than $1,000; and the median is about $500.

In short, the average GNI in sub-Saharan Africa is about a sixteenth of the $16,000 GNI in Israel. Accordingly, the $4,000 annual cost per child in an Israeli village would correspond to an average of $250 per child in Africa. If the GNI figures at the lower end of the scale seem unbelievably low, it might be salutary to recognise that in forty of the Organisation of African Unity countries people live on less than $100 a year (Saigon Times, 2001; MacPherson and Silburn, 1998; Overcoming Human Poverty,1998). Contrariwise, note that in New York foster families receive on the average about $28 a day for each child, a figure that is soon to rise (Kaufman, 2005). This comes to over ten thousand dollars per child per year, which is at variance with the oft-repeated argument that foster care is cheaper than institutional care. Similarly, it has been estimated that it costs adoption agencies $19,000 to arrange an adoption (Allpin *et al.*, 2001).

Again, it should be clear that GNI does not represent local costs, but insofar as it is even a rough approximation of differences in costs between Israel and the African countries being discussed, the cost of fifteen million children in villages (using an absurdly optimistic assumption that all of the children could and would be accommodated), would range between about $12 billion dollars - if the cost were that in Gabon - to $33 million dollars in the Democratic Republic of Congo. If the average cost of about $250 is used, all of the orphans could be settled into children's villages for less than four billion dollars a year. These upkeep costs do not include the initial investment in buildings and grounds, nor do they include the costs involved in training staff. The World Orphans organisation estimates that it costs about $8,000 to build a shelter or about $200 per child (World Orphans, 2005).

At first glance even the annual costs may sound like a formidable amount, given the small contributions that trickle in to organisations like UNICEF from member countries. But the United States alone spends $15 billion on development aid each year (Eviator, 2004). It has spent about $60 billion so far to fight the war in Iraq, and is spending almost $4 billion a month on the troops there. Tax cuts in the United States amount to about $20 billion a month (Sachs, 2004). Indeed, one of the bills introduced in the United States Senate calls for $3.35 billion for HIV/AIDS spending, which means that the $4 billion necessary to take care of is not a pie-in-the-sky amount (Zuniga, 2003).

On a more realistic note, it is clear that all of the orphans in Africa cannot and will not be accommodated. Consequently, cost figures must be reduced to fit a realistic child population in children's villages. With this in view it should be recognised that Europeans spend over $40 billion dollars a year on cigarettes; Americans spend about $60 billion a year on personal beauty products; in Britain over a billion pounds sterling is spent each year on pet food; and the world trade in drugs amounts to over $400 billion a year (Macarov, 2003). Even Ethiopia, with an annual health budget of $140 million, spends over a billion dollars a year caring for orphans (Eviator, 2004).

10. Conclusion

The relentless rise in the number of orphans - and particularly AIDS-related orphans - throughout the world, demands new methods of developmental help. The use of large-scale children's villages, instead of the presently preferred family-like settings, is indicated. There is no evidence that such villages are inherently less effective than much larger settings, and some reason to believe that they are as good, if not better, than the present method. The success of such villages is predicated on the existence of properly trained staff - personal, supervisory and administrative - which requires specialised training. Costs are not astronomical, and given the fact that not all of the orphans will be affected, can even be seen as reasonable. Failure to deal with the problem of the world's orphans may create more than a generation of rootless, amoral, illiterate persons, with implications of great social upheavals.

Despite the difficulties of conceptualisation and implementation of such programs, social planners should be aware of the admonition in The Ethics of the Fathers: *"It may not be given you to complete the job, but neither are you free to desist."*

References

Allpin, A., B. Simmons and A. Barth, 2001. Adoption of Foster Children: How Much Does It Cost Public Agencies? Children and Youth Services Review 23: 865-891.

Africa's Orphaned Generations, 2005, UNICEF, Geneva, pp. 9-11.

Barth, R., 2002. Institutions vs. Foster Homes: The Empirical Base for the Second Century of Debate. Chapel Hill, University of North Carolina.

Care and Support for Orphans and Families Affected by HIV/AIDS, 2004. http://www.unicef.org/aids/index/.orphans.html

Chow, J.C.-C. and P. Wyatt, 2003. Ethnicity, Language Capacity, and Perception of Ethnic-Specific Services Agencies in Asian American and Pacific Islander Communities. Journal of Immigrant and Refugee Services 1: 41-60.

Eviator, D., 2004. Spend $150 Billion per Year to Cure World Poverty. New York Times Magazine, November 7.

Fratter, J. and B.K. Ndagive, 2000. Meeting Health and Ethnic Needs in Placement Planning for African Children Affected by HIV. Adoption and Fostering 24: 34-39.

Gidal, N.T., 1957. Henrietta Szold. Jerusalem, Gefen.

Goodstein, L., 2005. Murder and Suicide Reviving Claims of Child Abuse in Cult. New York Times, January 5, p. 1.

Goodwin, D.K., 1994. No Ordinary Time. New York, Simon and Shuster (quoted by McCall, 1999).

Harber, M., 1999. Transforming Adoption in the 'New' South Africa in Response to the HIV/AIDS Epidemic. Adoption and Fostering 23: 10.

Kaufman, L., 2005. New York Finds Doctored Files in Foster Care. New York Times, January 15. p. 1.

Lachman, R., 2004. Review of Deja Views of an Aging Orphan: Growing Up in the Hebrew National Orphan Home, by S.G. Arcus. Philadelphia, Xlibris.

Lalor, K., 2004. Child Abuse in Kenya and Tanzania. Child Abuse and Neglect 28: 833-844.

Levy, Z., 2002. Creating a Powerful System of Residential Education and Care for Israeli Youth: The Lesson of Youth Aliyah. Child and Youth Care Forum 31: 157-161.

Levy-Shiff, R. and M.A. Hoffman, 1985. Social Behaviour of Urban and Kibbutz Preschool Children. Development Psychology 21: 1204-1205.

Lifton, B.J., 1988. The King of Children: The Life and Death of Janusz Korczak. New York, St. Martin's Griffen.

Macarov, D., 2001. Constructing and Deconstructing Utopia: The Israeli Kibbutz as a Case in Point. In: A. Shostak (ed.), Utopian Thinking in Sociology. New York, American Sociological Association.

Macarov, D., 2003. What the Market Does to People: Privatization, Globalization and Poverty. Atlanta, Clarity.

MacPherson, S., and Silburn, R., 1998. The Meaning and Measurement of Poverty. In: J. Dixon and D. Macarov (eds.), Poverty: A Persistent Global Reality. London, Routledge, pp. 1-19.

McCall, J., 1999. Research on the Psychological Effects of Orphanage Care: A Critical Review. In: R.B. McKenzie, R.B. (ed.), Rethinking Orphanages for the 21st Century. Thousand Oaks, Sage.

McKenzie, R.B., 1994. An Orphan on Orphanages. Wall Street Journal.

McKenzie, R.B., 1999. Rethinking Orphanages for the 21st Century. Thousand Oaks, Sage.

Overcoming Human Poverty, 1998. New York, United Nations Development Programme, 15 pp.

Porter, C., 2000. Report Predicts World's Orphans Will Exceed 40 Million by 2010. Fact Sheet, United States Embassy, Tokyo.

Rohde, D., 2005. Mix of Quake Aid and Preaching Stirs Concern. New York Times, January 22.

Sachs, J., 2001. A Miserly Response to a Global Emergency. Yale Global Online, December 18.

Saigon Times, 2001. March 5, p. 1.

Snarey, J.R., J. Reimer and L. Kohlberg, 1985. Development of Social-Moral Reasoning among Kibbutz Adolescents: A Longitudinal Cross-Cultural Study. Developmental Psychology 21: 3-17.

SOS, 2005. www.sos-usa.org.

Timaiaer, S., G.G. Sadler and A.J. Urquiza, 2004. Challenging Children in Kin versus Nonkin Foster Care: Perceived Costs and Benefits to Caregivers. Child Maltreatment 9: 251-262.

World Orphans, 2005. http://www.worldorphans.org.

Yaffe, N. (ed.), 2000. Kibbutzim - Statistical Six. Yad Tabenkin, Israel.

Zeria, A., 2004. New Initiatives in Out-of-Home Placements in Israel. Child and Family Social Work 9: 305-307.

Zuniga, J.M., 2003. Hope for Turning of the Tide. IAPAC Monthly 9, pp. 2.

Poverty, poverty alleviation, and capitalism in global and historical perspective: modeling a relationship between inequality and market maladjustment

Charles Powers
Department of Sociology, Santa Clara University, Santa Clara, California 95053, USA.
cpowers@scu.edu.

Abstract

Efforts to bolster market capitalism seem to reduce poverty in some countries and aggravate it in others. This may result from a relationship between (1) inequality and (2) distortions in market adjustment. Even if market adjustment produces generally beneficial outcomes in countries with relatively low levels of inequality, the "invisible hand of the market" may produce maladjustments when levels of inequality are high. The reason is that extreme disparities in disposable income leave many people without appreciable voice in the marketplace. Disparities of that kind can hamper the processes that might otherwise produce socially rational market adjustment. The central premise of this paper is that people who are far below the median for disposable income in the areas where they spend their money are to a considerable extent voiceless in the marketplace.

JEL Classification: B59, D43, D59, E13

Keywords: Gini Coefficient, market adjustment, Pareto distribution, poverty

1. The theoretical connection between market economics and socially rational goals

Mainstream economic thinking is predicated on the assumption that markets adjust in ways that promote economically efficient utilisation of resources to meet socially rational goals. The "socially rational goals" part of this claim is worth pausing to consider. When economics developed as a discipline, Adam Smith and his contemporaries shared a conviction that the earth would provide a better life for its people to the degree that the power of free markets could be unleashed (Smith, 1976). Social welfare would be optimised by allowing "the invisible hand" of the market to operate because, it was argued, market adjustment would encourage steadily more efficient use of resources in pursuit of generally more useful ends. The remedy for the lingering ills of feudalism, as Smith understood it, was reorganisation of economic activity on the basis of market principles so that real aggregate needs of the many (rather than extravagant whims of a spoiled few) would be addressed. He had faith that yesterday's unmet needs would be the target of today's new economic activity. From this point of view, global trade and freedom of capital movement are the most effective instruments of poverty alleviation.

The social rationality of free markets was never universally accepted as an article of faith. Many have characterised free markets as instruments for further marginalising the poor. From this point of view, global trade and freedom of capital movement can be viewed as contributing to poverty rather than alleviating it (Rodney, 1982). The apparent difference in these two positions (capitalism as an instrument of poverty alleviation and capitalism as the root of poverty) hinges on the social rationality of market adjustment. Most conventional economists have faith that markets encourage efficiency in pursuit of socially rational goals, while capitalism's sceptics tend to feel that capitalism serves only the interests of rich, to the exclusion of the needs of the many and disregarding matters of long-run sustainability.

The concept of market adjustment is at the core of this discussion. Market adjustment involves redeployment of effort following monetary incentive. There will, of course, be some discrepancy between yesterday's unmet needs and today's new activity. The rich obviously have more voice than the poor, and the very rich have much more voice than the very poor. Sachs (2005a) makes the point clear in his common sense analysis of research and development expenditures. There is a huge need for research on things like "off grid" renewable energy production, yet this need has received comparatively little attention because the need has (to date) been felt most dramatically by the world's most desperately poor. Their voices are inaudible in the global marketplace.

Despite such concessions to the role of inequality, most economists (see Meijer, 1987, for an overview of neo-liberals) and most business people (*e.g.*, McKenna, 2002) have faith that free markets tend to direct attention where aggregate needs are greatest, which ultimately makes "markets" allies of the poor because "the invisible hand of the market" is viewed as serving the common good. Socially rational market adjustment is an enticing concept because it seems to follow logically once we make certain assumptions about the marketplace in capitalist economies. The ideal-type market has the following standard textbook characteristics:

1. Actors engage in buying, selling, or trading of things that might be broadly thought of as "goods" and "services".
2. Aggregate demand does not discriminate. Demand reflects how many people really want something and how badly they really want it. Factors like race and gender are irrelevant where market adjustment is concerned. Producers (and potential producers) respond to changes in aggregate demand without regard to where that demand comes from.
3. There are many potential "buyers" and "sellers" of any particular good or service, so people in a marketplace always have a lot of choice. To the degree that choice is limited at any given moment, incentive can draw new producers into the market. This makes scarcity of suppliers a self-correcting problem.
4. People are free to make rational decisions. Tomorrow's exchanges are independent of today's exchanges.
5. There is transparency. People are, at least in general terms, sufficiently informed about pertinent matters to make interest-maximising decisions.
6. There are few barriers to inhibit market players from repositioning themselves.

This combination of factors makes market adjustment ("the invisible hand of the market") fluid and more or less friction free. Experiences of the twentieth century demonstrate this convincingly. Free markets have out-performed command economies of all kinds. Free markets have the power to change people's lives for the better because markets do, at least under some circumstances, encourage adjustments toward efficient and effective satisfaction of real needs (Backhaus, 2005). Markets have been the great poverty alleviation mechanisms of modern times specifically because they can direct entrepreneurial attention to areas of real need.

2. Illustrating that market adjustment can be socially rational by considering the failure of import substitution policies

The history of "import substitution" policies offers vivid evidence for the power of conventional economic analysis. Until very recently, policy makers in many countries defied conventional economic wisdom by using tariff barriers in order to encourage "import substitution," thereby protecting local industry. The argument for such "import substitution" policies was compelling. Tariffs could be used to make imports prohibitively expensive (definitely true). Local people would then be forced to buy domestically produced goods and services (probably true in the short-term). This would lead to industrial expansion and job creation (probably true in the short-term). Local producers would gain a much larger share of the local market (probably true in the short-term). Larger share of the local market would enable local producers to acquire valuable experience and to enjoy more favourable economies of scale so that prices could be reduced (a prediction which sounded reasonable enough) and growing experience in the domestic market would enable local producers to improve quality over time (a prediction which sounded reasonable enough). Reduced prices and improved quality would allow domestic producers to be more competitive in the global marketplace (a prediction which sounded reasonable enough).

During the mid-twentieth century governments in many countries (in Brazil, India and Ireland, for example) attempted to foster economic growth and development using import substitution policies. But generally speaking, such policies proved disastrous in the long-run (as anticipated by Pareto, 1984 [1921]). Higher tariffs initially help domestic producers by raising the price of foreign goods, but this diminishes competitive pressure for domestic product improvement and price control. The consequences are three-fold. First, domestic consumers end up having to pay more for those categories of goods enjoying protection, and this creates a net economic loss. Second, to the degree that domestic product quality deteriorates relative to global competition, local products lose rather than gain global markets. Third, to the degree that inferior products are infused into local infrastructure the domestic economy falters even further (Oatley, 2005). The last point may require a short illustration. Consider what would happen if all the offices and all the workers in a country were wired together with telephone equipment which did not transmit signals clearly. The resulting inefficiencies could reverberate throughout the economy.

In the final analysis, the weight of historical/comparative evidence tends to vindicate conventional economic analysis with regard to import substitution policies, and this makes for a powerful affirmation of mainstream economic thought. Protectionism often leads to outcomes which differ from those originally intended by the designers of protectionist policies. Allowing the "invisible hand of the market" to rationally adjust frequently produces significant benefits, while protectionist policies often bring about economic decline. Countries like Ireland and India have enjoyed much more prosperity, and indeed more effective poverty alleviation, by following the free trade policies of the present than they experienced while following the import substitution policies of the past. A good case can be made for relying on the "invisible hand of the market" to wage society's war on poverty.

3. Capitalism and poverty in historical perspective

Unfortunately, unleashing capitalism is far from being a universal cure for poverty. Current estimates are that 2.8 billion people, over 40% of the world's population, lives on less than two dollars (US) per day per capita (Robbins, 2005). While scholars debate what this really means after conversion rates and real prices for local staples are taken into account, there can be no doubt that a great many human beings live in dire conditions and have no protective safety net or buffer against the ravages of disaster (Chen and Ravallion, 2004).

To be sure, inequality and poverty were common long before the advent of modern capitalism (Dyer, 2000). Nevertheless, it seems accurate to say that many of the worst features of global inequality can be traced to the success of European mercantile capitalism. Starting with the early sixteenth century, Spanish colonial authorities depleted the Andean countryside to form work gangs for Bolivian silver mines. By the early seventeenth century millions of captives were being wrenched out of Africa, sold into slavery, and transported to the Caribbean to grow sugar. Later, in the eighteenth century, African slaves were used growing cotton and tobacco for a global market. At the beginning of the nineteenth century the Dutch government began using a form of taxation that compelled indigenous farmers in the East Indies to convert a certain portion of their crop land to the cultivation of those crops. Debt peonage ensnarled late nineteenth century rubber tapers and coffee growers in the world's equatorial regions. Where non-Europeans enjoyed a trade advantage, adroit action by European powers undermined that advantage. Illustrations include efforts of the British East India Company to undermine Indian textile production, and British encouragement of the opium trade (eventually turning a tenth of the population of China into addicts) in an effort to counteract the trade surplus China enjoyed from exporting tea. The poorest of today's poor are, disproportionately, descendants of those forced to mine the ores and grow the crops that were the basis of yesterday's global trade. And the least politically stable or economically prosperous of today's nation-states are those that were formed as sources of labour or agricultural or mineral output during the mercantile capitalist period (Robbins, 2005; Wallerstein, 2004).

In addition to lingering inequality left over from the past, today's global economy is producing new poor by further marginalising those semi-subsistence farmers with little or no land and those urban workers with little or no property or education. International mobility of labour suppresses wages in the affluent countries by importing workers from low-wage countries into high-wage countries, and by exporting assembly jobs from high-wage countries to low-wage countries (Anderson, 2000). At the same time, as capital moves to less prosperous countries and the economies of those countries become more export oriented, pressure increases on poor people to get out of the way of "progress" (Barker and Mander, 2001). This can be as simple as vacating property in sunbelt areas where Europeans and Americans vacation.

Coming to better understand how this happens is one of the major challenges confronting students of contemporary society (Stiglitz, 2002). Inflation is particularly devastating in low-wage countries where it makes meaningless what had already been the meagre market voice of the poor, leaving them without enough cash to make the kind of discretionary market choices that can drive socially rational market adjustment. Under these conditions, the predictable result is that the "invisible hand of the market" stops guiding events toward socially rational, need satisfying outcomes (Shiva, 2000). In order for a marketplace to act as a sorting mechanism for allocating resources on the basis of real need, the people with real need must have some discretionary income (1) with which to signal their priorities and (2) with which to alter their economic strategies. Without that, markets are unable to perform what Adam Smith understood as their most important function, which is to progressively realign economic activity and resources to better meet needs (Sen, 1997).

The fundamental insight is that in societies with little inequality, it does make sense to think that more money chasing after something is a genuine sign of a unmet need or aggregate want. But when a society is sharply divided between people who have a great deal of discretionary income and others who have none at all, there are no market incentives for finding better ways of meeting the needs of people without any money. This means market adjustments will occur, but they will not be socially rational.

Conventional economic analysis suggests that market adjustment produces constructive adjustment because markets search for more efficient and sustainable ways to satisfy greater need at less cost and with fewer negative side effects. But to the degree that a society is characterised by steep inequality, it may be more accurate to think of market adjustment in terms of conversion of resources away from meeting basic needs of the many to providing discretionary luxuries and entertainment for the few, while significant and widespread needs are ignored. Other things being equal, the greater the level of inequality in the distribution of resources then the more sociologists would expect real needs to fester (Parsons, 1966). To be realistic, one must anticipate that this situation could actually worsen with globalisation. To the extent that the most affluent people from the most affluent countries find opportunities for expressing their market voices in far-flung geographic areas of the world, the ability of local needs to drive adjustments in the local market is reduced. Whether a country is relatively isolated or rather well integrated into the global economy, income/wealth inequality among those participating in the local environment will tend to cause the market adjustment process to move in aberrant directions, away from socially rational allocation of resources (Powers, 2003). The greater the disparity of wealth and income, then the more obvious the risk that adjustments in the market will tend to redeploy time, energy, resources and entrepreneurial talent away from optimal efforts to meet real needs.

The fundamental point is straight-forward: The greater the income inequality is, then the more distorted market signals about aggregate societal needs will be, and consequently the more aberrant subsequent market adjustment will be. Given what we know about markets, it is reasonable to expect the hypothesised relationship between inequality and socially rational market adjustment to be curvilinear rather than linear. This follows from the basic premise of "Austrian" economics. Within broad limits, imperfect markets can perform as if they are perfect, or very nearly so. Economies can function very effectively even when there are some restrictions on private property and political freedoms, but as limits on private property and government control increase by arithmetic increments, market distortions make themselves apparent geometrically, which is why centrally administered economies are doomed to eventual failure (*e.g.*, Mises, 1966). Similarly, market economies with moderate amounts of inequality can be relatively effective in adjusting for socially rational pursuit of goals. However, where inequality is more extreme we should expect the market adjustment process to be subverted away form satisfaction of the genuine needs of ordinary people in favour of satisfying the ephemeral tastes of the privileged.

There are two dynamics through which the "invisible hand of the market" is directed away from meeting real needs when levels of inequality are extreme. First, the poor and businesses serving the poor are easy to displace when inequality is extreme, because poor people are often desperate and may be susceptible to the temptation of "buy out" offers (Chachage, 1998). This is especially true in the aftermath of natural disasters. Always living a precarious existence, any illness or natural disaster puts the poor at risk of utter, instant, and complete dispossession. Second, the desperately poor are easily tempted to absorb potentially devastating risks. The more desperate the family, the more likely family members are to risk health for short-term economic gain, accepting dangerous jobs (involving high accident rates or exposure to toxins, for example) or adopting non-sustainable economic practices (using dynamite to fish coral reefs, for instance). Consequently, beyond a certain threshold, income inequality should be treated as a limiting condition on socially rational market adjustment.

4. A model

A large segment of the world's population is now locked in poverty and lives without much economic voice or agency (Barker and Mander, 2001). The premise of this paper is that people who are far below the median for disposable income in the areas where they spend their money are to a considerable extent voiceless in the marketplace. They have real needs. Indeed, their circumstances constitute the best barometer of societal well-being. But in as much as they are essentially voiceless in the marketplace, normal market adjustments are unlikely to result in diversion of additional energy or resources to meet their needs.

The purpose of this paper is to posit an inverse relationship between inequality (as the independent variable) and the degree of social rationality evidenced in market adjustment (as the dependent variable). Using the Gini Index to represent inequality (where 0.0 represents complete equality in income or wealth distribution and 1.0 represents a total absence of equality in the distribution of wealth or income), market adjustment should be socially rational or nearly so where levels of inequality are at their lowest (in countries like Japan which is often cited as having a Gini score of between 0.25 and 0.3). By contrast, market adjustment might be expected to deviate significantly from socially rational allocation of resources where inequality is greatest (for example, in countries like Brazil with a Gini coefficient of around 0.60). Markets are predicted to function relatively well (that is, displaying a high degree of efficiency in pursuit of socially rational goals) where levels of inequality are low (where Gini is closer to zero than to 1.0). But gross distortions away from socially rational market adjustment should be expected where inequality is high (closer to 1.0 than to zero).

This suggests curvilinear relationship analogous to one "Austrian" economists posit between government control and aggregate economic performance. Increasing levels of government control may have comparatively little impact on aggregate economic performance until a threshold is past. But after some point, the inhibiting impact of government involvement becomes very obvious.

Curvilinear relationships of this kind, sometimes called Pareto distributions, are found everywhere. The challenge is to identify the empirical parameters for a given relationship. It seems premature to try to determine precise numerical parameters for the hypothesised relationship between inequality and socially rational market performance because of the difficulty we have in collecting comparable data on inequality and given obvious problems operationally defining the concept of socially rational market adjustment. Despite our inability to be precise at this time, it is possible to suggest some rough parameters that seem consistent with what we know about the world.

Inequality is often conceptualised as ranging between 0.0 (complete equal distribution of resources) and 1.0 (total lack of equality in the distribution of resources). If we (1) conceptualise social rationality in market adjustment on the same scale (1.0 being complete social rationality in market adjustment and 0.0 representing a total lack of social rationality in market adjustment), and (2) if we treat social rationality in market adjustment as a dependent variable to be predicted from changes in inequality, then (3) social rationality in market adjustment would be estimated by subtracting some function of inequality from 1 (because as inequality increases, socially rational market adjustment declines (from 1.0 as its highest possible value, declining toward zero as its lowest value). But what function of inequality (Gini) should be subtracted from 1.0? (4) The function needs to involve Gini to some power, in order to produce the hypothesised curve in the relationship between inequality and socially rational market adjustment, and (5) must be multiplied by some factor, in order to give the function sufficient weight to account for the variability we observe in the real world. We can arrive at a first approximation by noting that real world variability seems to be approximated by doubling (multiplying by a two) the square of the Gini coefficient. That is, the degree of social rationality in market adjustment = 1 - 2 x [(Gini coefficient) squared].

$$A = 1 - [2 \, (G^2)]$$

Where A = socially rational market adjustment and G = the Gini coefficient.

Using this equation, a predicted level of social rationality in market adjustment can be calculated for any given level of inequality as measured by Gini coefficients.

Plotting these values yields a Pareto distribution which visually illustrates the pattern of association being hypothesised in this paper.

Gini figures are sometimes calculated on the basis of income distribution, and sometimes on the basis of wealth. They could be calculated on the basis of other distributions as well. Whatever the basis of the distribution, Gini coefficients must be considered as rough estimates. In the case of Brazil, for example, so much economic activity takes place in the

Table 1. Gini coefficient values and predicted levels of social rationality in market adjustment associated with those values.

Gini coefficient value	Predicted level of social rationality coefficient in market adjustment
0.1	0.98
0.2	0.96
0.3	0.82
0.4	0.68
0.5	0.50
0.6	0.28
0.7	0.02

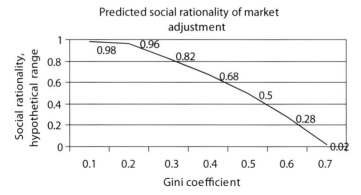

Figure 1. The hypothesised relationship between inequality and the social rationality of market adjustment.

"underground" economy that we are far from having Gini figures we can be certain about. Nevertheless, it seems reasonable to treat the Gini estimates that are available as roughly accurate gauges of inequality in different countries. Treating them as such, the formula advanced in this paper can be used to generate predictions about the expected degree of social rationality in market adjustment in economies having different levels of inequality. In Table 2 below, an incremental scale of inequality is outlined, with some actual counties arrayed in their approximate locations along this continuum (with relative positions based on Gini coefficients found at nationmaster.com). Hypothesised scores for social rationality of market adjustment were then derived by applying the formula advanced in this paper to Gini coefficients at standard increments of 0.5 along this continuum.

The cases chosen for this illustration were intentionally selected to make it clear that the independent variable is the degree of inequality, and not the size of a nation's GPD. The expectation would be that in countries as varied as Japan or Sweden the "invisible hand of the market" should produce adjustments more directly addressing real needs than in countries like Ghana or the United States. Similarly, the expectation would be that in Ghana or the United States the "invisible hand of the market" should produce adjustments more directly addressing real needs than in countries like Lesotho or Mexico. And countries with levels of inequality appreciably higher than that of places like Brazil or the Central African Republic might be expected to have almost completely ineffective market adjustments from the standpoint of socially rational needs. The Ottoman Empire could arguably have been a case in point (Freely, 1998).

This model also enables predictions based on change over time in a single country. In recent decades inequality has increased somewhat in both Japan and the United States. Based on this model one might predict a modest decline in socially rational market adjustment in Japan, which still has relatively little inequality in comparison with other countries. But

Table 2. Comparing predicted differences in social rationality of market adjustment based on increments of inequality as measured by Gini coefficients.

Score on the independent variable	Actual countries with that range of Gini score	Hypothesised comparisons of social rationality in market adjustment
Gini coefficient (approximate)	Countries often thought to be in the approximate range	Hypothesised value on the dependent variable
0.1		0.98
0.2		0.96
0.25	Japan; Sweden	0.88
0.3	Egypt; Germany	0.82
0.35	Algeria; Australia	0.76
0.4	Ghana; USA	0.68
0.45	Costa Rica; Philippine	0.60
0.5	Nigeria; Venezuela	0.50
0.55	Lesotho; Mexico	0.44
0.6	Central African Republic, Brazil	0.28
0.7		0.02

social rationality of market adjustment might be expected to appreciably decline in the United States, as inequality begins to approach what may be a tipping point. In the past, Gini coefficients for the U.S. were well under 0.4 by most estimates, but now they are well above 0.4 by some estimates. Consequently, market aberrations would be predicted to be greater in the United States than in Japan. Institutional factors are also relevant (Polillo and Guillen, 2005).

5. Market adjustment and poverty in global perspective

What seems to be good economic news in the short term can prove disastrous in the long-term. Conversion to coffee production in Brazil a little over a century ago, and in Rwanda a little over a decade ago, did generate foreign exchange revenue until world production overtook demand and prices dropped. But before the price of coffee dropped, production pushed the price of agricultural land farther out of reach of average farmers at the same time that it made peasant life seem less appealing. Small farmers were displaced and land holdings were concentrated (Eakin, 1998; Waters, 2001). Peasant life based on production of staple foods lost appeal, peasants left the countryside for the city, and food security diminished. The same scenario has played itself out in other countries as well.

Many countries have borrowed heavily in different periods and have found themselves confronting huge debts. Often labelling such countries inefficient and undisciplined, international agencies have sometimes advocated the use of "shock therapy" in the form of "structural adjustments." Structural adjustments most commonly include reductions in tariffs, opening up to more foreign investment, privatisation of public utilities, and reducing social safety-net spending (Anderson, 2000). This all comes with a promise of more jobs. But where that promise fails to materialise, the net effect of greater globalisation is more marginalisation of the poor.

Disheartening historical events not withstanding, economists tend to be people of great disciplinary faith. They want to believe that markets can be used to combat poverty. Their faith is based on recognition that markets have incredible power to bring about change. Under the right circumstances, the power of markets can be used to improve the living conditions of average people by bringing about socially rational adjustments in economic activity. But this tends not to happen automatically under conditions of extreme inequality (Sachs, 2005b). Promising institutional remedies include the use of micro-credit to allow the poorest of the poor to have access to small loans for the purpose of starting street businesses (Yunus, 1999), providing clear land title to people in shanty towns so that they are more secure when investing in their homes and can also use those homes as collateral (De Soto, 2000), creation of mutual funds oriented toward very small investors (Ghartey, 2005), and the use of insurance guarantees to protect marginal farmers against some risk while they innovate (Hoogeveen, 2001). In each case, institutional change is at the heart of efforts to combat poverty by empowering poor people to be market actors, and thereby bring market adjustment processes into alignment with their needs. These institutional innovations embody a "trickle-up" rather than a "trickle-down" vision of an economy capable of reducing poverty through socially rational market adjustment.

6. Conclusion

If the argument of this paper is correct, market adjustments will not be socially rational unless the vast majority of people have meaningful market voice. Extreme inequality mitigates against this, and consequently tends to distort market adjustment processes. The "invisible hand of the market" can be expected to facilitate relatively efficient pursuit of socially rational goals where levels of inequality are low to moderate. But where levels of inequality are high, market adjustment will normally move away from efficient pursuit of socially rational ends toward the pursuit of ephemeral interests of the rich.

Acknowledgements

Although solely responsible for any errors in this paper, the author has benefited from exchange of ideas with Jürgen Backhaus, Romanus Dimoso, Marilyn Fernandez, Michael Kevane, Reza Maghroori, Gerrit Meijer, Edward O'Boyle, Catlin Powers, and Tony Waters.

Valuable technical assistance was provided by Sandee Chiaramonte, Gloria Hofer, and Laurie Poe.

References

Anderson, S. (ed.), 2000. Views from the South; The Effects of Globalization and the WTO on Third World Countries. Oakland, California: Food First Books.

Backhaus, J.G. (ed.), 2005. Modern Applications of Austrian Thought. London: Routledge.

Barker, D. and J. Mander (eds.), 2001. Does Globalization Help the Poor? San Francisco: International Forum on Globalization.

Chachage, C., 1998. Land, Forests, and People in Finnish Aid in Tanzania. FAD Working Paper, Helsinki: Institute of Developmental Studies.

Chen, S. and M. Ravallion, 2004. How Have the World's Poorest Fared Since the Early 1980's? World Bank Policy Research Working Paper 3341.

De Soto, H., 2000. The Mystery of Capital; Why Capitalism Triumphs in the West and Fails Everywhere Else. New York: Basic Books.

Dyer, C., 2000. Everyday Life in Medieval England. London: Hambledom and London.

Eakin, M., 1998. Brazil: The Once and Future Country. New York: St. Martin's Press.

Freely, J., 1998. Istanbul, the Imperial City. New York: Penguin Books.

Ghartey, E., 2005. Monetary Policy on Ghana's Term Structure of Interest Rates; Effects and Implications. Presentation at the Eighth International ISINI Congress, Wageningen, The Netherlands, August 24-27, 2005.

Hoogeveen, H., 2001. A New Approach to Insurance in Rural Africa. The Geneva Papers on Risk and Insurance 26: 505-513.

McKenna, R., 2002. Total Access. Cambridge, Massachusetts: Harvard Business School Press.

Meijer, G., 1987. The History of Neo-Liberalism: A General View and Developments in Several Countries. Rivista Internazionale de Scienze Economiche e Commerciale, Volume 34, Number 7, 577-91.

Mises, L., 1966. Human Action; A Treatise on Economics. Third Edition, Chicago: Regnery. http://www.nationmaster.com/graph-T/eco_dis_of_fam_inc_gin_ind&int=-1 (Spring, 2005).

Oatley, T., 2005. The Global Economy. New York: Longman.

Pareto, V., 1984. The Transformation of Democracy. New Brunswick, NJ: Transaction [originally published 1921].

Parsons, T., 1966. Societies; Evolutionary and Comparative Perspectives. Englewood Cliffs: Prentice-Hall.

Powers, C., 2003. Accounting for the Persistence of Poverty in the Free Trade Era. In: J.G. Backhaus, W. Heijmann, A. Nentjes and J. van Ophem (eds.), Economic Policy in an Orderly Framework. Liber Amicorum for Gerrit Meijer. Berlin: LITverlag., pp. 361-372.

Polillo, S. and M. Guillen, 2005. Globalization and the State: The Worldwide Spread of Central Bank Independence. American Journal of Sociology 110: 1764-1802.

Robbins, R., 2005. Global Problems and the Culture of Capitalism. Third Edition. Boston: Allyn and Bacon.

Rodney, W., 1982. How Europe Underdeveloped Africa. Washington, D.C.: Howard University Press.

Sachs, J., 2005a. The End of Poverty. New York: Penguin.

Sachs, J., 2005b. Can Extreme Poverty be Eliminated, Scientific American 293: 56-65.

Sen, A., 1997. On Economic Inequality (expanded edition). Oxford: Clarendon Press.

Shiva, V., 2000. Stolen Harvest: The Hijacking of the Global Food Supply. Cambridge, Massachusetts: South End Press.

Smith, A., 1976. An Inquiry into the Nature and Causes of the Wealth of Nations. Oxford: Clarendon [1776].

Stiglitz, J., 2002. Globalization and its Discontents. New York: W.W. Norton.

Wallerstein, I., 2004. World System Analysis. Durham, N.C.: Duke University Press.

Waters, T., 2001. Bureaucratizing the Good Samaritan. Boulder CO: Westview.

Yunus, M., 1999. Banker to the Poor; Micro-Lending and the Battle Against World Poverty. New York: Public Affairs.

Families and changing life cycles

Kees de Hoog and Johan van Ophem
Department of Sociology of Consumers and Households, Wageningen University, P.O. box 8130,
6700 EW Wageningen, The Netherlands. Kees.deHoog@wur.nl.

Abstract

Until recently, the dominant family type, the nuclear family (husband, wife and their own children) followed a traditional life cycle. Nowadays, most modern-industrialised countries have entered an era of new biographic models. People have a wide choice in selecting their own life course menu. A typology consisting of four family types - the traditional, the modern, the egalitarian and the individualised - is used to explore the consequences of changing life cycles. In the second section the connection between traditional life cycle, wealth and well-being is analysed. In the period of honeymooners and the period of post parenthood households have a relative a high wealth and well-being. During both stages no children are living in the household. In the 1950s and 1960s a paradox emerged. The level of education of boys and girls increased. A first consequence was an increase in female labour force participation. But men and women become also less dependent on traditional family values and family life for fulfilling a variety of needs. This led to the emergence of other family types, next to the traditional one. There are two major problems with the non-traditional family types and lifestyles: fertility and divorce. Policy makers have to pay more attention to the pluralism of family lifestyles and family types, and especially to the position of children.

JEL classification: D10, I31, N30

Keywords: families, lifestyles, life cycle, well-being, wealth

1. Introduction

The traditional nuclear family was during the first half of the 20th century the safe harbor in a society in turmoil. Marriage was the gate to adulthood and maturity. Most couples had the same religion and the same political ideas. The husband was the only breadwinner, his wife was housewife and mother. He was the representative in the public domain, she was the manager of the domestic domain. Marriage was in almost every case an engagement for life.

The nuclear family (husband, wife and their own children) followed a traditional life cycle: bachelorhood (young adult living in the parental home or young single adult living apart from parents); honeymooners (young married couple without children); parenthood (married couple with at least one child living at home); post parenthood (an older married couple with no children living at home and dissolution (one surviving spouse) (Schiffman and Kanuk, 2004).

The demographic situation in that period was the outcome of the first demographic transition. This transition can be defined as a process leading from a combination of high levels of fertility and mortality in a population to lower mortality and fertility. This process of an old balance to a new balance took place in Western Europe and North America during the industrialisation in the 19th century. Mortality had declined, because of improved availability of food, better medicines and in general a better public health. The fertility change was more complex. It had to do with a growing wealth and a higher education level of the population.

The second demographic transition - from the late 1960s till now - (Van der Kaa, 1980) is also based on a complex of changes in demographic and social behaviour. Important changes are a decline of fertility in the late 1960s (below replacement), growing divorce and separation and a postponement of births in the 1970s; postponement of marriage until pregnancy in the early 1980s; and a delay of marriage even after the birth of children in the late 1980s and early 1990s. Other examples of demographic changes are the growing numbers of young people cohabiting or living alone and the ageing of society. The higher labour force participation of married women and a higher level of education of both men and women are major social changes.

The second demographic transition is coined by the term from convergence to diversity. Modern-industrialised countries have entered an era of new biographic models. People have a wide choice in selecting their own life course menu (Kuijsten, 2002). Through the second demographic transition especially the changing home leaving patterns, cohabitation, divorce and remarriage and the ageing of society the traditional family life cycle lost its ability to represent the stages which current nuclear families move through.

We will compare the consequences of the traditional life cycle and the new ones. These comparison is on the one hand based on a typology of today's family types (the traditional family type, the modern family type, the egalitarian family type and the individualised family type) (De Hoog and Vinkers, 1998; De Hoog and Hooghiemstra 2002) and on the other hand based on non-traditional living arrangements. Our main proposition is that differences between households, nuclear families and individuals being in a certain stage in their life cycle have implications for their wealth and well-being.

2. Life cycle, wealth and well-being

To analyse different stages during the life course sociologists, economists and demographers have been long attracted to the life cycle. The traditional family life cycle is based on three principles (Van Leeuwen, 1976). It supposes a connection between wealth, age composition and the different stages of the life cycle (Seebohm Rowntree, 1906). The second principle is based on a development process of children. Children have to learn by socialisation to be an adult (Erikson, 1972). The third principle supposes a connection between demographic events like the age of marriage, the birth of the first child, birth of the last child, leaving home of the children, the empty nest and the death of the partner and the different stages (Glick, 1947, 1955). A simple model of the traditional family life cycle gives, as we have seen, the following five stages: bachelorhood; honeymooners; parenthood; post parenthood and dissolution.

During two stages of this life cycle nuclear families have a relative high wealth and well-being. These stages are the period of the honeymooners and the period of post parenthood. During both stages no children are living in the household. During the stage of the honeymooners the standardised yearly income is rather high because both partners have an income, there are no children in the household and the costs of housing are rather low. The starting couple rents an apartment or a small house and they don't pay mortgage. They have an own lifestyle (Van Ophem & De Hoog, 1995). They spend a lot of money on leisure, cultural activities, food and clothes. It is reasonable to assume that all honeymooners show this pattern at their own income level.

The stage of post parenthood is the second period that couples have a relatively high wealth. The children have left the parental home and, if the children have finished their study and have their own income and the mortgage is low or has been paid off. Their lifestyle shows elements of the lifestyle of the honeymooners (vacation and cultural activities).

Three stages of the traditional life cycle show a more difficult financial situation. These stages are the period of bachelorhood, of parenthood and of dissolution.

During the bachelorhood the yearly income is rather low. The home leavers are following a study or starting a career. The bachelors who are staying at home ('hotel mama'), have also a low yearly income, but in most cases the costs of living are partly paid by their parents.
The period of parenthood is a stage with high costs. The birth of children is a turning point in life. The time costs of young children are considerable. Especially the mother will reduce her working hours or even leave her job. There are other financial changes. Starting families move to a better house or buy a home.

The Netherlands Institute of Budget Research (NIBUD, 2005.) computes the money costs of children to vary from € 205 per month for a child in a household living from a minimum income to about € 680 per month for a child in the highest income category. Taking a 18 years period, this results, if no present values are computed, € 44,200 for a child in the lowest income household to € 146,880 for a household in the highest income bracket.

The period of dissolution by the death of the partner, shows a decline in income. In most cases the man dies earlier than his wife. The pension of the widow is around 70 per cent of the pension of a couple. That is, if they have a 'good' pension, 50 per cent of the income before retirement. Sometimes there are high medical costs to be paid. Moreover a lot of the elderly above 80 years old do not have a good retirement pension. Other problems are: grieve, loneliness, decreasing mobility and growing dependency.

It is known that households contradict the pattern predicted in traditional economic life cycle theory, consisting of borrowing money in the stage of honeymooners, build up savings in money or real terms in the stages of parenthood, and draw from the accumulated savings in the later period of post parenthood and dissolution (Modigliani and Brumberg, 1954). Consumption tracks income at least within the working life, after cyclical and growth effects are taking out (Browning and Crossley, 2001), and even after retirement (Alessie *et al.*, 1997). This empirical regularity can be explained by some combination of presence of children and precautionary savings (prudence). Prudence leads households to treat future uncertain income cautiously and not to spend as much currently as they would if future income were certain (Browning and Crossley, 2001). Prudence fits reasonably well into the lifestyle of people following the traditional life cycle.

Various investigations show that the mean self-reported happiness of both husband and wife is higher than the one of single parents or divorced parents (Oswald, 1997; Argyle, 1999). It remains the question whether married people are happier than singles in the same age-income cohorts (Frey and Stutzer, 2005). Some studies show a decline of happiness after marriage attributed to getting used to pleasant stimuli as Frey and Stutzer (2005) do, while Groot and Maassen van den Brink (2000, 2002) report a decline of the wife's happiness while the score of the husband remains stable.

In a recent survey in the Netherlands it has been established that divorced people have lower mean self-reported happiness than singles or couples. For singles, as well as for divorced or married people children make them happier (Cornelisse-Vermaat, 2005).

3. Changing lifestyles

In the 1950s and 1960s the level of education was increasing. Through education girls acquired better skills for the labour market. In the labour market, the importance of education was growing. The differences between boys and girls with respect to attendance of secondary education disappeared. The difference in attending tertiary education came to an end in the 1980s. This rise in educational level, especially for girls, can be seen as a prerequisite for work outside the home. The increasing earning power and earning capacity of women can be seen as one of the important underlying forces causing changes in family life (Van Ophem and De Hoog, 1997).

Moreover functions such as education and socialisation of children, the economic and social security of the family have been partly taken over by state-supported systems and institutions (Manting, 1994). A consequence of these developments is that men and women become less dependent on traditional family values (Espenshade, 1985).

Individual freedom and personal self-expression became for adolescents the guiding principles in stead of the values of the traditional nuclear family. The changing values, attitudes and behaviour of the new generation, the baby boomers (born between 1945 and 1955), implies major demographic changes, the second demographic transition, consisting of a substantial decline in marriage and fertility as well as to a rise in divorce rates in most Western European countries. In the European Union one out of four couples of marriage cohorts from 1970s and 1980s had a divorce.

In their analyses of views of family types (De Hoog and Hooghiemstra, 2002; De Hoog and Vinkers, 1998) four distinct family types are discerned: the traditional, the modern, the egalitarian and the individualised family type.

In the traditional nuclear family the husband is breadwinner and the wife housewife. Motherhood is a dominant perspective in her life. The socialisation of children is governed by the principles of order, regularity and diligence. Traditional families are to be found among lower economic strata, non-western immigrants (Turkey, Morocco), orthodox Christians and among households in which both spouses are lower educated. It is estimated that about 25 per cent of the families are of a traditional nature. The traditional family of today differs from the one in the past. They are not longer a patriarchy. Husband and wife are seen as equal, although the wife focuses her efforts on household and children. The climate in the family is less authoritarian. But negotiation and bargaining between parents and children is not considered to be just.

Because of the wish of egalitarianism, the borderline with modern family type is fluid (Te Kloeze *et al.,* 1996). Togetherness is a main feature of the modern family type. The division of labour is more equal, but not completely. The husband is still the main breadwinner, works full-time, whereas the wife has a small part-time job next to her household work. Husbands perform domestic tasks, especially with the rearing of the children. Modern families are characterised by mutual affection, care and love. It is estimated that about 40 per cent of the families in the Netherlands are modern ones, mainly to be found in the middle economic strata.

The egalitarian family type is aimed at equality between the spouses. Its main feature is negotiation and bargaining. When children are present, considerable use is made of child care facilities, the wife works gainfully for a considerable amount of time. The family is inclined to communicate a lot and mutual aid is imminent. The socialisation of children is aimed at one with another and self actualisation. Equality between the spouses with respect to the division of labour is to be achieved in all stages of life and the family. About 25 per cent of the families in the Netherlands are egalitarian, mainly to be found in the middle/ upper-middle economic strata.

The fourth type is the individualised family, about ten per cent of all families. Both spouses are higher educated and career oriented. They are the relatively well-to-do. Meal preparation and home cleaning activities are outsourced. They spend a lot of money on different forms of child care. The nanny or au pair is frequently to be found. Motherhood as the most important social identity is rejected. They are convinced by their values, opinions and activities to be forerunners. This family is aimed at individual freedom and self actualisation. This type may not be the largest in size, but the credo of their cultural-liberal virtues is well received by policy makers and opinion leaders. In the latter the emancipation of women in this family type is seen as very successful.

A general feature of the traditional life cycle is the predictability of the individual life cycle. Adolescents are leaving the parental home to marry, to work or to study. Most of them will find a partner during their twenties. After a while they marry and children are born. About twenty years later the children are leaving home. The following stage is the period of the empty nest and during the last stage one of the partners will die.

In the 20th century two important changes occurred. The first change was that during the seventies the pattern to leave the parental home by marriage became less important and to study became much more important. The second change has to do with the decline of the number of children and a longer life expectancy. In the thirties of the 20th century widowing took in general place before all children had left the parental home. The stage of being one parent family by the death of the partner is nowadays less important (Niphuis-Nell, 1974). At the beginning of the 21st century two family forms - the traditional and modern family - will follow more or less the traditional life cycle.

Couples of the traditional family type have traditional ideas about the division of work and tasks and about marriage, education of their children and about the position of men and women, but also about financial management. Debt is to be avoided. Austerity is a virtue to be practiced. Children have to obey their parents. There are no or less negotiations between parents and children.

In the modern family type the ideas about marriage, socialisation and education of the children are traditional. But the family climate, especially the relationship between men and women is more democratic. Husbands take part in domestic work. Children should obey their parents, but they are listening to their wishes. Attitudes to debts are more rational, in the sense that in circumstances where debts can be repaid easily, indebtedness is permitted.

Two other family types follow a non-traditional life cycle: the egalitarian family type and the individualised family type. The egalitarian family type tries to achieve egalitarianism between the spouses, but the husband is still the main breadwinner. Wives have a considerable part-time or full-time job. In the individualistic family type husbands and wives have an equal task division. Both are working full time. Both are important decision makers.

4. Non-traditional life cycles

Egalitarian and individualistic family types are based on major changes during the second demographic transition. But we are still talking about nuclear families. The non-traditional life cycles know more non family stages than the traditional life cycle. Alders and Manting (1999) make use of three scenarios - individualisation, family and base line scenario - to predict the household composition. In all scenarios the number of persons living alone will grow and the total number of households increases, whereas the average household size declines.

The non family households consist of the following stages: unmarried bachelors, unmarried couples, divorced persons without children, single persons and widowed persons, in most cases the elderly. Cohabitation of young couples is a new stage in the life cycle. A majority of the starters in North West Europe will follow this pattern.

High separation rates too contribute to the dissolution of households before children are born. The growing numbers of these singles can also be seen as another new stage in the life cycle.

The duration of the stage of bachelorhood is growing fast. To delay first marriage is a new pattern, in general followed by men and women with a high educational level.
The longer life expectancy has an influence on the number of singles, especially for women of 75 years and over.

The family life cycle shows also major changes. New stages of the non-traditional family life cycle are: the growing number of childless couples, couples who are marry late and couples who have their first child in their late 30s. These patterns are mostly followed by couples with a high education.

Non-traditional life cycles and the egalitarian and individualised family types are connected to each other. It should be kept in mind that the educational level is high in both family types. Young adults will leave home to go to college or university. After graduation, they will start their career in their mid 20s. Career-oriented men and women are living together as a couple without marriage at the beginning of their 30s. This relationship must be perfect before they are to marry and to have children ['only the best is good enough']. This is the main reason for the high separation rates of young cohabitants. One of the results of this pattern is serial monogamy. It is the main reason, together with the career orientation, for the late start of the family stage in the egalitarian and individualistic family type. The couples have no children, but so-called kids. The kids give status to their parents.

During the stages of the new bachelors and the new honeymooners individuals will show an own lifestyle. This lifestyle is to be described as hedonistic. Material goods and services are important for singles and couples. Their cultural capital is high, social capital is important (Bourdieu, 1984). To enjoy life is generally accepted. New bachelors and cohabiting and married couples without children have the possibility to access many activities during their leisure time. Contrary, in the egalitarian and individualised family types leisure time is a scarce good. This has to do with the activities on the labour market, but also with child-oriented activities of these non-traditional families, for example quality time (Schulze and Tyrell, 2002).

Divorce, non-traditional life cycles and the egalitarian and individualised family types are also connected. The consequences of divorce for society, partners, other family members, and especially children are noteworthy (Whitehead, 1997). Women's increasing education, earning power and resulting increase bargaining power, is usually seen as important factors in explaining the rise in divorce rates (Beller and Kiss, 1999). Other factors are the diminishing barriers to an autonomous life due to a decline in fertility and the more wide-ranging acceptance of divorce as a solution to marital problems (Klein and Knopp, 2002). The overall legal and socio-economic environment also influences divorce decisions. Divorce risks have also to do with the expansion of the welfare state. Hoem (1997) comes to the conclusion that in Sweden the divorce risk has been concentrated in women with lower educational attainment. The reason is that in this welfare state personal independence is secured by state institutions. Klein and Knopp (2002) conclude that individual factors that account for a specific likelihood to divorce can change their theoretical impact depending on the institutional context.

The overall legal and socio-economic environment influences also divorce decisions. The costs of legal services related to marital dissolutions and trends in property settlements, payments to spouses (alimony) and child support payments as well as the availability of public assistance are examples of legal factors.

Ex-spouses are financially seen worse off after separation. This holds both for male as female. Financial assets, household durables are generally shared according to a one-time property settlement just as for pension and retirement income as well. Expenses for legal assistance have to be paid. The spouses have to move to lower quality housing. Even where nominal income (earnings) of the ex-spouse remains the same, (s)he normally has to pay extra monthly expenditures apart from incidental outlays: alimony for the ex-spouse, child support, payments for additional mortgage.

Moreover, the fixed costs of the household have to be paid out of the income of one spouse. It is a consequence of the loss of economies of scale incurred by a divorce. A divorce means that one house and set of fixed costs is substituted for two houses and accompanying fixed costs. In general, it leads to lower standards of living, especially in the domain of discretionary income expenditures. So, both partners are confronted with a sizable decline in economic capital, not only in the short run but in the long run as well. No wonder that separation/divorce is connected to poverty and poverty recidivism. According to Dutch data, low income is to be most likely in single-parent families with children under 18 years. They have the least favourable position in the chance of escaping poverty. Separation, divorce and widowhood give the highest risk of poverty recidivism (Vrooman and Hoff, 2004).

The most difficult questions about distribution when a marriage breaks up generally involve the children. Typically, the mother retains the physical custody of children, although joint custody is becoming much more common. Most children dislike a divorce. They become unhappy by this event. It is found that growing up in a single-parent family, the vast majority of which are headed by women, is disadvantageous for the children although receiving child support tends to reduce the extent of this disadvantage, for instance in school achievements. Pupils of single-parent families are less likely to graduate secondary education and less likely to attend higher education (Beller and Kiss, 1999).

5. Concluding remarks

In the egalitarian and individualised family types negotiation and, bargaining and looking for happiness in the self actualisation process are phenomena that demand time and effort. If there is not a win-win situation, the spouse is substituted for another happiness seeking individual. Shortly, it means that the logic of market choice has not only invaded the minds of people as producer or buyer of goods and services, but also the mind of people as family man or woman.

As wealth grows, there is more room for idiosyncratic turmoil that might spoil the internal relations of the family. In this respect we point to the growing importance of the emotional or emotions, which, today, are not only present in the experience economy of the producer/consumer relationship, but in the relationship between the spouses, as well. The parent-child relationship is excluded from this process. For various reasons, this relationship is governed by the principle of unconditional love. Anyhow, the divorce risk is higher for the egalitarian and individualised family type than for the other two types. This implies more non-traditional life cycles.

Between the traditional and modern family type on the one hand and the egalitarian and individualistic types on the other hand, profound differences in wealth and lifestyle do exist. Egalitarian and individualistic families have a better position on the consumer market than the traditional and modern families, because both partners have a well-paid job. Differences in leisure time and socio-economic position and status should be mentioned too.

The non-traditional life cycles know more periods of being single and these periods are longer than those stages during the traditional life cycle. This is important, because it shapes two different lifestyles for private forms of living (Koppetsch and Maier, 1998). Schulze and Tyrell (2002) draw the conclusion that: "*the dissociation between partnership and family is combined with differences in fertility of social classes.*" Strohmeier (1993) observes a shrinking 'family sector' and a growing 'non family sector'.

There are two major problems with the non-traditional family types and lifestyles: fertility and divorce. In comparison with the traditional types, the fertility of the egalitarian and individualised family types is low. There are strong indications that men and women with a higher education will not regard fatherhood and motherhood as the only desirable option.

It is a public task to implement fertility rising policies, like an improvement of child care facilities, an extension of care sabbatical and a rise of child benefits, especially for second and higher births.

In the Netherlands, estimations indicate that because of separation and divorce one million children less have been born. Separation and divorce is not to be forbidden, but real counselling could be a method to reduce the number of divorces. It is highly recommended in this respect that the Swedish model is introduced in more European countries.

In an institutional sense, policy makers have to pay more attention to the pluralism of family lifestyles and family types. An instrument to encourage this, is a Ministry of Family Affairs. An important task of this ministry is to analyse all policy measures with respect to their impact on family life, ranging from taxes to transport policies. Finally, in family policy the interest of the adult is less important than the one of children.

References

Alders, M.P.C. and D. Manting, 1999. Household scenarios for the European Union, 1995-2025.

Alessie, R.J.M., A. Kapteyn and F. Klijn, 1997. Mandatory pensions and personal savings in the Netherlands. De Economist 145: 291-324.

Argyle, M., 1999. Causes and correlates of happiness. In: D. Kahnemean, E. Diener and N. Schwarz (eds.). Well-being: the foundations of hedonic psychology. New York; Russell Sage Foundation

Beller, A.H. and D.E. Kiss, 1999. Divorce. In: J. Peterson and M. Lewis (eds.) The Elgar companion to feminist economics. Cheltenham: Edgar Elgar.

Bourdieu, P., 1984. Distinction. A social critique of the judgement of taste. London: Routledge & Kegan Paul.

Browning, M. and T.F. Crossley, 2001. The life-cycle model of consumption and saving. Journal of Economic Perspectives 15: 3-32.

Cornelisse-Vermaat, J.R., 2005. Household production, health and happiness. A comparison of the native Dutch and non-western immigrants in the Netherlands. Wageningen: Wageningen University.

De Hoog, K. and J. Vinkers, 1998. Van individualisering naar pluriformiteit. Analyses van gezinsbeelden in de programma's voor de Tweede Kamerverkiezingen. Den Haag: Nederlandse Gezinsraad.

De Hoog, K. and E. Hooghiemstra, 2002. Links en rechts aandacht voor het gezin. Gezinsbeelden in de partijprogramma's voor verkiezingen van de Tweede Kamer. Den Haag: Nederlandse Gezinsraad.

Erikson, E.H., 1972. Het kind en de samenleving [Child and Society]. Utrecht: Het Spectrum.

Espenshade, T.J., 1985. Marriage trends in America: estimates, implications and underlying causes. Population and Development Review 11: 193-245.

Frey, B.S. and A. Stutzer, 2005. Happiness research: state and prospects. Review of Social Economy LXIII: 177-207.

Glick, P., 1947. The family life cycle. American Sociological Review 14: 164-174.

Glick, P., 1955. The life cycle of the family. Marriage and Family Living 17: 3-9.

Groot, W. and H. Maassen van den Brink, 2000. Lusten en lasten; over economie en emotie [Joy and burden: on economics and emotion] Amsterdam: Prometheus

Groot, W. and H. Maassen van den Brink, 2002. Age and education differences in marriages and their effects on life satisfaction. Journal of Happiness Studies 3: 153-165.

Hoem, J.E., 1997. Educational gradients in divorce risks in Sweden in recent decades. Population Studies 51: 19-27

Klein, Th and J. Knopp, 2002. Divorce in Europe, a cohort perspective. In: F.-X. Kaufmann, A. Kuijsten, H.-J. Schulze and K.P. Strohmeier (eds.), Family life and family policies in Europe, Vol. 2. Oxford University Press: Oxford, pp. 149-174.

Koppetsch, C. and M.S. Maier, 1992. Individualisierung ohne Gleichheit? In: J. Friedrichs (ed.), Die Individualisierungsthese. Leske & Budrich: Opladen, pp. 143-164.

Kuijsten, A., 2002. Variation and change in the forms of private life in the 1980's. In: F.-X. Kaufmann, A. Kuijsten, H.-J. Schulze and K.P. Strohmeier (eds.), Family life and family policies in Europe, Vol. 2. Oxford University Press: Oxford, pp. 18-63.

Manting, D., 1994. Dynamics in marriage and cohabitation. An inter-temporal life course analysis of first union formation and dissolution. Amsterdam: Theses publishers.

Modigliani, F. and R. Brumberg, 1954. Utility analysis and the consumption function: an interpretation of cross-section data. In: K. Kurihara (ed). Post-Keynesian economics. Rutgers U.P.: New Brunswick, pp. 388-496.

NIBUD, 2005. Website

Niphuis-Nell, M., 1974. De gezinsfase. Amsterdam: Siswo,

Oswald, A.J., 1997. Happiness and economic performance. The Economic Journal 107: 1815-1831.

Schiffman, L.G and L.L. Kanuk, 2004. Consumer behavior, Chapter 10, References groups and family influences. Pearson Prentice Hall: Upper Saddle River, New Jersey, pp. 357-366.

Schulze, H-J. and H. Tyrell, 2002. What happened to the European family in the 1980's. In: F.-X. Kaufmann, A. Kuijsten, H.-J. Schulze and K.P. Strohmeier (eds.), Family life and family policies in Europe, Vol. 2. Oxford University Press: Oxford, pp. 69-119.

Seebohm Rowntree, B., 1906. Poverty; a study of town life. London.

Strohmeier, K.P., 1993. Pluralisierung und Polarisierung der Lebensformen in Deutschland. Beilage zur Wochenzeitung des Parlement B 17, pp. 274-282.

Te Kloeze, J.W., K. de Hoog, M. van Bergen and M. Duivenvoorden, 1996. Tussen vrijheid en gebondenheid: het postmoderne gezin ontdekt [Between freedom and commitment: the postmodern family discovered]. Leuven/Apeldoorn: Garant.

Van der Kaa D.J., 1980. Recent trends in fertility in Western Europe. In: R.W. Hoirns (ed.), Demographic patterns in developed societies. London: Taylor and Francis Ltd., pp. 55-81.

Van Leeuwen, L.Th., 1976. Het gezin als sociologische studie-object [The family as an object of sociolocical study]. Wageningen, Landbouwhogeschool.

Van Ophem, J.A.C. and C. De Hoog, 1995. Monetarisering in de huishouding: een analyse van de huishoudvoering van relatief welgestelden [Household monetarization. An analysis of household behaviour of relatively well-to-do], Huishoudstudies 5: 8-20.

Van Ophem, J. and K. De Hoog, 1997. Nuclear families and the changing income procurement role of married women. Associations, Journal of Legal and Social Theory 1: 279-295.

Vrooman, C. and S. Hoff (eds.), 2004. The poor side of the Netherlands. Results from the Dutch 'Poverty Monitor', 1997-2003, The Hague: Social and Cultural Planning Office.

Whitehead, B.D., 1997. The divorce culture. New York: Alfred A. Knopf.

Perceived inflation and actual price changes in The Netherlands

Gerrit Antonides, Wim Heijman and Marleen Schouten
Department of Social Sciences, Wageningen University, P.O. Box 8130, 6700 EW Wageningen, The Netherlands. Gerrit.Antonides@wur.nl.

Abstract

Price perceptions rather than the objective price level may affect consumer demand. We analyse which types of expenditures influence consumer perception of inflation. We use both consumer price indices (CPI) and series of perceived inflation of Statistics Netherlands in the 1996-2005 time period. Neither the introduction of the Euro nor the aggregate CPI significantly influenced perceived inflation. However, prices of transportation, appliances and food had a positive effect, whereas hotels and clothing had a negative effect on perceived inflation.

JEL classification: D12, D40

Keywords: perceived inflation, price change

1. Introduction

Consumer price indices are used frequently in economic research and economic policy. They may be used *inter alia* to forecast consumer behaviour, to compensate consumers for price increases, and to keep track of inflation. Hence, statistical bureaus regularly measure and report prices of consumer goods.

According to consumer behaviour theory (Blackwell *et al.*, 2001; Solomon, 2002), consumer perceptions mediate the effects of market stimuli on consumer decision making. In fact, price perceptions rather than the objective price level may affect consumer demand. Indeed, the Dutch Central Bank (DNB, 2004) states that household consumption decreased since the introduction of the Euro because perceived inflation exceeded actual inflation. Williams and Defris (1981) find that subjective measures of inflation positively influence consumer saving and negatively influence expenditures on other goods than motor vehicles and durables.

Some speculations concerning the deviation of perceived from actual inflation have been made, *i.e.*, prices of frequently purchased goods and steep price changes of particular goods would influence perceived inflation relatively much (Fluch and Stix, 2005; D'Elia, 2005).

Also, price perceptions appear to influence the perceived fairness of prices (Bolton *et al.*, 2004), possibly further contributing to changes in demand. When prices become too high, they may be considered as unfair, possibly resulting in lower demand.

To verify the earlier mentioned speculations, we will empirically analyse the relationships between perceived and actual inflation in the Netherlands. Next, we will give a brief overview of the literature on perceived inflation.

2. Literature

One of the first questions asked in consumer research concerning perceived prices was whether consumers were able to report on price changes at all (Gabor and Granger, 1961). For several food items, perceived price changes were found to be higher than actual price changes, due to exaggeration of price increases and a shortening, or telescoping, of the time interval over which the price changes had occurred (Bates and Gabor, 1986). Due to the availability heuristic (Tversky and Kahneman, 1974), the ease with which recent prices can be remembered is likely to inflate price changes over short intervals (*i.e.*, past month), leading to high perceived inflation in the short run.

Kemp (1987) also found slightly over-estimated inflation perceptions for the previous year but under-estimated perceived inflation for the previous 15 years. He also mentions the possibility that experience with purchases, *i.e.*, for frequently purchased items such as stamps, butter and telephone bills, tends to strengthen these effects, due to availability bias. In another study, Kemp (1991) found almost correct perceived inflation for the previous year (in contrast with his previous study) but again under-estimated perceived inflation for the previous 15 years. It appears that people remember recent prices quite well, and insufficiently adjust prices in previous periods because of their recent memories.

The results concerning last-year perceived inflation support the idea that questioning consumers about past prices should not refer to prices longer than a year ago. The results also suggest that perceived price changes concerning frequently purchased items may suffer more from availability bias (*i.e.*, lead to higher perceived inflation) than infrequently purchased items.

Given the under-estimation of price changes in the long run, consumers may consider current prices as relatively unfair (Bolton *et al.*, 2003). This may be true especially for infrequent purchases, the price of which may come as an unpleasant surprise at the time of purchase. Although non-buyers may still perceive little inflation for infrequent purchases, buyers may exaggerate perceived inflation. The fairness argument leads to different predictions regarding the influence of purchase frequency on perceived inflation than the availability argument.

Psychophysical theory studies quantified relationships between objective and subjective stimuli, *i.e.*, between actual and perceived prices. Weber's law implies that the ratio of a price change and the base price level should be perceived as a constant. Several authors have obtained results contradicting Weber's law. For example, consumers perceive 15% changes better for a 55ç product than for a 15ç product (Uhl, 1970). The probability of consumers changing to a 2ç lower priced gasoline brand is higher if the price is 42ç than if it is 28ç, contradicting Weber's law, too (Kamen and Toman, 1970). As an alternative, consumers may compare price offers to a 'fair' price. With a low 'fair' price, the consumers in the experiment above react adversely to a further price increase at 42ç, whereas they are quite tolerant to an increase at 28ç.

Fechner's law implies that the ratio of a price change and the base price level should equal the perceived price change. The just noticeable perceived price change is considered the unit of the subjective scale. Fechner's law results in a logarithmic perception function of prices. This idea is consistent with the common notion of consumers being 'penny wise and pound foolish'. In one version of this notion, Tversky and Kahneman (1981) observed that subjects generally were not willing to drive 20 minutes to save $5 on a calculator costing $125. However, they were willing to drive 20 minutes to save $5 on a calculator costing $15. Due to the curvature of the perception function, a discount of $5 has a greater impact when the price is low than when the price is high. However, Batchelor's results (1986), using perceived inflation data in different EU countries in different years, were inconsistent with Fechner's law. He found that the number of units of the subjective scale associated with the subjective sensation of 'moderate inflation' differed across countries and across different years.

Stevens' law (1957) implies that the ratio of perceived price changes and the base perceived price ($d\Psi / \Psi$) should equal the ratio of price changes and the base price level (dP / P):

$$d\Psi / \Psi = dP / P \qquad \text{(Eq. 1)}$$

Hence, by integrating Equation 1, the relationship between Ψ and P is found as:

$$\Psi = \alpha P^{\beta} \qquad \text{(Eq. 2)}$$

resulting in a linear relationship after taking logarithms of both sides of Equation 2. Equation 2 is similar to the well-known Cobb-Douglas specification. Due to its more realistic assumptions, we prefer Stevens' power law to Fechner's law in modelling relationships between perceived and objective inflation. However, we are not aware of empirical tests of Stevens' law in the area of price perception. In our empirical study, we attempt at estimating Equation 1 by using perceived and actual price change series. We use Equation 1 for estimating relationships both between perceived inflation and the aggregate price index, and between perceived inflation and price indices of a number of product categories. The multivariate specification is consistent with Hamblin (1973) who also applied a multiplicative power law in connecting perception and multidimensional objective stimuli.

Psychophysical theory mostly has been applied to individual perceptions, although it has also been applied to aggregate inflation perception data (Batchelor, 1986). Since we will use series of aggregate inflation perceptions, we will consider this series as indicating a representative consumer of the population behaving according to Stevens' law.

3. Data

Statistics Netherlands publishes monthly price statistics based on observations of 16,000 consumer items. Prices are weighted by expenditures on the items as measured in consumer budget surveys, resulting in the Laspeyres price index. The item weights are revised every 5 years. Price indexes are available at different levels of aggregation. We use price indices of thirteen consumer goods categories in the 1996-2005 time period, *i.e.*, (1) food and soft drinks, (2) alcoholic drinks and tobacco, (3) clothing and shoes, (4) housing, water and energy, (5) decoration and household appliances, (6) health, (7) transportation, (8) communication, (9) recreation and culture, (10) education, (11) hotels, cafes and restaurants, (12) other goods and services, and (13) consumption related taxes and government services. An overview of price changes in these categories is shown in Figure 1.

We observe that prices of alcohol, housing, education and hotels have increased considerably more than the overall consumer price index (CPI), whereas prices of appliances, food, communication, recreation and clothing have either decreased or increased considerably less than the CPI.

Since we will compare the price indices of the thirteen item categories with overall price perceptions, we use series of perceived inflation from Statistics Netherlands for the 1996-2005 period. Perceived inflation is measured by asking 1000 consumers in repeated monthly cross-section surveys the following question: "Do you believe prices have increased or decreased in the past 12 months?" The answers could be selected from the following categories: "Strongly increased," "Moderately increased," "Weakly increased," "Remained almost equal," "Decreased," and "Don't know." In our analyses, we use the percentage of consumers answering either "Strongly increased" or "Moderately increased" (PI1) and the percentage answering "Strongly increased," "Moderately increased," or "Weakly increased" (PI2). The development of the CPI and the two perceived inflation series is shown in Figure 2.

We observe that the CPI increased quite regularly, whereas the two perceived inflation series increased sharply after the introduction of the Euro (January 2002) until 2004, then returned to a relatively low level in 2005. Note that the scales of CPI and the perceived inflation series are different.

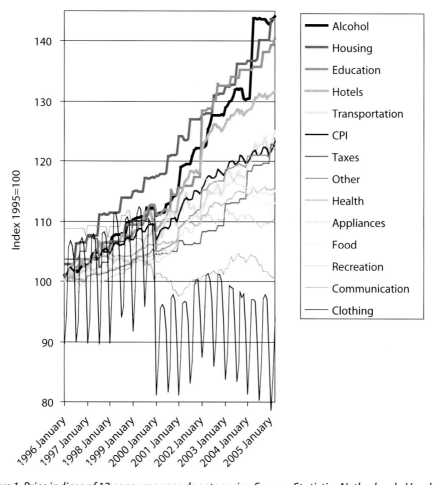

Figure 1. Price indices of 13 consumer goods categories. Source: Statistics Netherlands, Voorburg, The Netherlands.
Note: series legend in descending order of 2005 prices.

Next, we turn to our model estimating the relationships between perceived inflation and the price indices.

4. Model

Perceived inflation is indicated by the percentage of people believing that prices have increased in the past year. Hence, month-to-month changes in perceived inflation are expected to show considerable overlap, *i.e.*, autocorrelation. To remove autocorrelation, we take month-to-month percentage change in the perceived inflation series, denoted as dPI.

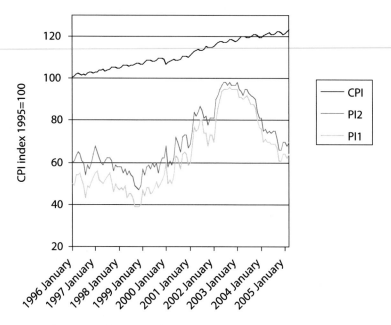

Figure 2. CPI and perceived price indices. Source: Statistics Netherlands, Voorburg, The Netherlands.
Note: PI1 denotes perception of strongly or moderately strongly increased prices; PI2 denotes perception of strongly, moderately strongly or weakly increased prices.

The CPI series concerns price changes with respect to price in the base year. To convert the CPI series to month-to-month changes in prices, we computed month-to-month percentage change in the CPI, denoted by dCPI. Also, by this method, autocorrelation is likely to be removed. Note that monthly percentage changes in perceived inflation and actual price changes are conceptually equivalent with the left-hand respectively right-hand sides of Equation 1, stating Stevens' law.

Perceived inflation and actual inflation are measured on different scales, even though both series are computed as month-to-month percentage changes. We assume a simple linear transformation to convert actual price changes into perception changes. Since we expect the introduction of the Euro to influence price perceptions, we also need to estimate the Euro effect. This leads to regression Equation 3.

$$dPI = \alpha_0 + \alpha_1 \, Euro + \alpha_2 \, dCPI + \varepsilon_1 \qquad \text{(Eq. 3)}$$

where Euro indicates a dummy which equals 0 before January 2002 and 1 thereafter, the α's are coefficients to be estimated, and ε_1 is an independent normal error term. We expect a significant coefficient α_2 since price changes should be reflected in price perception changes.

Next, we specify an extended model, taking into account the possibility that price changes in different goods categories may affect price perceptions in different ways. In fact, we assume linear scale transformations between each series of objective price changes and the series of perceived price changes. This leads to regression Equation 4.

$$dPI = \beta_0 + \beta_1 \text{ Euro} + \Sigma_i \beta_i \text{ dCPI}_i + \varepsilon_2 \qquad\qquad i = 1,...,13 \qquad\qquad\qquad \text{(Eq. 4)}$$

where Σ_i denotes summation over the thirteen terms associated with the different goods categories, the β's are coefficients to be estimated, and ε_2 is an independent normal error term. Based on speculations mentioned in our introduction (Fluch and Stix, 2005; D'Elia, 2005), we expect that categories with above-average price changes (alcohol, housing, education and hotels) are more strongly related to perceived price changes than categories with below-average price changes (appliances, food, communication, recreation and clothing). Also, prices in categories of frequently purchased items (alcohol, transportation, food, communication, recreation, and clothing) may be stronger related to perceived prices than infrequently purchased items (education, taxes, health, and appliances).

The relationship between weights in the Laspeyres price index (expenditure shares from budget surveys) and the weights estimated in the regressions of perceived price changes may be different. By definition the weights in the Laspeyres price index are all positive and add up to 1. Because of the different scales of perceived price changes and the series of actual price changes, the regression weights may not be comparable with the weights in the Laspeyres price index: there is no guarantee that the estimated weights are positive and that they add up to 1. In order to make these weights comparable, we use Social Judgment Theory (Cooksey, 1996). Applying Social Judgment Theory amounts to estimating the normalised marginal contributions of price changes in the item categories to the explained variance in actual overall price changes. This amounts to estimating the difference in R^2 between the full equation and the equation in which one of the item categories had been removed. Let the difference in R^2 be denoted by sr_i^2: the squared semi-partial correlation of price changes in the one category with the overall (objective) price change. The normalised 'objective' weights are then defined as $w_i = sr_i^2 / \Sigma_i sr_i^2$. Similar 'subjective' weights can be estimated from the regression of subjective price changes on the price changes in item categories. The 'subjective' weights then have similar meaning as the 'objective' weights.

5. Results

The estimation results of Equation 3 are shown in Table 1 for both perceived price series. Neither of the estimated coefficients was significant, implying that neither the introduction of the Euro nor the CPI influenced perceived prices. The Durbin-Watson statistic was close

Table 1. Regressions of perceived price changes on changes in CPI.

Variable	Prices strongly or moderately strongly increased		Prices strongly, moderately strongly or weakly increased	
	Coefficient	Absolute T-value	Coefficient	Absolute T-value
Constant	0.917	1.300	0.744	1.246
Euro	−2.397	0.360	−1.888	1.652
CPI	0.427	1.777	−0.053	0.053
Adjusted R^2	0.012		0.007	
Durbin-Watson	2.226		2.325	

to 2, showing that autocorrelation was successfully removed by taking month-to-month percentage changes in the series.

Table 2 shows the estimation results for Equation 4. It appeared that the introduction of the Euro did not significantly influence perceived inflation, given the development of the price series. The adjusted R^2 equalled 0.16 for perceived inflation as indicated by opinions of strongly and moderately strongly perceived price increases, and 0.19 for opinions of strongly, moderately and weakly increased perceived price increases combined. The explained variance was higher than in the regression estimated in Table 1 although it was still rather low. The Durbin-Watson statistics were around 2, indicating negligible autocorrelation. The computed variance inflation factor (VIF) scores were all smaller than 4, indicating that multi-colinearity was not a problem in the regressions (Hair *et al.*, 1998).

Only five of the consumer price series were significant in explaining perceived inflation. Transportation, appliances and food had a positive effect, whereas hotels and clothing had a negative effect on perceived inflation. We did not find evidence of frequently purchased items influencing perceived inflation more than infrequently purchased items. Neither did increasing series influence perceived inflation more than decreasing series.

As described in the method section, we applied Social Judgment Theory to compare objective and subjective weights. Table 3 shows the weights used in the Laspeyres price index, normalised 'objective' weights and normalised 'subjective' weights, respectively.

The weights used in the Laspeyres index appeared to be quite different than the 'objective' weights from Social Judgment Theory, the correlation between the two series equalled −0.434.

Table 2. Regressions of perceived price changes on price changes in consumption categories.

Variable	Prices strongly or moderately strongly increased		Prices strongly, moderately strongly or weakly increased	
	Coefficient	Absolute T-value	Coefficient	Absolute T-value
Constant	0.710	0.935	0.547	0.869
Euro	−1.322	0.976	−0.938	0.836
Alcohol	1.289	1.703	0.923	1.472
Housing	0.050	0.057	0.333	0.454
Education	0.098	0.140	0.172	0.295
Hotels	−3.569	3.149 [a]	−3.296	3.511 [a]
Transportation	1.691	2.094 [b]	1.515	2.264 [b]
Other goods	−2.080	0.843	−1.068	0.523
Taxes	−1.121	1.806	−0.884	1.719
Health	−3.293	1.731	−2.669	1.693
Appliances	7.325	2.801 [a]	5.901	2.724 [a]
Food	2.498	2.992 [a]	2.318	3.350 [a]
Communication	−0.439	0.555	−0.213	0.325
Recreation	−1.194	0.823	−0.685	0.570
Clothing	−0.247	2.378 [b]	−0.265	3.073 [a]
Adjusted R^2	.160		.191	
Durbin-Watson	2.191		2.352	

[a] $p<0.01$; [b] $p<0.05$.

The 'objective' and 'subjective' weights from Social Judgment Theory were slightly more comparable, their correlation equaled 0.272. Yet, large differences existed between the two series of weights.

Housing, water and energy received a relatively large objective weight (0.208) whereas the subjective weight was quite small (0.005). This result indicates that perceived inflation did hardly depend on housing expenditures although it received a relatively large objective weight. To a smaller extent, this was also true for transportation, communication and recreation.

Price changes in hotels, pubs and restaurants, and in decoration and appliances received relatively large subjective weights, whereas the objective weights were relatively small. To a smaller extent, this was also true for health price changes.

Table 3. Weights in Laspeyres index and weights from social judgment theory.

Item category	Weights used in Laspeyres index [a]	Normalised 'objective' weights	Normalised 'subjective' weights
Alcohol	0.040	0.024	0.037
Housing	0.268	0.208	0.005
Education	0.004	0.000	0.002
Hotels	0.055	0.045	0.208
Transportation	0.107	0.151	0.088
Other goods	0.063	0.013	0.007
Taxes	0.048	0.081	0.064
Health	0.005	0.001	0.053
Appliances	0.080	0.007	0.164
Food	0.137	0.141	0.198
Communication	0.019	0.007	0.002
Recreation	0.113	0.091	0.005
Clothing	0.061	0.231	0.169

[a] Source: Statistics Netherlands, Voorburg, The Netherlands

6. Discussion

Substantial deviations between actual and perceived inflation were observed, especially after the introduction of the Euro. Although the Euro overall did not significantly affect the level of perceived inflation, perceived inflation first increased substantially, then returned to normal level in 2005.

Several results and speculations in the literature deal with the effects of real price changes on perceived inflation. We have tested the hypotheses that perceived inflation is influenced relatively heavily by price changes in frequently purchased items and by items showing fast price increases. Neither of these hypotheses turned out to be fully true. Both frequent purchases (food, alcohol) and infrequent purchases (appliances) had a relatively large effect on perceived inflation. Also, some products with above-average price changes (housing, education) contributed relatively little, whereas some products with below-average price changes (food) contributed relatively much to perceived inflation. These results indicate that price perceptions may be influenced by other factors in addition to purchase frequency and price increase.

An additional explanation of our findings is that consumers compare prices with product benefits. If they believe to obtain value for money, perceived inflation may be relatively stable, even after a price increase. Another explanation is that price perceptions are associated with the way the prices are paid. In general, out-of-pocket payments may influence consumer price perceptions more than payments from bank accounts or credit cards (Davies and Lea, 1995).

We estimated both 'objective' and 'subjective' weights by applying Social Judgment Theory to the data. The objective weights represent the normalised marginal explained variance in actual price changes from price changes in the item categories. Likewise, subjective weights represent the normalised marginal explained variance in perceived price changes from price changes in the item categories. By comparing the two types of weights we are able to explain differences between actual and perceived inflation.

Housing, water and energy seemed to count less heavily in perceived inflation than in the CPI, despite substantial price increases, especially after the introduction of the Euro. Expenditures on this kind of items are made relatively infrequently (*i.e.*, monthly or bi-monthly), and usually are paid by standing order. Hence, price changes in this category may get unnoticed to some extent.

Transportation also obtained a relatively high objective weight, whereas its subjective weight is rather small. Since price changes in this item category were moderate (at least before the oil crisis starting in the fall of 2005), its effect on perceived inflation was relatively small. Although out-of-pocket costs may be associated with the use of transportation (*i.e.*, for buying tickets or gasoline), in the Netherlands many people buy season tickets using their bank accounts and standing orders, possibly reducing inflation perceptions. This may provide another explanation for this result.

Price changes in hotels, pubs and restaurants obtained a high subjective weight as compared with their objective weight in Social Judgment Theory. Remarkably, the effect of (above average) price changes in this category on perceived inflation was negative, implying that higher prices contributed to lower perceived inflation! One possible explanation of this result is that price increases in this category were not considered as unfair and possibly were compensated by higher quality services. Another explanation may be that this product category serves the consumer's hedonic needs for which higher prices are relatively easily accepted.

Price changes in decoration and appliances also obtained a relatively high subjective weight, although they count less heavily in the actual price index. Despite the low frequency of purchases in this item category, purchases may be quite memorable, contributing to perceived inflation.

Clothing and food both received relatively high objective and subjective weights, probably contributing less to differences between actual and perceived inflation. Food purchases were expected to contribute considerably to perceived inflation because they are frequently made, and are associated with out-of-pocket costs. The effect of food price changes on perceived inflation was positive, whereas for clothing it was negative. Clothing prices were highly variable though (see Figure 1), and its effects may have been hard to judge by consumers.

Although explanations from the literature to some extent supported our findings, the results were puzzling sometimes and not fully in line with theoretical expectations. This may be partly due to the fact that we used repeated cross-sections, whereas earlier empirical research employed single cross-section studies in which consumers were asked to state past prices for a limited number of items. On the other hand, the time series that we used may have been too short to find reliable results. In future research we plan to use longer series, possibly from different countries. Also, product category price indices summarise the information about individual product prices, thus preventing hypothesis testing for individual products. For example, the 'frequency hypothesis' is hard to test on the category of hotels, pubs and restaurants since hotel expenses may be less frequent than expenses on pubs.

We have provided several *ad hoc* explanations for our results, to be investigated in future research. In line with the theory, our results indicate that memorable expenses may affect perceived inflation to some extent. However, memorable expenses need not necessarily be associated with more frequently made purchases. For example, house decoration and appliance purchases may be memorable but infrequent purchases. Other factors may be the fairness of price increases and the way payments are made. However, the data used does not contain information concerning these factors.

Several policy implications of our results can be made. The consumer price index is based on price changes weighted by budget shares, whereas perceived inflation appears to be associated with price changes weighted in a different way. Our results show that prices in some product categories influence perceived inflation more than prices in other categories. In order to influence consumer spending, perceived inflation may be taken into account. This implies a policy focusing more on product categories with large subjective weights, for example appliances, and focusing less on categories with low subjective weights, for example, housing and transportation.

References

Batchelor, R.A., 1986. The psychophysics of inflation. Journal of Economic Psychology 7: 269-290.

Bates, J.M. and A. Gabor, 1986. Price perception in creeping inflation: Report on an enquiry. Journal of Economic Psychology 7: 291-314.

Blackwell, R.D., P.W. Miniard and J.F. Engel, 2001. Consumer Behaviour. Harcourt, London.

Bolton, L.E., L. Warlop and J.W. Alba, 2003. Consumer perceptions of price (un)fairness. Journal of Consumer Research 29: 474-491.

Cooksey, R.W., 1996. The methodology of social judgment theory. Thinking and Reasoning 2: 141-173.

Davies, E. and S.E.G. Lea, 1995. Student attitudes to student debt. Journal of Economic Psychology 16: 663-679.

D'Elia, E., 2005. Actual and perceived inflation. Working paper, ISAE and Statistical Office of the Municipality of Rome.

DNB, 2004. Annual report 2003. De Nederlandsche Bank, Amsterdam.

Fluch, M. and H. Stix, 2005. Perceived inflation in Austria-Extent, explanations, effects. Monetary Policy & The Economy Q3: 22-47.

Gabor, A. and C.W.J. Granger, 1961. On the price consciousness of consumers. Applied Statistics 10: 170-188.

Hair, J.F., R.E. Anderson, R.L. Tatham and W.C. Black, 1998. Multivariate Data Analysis. Prentice Hall, Upper Saddle River, NJ.

Hamblin, R.L., 1973. Social attitudes: Magnitude measurement and theory. In: H.M. Blalock Jr. (ed.), Measurement in the Social Sciences. Macmillan, London, pp. 61-121.

Kamen, J.M. and R.J. Toman, 1970. Psychophysics of prices. Journal of Marketing Research 7: 27-35.

Kemp, S., 1987. Estimation of past prices. Journal of Economic Psychology 8: 181-189.

Kemp, S., 1991. Remembering and dating past prices. Journal of Economic Psychology 12: 431-445.

Solomon, M., G. Bamossy and S. Askegaard, 2002. Consumer Behaviour. Prentice Hall, Harlow, UK.

Statistics Netherlands, Stattline Databank at http://www.cbs.nl. Voorburg

Stevens, S.S., 1957. On the psychophysical law. Psychological Review 64: 153-181.

Tversky, A. and D. Kahneman, 1974. Judgment under uncertainty: heuristics and biases. Science 185: 1124-1131.

Tversky, A. and D. Kahneman, 1981. The framing of decisions and the psychology of choice. Science 211: 453-458.

Uhl, J., 1970. Retail food prices: a study in consumer perception. Unpublished Paper, First meeting of the Association for Consumer Research, Amherst.

Williams, R.A. and L.V. Defris, 1981. The roles of inflation and consumer sentiment in explaining Australian consumption and savings patterns. Journal of Economic Psychology 1: 105-120.

Social policy and entitlements: a proposal for reform

Andries Nentjes
Faculty of Law, University of Groningen, The Netherlands. a.nentjes@wanadoo.nl

Abstract

Welfare states citizens have entitlements to a variety of social services provided for free or a price far below cost, such as education, health care, social security and housing. Every citizen benefits, but in their present organisation the social services also have major deficiencies: lack of choice, incentives encouraging over-consumption, X-inefficiency, in-transparency of benefit distribution and bureaucratic red tape. The paper proposes a radical reform by entitling every citizen with a fixed budget for lifetime consumption in the domain of social policy and by delegating the decisions on how to spend the budget to the budget holder.

JEL classification: H 42, H 53, H 55, I 38

Keywords: social policy reform, vouchers, public provided private goods, welfare state

1. Introduction

In the European welfare state citizens have entitlements - 'from the cradle to the grave' - to a broad range of social services, mainly financed by taxes and social insurance premiums. Major items in the list are: education, health care, housing, various income support arrangements (for example in case of loss of work, illness, and invalidity), basic old age pensions, and care for the elderly. The various arrangements have evolved in the second part of the twentieth century to cure and prevent individual need and deprivation and to protect citizens against economic and other insecurities of existence. They account for a large share of national welfare: no less than 30 to 40 percent of net national income is involved. The social services are highly appreciated by Europeans and their social benefits are enormous, but they do not come without a cost. In the first place there is the direct cost in the form of taxes and social premiums. Secondly, the present organisation of financing, producing and consuming social security and social care is fraught with inefficiencies. Rigidities in supply restrict choices for consumers, wrong incentives tend to encourage over-consumption, inactivity, free rides and waste and there is too much regulation and bureaucratic red tape. The X-inefficiencies and allocative inefficiencies are an additional unperceived cost next to the direct and visible cost of social policy. If social policy arrangements could be made more incentive compatible the change in citizens' behaviour would deliver a higher national income thus enabling substantial improvements in individual consumption of social services and market goods. This paper proposes such a change.

In recent years the efforts to reduce the and indirect cost of social policy have consisted in trimming the size of the schemes without radical makeover of their organisation. We take the opposite approach by maintaining the political commitment to the welfare state, taking present budgets for granted and focusing on a totally different organisation of how social security and care are financed, produced and consumed. The basic idea is that citizens maintain their claims on the existing variety of social services, but in contrast with present practice, can decide for themselves for which individual needs available funds are used. Together with the freedom to choose comes the responsibility for spending the funds properly and within the limits of the fixed individual budget. Instead of having entitlements to specific services, which are provided if certain criteria of need are met, the consumer holds a voucher to lifelong consumption of social services and security according to his or her own preferences.

Before presenting the details of the scheme and discussing its advantages in section 3 the structure of the present organisation of social policy and its problems are surveyed in section 2. Section 4 addresses potential bottlenecks of the new scheme. The conclusion is given in section 5.

2. The welfare state and its failures

In most OECD countries the welfare state has evolved in the period 1950 to 1980, bestowing on citizens entitlements to a broad range of provisions, running from old age pensions to health care and housing. From the nineteen eighties on political efforts have been made to mitigate the growth in social expenditure. They have been more or less successful in stabilising social expenditure as a percentage of national income or bringing the percentage somewhat down by eroding the size of the benefit, the length of time of entitlement, or by making the criteria to be met more stringent. Intensified monitoring and sanctioning should bring down abuse of welfare state facilities. However, in the process the organisation of social security and care has not been fundamentally changed.

The social expenditure items are in the following categories - taking the Netherlands as a case for illustration:

- Income during illness.
- Unemployment benefits.
- Public old age pensions.
- Income relief for the poor.
- Income for disabled persons.
- Education.
- Public health care.
- Care for the elderly and handicapped.
- Housing subsidies.

We shall follow the British social policy and administration tradition and subsume the whole set of arrangements under the label of social policy (see *e.g.* Culyer, 1991). A common characteristic of these provisions is that they are non-public goods: potential users can be excluded from consumption and the goods are predominantly rivalling in consumption. The reason for not leaving the allocation of the goods to the market but instead provide them through a centralised, collective allocation mechanism is not technical necessity but lies in a set of various political motives.

2.1. Benefits and costs

Altogether social expenditure can amount to as much as 40 percent of net national income. Considering the diversity of expenditure items and the huge sums that are involved there can be no doubt that social policy delivers substantial benefits for the inhabitants of the welfare state. Benefits in the form of having the security of an economic safety net and exemption from high personal expenditures for health care and education. The poor benefit from the vertical redistribution through the social arrangements; in particular through the expenditures on poor relief and public housing, but also by paying low, income dependent premiums and taxes while having entitlements to health care and old age pensions equal to the claims of those who pay high, income dependent premiums and taxes. But at the other end of income distribution the rich also benefit, for example by living longer and receiving the basic old age pension for many more years than the poor and by their higher participation in higher education. Next to that horizontal redistribution has been built in intentionally in a number of social arrangements. Income dependent premiums entitle their payers to income related benefits, for example in case of unemployment, illness and invalidity of wage dependent workers.

The benefits of social policy do not come without a cost, directly and indirectly. The direct costs, showing up in the taxes and social premiums paid in relation to benefits received are basically due to the restrictions on personal choice in spending the income that has been taken. The indirect costs are mainly caused by how the arrangements change behaviour of those who are involved as taxpayer, consumer/user, supplier of services or administrator and regulator. In the first place there is a cost, which can be encapsulated under the heading 'lack of choice'. Next to that there is for consumers an incentive to consume too much and for suppliers an incentive to waste resources and neglect consumer preferences. The regulator has to cope with lack of information, imperfect control and bias of its personnel. We shall discuss these types of social policy failure one by one.

2.2. Lack of choice

The total of taxes and premiums spent on social policy amounts to about Euro 12,000 per year for the medium income receiver in the Netherlands in 2005. That is an enormous amount of money, which cannot be freely spent according to a person's or household's own preferences. Instead the state decides on the destination of the taxpayer's primary income, it regulates for what and under which circumstances the taxpayer is eligible for consumption of social services and it also determines what criteria will be applied to assess his or her eligibility. Those regulations are very much of the type one size fits all. The discrepancies between the diverse private preferences and the standard, uniform type of service and security provided by the social arrangements imply a welfare loss; in particular when horizontal redistribution is involved. Insofar as vertical redistribution is supported by altruistic preferences, or solidarity of those who pay it is welfare increasing, but a higher share may be taken than the potential voluntary contribution and consequently the welfare losses of those who pay high taxes and premiums have to be subtracted from the welfare gains of the receivers of social support.

2.3. Wrong incentives for consumers: over-consumption

The services subsumed under social policy are of two types: insurance against the costs of certain economic risks and provision of subsidised goods. The distortion created in the consumption of the service is basically the same. Financing the provisions through the public budget or social insurance scheme signals to the consumer: these provisions are for free, whereas in fact they are not. Such signals encourage over-consumption. For an unemployed person the unemployment benefit or poor relief income is a subsidy on economic inactivity and tends to extend his period of being without a job. Housing rent subsidies undermine the incentive to search for suitable low rent housing. In this context over-consumption means that the marginal benefits to the consumer are less than the marginal cost of the service. The excessive part of consumption has negative net benefits, destroying national welfare instead of creating it. For social insurance there is the additional risk of moral hazard: a risk covered by entitlements to compensation in case the risky incident occurs, weakens the incentive to minimise the risk. Examples are risky behaviour that increases the probability of illness, invalidity and unemployment.

2.4. Wrong incentives for suppliers: X-inefficiency

The supply of social services, such as health care, care for disabled persons and education and housing by public and non-profit organisations tends towards X-inefficiency. It is mainly the consequence of not being directly paid by the client for services delivered but instead receiving a budget, which may be fixed, dependent on inputs or some performance indicator. Organisations which are not driven by the aim to maximise the surplus between revenue and cost pursue other aims. Formally their task will be to provide out-put according to need, but actually a second objective will slip in. The literature on the subject indicates that there is an incentive for participants within the organisation to create and consume internal surpluses, which may take the form of high salaries, low work loads, unnecessary expenditure on offices, the latest technology and so on. The result of such behaviour is excessive cost of output or shortly X-inefficiency. In particular input dependent and fixed budgets create

X-inefficiency incentives, output-indicator dependent finance does help to mitigate the incentive (Duizendstraal and Nentjes, 1994). Where professionals take pride in their job quality will not suffer but may even be higher than a consumer, who would have to pay the high cost, is willing to spend (Newhouse, 1970). On the other hand where suppliers have a monopoly position supply may be deliberately curtailed and queues of clients, waiting for service created (Nentjes and Schoepp, 2000). Such behaviour creates allocative inefficiency on top of X-inefficiency.

X-inefficiency means that inputs are used up for purposes, which do create welfare for the workers in the organisations that are involved, but it is lower than the welfare the inputs would have created in alternative use if X-inefficiencies had not distorted their allocation.

2.5. Rent seeking

Where suppliers are dependent from government finance there is an incentive for well organised professional groups to use their contacts with politicians, administrators and regulators to lobby for higher budgets (which will result in higher quality of output as well as in higher X-inefficiency) and also for regulation strengthening the position of professionals which is not necessarily in the interest of consumers. On the other hand specific client groups will support professionals in their demand for higher quality and quantity since the cost will be dissipated among premium and tax payers (Olson, 1965). Rent seeking actions use up inputs and if they are successful in their claims for a higher budget and more regulation it will add to X-inefficiency and over-consumption.

2.6. Bureaucracy

Where non-profit, public (and perhaps a few private) suppliers are mainly financed by the government or another national sponsor and competition between suppliers is weak and consequently consumer preferences cannot be revealed to suppliers a national bureaucracy is necessary to take over the functions of the market. The quantity and quality of the various social arrangements has to be planned, the budgets have to be calculated and distributed among suppliers. Next to planning and budgeting come monitoring of suppliers, auditing of their financial performance and applying sanctions for non-compliance. The bureaucracy also has the task to monitor consumers to prevent and correct over-consumption. The bureaucracy needed to direct production and consumption is a substantial overhead cost in the domain of social policy, which reduces the means available for delivery of services.

2.7. In-transparency of benefit distribution

A major difficulty with present social arrangements is the in-transparency of how lifetime benefits from social policy are distributed. For the Netherlands research at group level has been done into the lifetime benefits from collective arrangements according to six levels of education (ter Rele, 2005). The arrangements consist of income transfers, including the transfers due to housing arrangements and next to that the benefits in kind from education and care. They coincide with our social policy items. The group with university education has the highest benefits, Euro 321,600 in present value per person, and those with higher secondary education the lowest: Euro 251,700. The group with university degrees benefits about 20 percent more than the group with basic education only. Due to differences in taxation the arrangements clearly do redistribute net benefits between educational groups from 'rich' (university), which have negative net benefits of Euro 247,800, to 'poor' (basic education) with Euro 116,600 in net benefits.

The study is one of the very few researches on the lifetime benefits from public provided goods. However, at the level of the individual there still is an almost complete lack of information about the benefits measured over the whole lifetime. Social services are made available to individuals or families according to certain criteria of eligibility but a central registration of consumers and their use of services is lacking. Research in this area would reveal even bigger differences between educational and income groups and the differences within the groups. In-transparency of the redistribution at individual level brought about by present social arrangements makes it difficult to assess whether present social policy is fair, or not.

2.8. Conclusion

The above difficulties are not so much a consequence of the size of the social services. The problems are connected in the first place with weaknesses in the organisation of the welfare state: lack of consumer choice, wrong incentives for consumers, wrong incentives for suppliers, too much bureaucracy, too much rent seeking and an in-transparent distribution of the benefits of social policy.

3. Towards a flexible and transparent system of social entitlements

Is it possible to reform the organisation of the welfare state without sacrificing the economic and social protection it offers its citizens? In this section I intend to show that the following set of changes would create a new system in which the problems that plague present social policy have been reduced substantially or even eliminated:

- Every citizen is entitled to a broad range of social services over his life time, financed out of a personal budget with a fixed maximum in disinflated money terms: the social credit account.
- Consumers pay the market price for social services and social insurance and are allowed to use the individual social credit account for payment.
- The social services are supplied by private firms on a market with free entry and exit.
- The social credit scheme is funded by tax revenue.

The scheme replaces present social arrangements. Citizens maintain their claims on the existing variety of social services, but also get a maximum of consumer choice by deciding for themselves how to allocate the services to their various individual needs, within the constraint of their budget. Substitution between different types of social services is allowed. Together with having the final say in the consumption of social provisions comes the responsibility for spending the social credit account properly within the limits of the available individual budget. Using one's credit to finance consumption of social service A today means that there will be less available in the future for more A, or consumption of B, C, *etc.* The opportunity costs of the social services have been transferred from the collective level to that of the individual consumer.

The sum available for spending over a lifetime in substantial. Taking the Netherlands as an example, expenditure on social arrangements amounts to 40 percent of net national income, or Euro 12,000 per year per person above 17 years. The life expectation of the generation born in 2005 is 79 years. The total of entitlements is then 61 times Euro 12,000, which makes a total fund of Euro 750,000 in undiscounted value, available at your eighteenth birthday.

The social credit scheme in its pure form abolishes the present schemes of mandatory social insurance. Citizens can use their social credit as a personal safety net or financial buffer to meet the cost of unpredictable costly events, such as illness, invalidity, unemployment, *etc.* However, credit account holders are also free to use their funds to pay premiums for private insurance against the costs of heath care and loss of income due to unemployment, illness, disablement and old age. By taking insurance people can make their fixed fund flexible and more adjusted to such out-of-control events.

To avoid distortions between social account and private expenditures and to create the conditions for efficient inter-temporal choices within the social policy domain, account holders should receive a market conform rate of interest (equal to the rate for savings deposits in a solid bank) for the unspent money in their social credit account.

An essential building block of the scheme, necessary to give consumer sovereignty real content, is the organisation of a market with free entry and exit. It means getting rid of existing regulation, such as rent control in housing and price regulation in health care. Suppliers should be able to cover their cost by revenue. Privatisation of suppliers is the best guarantee to prevent hidden cross-subsidies. A Competition Authority should monitor and discipline the social service sector, focusing on conspiring suppliers and abuse of market power, in a way not different from its surveillance of markets in other branches of economic activity.

The choices people actually make will reflect their values, economic capabilities and lucky and adversary conditions they have to face during their lifetime. Very different patterns of lifetime consumption will appear. One path is spending large amounts for a good education at early age, followed later on by the use of funds for replacing or supplementing income in times of illness and periods of unemployment, to pay for health care, to finance education of children (until they are 18 years of age) and for a basic old age pension and care in the last stage of life. A very different pattern emerges for a person who starts working and earning an income at the age of 18. He or she may use in his/her thirties funds for renting a house of good quality, early retirement when 55 and old age pension from 65 on. For a person addicted to alcohol or drugs funds will be mainly used as a basic income and for paying the costs of health care and later on care for the disabled and mentally ill people. It is even an option to charge the social credit of imprisoned persons for the costs of their incarceration, at least for a part of it.

3.1. Transparent distribution of benefits

The proposed alternative arrangement will not remove the disincentives and distortions caused by the burden of a high rate of taxes plus social premiums, since the total of entitlements to social security and care is maintained. However, the other bottlenecks of the present organisation of social policy will either be eliminated or very substantially be reduced. First of all the in-transparency of the distribution of the benefits of social entitlements is transformed into transparency. Over their lifetime all citizens enjoy entitlements, which in terms of value are equal. Equal benefits and financing the budget through proportional or progressive taxes implies that horizontal redistribution of income within the same income group is terminated. What remains is a reasonably transparent vertical redistribution. Taxes from high-income groups paid over their lifetime are higher than their lifetime social credit. The tax surplus serves to supplement the taxes contributed by the low-income groups. For the Netherlands it would imply a larger vertical redistribution from high-income groups to low-income groups than occurs in present social policy.

3.2. Choice

One of the major objections against the existing organisation of social entitlements is the lack of choice citizens have in when and how to realise their potential claims. In the alternative scheme people are free to choose between the options to which the social credit account entitles them, if only they remain within the limits of their individual budget. The consumer can decide whether he wants high quality and consequently expensive care, education, *etc.* or a lower quality at a lower price, thus saving money on the social credit account. People can decide whether they consider their social credit as a sufficient buffer against uncertain high cost incidents, or use part of their fund for insurance. The choice options enable citizens to tailor social security and care to their individual needs. By doing so the scheme avoids the welfare losses of discrepancies between uniform public supply and diverse individual preferences.

3.3. Preventing over-consumption

Wrong incentives, encouraging over-consumption are caused by the false signal that social provisions are for free since the user does not or only partly pay. In contrast the social credit scheme allows choice with regard to consumption of social services while confronting the consumer with opportunity costs: present consumption withdraws money from the individual social credit account thus diminishing options for other social consumption presently or for use later on in life. The consumer will balance the marginal benefits of the consumed item against the marginal costs of the sacrificed opportunity of other present or future consumption and it will contain consumption compared to the seemingly costless consumption in traditional social policy. The economic model of rational individual choice of mainstream economics predicts that the unemployed person will search harder for a new job and also that people will take less risk to run into loss of income or high costs of care. Although the opportunity cost, in the form of subjective individual valuation of sacrificing alternative social consumption, is not identical with the taxpayer's valuation of his consumption sacrifice it can serve as a substitute that contributes to making social consumption allocatively more efficient.

It cannot be denied that if citizens choose to take voluntary private insurance against the economic consequences of unemployment, illness *etc.* the opportunity costs of over-consumption tend to disappear. However, private insurance schemes try to counter the over-consumption and moral hazard incentives by differentiation of insurance premium, such as no-claim reductions and 'own risk' clauses. In this way part of the opportunity costs of consumption is reintroduced in a different form.

3.4. Mitigating X-inefficiency and rent seeking

To counter the X-inefficiency of today's organisation of supplying social services through public or non-profit firms we have proposed privatisation and liberalisation. Privatisation should restore incentives. The blueprint for the supply side requires that firms go for maximum profits, which also means cost minimisation. Liberalisation should bring competition to the market for social security and care. A market with free entry and exit and sufficient actual or potential competition prevents abuse of market power and encourages innovation. Such a reorganisation of the supply side will terminate the problem of X-inefficiency. It also ends the pressure of professional lobbies for higher budgets, since the consumers and their insurers determine the demand for social services.

3.5. A different and smaller bureaucracy

Reform of social policy, which establishes consumer sovereignty and creates a market where suppliers compete, has enormous consequences for the welfare state bureaucracy. When markets discipline suppliers and consumers, civil servants engaged in central planning, budgeting, monitoring and enforcement loose their tasks. On the other hand the coordination of demand and supply through markets occurs within a framework of rules, which requires a bureaucracy of its own. It will have tasks totally different from the former central planning bureaucracy. After the initial work of investment in the preparation and introduction of the social credit account system has been done a bureaucracy will be needed to create social accounts for newly entering citizens and to close accounts of those who died. Social account transactions have to be registered and consumers have to be informed on changes in their budget. With regard to consumers, checks have to be applied to make sure that social account money is not spent outside the domain of specified social services. A register of certified suppliers will reduce largely the bureaucratic work in the domain of monitoring consumers. Certification of suppliers implies monitoring whether a basic quality of service is supplied, whether information on performance in quality of service and financial position is sufficient and whether its owners and managers have not a criminal record. Such monitoring should not be overdone, since consumers themselves and consumer organisations will assess quality. Monitoring and fighting abuse of market power is in the domain of the Competition Authority. All this suggests that the new social credit account system would require only a fraction of new bureaucracy compared to the old bureaucracy of social policy.

3.6. Conclusion

In this section we have discussed whether and how the social credit account scheme mitigates the problems that plague social policy in European welfare states. We have argued that the alternative with its equal entitlements for all brings full transparency of social expenditure incidence. The lack of consumer choice of present social arrangement makes way for choice: users have the option to substitute one arrangements for the other, they can choose between various qualities per arrangement and decide to what degree they want to reduce uncertainty by taking insurance. The social credit account scheme mitigates over-consumption, inclusive the moral hazard problem, substantially by confronting the users of social security and care with the opportunity costs. Privatisation and liberalisation of the supply side force suppliers to compete, to be X-efficient and to meet consumers' demand in order to survive. The bureaucratic overhead cost of social policy will be smaller because its role will change from central planner to being monitor. We conclude that the social credit account scheme eliminates the in-transparency of who benefits from social policy, ends the lack of choice for citizens and largely overcomes its problems of over-consumption, X-inefficiency and high overhead cost of bureaucracy.

4. Potential bottlenecks

Free lunches do not exist and therefore it is impossible to devise a scheme of social policy with benefits only and no costs. So what new problems might arise after the introduction of the social credit account scheme has erased the present ones?

4.1. Premature depletion: can people choose?

An obvious problem is that the fixed fund may be depleted prematurely, leaving people who are without means of their own without any form of social support. To assess how many persons might be involved and how the problem can be prevented one has to look at the causes of premature depletion. These are very diverse. In the first place a distinction should be made between depletion due to personal mismanagement and on the other hand premature depletion of a prudently managed account, caused by an exceptional accumulation of bad luck, such as unemployment, illness and disability, or simply by living long. The two categories ask for different approaches and solutions.

We do not deny that there are people who have not the capability to manage their social credit account properly. Although monitoring prevents spending on items outside the domain of social policy, they would spend too quickly or they do not use their entitlements where for their own good they should. In the category of persons who cannot help themselves properly are in the first place the homeless: 45,000 in the Netherlands in 2005, of which 30,000 without a post address. Most of them are alcohol and/or drug addicts and mentally ill. An unknown part of them is under guardianship. Those who are not do already remain outside the present schemes of transfers and public care. They form the hard core of persons unable to manage their social credit account. Partly overlapping with this category are those who (Dutch) law puts under guardianship: the mentally ill and addicted persons. It also is a relatively small group, of about 50,000 persons in the Netherlands in 2001 (NRC Handelsblad 19-7-2005, p. 3), or less than 0.4 percent of the population over 17. For such persons the guardian manages the social credit account and mismanagement is basically not a problem.

A second subgroup consists of those who are unable to manage their own financial situation and by spending more than their income allows have built up a debt which forces them into debt sanitation under a form of financial guardianship. Entering (legal) debt sanitation have been on average 10,000 persons per year in the Netherlands in the past decade. The number fluctuates, depending on the general economic situation. Assuming that such a position exists for about five years in average the total number is about 50,000 households. About half of them live on poor relief. Although falling in heavy personal debt is not identical with premature depletion of the social credit account the number of persons in debt sanitation can be seen as an indicator of the size of the group of persons who should not be left on their own in managing the social credit account.

The numbers suggest that the most vulnerable group is no more than one percent of the population at any moment. A more pessimistic view might see this as the lowest estimate and want to include all persons living on poor relief: in the Netherlands on average 300,000 in the past decade (1995-2005). This would really be an upper estimate. Many divorced and unmarried mothers who prefer to care for their children instead of taking a paid job are among them and there is nothing wrong with their capability to manage a budget.

It would be absurd not to introduce a system that includes all citizens for the reason that 1 to 3 percent of the population has difficulties in handling its account. A more fruitful approach is to build in checks to identify potential problems in an early stage, to support those persons in their account management by way of advice and ultimately by forms of guardianship, running form light to strict. The database for an early warning system is provided by electronic monitoring of the depletion of every personal account and the items on which it is expended. For example the sums used for income relief above a certain limit per period may be signalled. Mandatory counselling before further expenditure can be done would follow and possibly certain types of account expenditure could be restricted. The guidelines for such intervention should be clear and publicly available and appeal should be possible.

The second category includes persons with premature depletion despite proper management, due to accumulation of adversary conditions during life. It should be reminded that an effective way to prevent such a development is to take insurance, in particular when personal income is too low to absorb big financial shocks. Not taking such insurance is then not far from irresponsible account management. Introduction of the social credit account scheme should be accompanied by a campaign that provides people with relevant information. The advantages of using your account for paying private insurance premiums should be made clear as an option method to prevent premature depletion due to accumulation of adversary life events; in particular for people with low incomes. A system of early warnings, and where necessary increasingly strict monitoring and tutelage of how a person spends his social credit account, can reduce premature depletion to the level of the exceptional incident. Where it happens it will reflect the person's willingness to accept risks. If such a person has means of his own which are sufficient for life above the existence minimum there is no reason for public support. If personal wealth and income are lacking a safety net of public poor relief should provide the necessary at strict minimum level, with close monitoring, counselling and if necessary guardianship. The same basic provision is of course also available for the first category of persons unable to manage their account

4.2. 'Big brother is watching you'

The suggestions we did for individual monitoring of social credit account expenditure, early warning signals, counselling and guardianship may instil the fear that the scheme drives society towards a 'big brother is watching you' state. In George Orwell's '1984' big brother is the dictator who interferes with force in the private lives of citizens. In the proposed scheme supervision and guidance are imposed on those who have problems in managing their budget. It certainly is a strong infringement on personal lives and liberties, but the unavoidable consequence of providing private goods through a public arrangement.

In present arrangements similar interferences occur. For example, for every person living on poor relief the present monitoring is really intrusive, and necessarily so because of the incentive to take free rides on or even abuse the system. It is largely eliminated in the social credit account scheme and interference of the public authority comes in only if expenditure on poor relief is excessive.

4.3. More inequality

A third objection against the social credit account scheme could be that it will increase inequality compared to the present structure and organisation of social policy. Implicitly the criticism is that such a change would be unfair. For the Netherlands there is at group level no empirical base for such an assertion. The opposite is true. The social credit scheme, with its equal financial entitlements for each person, creates more redistribution from rich to poor than the present arrangements which allot higher social policy benefits to the group with university education and with higher vocational training than to the group with basic and secondary education (ter Rele, 2005).

The fear for an unacceptable increase in inequality in society may also be inspired by the suspicion that very specific small groups and individuals will see their economic position deteriorate. For example persons who have big handicaps from childhood on: for them taking insurance is not an option and a lifelong basic income of Euro 12,000 will not suffice when high costs of care have to be paid. For this category of 'young handicapped' - in the Netherlands about 140 thousand persons, or 1.1 percent of the population above the age of 17 - a special arrangement would have to be made; for example providing an additional budget on a yearly base with the flexibility to add an annual surplus to the social credit account.

4.4. Public expenditure control

One may wonder whether the scheme will make public expenditure uncontrollable, in particular on an annual base, since citizens with entitlements determine how much is spent and not the state through its annual budget.

It is true that the social credit expenditure can fluctuate from year to year although the long-term commitments of the government are clearly defined and quite stable. But is such 'volatility' a real economic problem? Social credit expenditure will fluctuate counter-cyclically through its function of providing income support during unemployment or low income from private business in times of a downturn in the business cycle. In this way the scheme will operate like a built-in stabiliser of national income, which should be welcome.

Some may worry that in the long run the scheme may be beyond the capacity to finance the high level of social expenditure, which has been promised. In an economy with long term growth in real GDP the problem can hardly arise. In an economy with decreasing population it is a transitory problem since long-term government expenditure commitments for the social credit scheme also will decrease. In a stagnating economy with structural negative productivity growth the continuity of the scheme comes under threat and a reduction of the fixed fund per person will be inevitable. The cuts should be made on the basis of an equal cut per remaining year, running from 61 times the annual cut for the new generation of 18 years old to zero for persons of 79 years and older.

One of the problems of present social policy is the almost permanent political pressure to improve existing arrangements. Would this continue or perhaps even increase under the social credit account scheme? In the first place it has to be noted that all specific arrangements have been terminated on the introduction of the new scheme. This reduces the scope for rent seeking by special interest groups. Proposals for improvement will have to focus on a general increase of the personal budgets. However, to remain credible a politician cannot do so without a proposal where to find the means to finance the extra expenditure. It may discourage such expenditure proposals; there is however also the possibility for voters at the lower end of the income and tax scale to exploit the higher income and tax group.

4.5. Political feasibility

The perhaps most formidable argument against the social credit account scheme is that is politically unfeasible. The existing welfare states have gradually built up and adapted their social arrangements over the past sixty years. Politicians and administrators have knowledge of how it works, how to manage it and they have learned to live with its weaknesses and strengths. They will not be willing to give it up for the new and untried blueprint of a social credit account. The necessary investments in changing the legal framework, installing the new administration, learning to run the administration: all this will look too much since the advantages the system should bring can only be hoped for and will therefore be distrusted. One could define the situation as an institutional lock-in (Mahoney, 2000; Pierson, 2000; Woerdman, 2004). An institutional break-out will have only a chance of occurring when it becomes apparent that the small, stepwise adjustments and efforts to trim the present system of social arrangements have little effect in suppressing the negative incentives discussed in section 2, and their welfare depressing impacts are more intensively perceived and repelled. The political non-feasibility of the social credit scheme reflects the present political climate and that can change; even quite drastically and abruptly as we have seen with the rise of the Reagan and Thatcher era and the fall of communist economic systems.

5. Conclusion

The social account scheme adheres to the motives, which in the past have given rise to the present system of social services and social security. It embraces the idea of equal access to a pool of technically private goods, but publicly provided to make them less dependant on private income, financed by income-dependant contributions. Equal claims are guaranteed by entitling every person to an equal fixed fund available for lifelong consumption. Solidarity is implied in financing the scheme from income taxes and VAT, where total taxes paid mainly depend on the taxpayer's income. The major distinction compared to present schemes is the tearing down of walls between the various schemes and the translation of scarcity of available means from the collective level to the individual level, thereby carrying over the responsibility for proper management of funds and the use of welfare provisions from the state to the individual citizen.

The arguments in favour of the scheme are of two different kinds. Welfare economic arguments are involved, but also arguments of a psychological and ideological nature. From a strict welfare economics point of view the lump sum available for life time consumption enables consumers of social services to maximise utility from social services under the constraint of their lump-sum fund plus their after tax private income. The lump-sum constraint introduces liberty of choice and together with that it brings the opportunity costs of consumption from the fund into a person's decision, thus raising individual and national welfare.

Next to the economic argument the social psychological, ideological and political argument, comes in. Our proposal for an alternative organisation of social policy takes it for granted that, apart from a relatively small minority, citizens are able to take responsibility and can manage their resources to serve their ends. This author is even willing to defend the view that such responsibilities should be given back to people. Independence from state tutelage, managing ones' own budget, accepting the consequences of ones own choices, including mistakes made, helps to develop and strengthen people's self-reliance and to respect themselves as responsible citizens. Financial responsibility stimulates to be alert and active; it discourages passivity and relapse in the role of the helpless victim dependent on others. The scheme makes citizens more adult by addressing them as persons who can take responsibility.

References

Culyer, A. J., 1991. The political economy of social policy. Gregg Revivals, Aldershot.

Duizendstraal, A., Nentjes, A., 1994. X-inefficiency in subsidized organizations. Public Choice 81, 297 - 321.

Mahoney, J., 2000. Path dependence in historical sociology. Theory and Society 29, 507 - 548.

Nentjes, A., Schoepp, W., 2000. Discretionary profits in subsidized housing markets. Urban Studies 31, 181 - 194.

Newhouse, J.P., 1970. Towards a theory of non-profit institutions: an economic model of a hospital. American Economic Review 50, 64-74.

Olson, M., 1965. The logic of collective action: public goods and the theory of groups. Harvard University Press, Cambridge Mass.

Pierson, P., 2000. Increasing returns, path dependence and the study of politics. American Political Science Review 94, 251 - 267.

Ter Rele, H., 2005. Measuring lifetime redistribution in Dutch collective sector arrangements. C.P.B. Document no. 79, CPB, The Hague.

Woerdman, E., 2004. The institutional economics of market-based climate policy. Elsevier, Amsterdam.

Corporate issues

Empowering ultimate owners as a means to improve corporate governance

Tsjalle van der Burg
Institute of Governance Studies, University of Twente. PO Box 217, 7500 AE Enschede, The Netherlands. t.vanderburg@utwente.nl

Abstract

In this paper, a new system of shareholder empowerment is proposed. In this system, the responsibility for trading shares remains where it is today, but the responsibility for voice is given to the ultimate owners of the shares who delegate it to proxy voting institutions. The system improves corporate governance because it solves the collective action problems relating to voice. Besides, managers can be encouraged to provide better information. This will also help shareholders to discipline managers by means of exit and entry, and it improves the allocation of resources by means of capital markets.

JEL classification: G34

Keywords: corporate governance, private benefits of control, voice and exit, shareholder democracy, collective action problems

1. Introduction

Different countries have different corporate governance systems. In some countries, shareholders have a legally dominating position, and managers are supposed to maximise shareholder wealth. Elsewhere, other stakeholders, such as labour and the government, also have much power. This paper will not discuss which system is best (For a comparison of different systems of corporate governance, see La Porta *et al.* 1999; Roe, 2003; Denis and McConnell, 2003; Monks and Minow, 2004). Rather, given a situation in which it is considered desirable that shareholders have a certain amount of influence, the question is how the desired influence of the owners can be realised. Section 2 discusses corporate governance, and the problems faced by (especially) shareholders. Section 3 presents a proposal for a new system of shareholder empowerment. Section 4 discusses how this system can improve corporate governance. Section 5 concludes.

2. Problems of corporate governance

2.1. Introduction

Managers do no always work for shareholders (and others) as they should do. They may shirk, or simply be incapable while remaining in office. They may get excessive remunerations.

Besides, a manager may, for his own satisfaction, aim at too much firm expansion. He may also trade shares of his own firm at the cost of uninformed shareholders, or favour a dominating shareholder at the cost of other shareholders or stakeholders. The term 'private benefits of control' is used to denote the private benefits which managers and dominating shareholders get in relation to these problems (For an overview of these problems, see Shleifer and Vishny, 1997; Denis and McConnell, 2003).

Inspired by Hirschman (1971), we distinguish two methods which shareholders can use to improve their situation: voice and exit and entry. Exit and entry concern selling and buying shares. Voice concerns all other means of exerting influence. The title of Hirschman's book is 'Voice, Exit and Loyalty'. Essentially, however, loyalty is important through its effects on voice and exit.

2.2. Exit and entry

Shareholders that get unfavourable information about a company may sell their shares so that the price decreases, and *vice versa*. This disciplines managers in two ways. First, their remuneration is (often) dependent upon the share price. Second, the possibilities for attracting new capital decrease, so that expenditures (including those on prestigious expansion for instance) remain limited. Clearly then, shareholders can better discipline managers by means of exit and entry if they have good information.

When some investors (or traders) obtain information about a firm initially, their subsequent trades cause the information to be reflected in the stock price, and as such it becomes available for all investors. Thus, if firms provide good information to some investors at least, share prices will reasonably reflect the true value of firms. People can then safely buy shares, the stock market will function and managers will be disciplined. In addition, resources will be allocated efficiently, which is important for the economy at large (Diamond, 1967; Fama, 1970). Thus, exit and entry also are a mechanism for realising an efficient allocation of resources. From this perspective too, it is important that investors obtain good information.

There is no universal standard for reporting on firm performance. Besides, even if all firms used the same standard (*e.g.* US GAAP), there would remain much room for flexibility and interpretation. For instance, profits can take significantly different values depending on the auditor's choices (Monks and Minow, 2004). Even more serious problems relate to less tangible results, such as human capital and knowledge capital. Such results can have a large impact on future profits, yet they are very difficult to value. Therefore, it is very difficult to publish reliable information about these results.

Information on short-term profits, which is the least unreliable in principle, has a significant impact on the stock price. A high stock price is advantageous for the firm as it reduces the cost of capital. Besides, it has advantages for managers pursuing personal gains (see above). Therefore, all managers have an interest in projects that foster short-term profits. In relation to this, they may invest too little in projects with less tangible results. Such 'short-termism' can be damaging to shareholder value in the long term. For a discussion of this issue see Jacobs, 1991; Porter, 1992; Laverty, 1996; Palley, 1997; Grinyer *et al.*, 1998; Segelod, 2000.

Another problem is that managers have various incentives for providing inadequate or even false information. First, too optimistic information can lead to a higher stock price, which, as discussed above, has advantages for the firm as well as for managers pursuing personal gains. Second, too positive information can improve the firm's (short-term) image, which has various advantages for the firm and its relations with stakeholders and which can give managers personal satisfaction. Finally, mismanagement, excessive private benefits of control or fraud may be reasons for obstructing the information flow. On the other hand, many managers have high moral standards. In addition, reliable information can foster a firm's reputation, which has positive long-term effects on the stock price, firm performance, and the personal satisfaction of managers. In relation to these different, opposing incentives, firms exhibit large differences regarding their information policies.

In this context, auditing can be an important instrument to protect shareholders and to help managers to foster the firm's reputation (Jensen and Meckling, 1976). Unfortunately, auditing itself is not always reliable due to a principal-agent problem (Loitlsberger, 1968; Antle, 1982, Parkash and Venable, 1993). The legal system can also encourage reliable information. Unfortunately, even a well-functioning legal system cannot fully ban out bad reporting and fraud, and the legal system is far from perfect in many countries (Shleifer and Vishny, 1997; La Porta *et al.*, 1998). In addition, auditing and laws can never lead to perfect information about intangible results.

In view of these complexities, it is crucial that investors spend time and resources to obtain information. Rational investors will acquire information up to the point where marginal benefits equal marginal costs. Unfortunately, it is generally irrational for small investors to search for much information as searching often involves significant costs while private benefits are low. Besides, free riding on the information of others is often possible (see also Hirshleifer and Riley, 1992).

Large investors and specialised traders often do search for information. There are two reasons for this. First, superior information may enable them to buy and sell at the cost of uninformed traders (Grossman and Stiglitz, 1980). Second, information can also be used for voice, which can give them additional benefits (see Section 2.3). Thus, large shareholders and specialised traders get relatively much information, so that they can better discipline managers while resources are allocated more efficiently (Porter, 1992; Adam-Müller, 2002).

2.3. Voice

Voice has a number of elements: voting at shareholders meetings, forming shareholders coalitions, meeting with board members, becoming a non-executive director or a manager, and engaging in takeovers. For the average small shareholder, voice is not popular because of the following. To the extent it results in higher profits, the benefits are merely proportional to the small size of his stake. He incurs costs to gather information. In relation to this, collective action problems arise similar to those for exit and entry. Voice, however, can also involve significant costs outside information gathering, and in relation to this additional collective action problems arise.

For a large investor, voice can be more interesting. First, if it has positive effects on performance and stock price, his benefits will be large because he owns many shares. Still, since he does not own all shares some collective action problem may remain (Webb *et al.*, 2003). Second, because he has many shares he has many votes, so his voice can be more effective. Therefore, the chance of (perceived) improvements is higher. Third, some large shareholders can be effective by using the threat of a takeover (Shleifer and Vishny, 1986; Butz, 1994). Fourth, when a takeover occurs, the new owner has large powers to bring about improvements. Fifth, a large investor may get private benefits of control as a result of his influence (Shleifer and Vishny, 1997).

However, there are also factors that set a limit to voice by large shareholders. To have an impact, a shareholder needs a large holding. However, this reduces his possibilities for diversification, and so his costs of risk increase (Demsetz and Lehn, 1985). Besides, it is difficult to sell a large stake without negative effects on the price, or to accumulate a large holding without increasing it (Webb *et al.*, 2003). Finally, some large shareholders face specific obstacles. In the US, for instance, legal constraints and corporate culture limit shareholders activism (Edwards and Hubbard, 2005; Monks and Minow, 2004).

The effects of the factors discussed above on voice depend on the country. In the US, the legal system offers shareholders good protection in principle, so that they have fewer problems - and therefore fewer incentives for voice and for large holdings that facilitate voice. Indeed, in the US ownership concentration is lower than in many other countries (La Porta *et al.*, 1998). Nevertheless, there still are a significant number of large investors (see also La Porta *et al.*, 1999). There also are serious managerial failures (still). Many large investors are not very active in correcting these failures; other large investors, however, are (Porter, 1992; Monks and Minow, 2004; Edwards and Hubbard, 2005).

Some of these active large shareholders become manager, or appoint a person they control as a manager. Here, there are four types of manager: (1) the manager who is appointed following a takeover; (2) the manager who has been appointed by a large shareholder; (3) the founder of a company who sold part of his company but kept a large holding; and (4) the manager who has a large holding for other reasons. The large stakes of these managers may help solve a number of agency problems. In addition, some of these managers have special qualities. As a result, these managers have increased firm value in some cases. In other cases, however, they have had a negative impact, partly because they could reap private benefits of control (Monks and Minow, 2004; Morck *et al.*, 1988; McConnell and Servaes, 1990). Some other large investors use other means, such as activism at General Meetings. Such activism can include voting, submitting proposals and nominating candidates for the board. This has increased firm value in some cases (Porter, 1992; Economist, 2004; Monks and Minow, 2004; Van Nuys, 1993; Strickland *et al.*, 1996; Karpoff, 2001; Edwards and Hubbard, 2005).

Outside the US, voice sometimes functions differently. In countries where shareholders get little protection against managers, ownership is more concentrated than in the US and voice by large shareholders is more important (La Porta *et al.*, 1998, 1999). In corporate governance systems in which managers are supposed to work for both shareholders and stakeholders, shareholders seek to protect their interests against stakeholders. For instance, it has been argued that German codetermination, by which, for instance, labour takes half of the seats on the board in some of the largest firms, stimulates concentrated ownership - as a means to protect shareholders against labour (Roe, 2003). A thorough analysis of voice by shareholders in different countries is beyond the scope of this paper (For an overview see Shleifer and Vishny, 1997; Denis and McConnell, 2003).

Some final remarks on the private benefits of control are useful. As noted above, the possibility of reaping such benefits can stimulate large shareholders to gather information and to help discipline managers. However, private benefits of control may be regarded as unfair. They can also reduce the willingness to invest of other shareholders, thereby reducing the inflow of capital. It depends on the country whether the positive effects outweigh the negative ones. In countries with poor shareholder protection, excessive private benefits of control may well be the major problem of corporate governance (Shleifer and Vishny, 1997; Denis and McConnell, 2003).

3. Empowering ultimate owners

In this section, a new system of shareholder empowerment will be described. We start with some definitions concerning the ownership of shares. The 'direct owner' is the person or institution that can sell the shares. The 'ultimate owner' is the person who has ultimately provided the money to buy it. For instance, in case a person directly buys the shares of a firm, he is direct owner and ultimate owner at the same time. In case he invests in a mutual fund that buys shares of firms, he is (together with others who invest in the mutual fund) the ultimate owner of these shares, the mutual fund being the direct owner. A final example: consider the case where people pay money to an insurer that buys shares in firms to provide for future indemnities or pension payments. In that case, the insurer is the direct owner and the people are the ultimate owners of the shares.

The proposed system has the following elements. First, the responsibility for trading shares remains where it is today. Second, the responsibility for voting at shareholders meetings is given to the ultimate owners, subject to the following constraint: every ultimate owner delegates his votes to a proxy voting institution, or he is not allowed to vote. Third, every proxy voting institution represents certain general principles, and it promises to vote at shareholders meetings on the basis of these principles. For instance, a proxy voting institution could represent the principle that every firm should maximise it own profits. Another proxy voting institution could stand for corporate social responsibility combined with fair profits. The general principles for which a proxy voting institution stands should be applied to all firms. Consider, for instance, a proxy voting institution that stands for maximisation of profits only. It cannot merely vote for proposals that increase the profits of Microsoft. It must vote for any proposal at the General Meeting of any firm that increases the profits of that firm. Fourth, a proxy voting institution can use its own judgment to vote on specific issues, while taking account of firm-specific information and its general principles.

The election of proxy voting institutions could be confined to limited time periods, such as the last three weeks of every even calendar year. During an election period a person can vote for a proxy voting institution, which then keeps the proxies until the next elections.

For ultimate owners that are direct owners at the same time the procedure is as follows. First, every ultimate owner votes for a proxy voting institution. Second, his choice, and the numbers of the shares of individual companies he owns, is conveyed to the preferred proxy voting institution. Banks and brokers can be made responsible for this second step.

In case the ultimate owner is not identical to the direct owner, the direct owner is made responsible for the practical procedure. More specifically, a direct owner could act as follows. First, he asks every ultimate owner financially related to him to vote for a specific proxy voting institution. Second, he calculates, for every related ultimate owner that has chosen to vote, the percentage of all shares of the direct owner to which the relevant ultimate owner is entitled. Essentially, this percentage is equal to the ratio between the money this ultimate owner has paid to the direct owner and the money all ultimate owners taken together have paid. Third, for every proxy voting institution that has obtained votes, he calculates the sum total of the percentages of all shares of the direct owner to which ultimate owners that have chosen this proxy voting institution are entitled. This sum total is called the voting percentage of the relevant proxy voting institution. Fourth, for every General Meeting of a firm in which the direct owner has invested, he calculates the number of proxies to be used by each proxy voting institution (one proxy corresponding to one share). The number of proxies given to a proxy voting institution equals the voting percentage of this proxy voting institution multiplied by the number of shares of the firm in the possession of the direct owner.

The practical procedures, as well as the work of the proxy voting institutions, involve costs. All ultimate owners, including those who do not vote, could be obliged to make a contribution to cover these costs. This is because they all benefit from better disciplined managers governance, and free-riding should be avoided.

4. Effects on corporate governance

4.1. General remarks

It is widely accepted that shareholders should not make decisions about all but the most general issues facing the firm. Specific decisions are to be left to managers, who can be dismissed if overall results are unsatisfactory. This limited authority for shareholders (and its companion limited liability) stems from the lack of knowledge of shareholders and the related problems of controlling specific decisions. The background is that, because most firms need large amounts of capital while most shareholders prefer to spread their risks, the typical individual shareholder of a firm has a small stake only. This makes information gathering and monitoring relatively costly for him, while there is a free-rider problem (Monks and Minow, 2004).

In the proposed system, an individual shareholder can no longer vote at the General Meeting of a firm, although his representative can. In view of the principle of limited authority, this new limitation of the authority of individual shareholders is not revolutionary, especially not if one takes into account that their representatives can be more effective in shaping decisions than individual shareholders (see below).

Various proxy voting institutions could meet the preferences of various groups of ultimate owners. Profit-oriented proxy voting institutions could attract owners that focus on profits only. Environmental proxy voting institutions could attract environmentalists. Other ethical institutions could meet other demands. Many combinations are possible. The specific (combination of) topic(s) of a proxy voting institution, combined with the names of affiliated people and (after some time) the reputation of the proxy voting institution, will attract specific voters. A person only needs to investigate which institution comes closest to his preferences and is trustworthy. This reduces the costs of information gathering.

4.2. Effects on corporate governance

As discussed in section 2, shareholders face various obstacles for getting the influence they are intended to have (given the legal system in which the company operates). First, shareholders get far from perfect information, which is an obstacle for voice as well as for exit and entry. This is partly the result of collective action problems, which are most serious for small investors. Besides, it is intrinsically difficult for managers to provide reliable information, especially in the field of less tangible results. In addition, some managers suppress information, and auditing is not always an adequate solution. Second, for voice there are (additional) collective action problems outside information gathering, again for small shareholders especially. Third, as large shareholders often have more influence than small shareholders, the former may reap excessive benefits of control.

In the new system, the proxy voting institutions solve the collective action problems for voice (essentially). Thus, the quality of voice will improve. Small shareholders will become more powerful *vis-à-vis* large shareholders. As a result, the private benefits of control can be reduced. The proxy voting institutions, which (as a group) fully dominate General Meetings, will better succeed in disciplining managers and improving firm performance than shareholders do under the present system.

The only possible exception concerns cases where voice by large shareholders has (particularly) positive impacts on the performance of managers and firm value under the present system. Are such cases exceptions indeed? As discussed in section 2, some large shareholders become manager, or appoint a person they can control as a manager. In such cases, the manager gets his position because of a takeover, because he is (appointed by) a large activist investor, because he has brought the firm to the stock market, or for other reasons. As a result, these managers have increased firm value in some cases. In other cases, however, they have had a negative impact. Will the positive impacts disappear when shareholder meetings are dominated by proxy voting institutions? When a person is a good manager, it is rational for the proxy voting institutions to make him manager. One of the factors that make him qualified may be the possession of a large holding (which solves some agency problems), or a history as a founder. In any case, if a person is the best candidate, the proxy voting institutions will probably vote for him, and the new system is not inferior to the present one in this respect.

Large shareholders presently also influence management by other means, such as activism at shareholder meetings. As discussed in section 2, this has had favourable effects in some cases. However, there is no reason why proxy voting institutions can not have similar effects. Indeed, at shareholder meetings their votes may be more effective in influencing management. All in all, the advantages generated by large investors under the present system can also be generated under the proposed system.

Another point is that the proposed proxy voting institutions can improve the information flow - by pressuring managers to disclose information, by encouraging the independence of auditors, and also by sharing their information with direct owners. As a result, voice as well as exit and entry can function better. Here, it may be recalled that a well-functioning exit and entry mechanism not only helps discipline managers, but it also improves the allocation of resources in the economy at large.

Finally, the problem of 'short-termism' can be mitigated. As discussed in section 2, managers may presently invest too little in projects with less tangible results. Proxy voting institutions can stimulate them to increase such investments, while furthering Porter's (1992) proposal of improving the provision of information about less tangible results. This could increase long-term firm value, while the short-term stock price needs not decrease (much) because of the improved information.

All in all, the proposed system solves or mitigates many of the problems of present corporate governance systems, especially with regard to the way shareholders discipline managers.

5. Conclusions

In this paper, a new system of shareholder empowerment has been proposed. In this system, the responsibility for trading shares remains where it is today. The distinguishing characteristic is that the responsibility for voice is given to the ultimate owners of the shares. However, the ultimate owners delegate it to proxy voting institutions that vote at shareholders meetings according to their own judgment.

For corporate governance, the system solves the collective action problems relating to voice. As a result, the quality of voice can improve, managers can be better disciplined, private benefits of control can be reduced, and 'short-termism' can be mitigated. Besides, managers can be encouraged to provide better information, which has three advantages: it further improves voice, it helps shareholders to discipline managers by means of exit and entry, and it helps improve the allocation of resources by means of capital markets.

It is beyond the scope of this paper to analyse the implications of this system for problems beyond the boundaries of the corporation. For a discussion, we refer to Van der Burg and Prinz (2004). However, it can be noted that the new system has an interesting consequence: the ultimate owners can, without financial repercussions for themselves, choose proxy voting institutions that encourage corporate social responsibility to possibly very large extent.

As the system has not been used as yet, it is, of course, difficult to imagine how exactly it will function in practice. In this context, it could be useful to start experiments with the more modest system proposed by Van der Burg and Prinz (personal communication). This system differs from the system discussed above in that the opportunity to delegate votes to proxy voting institutions is given only to small shareholders who invest directly in individual firms. Experiments with this relatively simple system could generate useful insights. Finally, it would also be useful to explore the system proposed in this paper on the basis of formal models.

Acknowledgements

This paper is based on Van der Burg and Prinz (2004) to a large extent. The author likes to thank Aloys Prinz for extensive text suggestions, and an anonymous referee for useful comments.

References

Adam-Müller, A.F.A., 2002. Stock Option Plans für das Topmanagement [Stock option plans for the top management]. In: M. Ruffner (Ed.), Corporate Governance, Shareholder Value and Finance, Vahlen, Zürich, pp. 331-362.

Antle, R., 1982. The auditor as an economic agent. Journal of Accounting Research 20: 503-27.

Butz, D.A., 1994. How do large minority shareholders wield control? Managerial and Decision Economics 15,:291-298.

Demsetz, H. and K. Lehn, 1985. The structure of corporate ownership: causes and consequences. Journal of Political Economy 93: 1155-1177.

Denis, D.K. and J.J. McConnell, 2003. International corporate governance. Journal of Financial and Quantitative Analysis 38: 1-36.

Diamond, P.A., 1967. The role of a stock market in a general equilibrium mode with technological uncertainty. American Economic Review 57: 759-76.

Economist, 2004. Activist funds. Profit huggers. Economist, April 3, pp. 69-70.

Edwards, F.R. and R.G. Hubbard, 2005. The growth of institutional stock ownership: a promise unfulfilled. In: H. Chew and S.L. Gillan (Eds.), Corporate Governance at the Crossroads. McGraw-Hill, New York, pp. 347-359.

Fama, E.F., 1970. Efficient capital markets: A review of theory and empirical work. Journal of Finance 25: 383-417.

Grinyer, J., A. Russell and D. Collison, 1998. Evidence of managerial short-termism in the UK. British Journal of Management 9: 13-22.

Grossman, S.J. and J.E. Stiglitz, 1980. On the impossibility of informationally efficient capital markets. American Economic Review 70: 393-408.

Hirshleifer, J. and J.G. Riley, 1992. The Analytics of Uncertainty and Information. Cambridge University Press, Cambridge.

Hirschman, A.O., 1970. Exit, Voice, and Loyalty. Responses to Decline in Firms, Organizations and States. Harvard University Press, Cambridge, MA.

Jacobs, M.T., 1991. Short-term America: The Causes and Cures of our Business Myopia. Harvard Business School Press, Boston.

Jensen, M.C. and W.H. Meckling, 1976. Theory of the firm: Managerial behaviour, agency costs and ownership structure. Journal of Financial Economics 3: 305-360.

Karpoff, J.M., 2001. The impact of shareholder activism on target companies: A survey of empirical findings. Working Paper, University of Washington, Washington.

La Porta, R., F.F. Lopez-de-Silanes and A. Shleifer, 1998. Law and finance. Journal of Political Economy 106: 1113-1155.

La Porta, R., F.F. Lopez-de-Silanes and A. Shleifer, 1999. Corporate ownership around the world. Journal of Finance 54: 471-516.

Laverty, K.J., 1996. Economic "short-termism": The debate, the unresolved issues, and the implications for management practice and research. Academy of Management Review 21: 825-860.

Loitlsberger, E., 1968. Die Buchprüfung als spieltheoretisches Problem [Auditing as a game theoretic problem]. Der Österreichische Betriebswirt, 137-179.

McConnell, J.J. and H. Servaes, 1990. Additional evidence on equity ownership and corporate value. Journal of Financial Economics 27: 595-612.

Monks, R.A.G. and N. Minow, 2004. Corporate Governance. Blackwell, Oxford.

Morck, R., A. Shleifer and R.W. Vishny, 1988. Management ownership and market valuation. An empirical analysis. Journal of Financial Economics 20: 293-315.

Palley, T.I., 1997. Managerial turnover and the theory of short-termism. Journal of Economic Behaviour & Organization 32: 547-557.

Parkash, M. and C.F. Venable, 1993. Auditee incentives for auditor independence: The case of nonaudit services. Accounting Review 68: 113-133.

Porter, M., 1992. Capital disadvantage: America's failing capital investment system. Harvard Business Review 70: 65-82.

Roe, M.J., 2003. Political Determinants of Corporate Governance. Oxford University Press, Oxford.

Segelod, E., 2000. A comparison of managers' perception of short-termism in Sweden and the U.S. International Journal of Production Economics 63: 243-254.

Shleifer, A. and R.W. Vishny, 1986. Large shareholders and corporate control. Journal of Political Economy 94: 461-488.

Shleifer, A. and R.W. Vishny, 1997. A survey of corporate governance. Journal of Finance 52: 737-783.

Strickland, D., K.W. Wiles and M. Zenner, 1996. A requiem for the USA. Is small shareholder monitoring effective? Journal of Financial Economics 40: 319-338.

Van der Burg, T. and A. Prinz, 2004. Improving political and corporate governance: The separation of voice from exit and entry for shareholders. Westfälische Wilhelms-Universität, Volkswirtschaftliche Diskussionsbeiträge Beitrag Nr. 359, Münster. Available at: www.wiwi.uni-muenster.de/vwt/vwd/pdf/359.pdf.

Van Nuys, K., 1993. Corporate governance through the proxy process. Journal of Financial Economics 34: 101-132.

Webb, R., M. Beck and R. McKinnon, 2003. Problems and limitations of institutional investor participation in corporate governance. Corporate Governance 11: 65-73.

Vulnerability of a high-trust society: the collapse of Enron

Eiji Furuyama
Nihonbashi Gakkan University, Faculty of Human Sciences & Business Administration, 1225-6 Kashiwa, Kashiwa-shi, Chiba 277-0005, Japan. fury@nihonbashi.ac.jp

Abstract

A corporation, which had won the most innovative firm award by *Fortune* six-times and ranked the 7th among the 500 largest U.S. corporations, imploded and plunged into bankruptcy. The dramatic rise and the scandalous fall of a large corporation took place in a high-trust society. The paper describes a series of the events, which led the corporation to a large scale deception of the security markets and investors, and then attempts to analyse the background of such a deception in a socio-economic framework.

JEL classification: M14

Keywords: Enron, market deception, business ethics, high-trust society

1. Democracy, trust and securities market

Fukuyama (1992) describes a universal history of mankind from two aspects. One is an empirical argument that the number of liberal democracies increased from three in 1790 (United States, Switzerland and France) to 36 in 1960 and then to 61 in 1990 (Fukuyama, 1992:.49). The other is a Hegelian argument to see history as a dialectic of the two classes, *i.e.*, master and slave; master, the thesis and slave, the antithesis, are lifted up to a synthesis, in which both can live in peace, ending the battle between man's desire for recognition and his fear of violent death, which forces him to accept a life of slavery in return for security. Socially this synthesis, according to Fukuyama, has been realised only in a political system adopting the parliamentary democracy.

Fukuyama was often misunderstood as he claimed that the history ended in 1991, when the Soviet Union imploded as a political system and disappeared as a sovereign state. The misunderstanding was, probably due to the fact that a book so superbly titled was published in 1992, that some people referred to the book having a look only at the book title without reading the content. Fukuyama argues that history ended in 1789 with the French Revolution, which initiated the parliamentary democracy. Since then no other political system was superior to the parliamentary democracy, politically, economically as well as ethically (Fukuyama, 1992: Part III Chapter 19). In this argument is also expressed Fukuyama's confidence in the American democracy, which came out of the American Revolution, a cousin of the French Revolution.

Fukuyama analyses in his next book (Fukuyama, 1995) the key factors, which promise the democracy a high economic prosperity. He argues that trust is essential for those who trade and the most rudimentary form of trust is the one resting on kinship. Kinship-based trust is limited in its extension. Fukuyama argues that the culture of spontaneous sociability allows business to grow beyond family. Fukuyama tests his thesis by comparing various economies and presents a rather unorthodox list of "high-trust societies", which are the US, Germany, and Japan and "low-trust societies", which are Italy, France, Korea, and Taiwan (Fukuyama, 1995: Part II and Part III).

The securities market is a place where the characteristics of the high-trust societies are most typically exhibited. In the capitalist economy savings are channelled to business enterprises, which need financial resources for business creation and expansion. Securities markets play a key role in this circulation. Investment in securities is a form of fund transfer from the investors to the sponsors. Lending is another form of fund transfer. However, in terms of the degree of risk bearing there is a difference between investments in securities and lending. A lender's risk is low when lending is covered with the collateral. However, investors' decision-making to transfer his fund rests much with his unilateral trust in the sponsor, who issues the securities. The investors' decision-making is based on the information that is publicly available and it is assumed and almost taken for granted, especially in a high-trust society, that business enterprises publicly disclose full and complete information of their present and future value. In actuality, however, the financial disclosure is not always full and complete. It might intentionally hide information implying risk for investors.

2. Securities market deceived

The 2000 Enron annual report announced that the corporation had built unique and strong business with tremendous opportunities for growth in the business of wholesale as well as retail energy services, broadband services, and transportation services. It further stated that their market opportunities would triple over the coming five years. Such an announcement appeared substantiated through the Enron and subsidiaries consolidated income statement, which reported the total revenues of US$101 billion, US$2.5 billion income (before interest and income taxes) and net income of US$979 million (Enron, 2000). In the 500 Largest U.S. Corporations by *Fortune* Enron ranked the 7th, only one rank below CITIGROUP, whose revenues were US$112 billion (Fortune, 2001).

When Enron boasted "tremendous opportunities for growth" in the 2000 annual report, it must have been known to the insiders that their overseas ventures such as the Dabhol power plant in India had caused the corporation an enormous financial distress (Swartz and Watkins, 2003: 206). Blockbuster 20-year deal to provide video-on-demand service to consumers over high speed Internet lines announced in July 2000 and incorporated in their financial statement as part of revenue and income existed only on book and was never realised (Healy and Palepu, 2003: 10). All such negative information was intentionally hidden and those investors who trusted window-dressed financial reports continued to buy Enron's stock to bring its price to an all-time high of US$90.56 in August 2000 (Fox, 2003: ix).

Behind Enron's deceptive practices there was abuse of accounting techniques, excessive emphasis on mark-to-market accounting that led the corporation to an obsession with the stock prices, and personnel evaluation system called PRC (Performance Review Committee), which spurred employees to an endless competition to enhance their sales even at the risk of committing unethical behaviour (Bryce, 2003: Chapter 17).

Enron formed off-balance sheet partnerships called SPE's (special purposes entities) one after another, in which the accumulating loss was cunningly disguised (Powers *et al.*, 2002). One year and two months after its stock price had hit an all-time high, the SEC began a probe of the corporation's management of the SPE's. When the news was revealed, Enron's stock price fell to US$20.65. Dynegy, the second largest energy trader next to Enron, announced a deal to purchase Enron. However, as major credit rating agencies downgraded Enron's bonds to a junk status, Dynegy terminated its deal to buy Enron (CNN News, 2001) and its stock price plummeted, opening at US$3.69 and closing at US$0.61 on November 28, 2001 (Cruver, 2002: 185). On December 2, 2001 Enron filed for Chapter 11 bankruptcy protection. The court assessed the Enron's debt at US$63 billion and its disposable asset at US$12 billion (Enron, 2001).

The Enron collapse was not only scandalous, but also suspected as constituting such crimes as fraud, conspiracy, insider trading, money laundering, obstruction of justice and so forth (U.S. Department of Justice, 2004). The sudden and dishonourable implosion of a large corporation was as shocking as the September 11 terrorist attack, both taking place in the first year of the new century. The two incidents severely shook the confidence in a high-trust society.

3. The birth of Enron

Had it not been for constant and accelerated social, economic and political trends of deregulations, Enron would not have been born. In the recent decades in the US, UK, and other countries the financial, transportation and telecommunication sectors have been extensively deregulated. The late comer in this series was the energy sector, which started being deregulated toward the late 1970's and the early 1980's (David and Wen, 2001; Munson, 2005).

Kenneth Lee Lay (1942-2006), the founder of Enron, was born to a rural family in Tyrone, Missouri in 1942. His father was a minister of Southern Baptist church but had to hold other jobs besides ministry in order to support his family. With scholarship grants, loans, and money earned through his part time jobs Lay was able to attend the University of

Missouri at Columbia. He continued his study at the graduate school to obtain his M.A. in economics in one year. He started the career as a corporate economist with Humble Oil in Houston (Fusaro and Miller, 2002: 151-152). The young economist was much attracted to the energy industry, especially by the industry's highly capital intensive nature. He is said to have told one writer: *"It required a lot of long-range planning and interface with government and regulatory bodies, which also tended to fit into my economics training."* (Fox, 2003: 8)

He joined the Navy in 1967 as a supply officer, and later accepted to a position at the Pentagon as an economist. He served for three years as the Assistant Secretary of the Navy for Financial Management. During this service Lay made a research on the economic impact of defence spending, on which he wrote a Ph.D. dissertation to be presented to the University of Houston (Kenlayinfo, 2006). After his discharge from the Navy in 1971 he found a job with the Federal Power Commission, which later became FERC or Federal Energy Regulatory Commission. At the Power Commission he was an assistant to his former M.A. supervisor, Pinkney Walker, who became the head of the Commission after quitting the University of Missouri (Columbia Daily Tribune, 2002). In Washington he also taught the graduate courses of the George Washington University in economic theories as well as government-business relations (Kenlayinfo, 2006).

With the knowledge of theories in economics, government-industry relationships, and experience-based insights into the energy industry, Lay joined a natural gas utility Florida Gas in 1973 as vice president. In 1981 he moved to Transco, a Houston-based pipeline company supplying gas to the New York-New Jersey area. Lay was put in the position of president and Chief Operations Officer of Transco. The majority of U.S. natural gas wells are drilled in five major regions: Texas, Louisiana, Gulf Coast, West Texas and New Mexico. Other wells are scattered in a huge area stretching from Kansas to Oklahoma, the Rocky Mountains, and Western Canada. End users are divided into two categories, household and industries. More than 60 percent of natural gas is consumed as factory fuels, fuels for electric power generation and organic chemicals materials. The gas processing plants located near the wells are linked with end users via a vast network of pipelines stretching to 300,000 miles (Shively and Ferrare, 2003: 35).

Technically, gas transmission is far more difficult than the transportation of oil, which is liquid and storable in barrels or tanks and transportable by vehicles, trains or ships. Gas distribution systems consist of pipe, compressors to boost pressure, regulators to reduce pressure, valves to control flow and metering to measure flow quantity at each customer location. Furthermore, there must be SCADA, *i.e.*, Supervisory Control and Data Acquisition systems. A SCADA system provides the capability to monitor and remotely control components of the distribution system. The industry was tightly regulated by the government. Gas producers had to drill and pump gas in accordance with the regulations and sell gas at the prices set by the federal government. Under such strict governmental controls there was no competition and consequently, no market in the natural gas industry.

The contracts between suppliers and users were take-or-pay, which meant that the buyer would still pay some amount even if the product or service was not provided (Shively and Ferrare, 2003).

By the time Lay was at Transco, the situations were going to change toward deregulations. In the background of this change there was a shortage of natural gas. While gas demand was steadily increasing, there was no incentive on the part of suppliers to increase supply since prices were regulated. In 1978 the government started to remove its price control, enabling natural gas producers to set the sales prices at their wells. The 1978 deregulation worked well and gas production increased. However, shortly after gas production increase, a recession set in and gas demand dropped to press the prices down from US$6 per 1000ft^3 to US$3 per 1000ft^3 (LIHEAP, 1999).

It was a rare opportunity for Lay to test his expertise of economic theories and receive feedback from the actual economy. Lay moved from Transco to Houston Natural Gas or HNG in 1984. He finally assumed the position of chairman and Chief Exexutive Officer (CEO) at HNG. When Lay joined HNG, the company had just narrowly survived a takeover attempt by one of the competitors, Coastal Corp (Houston Chronicle, 2002). The late 1980's were the stormy period for gas companies as take-over and M&A were rampant in the industry. In such a period HNG was more offensive than defensive under the leadership of Lay. It spent US$1.2 billion to buy out Transwestern Pipeline and Florida Gas Transmission. By purchasing those two pipeline systems, HNG expanded its network from Oklahoma and West Texas to California and to the entire area in Florida (Bryce, 2003: Chapter 3). HNG was not a local pipeline company in Texas anymore. It became one of the largest pipeline companies in the United States. All such set-up completed, the second wave of energy deregulation was announced in 1985. The order came from FERC to the effect that local utilities could buy gas from the producers and pay the pipeline companies just for transporting the gas (FERC, 1985). Separation of gas trading and gas transmission also meant that government controls would remain in the pipeline safety, which was and still is regulated by the U.S. Department of Transportation, while gas trading was then left to the free market.

Lay grasped that the second wave of deregulation would provide a tremendous business opportunity with HNG. The pipeline industry is a natural monopoly and could enjoy monopoly rent under free market. However, since it is regulated by the government, the rent would remain residual. On the other hand, gas trading is deregulated to function freely in a competitive market. If a firm holds the control of both functions, *i.e.*, gas trading and gas transmission, the residual rent in gas transmission would be managed to realise in gas trading or at least it could be used as a competitive edge. This vision further prompted Lay to enhance the degree of monopoly of the pipeline network of HNG and this was the motive to merge HNG with InterNorth, a pipeline company much larger than HNG, based in Omaha, Nebraska. In May 1985 the two companies released news that InterNorth would buy HNG for US$2.26 billion in a friendly transaction (Time, 1985).

Samuel Segnar, the chairman and CEO of InterNorth, assumed the CEO of the merged company. It was agreed that Segnar would remain in that position until 1987 and then be succeeded by Lay. The new company was re-named as Enron and its headquarters were moved from Omaha to Houston.

4. Growth of Enron

Enron started with a shaky financial foundation. HNG had already been deeply in debt when it had purchased Transwestern Pipeline and Florida Gas Transmission. In 1987 Enron issued US$585 12-year debentures and paid off a part of the long-term debt with the revenue from the debenture sales and yet the balance of the long-term debt at the end of 1987 was as high as US$3.4 billion (Gillan and Martin, 2002).

Enron owned 37,000 miles of pipeline network nationwide, occupying 13% share in the market. Besides gas trading and transmission units, Enron also possessed gas processing plants that drilled and extracted methane, ethane, and propane gas. In 1987 Enron registered US$5.9 billion revenue and US$53.7 million net profit before tax, in which the net profit margin was yet as low as 0.9% of the revenue (Gillan and Martin, 2002: 42).

Richard Kinder, who was a fraternity brother of Lay at the University of Missouri, joined Enron as Vice Chairman. Kinder was a demanding business administrator, under whose management all the staff and employees had to work so hard that the ends were necessarily made to meet. From 1989 Kinder was Chief Operations Officer and stayed in that position until 1996, when he left Enron as he felt uncomfortable with Jeff Skilling's management style (Swartz and Watkins, 2003: 98-100). The sales and net profits of Enron during Kinder's administration are shown in Table 1.

In the late 1980's the whole natural gas industry faced one problem of the interaction between sellers and buyers of natural gas. The contracts between sellers and buyers were mostly on a long-term basis, when the industry was under the government control. After deregulation, however, the deals were made more and more on a spot basis. Price settlement for one month supply was done in a frantic few days at the end of every month. The spot

Table 1. The sales and net profits of Enron during Kinder's administration in Million US Dollar.

Year	1990	1991	1996
Sales	5,300	5,700	13,300
Net Profits	202	232	584

Source: Enron Annual Reports

market was volatile and fluctuated depending on weather. Such uncertainty discouraged some users to switch from gas back to oil and coal.

Enron was trying to convince the industry to move back to long-term contracts like those days when the industry was regulated, except for the prices which were to be negotiated between sellers and buyers. Enron established a new corporation called Enron Gas Marketing for such purposes. It made a long-term sales contract with the customers and purchased gas on a spot basis from the gas producers. The system was welcome to the gas users, but it increased risks on the part of Enron.

Then, the idea of Gas Bank was introduced by Jeff Skilling, a McKinsey consultant, who later became CEO of Enron Gas Marketing (McLean and Elkind: 2003 Chapter 14). The idea of gas bank is as follows. Gas producers make contract with Enron to sell their gas to Enron, which is a bank and producers are depositors so to speak. Customers who buy gas from Enron are borrowers. The bank or Enron will obtain profits, which result from difference between the price at which it acquires the gas and the price at which it sells the gas to the customers, just as a bank earns the spread between interests it charges on borrowers and interests it pays depositors. In the beginning the system did not work as designed. When the gas market was weak, suppliers were willing to sell gas at the contracted prices to Enron, but when the market was strong, they tended to renegotiate their sales prices. Skilling solved this problem by changing Enron's payment method. Instead of paying the gas suppliers on a delivery basis, Enron then would pay cash in return for a long-term contract. Not all of gas producers were financially strong and Enron provided loan with financially weak suppliers so that they were contractually and also financially bound to extract, process, and deliver gas exclusively to Enron.

The gas bank finally began to work. Enron was a pioneer among the gas traders which had introduced a system of long term contracts to give more stability to the post-deregulation gas market. Skilling's innovation went one step further. While the long term contracts were more and more standardised in terms of price and delivery conditions, the contract itself could be traded. That sort of business had long since been practiced in the oil market, namely, oil future market. Natural gas, which was once strictly regulated by the federal government, finally became one of those commodities, which were traded in a commodity market (Eichenwald, 2005: 43).

5. Failure of Enron

If Enron had stayed as a gas trader in the US natural gas market, "*the amazing rise and scandalous fall of Enron*" (McLean and Elkind, 2003) would not have taken place. Lay was convinced that deregulations would open new business chances. He envisioned that the next industry that would be deregulated after natural gas would be the electric power industry. In the 1980's, the electricity supply industry was undergoing a rapid change. A significant feature in these changes was an attempt to introduce competition among generators and distributors of electricity to reduce costs.

The deregulation process in electricity was slow and there were and still are strong opinions that it should not be left to the hands of free market, because the stability of its supply is so vital to people's life. Furthermore, there are many technical difficulties in trading electricity in a market, because it cannot be stored and vastly lacks the flexibility to adjust supply capacity in response to the change in demand (Munson, 2005: Chapter 9).

The UK was an earlier starter of electricity deregulation (Perl *et al.*, 1996). The industry was privatised and power generation was separated from power distribution. With one of the private power generation companies in the UK, National Power and ICI Chemicals, Enron decided to build a natural gas powered electric generating plant. The site for a new plant was Teeside in northern England, where ICI Chemicals had a factory and its capacity was estimated 1,875-megawatt. The project was signed in 1990 and the plant was completed in 1993. The power generation project itself was not a failure for Enron, but its deal with the so-called J-Block in the North Sea oil field proved to be a fiasco (Enron, 1996).

Enron committed to supply the Teeside plant 300 million ft^3 of gas per day from two new fields under the North Sea. Enron agreed to buy natural gas from the J-Block under a long term contract and the J. Block supplier, Phillips Petroleum, agreed to supply 260 million ft^3 per day. The contract was a take-or-pay, which caused Enron a US$450 million loss as the oil prices fell sharply after the contract (Fidler, 2002).

The next stage of Enron's international venture was India. India was then opening up its power market to foreign investors. In 1993 Enron proposed to build a gas-powered electric plant in Dabhol, about 100 miles from Mumbai (Bombay). Two other US firms joined the project, General Electric and Bechtel Engineering. The share of participation was 80% for Enron and 10% each for General Electric and Bechtel. The total planned capacity was 2,015-megawattts divided into two phases and the project required US$2.9 billion. The first phase would provide 695 megawatts, fuelled with naphtha and the second phase with 1,320 megawatts fuelled with LNG. From the beginning there was a resistance to this project on the local side. The Indian partner insisted that the International Bank for Reconstruction and Development (IBRD) should be invited to provide a loan. In 1993 the IBRD examined the project and concluded that the project was not economically feasible. The IBRD was critical about the plan to supply fuel for the second phase with LNG, which is the only alternative means of gas transportation when pipeline cannot be used. Enron proposed to supply LNG from Qatar to Dabhol, but the IBRD judged that the idea would not be economically feasible (Allison, 2001).

The project was viewed by those who opposed it that the foreign capital was exploiting people in India by forcing them to buy higher priced electricity. In May 1995 a crowd of several hundred protesters threw rocks and stones to the workers in the project site. The project was suspended and the Indian partner wanted to cancel the contract. The case was brought to arbitration in London (Human Rights News, 2002). While the construction of the phase one was being suspended, interest accrued from the loans at the rate of US$250,000 per day (Fox, 2003: 53).

The above description is a sort of *post-mortem* examination of the Enron's failed overseas ventures. How, then, were these projects officially reported to the investors?

"The Dabhol power project in the state of Maharashtra is the cornerstone of Enron's activities in India and is expected to be a strong contributor to Enron's earnings in 1999 and beyond. Upon achieving full commercial operation in 2001, 2,450 megawatts facility, which will include India's first-ever liquefied natural gas (LNG) terminal and regasification facility, will be the largest independent power project in the World." (Enron, 1998: 18)

It was an irony that Enron bankrupted before the project *"achieved full commercial operation in 2001."*

In 1994 Enron bundled together all its overseas ventures into one limited partnership called Enron Global Power Pipeline (EGPP). Enron retained 52% of EGPP, investing its own stock, and the remaining 48% stake was sold in the securities market. The offering of EGPP shares raised US$200 million cash for Enron, which transferred all its overseas projects, their assets as well as debts, to EGPP (Swartz and Watkins, 2003: 69). It meant that the investors in EGPP paid cash to purchase huge debts of Enron. Economic journalism was partially responsible in misleading the investors. One article referred to the EGPP stocks as a good buy, to which Wall Street had not paid enough attention yet (Fortune, 1995). The facts about Dabhol and the J. Block were known to economic journalists. However, their articles were editorialised and biased that Enron, which was a dynamic and innovative company, would eventually overcome such difficulties (Hurt, 1996).

Enron established subsidiaries one after another. Just to name them, they were Enron Capital & Trade Resources (ECT), Enron Communications, EnronCredit.com, Enron Development Corp., Enron Energy Services, and Enron Renewable Energy Corp. New ventures required huge initial capital investments, which were not expected to generate earnings or cash flow on a short run and that would place an immediate pressure on Enron's balance sheet. In order to fund the new investments, Enron resorted to a financial practice, which could raise fund without affecting their consolidated balance sheet. That was to establish special purpose entities (SPE's). SPE is a practice approved by Financial Accounting Standards Board (FASB). When the sponsor itself sets up an SPE, its "independence" from the sponsor's consolidated balance sheet can be maintained, according to the FASB rules, if 3 percent capital of the SPE comes from an independent party. This is what accountants call the *"non-consolidation equity requirement of SPE"*. There is no rationale why it is 3% (McLean and Elkind, 2003:157).

Enron's practices of SPE management were highly complicated involving mesh-like re-financing and re-investment. The following is a simplified version of the JEDI case. JEDI (Joint Energy Development Investment) was established in 1993 with joint participation of the California Public Employees Retirement System (CalPERS), which paid up with cash US$250 million and Enron, which invested US$250 million worth of its own stock. By 1997, JEDI had invested its entire fund here and there and Enron needed CalPERS to invest in a second similar fund. CalPERS insisted to sell the stakes of JEDI to someone else before establishing a second JEDI. The two parties agreed to assess the CalPERS portion of JEDI current value at US$380 million. Enron had to find an entity, which would pay CalPERS US$380 million in cash. An SPE called Chewco was established. An Enron employee, Michael Kopper, was the founder of Chewco, but he personally possessed only US$125,000, which he paid in Chewco. Barclays, a British bank, provided Chewco US$240 million with a guarantee given by Enron. Then, JEDI advanced Chewco US$132 million under a revolving credit arrangement and the remaining US$11.4 million came from Barclays, structured in such a way as to be recorded as a loan on Barclay's books and as equity by Chewco (Powers *et al.*, 2002: 43-47). Chewco was perfectly in compliance with the 3 percent rule, except that Michael Kopper was an Enron employee, who was not an entirely independent entity. The stakes of CalPERS in JEDI were transferred to Chewco and US$380 million was paid to CalPERS.

6. An analysis of the case

For a period from its establishment till early 1990's Enron was a judicious corporation, trading natural gas in the U.S. domestic market. Decay gradually crept into the corporation toward the middle of 1990's, when it started being involved in reckless and misjudged overseas ventures. Although decay was further accelerated inside as the firm resorted to unorthodox and doubtful financial techniques to alleviate the financial distress, the public reaction to the risks, which were incurred by the firm and reported publicly, was surprisingly sympathetic.

Trust, as Fukuyama (1995: Chapter 3) points out, is nurtured through spontaneous sociability, which depends upon the ability of the member of a society to share common values on a large scale. In a sense there existed a concordance between Enron and the public opinion until March 2001, when Bethany McLean (McLean, 2001) wrote an article in *Fortune*, seriously questioning the profitability of Enron and concluded *"it boils down to a question of faith"* (McLean, 2001: 126). An article, also contributed to *Fortune* in 1996 (Hurt, 1996), contrasted clearly with the article by McLean. It supported the contents of Enron's annual reports almost at their face value. In this article he wrote: *"Enron has shaken up the sleepy gas pipeline and power business by aggressively embracing risk and continually remaking itself."* (Hurt, 1996: 94) In such a concordance even the abuses of SPE's were interpreted as innovative financial engineering.

To describe such a concordance as existed between those who deceived the market and those who were deceived, we find some fitting expressions among the phrases, which Kindleberger (2000: 25) culls from the past literature of manias and panics. They are wishful thinking, intoxicated investors, turning blind eye, people without ears to hear or eyes to see, investors living in a fool's paradise, and overconfidence.

7. Conclusion

On one hand a high-trust society is economically efficient, but on the other hand it is vulnerable to bubbles and manias because of its wide and strong basis of spontaneous sociability. In a cultural characteristic of the friction-free economies the same momentum as provides corporations with an ability to siphon huge financial resources from securities market can also function as an incubator of the fools in a paradise. The momentum itself is value-neutral and therefore, for desirable development of a high-trust society there needs to be an anchor, which is normative. A sure anchor to prevent a high-trust society from drifting toward easy credibility and over-speculation would be business ethics.

Among business people, ethical egoism would be a most widely accepted moral principle. It claims that for a moral action it is necessary to maximise one's self-interest. Instead of "maximisation" it can also be stated that one should achieve a certain level of profits or welfare. Ethical egoism may give us an impression that it is different from such traditional moral principles as Kantian deontology and Benthamian utilitarianism; those traditional principles place some weight on the interests of others. Well examined, however, ethical egoism is not so much different from deontology and utilitarianism in terms of its relationships to interests of others. Each person needs the cooperation of others to obtain such an offering as friendship. If one acts with no consideration of others at all, others will not cooperate with him. Suppose that one breaks his promise to others, because by doing so his self-interest is maximised. After such a break of promise, others will not accept his promise anymore and it will not be of his self-interest. Therefore, he must do his best to keep his promise with weight to others. The principle "we treat others as we expect to be treated ourselves" can also find a comfortable place in ethical egoism.

Ethical egoism, if interpreted correctly, and backed-up by a proper data basis, can function as an effective guiding principle of business people and a steadfast anchor for a high-trust society.

References

Allison, T., 2001. Enron's eight-year power struggle in India. Asia Times, January 18, 2001. (http://www.atimes.com/reports/CA13Ai01.html)

Bryce, R., 2003. Pipe Dreams: greed, ego, jealousy and the death of Enron. Cambridge MA, The Perseus Books.

CNN News, 2001. Standard & Poor announced to lower Enron Corp's rating to "junk"status. ET. November 28, 2001: 3:40 p.m. (http://money.cnn.com/2001/11/28/companies/v_enron_analyst/).

Columbia Daily Tribune, 2002. January 26, 2002. (http://archive.showmenews.com/2002/jan/20020126busi003.asp).

Cruver, B., 2002. Anatomy of greed the unshredded truth from an Enron insider. New York, Carroll & Graf Publishers.

David, A.K. and F. Wen, 2001. Transmission Open Access. In: L.L. Lai (Ed.), Power System Restructuring and Deregulation. New York, John Wiley & Sons.

Eichenwald, K., 2005. Conspiracy of Fools. New York, Broadway Books.

Enron, 1996. Enron's Press Release on April 3, 1996. (http://www.enron.com/corp/pressroom/releases/1996/jblcklit.html.).

Enron, 1998. ENRON Annual Report 1998. (http://www.enron.com/corp/investors/annuals/annual98/pdfs/1998_Annual_Report.pdf)

Enron, 2000. ENRON Financial Report 2000. (http://www.enron.com/corp/investors/annuals/2000/financial.pdf).

Enron, 2001. Enron's Press Release on February 12, 2001. (http://www.enron.com/corp/pres-room/release/2001/press_chron2001.html.)

FERC, 1985. FERC Order 436: Open Access Blueprint (1985) Energy Information Administration. (http://www.eia.doe.gov/oil_gas/natural_gas/analysis_publications/ngmajorleg/ferc436.html.)

Fidler, S., 2002. Enron in depth: Enron chief scorned asset division. Financial Times, February 11, 2002. (http://specials.ft.com/enron/FT3AB0FQKXC.html.)

Fortune, 1995. April 3, pp.136.

Fortune, 2001. The Fortune 500 Largest U.S. Corporations. April 16.

Fox, L., 2003. ENRON the Rise and Fall. Hoboken, New Jersey, John Wiley & Sons.

Fukuyama, F., 1992. The End of History and the Last Man. New York, Free Press.

Fukuyama, F., 1995. Trust. New York, Free Press.

Fusaro, P.C. and R.M. Miller, 2002. What went wrong at Enron. Hoboken, New Jersey, John Wiley & Sons.

Gillan, S.L. and J.D. Martin, 2002. Financial Engineering, Corporate Governance, and the Collapse of Enron. Working Paper Series WP 2002-001, Center for Corporate Governance, College of Business & Economics, University of Delaware (http:www.be.udel.edu/ccg/).

Healy, P.M. and K.G. Palepu, 2003. The Fall of Enron. Journal of Economic Perspectives 17: 3-26.

Houston Chronicle, 2002. Enron timeline. January 17. (http://www.chron.com/disp/story.mpl/special/enron/1127125.html).

Human Rights News, 2002. Corporate Complexity in Human Rights Violation Press Release January 23. (http://www.hrw.org/reports/1999/enron/)

Hurt, H., 1996. Power Players. Fortune, August 5.

Kenlayinfo, 2006. On February 16, 2006 Ken Lay himself writes in his own website. (http://www.kenlayinfo.com/public/HSWOK534332323.aspx.)

Kindleberger, C.P., 2000. Manias, Panics, and Crashes. A History of Financial Crises. 4th edition. New York, John Wiley & Sons, Inc.

LIHEAP, 1999. Low-Income Home Energy Assistance Program, an overview and history of gas deregulation. Compiled by the LIHEAP Clearinghouse. (http://www.liheap.ncat.org/dereg/gasoview.htm.)

McLean, B., 2001. Is Enron overpriced? Fortune, March 5, 2001.

McLean, B. and P. Elkind, 2003. The smartest guys in the room: the amazing rise and scandalous fall of Enron. New York, Portfolio.

Munson, R., 2005. From Edison to Enron: the business for power and what it means for the future of electricity. Westport, Praeger Publishers.

Perl, L.J., G. Yarrow, T. Nambu, A. Furukawa, 1996. International Comparison of Privatization and Deregulation among the USA, the UK and Japan Volume: Country and General Overview. In: The Keizaibunseki (The Economic Analysis) 144, Economic Research Institute, Economic Planning Agency, Tokyo.

Powers, W.C. Jr., R.S. Troubh and H.S. Winokur, 2002. Report of Investigation by the Special Investigative Committee of the Board of Directors of Enron Corp. Austin Texas.

Shively, B. and J. Ferrare, 2003. Understanding Today's Natural Gas Business. San Francisco, Enerdynamics.

Swartz, M. and S. Watkins, 2003. Power Failure: The Inside Story of the Collapse of ENRON. New York, Doubleday.

Time, 1985. May 13. (http://www.time.com/time/archive/preview/0,10987,1101850513-141737,00.html).

U.S. Department of Justice, 2004. The press releases by the U.S. Department of Justice on February 19 and July 8, 2004 list the criminal charges against Kenneth L. Lay and Jeff K. Skilling in full details. (http://www.usdoj.gov/opa/pr/2004/htm/).

The effect of changes in ownership structure on performance: evidence from the building societies' demutualization in the UK

Radha K Shiwakoti
Kent Business School, The University of Kent, Canterbury, Kent CT2 7PE, United Kingdom.
R.K.Shiwakoti@kent.ac.uk

Abstract

We tested the justifications for demutualisation of building societies in the UK, and other reasons generally found in the literature for conversion from mutual to plc status, under five hypotheses, and included the efficiency versus expropriation, access to capital, risk, corporate growth and diversification hypotheses. Our estimates provide mixed evidence. They support the risk and efficiency hypotheses but reject most of the justification argued at the time of demutualisation, including the access to capital, achievement of higher growth and diversification hypotheses.

JEL classification: G21

Keywords: building societies, demutualisation, performance, ownership structure

1. Introduction

The Building Societies Act 1986 gave an option to building societies to convert into a public limited company (plc) form of ownership. A number of large societies took advantage of this and opted to give up their mutual status either by flotation as independent companies or through acquisition by other banks. The first demutualisation took place in 1989. In 1997 alone, five larger building societies with more than 60 percent of industry assets converted to banks. Just two of the then ten largest building societies have remained mutual. It is important to note that in the UK, building societies have been structured as mutual (*i.e.* unincorporated) organisations since 1775, when they first came into existence. As a consequence, all building societies are mutual organisations owned by their members. However, a conversion from mutual to a plc changes the ownership structure from one owned by members to one owned by shareholders.

In the UK, converting building societies have provided several business reasons to justify their conversion. Among them, diversification of business, access to capital, a less restrictive regulatory structure, enhanced ability in a competitive market, a need to maintain their position in the market, a desire for market discipline were important. These justifications for conversion will be grouped under the headings of efficiency and expropriation, access to capital, growth, diversification and risk hypotheses as described below. We should note that most of the reasons for conversion of savings and loans in the US are quite different from the reasons for demutualisation of UK building societies. For example, Peristiani and Wizman (1997) documented that in the 1980s mutuals were driven to convert as a result of a thrift crisis, and this was part of a general program to increase loanable funds for the purpose of increasing investment opportunities raised by deregulation, and in the 1990s conversions were driven by the need to raise equity capital. This situation did not prevail in the UK. There was no crisis in the building societies in the UK, and only Abbey National Building Society raised additional equity capital at the time of flotation.

However, demutualisation changed building societies from mutual form of organisation and they became a plc. The question is whether such a conversion had any impact on performance. For example, Jensen and Meckling (1976) predicted that organisational change takes place when economic efficiencies are to be achieved. Armitage and Kirk (1994) argued that there are reasons to believe that the form of ownership of an organisation may have an impact on performance. In light of these issues, the main objective of this research is to examine whether demutualised building societies realised their objectives as stated earlier. This research aims to provide UK evidence. This paper begins with hypotheses development. It is followed by a sample and data and the methodology used in the research. Section 5 presents the empirical results and section 6 provides a research summary and conclusions.

2. Hypotheses development

There is considerable literature on the effect of organisational change on performance; however, in this section we summarise only the major hypotheses and evidence of the relationship between different organisational forms, and their implications for the performance and behaviour that are relevant to the research objectives identified in the previous section, and we develop testable hypotheses.

2.1. Efficiency versus expropriation hypothesis

Two possible competing explanations of demutualisation are the desire for greater efficiency and expropriation, both of which have been tested in many studies since Mayers and Smith's (1986) seminal study. They explained that efficiency is the 'positive change' in the value of the firm and expropriation is the 'non-positive change' in the value of the firm. These hypotheses have focused on the efficiency of different forms of organisation, and are based on the context of agency theory. Mayers and Smith (1986) found that changing from a stock to a mutual ownership structure is on average efficiency enhancing. McNamara and Rhee (1992), provided evidence that change in organisational form reflects a move toward efficiency rather than expropriation of wealth between claim holders of the insurers. This evidence supports the hypothesis that the motivation behind demutualisation is efficiency rather than expropriation. However, Cagle *et al.* (1996) examining the pre and post demutualisation of insurance firms concluded that the change in organisational form appeared to be a neutral mutation. In the UK, building societies' reasons for demutualisation consist, among others, of freedom from legal restriction, enhanced competitive position, and maintaining their position in the market. This suggests the first testable hypothesis:

Hypothesis 1. Demutualisation is motivated by the desire to gain efficiency rather than expropriation of wealth around the time of conversion (efficiency versus expropriation hypothesis).

2.2. Access to capital hypothesis

The access to capital is usually the major reason for demutualisation into a plc form of ownership. Indeed, all institutions that have converted from mutual status have given this as one of the reasons for conversion. For example, Llewellyn and Holmes (1991) reported that access to capital is central in the debate about the conversion of mutuals. It is to be noted that in the UK, building societies have no publicly traded ownership and as a result cannot access equity capital by issuing shares. Hemmings and Seiller (1995) who argued that demutualisation is a viable model to gain access to capital however, also warned that it is not the only way to gain access to capital. Evidence provided by Carson *et al.* (1998) does not support the access to capital hypothesis for the motivation for demutualisation. They report the potential for wealth expropriation appeared to be immense in the demutualisation process. However, in the UK's building societies' demutualisation into plc's, access to capital was one of the reasons given to justify the conversion. This suggests the second testable hypothesis.

Hypothesis 2. Demutualisation is motivated by a desire for access to capital (access to capital hypothesis).

2.3. Risk hypothesis

This hypothesis assumes that incentive for risk taking varies with different forms of organisational structure. Fraser and Zardkoohi (1996) report that shareholder owned savings and loan associations appeared to take substantially more risks than mutual savings and loan associations. Furthermore, they reported that greater risk taking in saving and loan associations has come from ownership change. They posit that demutualisation provides the incentive to take greater risk. Esty (1997) argued that adoption of a risky financial strategy depends on separability of residual and fixed claims and further argued that in mutual thrifts, residual claims and fixed claims are not separable and increased risk will not affect the total wealth. In addition, in the UK, building societies are regulated and barred from taking risky assets. After conversion, converted societies can undertake risky business outside their traditional residential lending. This suggests the third testable hypothesis.

Hypothesis 3. Demutualised firms will operate with a greater degree of risk (risk hypothesis).

2.4. Corporate growth diversification hypotheses

Hadaway and Hadaway (1981) stated that growth is an important goal irrespective of organisational form. However, such growth should accelerate after demutualisation, as demutualisation provides more operational flexibility. O'Hara (1981) argued that mutual and stock savings and loans, in addition to others, differ in growth. She argued that efficient use of resources and aggressive pursuit of profit depends upon the objectives of the firms. It is hypothesised that plc status, with its greater access to equity capital and more flexibility in operation of business, can accelerate their growth than mutuals. It is to be noted that the constitution of building societies in the UK restricts them in the composition of business mix. As a result, growth should accelerate after demutualisation as they are free to choose the composition of business mix. This suggests the fourth and the fifth testable hypotheses.

Hypothesis 4. Demutualisation is motivated to achieve higher growth (growth hypothesis).

Hypothesis 5. Demutualisation is motivated by a desire to diversify the business (diversification hypothesis).

3. Sample and data

The sample of this study consists of those building societies that demutualised independently in 1997. In that year, more than 60 per cent of the total industry assets were converted to the banking sector. It is important to note that in the UK, most financial institutions are quite large and few in numbers, which contrasts with the US. For example, Cole and Mehran (1998) studied 88 'thrifts', but they comprised only 19% of the thrifts that converted from mutual to stock ownership during 1983-87. Most of the largest building societies in the UK chose to convert to plc status. This study considers only four building societies' demutualisation; however, this sample constitutes more than 57 per cent of all demutualisations in the UK.

We analysed the financial variables of four demutualised societies for an eight-year period to estimate pre-and post-conversion performance. For control purposes we also observed changes in operating behaviour of the remaining building societies, and for this purpose we collected the data for 40 mutual building societies with assets greater than £200 million. The sample of 40 matching building societies considered in this study constitutes about 95 per cent of the total assets of the remaining mutual building societies.

Time series data were collected for each of the demutualised building societies from the year 1993 to 2000, *i.e.* four years before and four years after demutualisation, including the year of demutualisation. Cagle *et al.* (1996) argued that the use of time series data controls for firm-specific characteristics that are not related to organisational form and provide a more powerful test of the relative performance compared with cross-sectional studies. However, such comparison also raises some questions. For example, it may be confounded by different economic conditions existing in the four years before demutualisation compared to the four years after demutualisation. Performance might have changed either as a result of demutualisation or due to some other factors in the economy. To overcome this problem, for control purposes, performance of the remaining building societies that did not demutualise in the same period was computed.

Most of the data was collected from annual reports and accounts of the firms which demutualised, and data for those building societies whose annual reports were unavailable were collected from the building societies' yearbook. Substantial parts of the data for building societies were provided by Thedata ltd[1]. Seventeen financial variables were examined to compare the performance of these four companies after demutualisation to their performance before demutualisation, and also to compare the performance of demutualised firms' with the remaining mutuals.

4. Methodology and variables

The approach of this study is to compare the performance of the same organisation in two different organisational structures, where before demutualisation they were mutual organisations, and after demutualisation they gained a plc status. Schwert (1981) and Mayers and Smith (1986) argued that a better comparison of mutual and stock organisations would be to examine the same firms in alternative organisational structures.

We used a non-parametric test to analyse the pre- versus post-demutualisation performance of demutualised building societies. The Wilcoxon Signed Rank test is designed to test hypotheses. It is very commonly used in this type of pre- versus post-performance study. For example, McNamara and Rhee (1992) used the Wilcoxon Signed Rank test to measure the pre- versus post-demutualisation performance of reserve life insurers. Cole *et al.* (1995) also used the Wilcoxon Signed Rank test to analyse the pre- versus post-demutualisation level of undistributed cash flow.

To determine the justification for demutualisation and the effect of changes of ownership on performance, we tested the different hypotheses described in the hypotheses development section. The variables included in the analysis cover profitability, efficiency, risk exposure,

---

[1] Thedata ltd. (the Housing and Mortgage Information Service) is a Company based in Edinburgh and provides financial data.

capital and diversification. The efficiency versus expropriation hypotheses are measured from return on equity (ROE), return on assets (ROA), return on all earnings after interest payments (AEIP), return on assets on net of loan loss reserve (ROANL), return on operating income (NOI), and return on net income (NI). To reiterate, efficiency is measured through management expenses (MEXP) and cost to income ratios (COINC) before and after conversion. In order to estimate pre- and post-conversion performance, the growth hypothesis is measured from profit growth before (PGRB) and after tax (PGRA), and assets growth (ASTG). The risk hypothesis is tested from provision for bad debts (PBADT) and loan loss reserve (BAD). The access to capital hypothesis is measured from primary capital to assets (COCAP) and capital formation (CAPFO). Finally, the diversification hypothesis is measured from non-interest-growth (NONIN) and non-interest to total income (NONTO). These variables are also used to compare the performance between building societies and converted societies.

5. Results

Empirical results are analysed and reported in two sub-sections. Sub-section 1 reports the performance of converted societies in two different organisational forms, where in the first period they were mutual organisation, and in the second period they became a plc. Sub-section 2 examines the performance differences between demutualised and matching building societies for both periods.

5.1. Performance of converted societies in two different organisational forms

Table 1 examines the five hypotheses discussed earlier of demutualised societies in two different organisational forms.

In testing the efficiency and expropriation hypothesis, six profitability and two efficiency variables were examined. The results reported in Table 1 suggest that only return on equity has significantly improved after demutualisation. ROE can be distorted for example, by keeping very low capital ratios. Capital is slightly lower prior to demutualisation and assets growth also went down compared to the pre-demutualisation period, and that might have contributed to the increase on ROE. Other remaining profitability variables are not significantly different. The findings of this study show very weak evidence for the efficiency hypothesis. ROANL, AEIP, NOI, and NI variables increased after demutualisation and only ROA slightly went down. Using the results for profitability failed to provide support for the efficiency or expropriation hypotheses. This finding is consistent with Cagle *et al.* (1996) where they found little support for conversion from a mutual to a stock motivated by either efficiency or expropriation of wealth. They concluded that changes in organisational form appeared to be a neutral mutation. In our view, this is the trade-off between the benefits of mutual and stock forms of organisational structure as suggested by Fama and Jensen (1983).

Table 1. Comparison of performance before and after demutualisation for demutualised societies.

Hypotheses	Efficiency versus expropriation								Access to capital		Risk		Growth			Diversification	
Hypotheses tested	1								2		3		4			5	
	ROE	ROA	ROANL	AEIP	NOI	NI	MEXP	COINC	COCAP	CAPFO	PBADT	BAD	PGRB	PGRA	ASTG	NONIN	NONTO
Mean 93-96	22.34	6.13	5.93	1.45	1.25	0.75	1.48	47.14	5.53	13.85	0.20	0.58	21.14	19.12	12.85	39.04	26.53
	(3.33)	(0.59)	(0.52)	(0.13)	(0.16)	(0.12)	(0.89)	(11.91)	(0.74)	(2.90)	(0.16)	(0.14)	(20.40)	(20.64)	(11.08)	(22.32)	(10.32)
Mean 97-00	25.81	6.12	6.03	1.46	1.37	0.86	1.27	43.99	5.06	7.67	0.09	0.38	12.17	17.89	9.88	43.60	30.01
	(2.26)	(0.75)	(0.74)	(0.25)	(0.23)	(0.19)	(0.70)	(10.93)	(0.93)	(4.22)	(0.03)	(0.12)	(24.16)	(30.99)	(4.66)	(10.56)	(5.10)
Wilcoxon test	-2.379	.259	-.259	-.414	-1.396	-.603	2.844	2.172	1.655	3.464	2.689	3.516	1.603	.517	.724	-1.034	-1.655
(p-value)	(.017)**	(.796)	(.796)	(.679)	(.163)	(.109)	(.004)	(.030)**	(.098)	(.001)	(.007)	(.000)	(.109)	(.605)	(.469)	(.301)	(.098)
							***			***	***	***					

*** Significant at 1% level of confidence. ** Significant at 5% level of confidence. Standard deviation in the bracket.

The efficiency and expropriation hypothesis is further investigated through direct efficiency ratios *e.g.* management expenses (MEXP) and cost to income ratio (COINC). MEXP and COINC went down and both are significant and support the efficiency hypothesis. A decline in the expense ratio could provide evidence of greater operational efficiency. However, considering profitability and efficiency ratios measured from COINC and MEXP taken together, we find only weak evidence to support the Hypothesis 1 for change from the mutual to the plc status.

Access to capital is mostly cited reason for conversion in all types of industry. It is argued that a key advantage of the plc form of ownership is access to capital markets. Earlier studies, for example, Hadaway and Hadaway (1981), and McNamara and Rhee (1992) provide evidence that capitalisation increases after demutualisation. Surprisingly, results presented in Table 1 do not support the access to capital market hypothesis (Hypothesis 2). We found that the capital to assets ratio and capital formation both went down after demutualisation and this is not consistent with generally cited reason for conversion. There might be several reasons for this. For example, in the US, mutual savings and loan associations were granted conversion to stock form in an effort to attract private capital into the industry. This was not the case in the UK. None of the demutualised building societies considered in this study raised additional equity capital at the time of flotation[2]. Needleman and Westall (1991) argue that a decision to demutualise to raise capital arises when either the company feels that they do not have sufficient resources to compete, or there are opportunities which cannot be realised with the available resources. This second argument of Needleman and Westall seems reasonable when considering building societies' demutualisation. Furthermore, Dannen (1984) predicted that access to additional capital was especially important to the smaller firms. In the UK, all demutualised building societies except Northern Rock were larger building societies.

Generally, it is hypothesised that risk taking is greater in the plc form of ownership compared to the mutual form of ownership, because of the separability of fixed and residual claims. Consequently, risk taking should increase following the conversion from mutual to plc status (Hypothesis 3). In this study, risk exposure was measured through the loan loss reserves to assets (BAD), and provision to loan losses to asset ratios (PBADT); both went down significantly (see Table 1). However, we should be cautious when explaining these variables. In the early years of study, the industry as a whole had high provision and loan loss because of negative equity and higher possession rate, something which has improved in the subsequent years. This result is not consistent with most of the earlier studies (see Esty, 1997). We have further analysed this hypothesis in the next section and compared it with matching mutuals.

---

[2] Only Abbey National which demutualized in 1989 raised about 900 million at the time of flotation.

Building societies as mutual organisations do not have equal flexibility in the operation of business compared with banks. Consequently, one of the main cited reasons/justifications is that conversion enables building societies to diversify into new areas of business. Hadaway and Hadaway (1981) suggest that growth should accelerate after demutualisation, as demutualisation provides more operational flexibility to demutualised building societies. Therefore, Table 1 also provides evidence for the growth and diversification hypotheses (Hypothesis 4 and 5). Results do not support the growth hypothesis. All variables considered to measure growth went down after demutualisation. This might have resulted because demutualisation did not bring new capital to the converted firms.

After conversion, converted societies enjoy more flexibility in their business operation, and it should help to diversify their business. Two proxies non-interest growth (NONIN) and non-interest to total income (NONTO) were tested for diversification hypothesis. Results were statistically insignificant; however, both variables went up after conversion. The results suggest that business mix has not changed significantly after demutualisation. This finding clearly does not support the diversification reason (hypothesis 5) for demutualisation to plc status.

5.2. Comparative performance of converted societies and matching mutuals

The same hypotheses described earlier were examined to assess whether a mutual or a plc form of organisation is more efficient and profitable. The results are reported in Tables 2 and 3.

When both demutualised and matching mutuals were mutual (see Table 2), we noticed three significant differences. Demutualised firms were more diversified, they had lower capital to assets ratios, and higher capital formation compared to matching mutuals. Profitability ratios showed the mixture of differences *i.e.* ROE was higher for converting firms. Return on assets (ROA), *i.e.* all earnings before interest payments, provisions to loan losses and taxes, and (ROANL) *i.e.* all earnings net of provision to loan loss reserve, were found to be the same. However, when interest payments are made, subsequently demutualised firms have higher returns. This was also found in net operating income to assets and net income to assets. Profit growth for both before and after tax was higher for converting firms whereas asset growth was the same. Both demutualised and matching mutuals are equally exposed to risk, and no difference was noticed. Efficiency ratios are also mixed. Management expenses have no significant differences, but the cost to income ratio is higher for those building societies which did not demutualise.

All ratios of profitability variables became significant after conversion. We should note that in the plc form of structure ownership can be concentrated and shareholders have direct incentives to monitor management performance. We could argue that absence of such pressure in mutual building societies might have resulted in lower earnings. The differences

Table 2. Comparison of performance before demutualisation for both demutualised and matching mutuals.

Hypotheses	Efficiency versus expropriation								Access to capital		Risk		Growth			Diversification	
Hypotheses	1								2		3		4			5	
tested	ROE	ROA	ROANL	AEIP	NOI	NI	MEXP	COINC	COCAP	CAPFO	PBADT	BAD	PGRB	PGRA	ASTG	NONIN	NONTO
Mortgage Banks	22.34 (3.33)	6.13 (0.59)	5.93 (0.52)	1.45 (0.13)	1.25 (0.16)	0.75 (0.12)	1.48 (0.89)	47.14 (11.91)	5.53 (0.74)	13.85 (2.90)	0.20 (0.16)	0.58 (0.14)	21.14 (20.40)	19.12 (20.64)	12.85 (11.08)	39.04 (22.32)	26.53 (10.32)
Building societies	14.42 (3.82)	6.05 (0.60)	5.87 (0.54)	1.14 (0.28)	0.96 (0.28)	0.63 (0.19)	1.28 (0.29)	52.97 (8.95)	6.81 (2.19)	9.53 (2.57)	0.18 (0.20)	0.47 (0.33)	10.37 (38.29)	10.43 (38.31)	7.11 (5.29)	16.49 (11.86)	13.34 (8.22)
Wilcoxon test (p-value)	5.861 (.000)	.669 (.503)	.463 (.643)	4.611 (.000)	4.349 (.000)	3.067 (.002)	.931 (.352)	2.233 (.026)	3.577 (.000)	4.909 (.000)	1.328 (.184)	1.774 (.076)	2.383 (.017)	2.074 (.038)	1.883 (.060)	4.858 (.000)	4.858 (.000)
	***			***	***	***		**	***	***			**	**		***	***

*** Significant at 1% level of confidence. ** Significant at 5% level of confidence. Standard deviation in the bracket.

Table 3. Comparison of performance after demutualisation for both demutualised and matching mutuals.

Hypotheses	Efficiency versus expropriation								Access to capital		Risk		Growth			Diversification	
Hypotheses	1								2		3		4			5	
tested	ROE	ROA	ROANL	AEIP	NOI	NI	MEXP	COINC	COCAP	CAPFO	PBADT	BAD	PGRB	PGRA	ASTG	NONIN	NONTO
Mortgage Banks	25.81 (2.26)	6.12 (0.75)	6.03 (0.74)	1.46 (0.25)	1.37 (0.23)	0.86 (0.19)	1.27 (0.70)	43.99 (10.93)	5.06 (0.93)	7.67 (4.22)	0.09 (0.03)	0.38 (0.12)	12.17 (24.16)	17.89 (30.99)	9.88 (4.66)	43.60 (10.56)	30.01 (5.10)
Building societies	10.62 (3.23)	5.63 (0.59)	5.60 (0.57)	0.76 (0.17)	0.72 (0.15)	0.46 (0.12)	1.20 (0.33)	61.69 (8.87)	6.67 (1.73)	7.14 (2.31)	0.04 (0.07)	0.23 (0.12)	7.82 (35.19)	13.84 (85.56)	9.87 (5.48)	22.14 (25.93)	15.66 (12.44)
Wilcoxon test (p-value)	6.587 (.000)	2.640 (.008)	2.511 (.012)	6.567 (.000)	6.546 (.000)	6.319 (.000)	.710 (.478)	5.229 (.000)	4.472 (.000)	2.444 (.015)	3.669 (.000)	4.091 (.000)	.782 (.434)	1.171 (.242)	.340 (.734)	4.961 (.000)	4.961 (.000)
	***	***	**	***	***	***		***	***	**	***	***				***	***

*** Significant at 1% level of confidence. *** Significant at 5% level of confidence. Standard deviation in brackets.

in cost to income ratios of the two groups significantly widened after demutualisation. Hart and Moore (1996) argued that mutual organisations are more efficient at serving a homogenous clientele compared to stock organisations. After the demutualisation period (1997-2000), the remaining building societies were earning significantly more non-interest income and serving a more heterogeneous clientele. As a result, mutual organisations might be less efficient in servicing a heterogeneous clientele.

No differences were noticed in either profits growth before tax or after tax following conversion and also for assets growth. The previous period results hold for both diversification variables and capital ratios. Interestingly, we noticed that after conversion, converting firms were more exposed to risk, and both provision for loan loss and loan loss reserve became significantly different after conversion, whereas there was no difference when they were in the same group. With a short period of conversion, the converter has more assets of bad quality. This is consistent with Fraser and Zardkoohi (1996) where they report greater risk taking from the ownership change of savings and loans.

Overall, comparison of demutualised and matching building societies' results for before and after demutualisation provides some interesting results. The study confirms that risk taking behaviour changes when the organisational structure is changed, and is consistent with most of the earlier studies (see Esty, 1997). Most of the profitability ratios have improved and became significant after demutualisation. These can be interpreted as indicative of improvement in the efficiency of the plc form of organisation. However the study rejects the access to capital, growth and diversification hypotheses as described earlier.

6. Conclusions and discussion

This paper has empirically examined the reasons given by the demutualised building societies, and different hypotheses found in the literature on the effects of ownership change from a mutual to a plc form of ownership structure, by studying the demutualisation of building societies in the UK. For this purpose, this study analysed the financial performance and operating behaviour of demutualised building societies as a distinct group, and comparison was made before and after demutualisation with matching mutuals.

Most of the reasons for demutualisation given by demutualised societies at the time of conversion are not empirically supported. Examining the demutualised firms as a distinct group, neither the access to capital hypothesis nor the growth hypothesis is supported. Our study supports the efficiency hypothesis. The risk hypothesis is rejected as the risk ratio went down. However, we should be cautious, when coming to this conclusion because of the industry trends.

Many interesting results are noticed when the performance of demutualised societies and matching mutuals are compared. For the first half period of study (1993-1996), most of the profitability ratios were higher for the demutualised societies compared with matching mutuals. Both groups were equally exposed to risk, and we did not notice any differences on return on assets and return on assets on net of provision for bad debts and doubtful debts. The cost to income ratio was higher for remaining mutuals. The demutualised societies were more diversified. This study found some behavioural changes in converting firms after demutualisation. No significant relationship between performance and organisational form is found. This result supports the view that organisational specific costs and benefits should be balanced within each organisational form. Finally, rejection of many hypotheses as discussed earlier suggests that some other factors, for example directors' remuneration, might have contributed to the decision to change ownership structure of a firm and needs further investigation.

Acknowledgements

The author wants to thank Professor Krishna Paudyal for his helpful comments and suggestions on the earlier draft of the paper. I also want to thank conference participants at the Eighth International Society for Intercommunication of New Ideas Conference (ISINI), held in Wageningen, The Netherlands, August 24-27, 2005. The usual disclaimer applies.

References

Armitage, S. and P. Kirk, 1994. The Performance of Proprietary Compared with Mutual Life Offices. The Service Industries Journal 14: 238-261.

Cagle, J.A.B., R.L. Lippert and W.T Moore, 1996. Demutualisation in the Property-Liability Insurance Industry. Journal of Insurance Regulation 14: 343-369.

Carson, J.M., M.D. Forster and M.J. McNamara, 1998. Changes in Ownership Structure: Theory and Evidence from Life Insurer Demutualisations. Journal of Insurance Issues 21: 1-22.

Cole, C.S., M.J. McNamara and B.P. Wells, 1995. Demutualisations and Free Cash Flow. Journal of Insurance Issues 18: 37-56.

Cole, R.A. and H. Mehran, 1998. The Effect of Changes in Ownership Structure on Performance: Evidence from the Thrift Industry. Journal of Financial Economics 50: 291-317.

Dannen, F., 1984. Is Time Running Out for the Big Mutual? Institutional Investors 23: 159-164.

Esty, B.C., 1997. Organisational Form and Risk-taking in the Savings and Loan Industry. Journal of Financial Economics 44: 25-55.

Fama, E. and M. Jensen, 1983. Agency Problems and Residual Claims. Journal of Law and Economics 26: 327-349.

Fraser, D.R. and A. Zardkoohi, 1996. Ownership Structure, Deregulation, and Risk in the Savings and Loan Industry. Journal of Business Research 37: 63-69.

Hadaway, B.L. and S.C. Hadaway, 1981. An Analysis of the Performance Characteristics of Converted Savings and Loan Associations. The Journal of Financial Research IV: 195-206.

Hart, O. and J. Moore, 1996. The Governance of Exchanges: Members' Cooperatives Versus Outside Ownership. Oxford Review of Economic Policy 2: 53-69.

Hemmings, R.A. and R.S. Seiler, 1995. An Economically Viable Model For Insurers to Demutualise. Best's Review-Life/Health Insurance edition November, 96, 7, 45-49.

Jensen, M.C. and W.H. Meckling, 1976. Theory of the Firm: Managerial Behaviour, Agency Costs and Ownership Structure. Journal of Financial Economics 4: 305-360.

Llewellyn, D.T. and M.J. Holmes, 1991. In Defence of Mutuality: A Redress to an Emerging Conventional Wisdom. Annals of Public and Co-operative Economics 62:319-354.

Mayers, D. and C.W. Smith, 1986. Ownership Structure and Performance: The Mutualisation of Life Insurance Companies. Journal of Financial Economics 16: 73-98.

McNamara, J.M. and G.S. Rhee, 1992. Ownership Structure and Performance: The Demutualisation of Life Insurers. Journal of Risk and Insurance 59, Part 2: 221-238.

Needleman, P.D. and G. Westall, 1991. Demutualisation of a United Kingdom Mutual Life Insurance Company. J.I.A. 188: 321-428.

O'Hara, M., 1981. Property Rights and Financial Firm. Journal of Law and Economics XXIV: 317-332.

Peristiani, S. and T.A. Wizman, 1997. Mutual-to-Stock Conversions in the Thrift Industry in the 1990s. Journal of Economics and Business 49: 95-116.

Schwert, G.W., 1981. Using Financial Data to Measure Effects of Regulation. The Journal of Law and Economics 24: 121-158.

The incremental contribution of financial reporting on the internet to business reporting

Samir Trabelsi

Brock University, 500 Glenridge Avenue, St. Catharines L2S 3A1 Ontario, Canada. samir.trabelsi@brocku.ca

Abstract

The Website is a space which offers the firm the possibility of presenting financial and non-financial information as well as mandatory and standardised information already published in traditional media. This paper shows that the inadequate methodologies and theories employed in measuring the Internet's specific contribution to financial reporting (FR) leaves us with very little knowledge on the question. Prompted by this observation and by the fact that this research topic is relatively unexplored, we propose avenues for gaining a better understanding of the ins and outs of the Internet's incremental contribution to the process of financial reporting.

JEL classification: G14, M41, M45

Keywords: internet reporting, paper based reporting, voluntary disclosure

1. Introduction

Internet financial reporting (IFR) is currently a hot topic in professional circles and among standardisation and regulatory bodies. It is also a topic of more and more widespread academic research (Lymer, 1999; Lymer *et al.*, 2002; Gowthorpe, 1999). The Website is a space where the firm can present financial and non-financial information as well as mandatory and standardised information already published in traditional media. Were a firm content with this, it would be like putting old wine in new bottles. On the other hand, the firm also has the possibility of creating new wine by using multimedia Internet technology to enrich the information provided.

This dilemma raises the following questions: What precisely does the Internet have to contribute to financial reporting? Are its determinants the same as those for traditional financial reporting? Combing through the research done on Internet financial reporting IFR) in Canada and in other parts of the world, this article looks at how the Internet influences or modifies the firm's financial reporting strategy. We first note that studies on use by firms of the Internet for financial reporting can be classified under three main complementary groups. The first group is descriptive and its goal is to take stock of the procedures used by firms in reporting their financial information on Websites (Patten, 2002; Ettredge *et al.*, 2001; Business for Social Responsibility, 2000; Hindi and Rich, 2000; FASB,

1999; IASC, 1999; Trites, 1999; Deller *et al.*, 1999; Gowthorpe and Amat, 1999; Heldin, 1999; Prentice *et al.*, 1999; Brennan and Hourigan, 1998). The disclosure index developed by FASB (in its original or modified version) is often used for to survey firm's website. These studies document a widespread and growing use of the Internet to publish both mandatory and voluntary disclosure. Mandatory information is financial or non-financial information which an entity is obliged to publish in accordance with the requirements of regulatory authorities. Voluntary disclosure applies to financial or quantitative/qualitative accounting information, which a firm may or may not choose to publish, depending on the latitude granted by regulatory authorities.

The second group of studies attempts to pinpoint the factors explaining the variability observed in the information available on Websites (Patten, 2002; Debreceny *et al.*, 2002; Ettredge *et al.*, 1999, 2002; Pirchegger and Wagenhofer, 1999). Finally, the third group tries to distinguish between firms that do use the Internet to report financial information and those that do not (Ashbaugh *et al.*, 1999; Marston and Leow, 1998). These last studies are no longer of much interest, since the great majority of firms now use the Internet for financial reporting. We have thus excluded them from our analysis.

This analysis leads us to conclude that the inadequate methodologies and theories employed in measuring the Internet's specific contribution to financial reporting (FR) leave us with very little knowledge on the question. Prompted by this observation and by the fact that this research topic remains relatively unexplored, we propose avenues for gaining a better understanding of the ins and outs of the Internet's incremental contribution to the process of information reporting.

2. Internet's contribution to financial reporting

Standardisation/regulatory bodies and practitioners obviously agree on a number of IFR characteristics. Firms can in fact use their Websites to improve and accelerate access to financial information and to make it more widely available. They can also cut down on the printing and distribution costs inevitably associated with TFR on paper format (Beattie and Pratt, 2003).

In France, the Yolin report (Yolin *et al.*, 2001) on 'Internet and Business' sponsored by the Ministry of Economic Affairs identifies three main advantages provided by the Internet. First of all, the Internet has global reach; it allows you to navigate as easily from one continent to the next as from one site to the next. Next, it costs relatively little, and its cost is falling rapidly. Finally, compared to TFR, the Internet offers new options and makes it possible to report information on a much larger scale. The Canadian Securities Authorities (Autorités Canadiennes des Marchés, 1999: Preface CNP 11-201) also points out that: *"Developments in information technology provide market participants with the opportunity to disseminate documents to security holders and investors in a more timely, cost-efficient, user-friendly and widespread manner than by use of paper-based methods."*

The Website is thus a space which the firm can use simply to reproduce the financial/non-financial, mandatory, and standardised information it has already published in traditional media. But it is also space in which this information can be enriched by taking greater advantage of the multimedia possibilities of Internet technology (Jones and Xiao, 2003; Yolin, 2001; Lymer *et al.*, 2002; Trites 1999)

3. Descriptive studies of corporate websites

Descriptive studies of IFR focus on two important dimensions: the content and the presentation of Website financial information. Figure 1 shows these two dimensions. As to content, the Website can reproduce the TFR process, presenting standardised mandatory information along with other discretionary details already available on paper or on regulatory sites such as SEDAR in Canada or EDGAR in the United States. Windows I and II of the diagram refer to this approach. Companies can also enrich traditional information by publishing more detailed or incremental information on their Websites (Windows III and IV).

As to its presentation, the Website may display a static version (including graphics) of what was already available on paper (Windows I and III). Or more enterprising and opportunistic firms may choose to use sound or video (Windows II and IV of the same diagram) to make

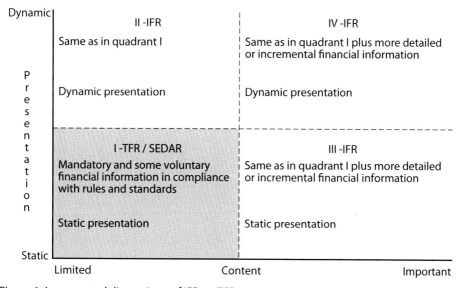

Figure 1. Incremental dimensions of IFR vs. TFR.

a dynamic presentation that would not be possible on paper. We use these two dimensions proposed by FASB (1999) to analyse the findings of the descriptive work done on IFR.

3.1. Studies on the content of corporate websites

Studies describing the content of corporate Websites can be classified into two categories: studies documenting the emergence of the Internet as a "new" medium of communication (period before 1999) and studies taking an inventory of the content of the Websites (period after 1999).

3.1.1.Emergence of the Internet as a reporting medium

Studies on the emergence of the Internet as a medium of communication have been principally piloted by national (FASB, 1999; Trites, 1999) and international (IASC, 1999) standards boards. To our knowledge, the IASC study is the only one to have looked at France and other European countries.

This IASC (International Accounting Standards Committee) study (1999) recorded the IFR practices of the 30 largest firms in 22 countries, including France. An analysis grid was developed to take stock of all the financial information reported as well as the technologies used to do so. The disclosure index required checking for the existence of one of the attributes selected. The international findings show that, at that time, 84% of these firms already have a Website. Among these firms, 100% of the large Canadian, German, Swedish, and American corporations also make voluntary disclosures. And 100% of French firms do so as well. So, 62% of the whole sample uses IFR as a reporting instrument.

Adopting the same methodological approach as IASC, the CICA put Gérald Trites in charge of a pilot project (1999) designed to examine Internet financial reporting and its modes of presentation. The findings from an inventory of 370 Websites of corporations listed on the TSX, the NYSX, and NASDAQ reveal that, in December 1998, 69% of the firms in the sample do have a Website and that 51% of them also present some financial information there. In March 1999, this percentage rises to 70%. And in December 1998, 74% of the firms are presenting their entire financial statement on their sites.

For its part, the task force formed by the FASB (1999) developed an inventory grid of 325 attributes to analyse the content of the Websites of the 100 largest firms. The findings indicate that 99% of the corporations studied do have a Website and that 96% of them publish their annual accounts on the Internet. In terms of content, most of the firms reproduce all the information reported on paper. However, other firms do enrich this information. In this sense, some firms now offer all users information previously meant only for analysts and institutional investors: presentations given by managers, teleconferences or the calendar of future events. Other firms use e-mail lists to alert users to all the information placed on the Website. The task force selected 15 firms to be interviewed by telephone and to answer a questionnaire on their view of the future orientation of IFR. The findings revealed three trends: (1) IFR as a complement to the paper format; (2) IFR as a substitute for the paper format; and (3) IFR as an innovation over and above the paper format.

3.1.2. Content of corporate websites

Academic and professional studies describing the content of corporate Websites report that firms use such sites to provide financial information (Richardson and Scholz, 1999; Hindi and Rich, 2000) as well as social and environmental information (Oxibar, 2003; Business for Social Responsibility, 2001; Patten, 2002).

Richarson and Scholz (1999) have analysed 400 Websites of American firms, in order to determine the volume and type of information reported. Their inventory has shown that most of the firms just report the information already given by traditional media rather than new or continuous information. In this sense, the authors note that 54% of the firms display their quarterly reports, 45% display their complete annual reports, and 3% display their monthly sales figures.

Hindi and Rich (2000) have used the FASB grid to inventory the Websites of 100 of the largest Fortune 500 firms (17 April 2000 issue). Their results show that 100% of these firms disseminate financial information on their Website (96% in the FASB study) and that there is a wide variation in both the content and design of the information reported.

The Business for Social Responsibility group (BSR) has analysed the dissemination of environmental and social information on the Websites of businesses belonging to Fortune 500. The findings show that 86% of such firms publish social and environmental information. Moreover, 40% of these firms also describe their strategies and commitments regarding social responsibility and 31% of them give an analysis comparing their commitments and achievements in environmental matters. And 22% of these firms provide an evaluation of their environmental performance.

Patten (2002) has made an inventory of the Websites of 40 insurance companies. His findings show that 25% of these firms do no financial reporting on their Websites. But they do disseminate information on ethics, human resources, their community commitments, and their environmental practices.

3.1.3. Format of corporate websites

Technologies for presenting information on the Web are tools managers can use to gain latitude or flexibility in handling financial information on the Web. The exploratory findings of IASC (1999), Trites (1999), FASB (2000), and Hindi and Rich (2000) show that firms are at different stages in their use of these technologies.

The IASC study (1999) identifies three groups of formatting technologies for presenting financial information on Websites:

- Static technologies such as documents in the form of downloads, electronic paper and HTML (Hypertext Mark-Up Language).
- Multimedia technologies such as 3D or Pulls.
- Technologies allowing interaction with the user: access to research tools and smart software, programming with JavaScripts, Java and Active/X, use of XML language (eXtensible Markup Language).

In July 2000, the American Institute of Certified Public Accountants (AICPA) published a first version of the universal electronic financial reporting language called Extensible Business Reporting Language (XBRL) which uses the XML language format. According to the committee that runs this international project, this Internet financial reporting language makes it possible to improve and accelerate access to information. It helps satisfy the needs of users by providing them with credible information more quickly (Debreceny and Gray, 2001).

The IASC task force observes that corporations do not use the full potential of Internet technology. Most corporations reproduce their financial statements in an Adobe Acrobat document (13%) or use HTML formatting and allow users to download the data reported (19%). On the other hand, some corporations make substantial improvements in the information reported on paper, by disseminating management PowerPoint presentations, conferences, and Web broadcasts.

In order to measure IFR interactivity, Trites (1999) used four indicators: question forums (QF), e-mail addresses, telephone numbers, and fax numbers. The findings show that in March 1999, a large number of firms did give a telephone number (92%) and an e-mail address (96%).

The FASB task force notes that most firms group financial information under the section "relation with investors." Some firms adopt a static presentation, whereas others opt for a dynamic format including video reports. And to make it easier to locate, access, and download financial data, some firms are now collaborating with AICPA to develop a standard model for preparing and exchanging financial data.

Finally, Hindi and Rich (2000) show that 59% of firms report using an HTML format, whereas 71% report using the PDF format. And to help the user gain access to the "investor relations" section, 97% of firms provide a table of contents while 66% allow access to this section by means of a search engine.

3.1.4. Contribution and limits of descriptive studies on IFR

The main contribution of the preceding descriptive studies is the yardstick they give for assessing first the emergence and then the evolution of the use of Websites for financial reporting (Lymer, 2002). However, according to Lymer (2002), most of these studies, given their exploratory nature, are without any theoretical foundations. It is that context which prompts Lymer to call for more in-depth academic studies.

We may add that these studies also fail to isolate the Internet's impact on financial reporting. Some measurement of this impact is needed in attempting to answer the research question raised in the introduction. It is also necessary to measure the Internet's incremental contribution to financial reporting, so as to see whether its determinants are the same as those for TFR. Standard-setters also need information on this matter in order to guide their reaction to the evolution of this medium of financial reporting.

4. Study of the determinants of reporting on websites

In this part, we present the works designed to gain a better understanding of IFR determinants: In section 4.1, we shall try to show that, in general, these studies are weakened by their problem with the specification of the dependent variable they use to measure IFR. As concerns determinants (section 4.2), these studies are rather unanimous. In general, they show that size, sector of activities, sophistication of users, performance, and widely dispersed ownership will explain the variability of the two IFR dimensions presented in Figure 1: content and presentation of financial information on corporate Websites.

4.1 The determinants of reporting on websites

4.1.1. Size

Most of the research on the determinants of IFR dimensions (Craven and Marston, 1999; Ashbaugh *et al.*, 1999; Ettredge *et al.*, 1999; Pirchegger and Wagenhofer, 1999) document a positive and significant association between the dissemination of financial information on the Internet and the size of the firm.

This relationship would be explained notably by the information asymmetry existing between the managers of these firms and users of the financial information, who are often widely dispersed shareholders. To reduce the agency costs resulting from this asymmetry, large firms would tend to adopt more elaborate IFR practices. Ashbaugh *et al.* (1999) also use the notion of economies of scale to justify a positive association between the size of the firm and the probability that a firm will disseminate financial information on its Website. They obtain their results based on a sample of 290 non-financial firms. Using a logistic regression they document a positive relation between IFR and the size of the firm. The dependent variable is dichotomous and equal to 1 if the corporation reports its financial information on the Internet and 0 if it does not.

Craven and Marston (1999) analyse IFR for a sample of 206 firms classified by the Financial Times according to their market capitalisation as reported in July 1998. The authors report that 153 of these firms (74%) have a Website, 109 of which do present financial information. Out of these 109 firms, 67 report detailed financial information whereas 42 present a portion of their annual report. Kruskal-Wallis comparative average tests show that a significant statistical difference exists between the size factors (turnover of personnel, number of employees, total assets and market value) of firms disseminating financial information on their Websites and those that do not adopt such practices.

Based on a sample of 660 firms from 22 countries, Debreceny *et al.* (2002) have tested the relation between the presentation format, the Website's content (measured by an ordinal variable equal to 0 if the corporation does not use a Website, to 1 for a succinct presentation of accounting data, to 2 for a reproduction of the information presented on paper, and to 3 for the presentation of additional information), and the size of the firm measured by its market capitalisation. The results of the ordinal logistic regression models show that the presentation format and the reporting practices are positively and statistically associated with the size of the firm. The authors conclude that large firms are more likely to adopt various media, including their Website, to disseminate more information at lower costs in a more convivial manner. Large firms have many widely dispersed shareholders and the Internet provides an ideal tool for reaching them.

4.1.2. Sector of activity

Empirical studies show mixed results as to the influence of sector of activity on IFR. Marston and Leow (1998) document a significant association between the electronic dissemination of information and the firm's sector of activity. Their contingency table shows that firms in the financial sector tend to report summary financial data. In contrast, those in the service sector tend to present their entire annual report. Ashbaugh *et al.* (1999) show a significant statistical difference for size and performance between those industrial, service, and food-processing corporations that do disseminate financial information by Internet and those that do not. Craven and Marston (1999) find no significant statistical difference between firms from various industrial sectors when it comes to IFR.

4.1.3. Performance

The studies by Ashbaugh *et al.* (1999) and Ettredge *et al.* (2002) find no positive and significant statistical relation between performance and IFR. Ashbaugh *et al.* (1999) have analysed this relation using earnings on assets to measure the firm's operational performance. Their univariate analysis shows a statistically significant difference between the performance of firms disseminating financial information by Internet and those that do not. However, in their logistic regression analysis, the sign is positive but not statistically significant.

The study by Ettredge *et al.* (2002) distinguishes the dissemination of mandatory information in annual or quarterly reports from voluntary disclosure. Their regression analysis shows no statistically significant association between the two types of financial reporting and the firm's performance measured by market returns.

4.1.4. Shareholding structure

According to Pirchegger and Wagenhofer (1999), the shareholder with only a few shares in the firm's capital will tend to use its Website to the extent that the use of other sources, such as analysts and brokers, are more costly. Consequently, IFR is more advantageous for widely held firms. However, Ettredge *et al.* (1999) argue from the notion of information overload to suggest that the individual investor will find an abridged annual report more useful that a detailed annual report. Consequently, these authors expect the dissemination of an abridged annual report on corporate Websites to be positively associated with the number and dispersal of a firm's small investors.

Pirchegger and Wagenhofer (1999) have analysed the relation between several dimensions of IFR and the shareholding structure of a sample of 31 Austrian and German firms. They compiled indices grouping these dimensions into 4 categories: reporting procedures used on the Web; technologies used; synchronisation; and support provided to users. Their results document a positive and statistically significant association between IFR dimensions and the dispersal of shareholders. However, this finding contradicts those of Ashbaugh *et al.* (1999) who find that the probability that a firm will use IFR is not significantly linked to its shareholding structure as measured by the median of the percentage of shares held by individual investors.

The research conducted by Ettredge *et al.* (1999) also seeks to understand why some corporations bear additional IFR costs when the information is already available in other media. Their study is based on a survey of 203 British corporate Websites. They draw up a list containing 15 items designed to capture the different properties (whether subjective or objective) of the information reported in the complete annual report or in a summary.

Using a Probit model (estimated by Ettredge *et al.* (1999) as: Information $(1.0) = f$ (No. of individual investors, No. of financial analysts, size of firm), they show that the presentation of a complete annual report is positively associated with the number of analysts monitoring the firm, when controlling for size. When summary information is presented, the relation is the same with the number of individual investors but the results indicate a negative and statistically significant relation with the number of analysts monitoring the firm. The results also show that firms monitored by a large number of financial analysts provide more objective financial information. Firms with a large number of individual investors tend to provide more subjective financial information. In sum, Ettredge *et al.* (1999) interpret the variability observed in IFR practices as a reflection of the user's degree of sophistication.

4.1.5. Debt

Debreceny *et al.* (2002) draw on the agency framework of Jensen and Meckling (1976) to analyse the association between IFR dimensions and debt. The argument is that managers can use voluntary disclosure on their Website to reassure lenders of the firm's ability to repay its debt on time. Besides, the firm's Website is a window through which lenders can keep a close watch on the firm's activities. However, the results of an ordinal logit analysis fail to document any statistically significant association between IFR and debt.

4.2. Limits of studies on IFR determinants

Our analysis of the literature reveals that, in general, IFR dimensions will vary with size. For the factors—such as sector of activity, performance, shareholder dispersal, sophistication of users, and debt—the results are not as robust. In our opinion, these mixed results could be explained in several ways. First, using mainly dichotomous or ordinal measurements to determine IFR dimensions (as in Figure 1) or, to a lesser degree, calculating the score based on an analysis grid do substantially reduce the variability actually measured as compared to the real diversity of the IFR strategies used by corporations. This makes it difficult to characterise corporations according to the level of their IFR.

Second, when authors use an analysis grid for IFR dimensions, they often only take stock of the reporting procedures used. These studies are thus more concerned with technical aspects than with the presentation and content of IFR which require a more direct and exact evaluation.

Third on most of these studies on IFR, dimensions related to presentation, technology used, user support, and synchronisation often lack any rigorous theoretical justification. This lack of theory sometimes leads to the use of poorly specified econometric models. This means, notably, that these models do not take account of several variables identified in the literature on determinants of voluntary disclosure (Lang and Lundholm, 1993; Clarkson *et al.*, 1999; Healy and Palepu, 2001). The models tested are thus relatively weak in explanatory power. Finally, some researchers such as Pirchegger and Wagenhofer (1999) and Ettredge *et al.* (2002) exclude from their analysis corporations that do not disseminate financial information by Internet. This implies a selection bias which may compromise the interpretation of the results of the models estimated (Greene, 2003; Gouriéroux, 1989).

5. IFR: The incremental contribution to business reporting

The studies reviewed in this article show that there is great heterogeneity in the presentation and content of the financial information disseminated on Websites. On the one hand, descriptive studies indicate that corporations are at various stages in adopting the Internet to report financial information on their Websites. On the other hand, works on the determinants of this heterogeneity obtain several contradictory results, except as concerns firm size which they almost all identify as the main explanatory factor.

Sections three and four of this paper show the essentially descriptive nature of the research conducted on this matter. They also show the weakness of the methodologies employed and the inadequacy of the hypotheses suggested to explain recourse to Internet Repetition. The methodologies are generally simplistic because they are solely designed to explain why the business does or does not use the Internet. The hypotheses are poorly adapted to the research problem, because they do not differ from those stated in studies seeking to explain voluntary disclosure practices not connected with Websites. They do not take into account the specific features of the Internet.

Most of the previous works on IFR have not isolated the impact of the Internet—as compared to that of traditional financial reporting (TFR) media—on a firm's financial reporting strategy. The research work of Oxibar (2003) and Trabelsi *et al.* (2004) seeks to remedy this weakness. Oxibar (2003) has compared the social information published on the Internet to that published in the annual report for 49 French firms. The results show that the social information available on the Internet is comparable to that published in the annual report. Trabelsi *et al.* (2004) have compared financial information disclosed in traditional financial reporting (TFR) as compared to websites disclosures of a random sample of Canadian companies. The results document a significant difference between TFR and IFR as well as a wide variability among the sample firms in their use of IFR content, format and technology. Trabelsi *et al.* (2004) interpret this variability in the incremental difference of IFR over traditional financial reporting (TFR), as an indication that a firm's ritualistic or opportunistic behaviour under IFR is not different from its behaviour under TFR.

6. Conclusion and avenues of research

Our review of the literature has led us to conclude that the question as to whether or not the financial information reported on the Internet is identical to that available in traditional formats remains an empirical one. The study by Trabelsi *et al.* (2004) tends to support the fact that financial reporting on the Internet contributes to business reporting at least by allowing firms to disclose additional voluntary disclosure.

Several questions remain unanswered. Future research could try to gain a more exact understanding of how the Internet affects the behaviour of managers with regard to voluntary disclosure. There would be a need to improve the measurement of IFR dimensions which are often dichotomous and aimed mainly at its technical aspects, in order to better understand how its incremental role compares with that of TFR. For example, SEDAR, though also accessible on the Internet, could be used to represent TFR, since the firm is obliged to publish all regulatory information there, independently of its decision to also use its Website for financial reporting. The analysis could thus truly focus on the incremental impact of IFR as compared to this image of TFR.

Like the works of Clarkson *et al.* (1999) on management reports (MD & A) and of Frankel *et al.* (1999) on conference calls, future studies could aim at determining whether firms consider the Internet— a medium of voluntary disclosure— as an integral part of their financial reporting strategy and, if yes, how they go about achieving this end. It would also be necessary to test the content of the information published on corporate Websites using the methodology with which Bryan (1997) measured the incremental informational content of management reports.

Finally, up to now, research studies have examined only a fraction of the variables that are presumed to be determining in the literature on voluntary TFR. Such studies have not proposed a specific model designed to obtain a clearer understanding of the determinants of IFR. By analogy, the study by Bushee *et al.* (1999) shows that the decision to broaden access to conference calls will depend on the composition and demand of the firm's clientele of investors as well as on the complexity of the information disseminated. By extension, future research could test simultaneously the reasons determining the decision to broaden access to financial information through Internet publication as well as those determining the scope of the information published.

Acknowledgements

We acknowledge support from SSHRC's Initiative on the New Economy program. This paper is partly based on my dissertation at HEC Montreal. I wish to thank the members of my dissertation committee for their many insightful comments and suggestions: My supervisor Réal Labelle, Gaétan Breton, Pascal Dumontier, Claude Laurin and Robert Gagné. This paper has benefited from the comments of the participants in the Brock University workshop, the Eight ISINI International Conference, the 2005 Canadian Academic Accounting Association annual meeting and the 2006 ABR (Business) Conference sponsored by the Clute Institute for Academic Research, as well as from those provided by John Core, Gordon D. Richardson, Steven E. Salterio, Dan Simunic, Gerald Trites, and Sameer Mustapha. The usual caveat applies.

References

Ashbaugh, H., K.M. Johnstone and T. Warfield, 1999. Corporate reporting on the Internet. Accounting Horizons 13: 241-257.
Autorités Canadiennes des Marchés, 1999. Instruction Canadienne 11-201: La transmission de documents par voie électronique. Bulletin de la Commission de Valeurs Mobilières du Québec, XXVIII (24).

Beattie, V. and K. Pratt, 2003. Issues Concerning Web-Based Business Reporting: An Analysis of the Views of Interested Parties. The British Accounting Review 35:155-187.

Brennan, N. and D. Hourigan, 1998. Corporate Reporting on the Internet by Irish Companies. Accounting Ireland. December, pp. 18-21.

Bryan, S., 1997. Incremental Information Content of Required Disclosures Contained in Management Discussion and Analysis. The Accounting Review 72: 285-301.

Bushee, B.J., D.A. Matsumoto and G.S. Miller, 2003. Open Versus Closed Conference Calls: the Determinants and Effects of Broadening Access to Disclosure. Journal of Accounting and Economics 34: 149-180.

Business for Social Responsibility Education Fund (BSR), 2000. Social and Environmental Internet Reporting among Fortune 100 Companies. The Fund, San Francisco.

Clarkson, P.M., J.L. Kao and G.D. Richardson, 1999. Evidence that Management Discussion and Analysis (MD&A) is a Part of a Firm's Overall Disclosure Package. Contemporary Accounting Research 16: 111-134.

Craven, B., and C.L. Marston C. L., 1999. Financial Reporting on the Internet by Companies. The European Accounting Review 8: 321-333.

Debreceny, R. and G.L. Gray, 2001. The Production and the Use of Semantically Rich Accounting Reports on the Internet: XML and XBRL. International Journal of Accounting Information Systems 2:47-74.

Debreceny, R., G.L. Gray and A. Rahman, 2002. The Determinants of Internet Financial Reporting. Journal of Accounting and Public Policy 21: 371-394.

Deller, D., M. Stubenrath and C. Weber C., 1999. A Survey on the Use of Internet for Investor Relations in the USA, the UK and Germany. The European Accounting Review 8: 335-350.

Ettredge, M., V.J. Richardson and S. Scholz, 1999. Financial Data at Corporate Websites: Does User Sophistication Matter? Working Paper. Available at SSRN: http://ssrn.com/abstract=142936

Ettredge, M., V.J. Richardson and S. Scholz, 2001. The Presentation of Financial Information at Corporate Websites. International Journal of Accounting Information Systems 2: 149-168.

Ettredge, M., V.J. Richardson and S. Scholz, 2002. Dissemination of Information for Investors at Corporate Websites. Journal of Accounting and Public Policy 21: 357-369.

Financial Accounting Standard Board (FASB), 1999. Business Reporting Research Project: Electronic Distribution of Business Reporting Information.

Frankel, R., M.S. Johnson and D.J. Skinner, 1999. An Empirical Examination of Conference Call as a Voluntary Disclosure Medium. Journal of Accounting Research 37: 133-150.

Gouriéroux, C., 1989. Économétrie des variables qualitatives. 2ième edition, Economica, Paris.

Gowthorpe, C., 1999. Corporate Reporting on the Internet: Developing Opportunities for Research. The Journal of Applied Accounting Research 5: 2-28.

Gowthorpe, C. and O. Amat, 1999. External Reporting of Accounting and Financial Information Via the Internet in Spain. The European Accounting Review 8: 365-371.

Greene, W.H., 2003. Econometric Analysis. 5th edition, MacMillan Publishing Company, New York.

Healy, P.M. and K.G. Palepu, 2001. Information Asymmetry, Corporate Disclosure, and Capital Markets: A Review of Empirical Disclosure Literature. Journal of Accounting and Economics 23: 405-440.

Heldin, P., 1999. The Internet as a Vehicle for Investor Relations: the Swedish Case. The European Accounting Review. 8: 373-381.

Hindi, N. and J. Rich, 2000. Financial Reporting on the Internet: The Future or the Present. Accounting Information Systems Educators Conference, Denver, CO, pp. 175-176.

International Accounting Standard Committee (IASC), 1999. Business reporting on the Internet.

Jensen M. and W. Meckling, 1976. Theory of the Firm: Managerial Behaviour, Agency Costs and Ownership Structure. Journal of financial economics 3: 305-360.

Jones, M. J. and Xiao J. Z., 2003. Internet Reporting: Current Trends and Trends by 2010. Accounting Forum 27: 132-165.

Lang, M. H. and Lundholm R. J., 1993. Cross-Sectional Determinants of Analyst Ratings of Corporate Disclosures. Journal of Accounting Research, 31: 246-271.

Lymer, A, 1999. The Internet and Future of Corporate Reporting in Europe. The European Accounting Review 8: 289-301.

Lymer, A., J. Xiao and M. Jones, 2002. Immediate trends in Online Corporate Financial Reporting. European Accounting Review 11.

Marston, C. and C.Y. Leow, 1998. Financial reporting on the Internet by leading UK companies. Paper presented at EAA'98, Antwerp.

Oxibar, B., 2003. La diffusion d'information sociétale dans les rapports annuels et les sites Internet des entreprises françaises. Thése de Doctorat. Université Paris Dauphine.

Patten, D.M., 2002. Give or Take on the Internet: An Examination of the Disclosure Practices of Insurance Firm Web Innovators. Journal of Business Ethics 36: 247-260.

Pirchegger, B., and A. Wagenhofer, 1999. Financial Information on the Internet: A Survey of the Homepages of Austrian Companies. The European Accounting Review 8: 383-395.

Prentice, R.A., V.J. Richardson and S. Scholz, 1999. Corporate Website Disclosure and Rule 10b-5: An Empirical Evaluation. American Business Law Journal 36: 531-579.

Richardson, V.J. and S. Scholz, 1999. Corporate Reporting and the Internet: Vision, Reality and Intervening Obstacles. Pacific Accounting Review 11: 153-159

Trabelsi, S., R. Labelle and C. Laurin, 2004. The Management of Financial Disclosure on Corporate Websites: A Conceptual Model. Canadian Accounting Perspectives 13: 235-259.

Trites, G., 1999. The Impact of Technology on Financial and Business Reporting. Canadian Insititue of Charted Accountants. Toronto.

Yolin, J.M., J. Merlin, G. Postel-Vinay and C. Scherer, 2003. Internet et entreprises, mirages et opportunités. Rapport de la mission conduite pour le Ministère de l'Économie, des Finances et de l'Industrie-France.

Environment

An evolutionary defense of emissions trading

Edwin Woerdman and Frans P. de Vries
University of Groningen, Faculty of Law, Department of Law and Economics, P.O. Box 716,
9700 AS Groningen, The Netherlands. e.woerdman@rug.nl.

Abstract

Based on static arguments, 'standard' environmental economics considers emissions trading to be more effective and efficient than other policy instruments. However, in one section of a much broader article on sustainable development policies, Rammel and Van den Bergh (2003) argue that the economic superiority of tradable permits is not evident from an evolutionary perspective when factors like diversity, risk and path dependence are taken into account. However, contrary to their conjecture, we conclude that tradable permits are also efficient from a long-term, evolutionary point of view. Path dependence and lock-in rather provide additional, dynamic arguments in favour of emissions trading.

JEL classification: B52, K32, L51, Q58

Keywords: emissions trading, institutional diversity, evolution, path dependence, lock-in

1. Introduction

There is a large diversity of environmental policy instruments that perform rather differently in terms of efficiency and effectiveness. Emissions trading is one of these instruments that is becoming increasingly popular as a regulatory tool, for instance in climate policy. Imposing an environmental standard usually implies relatively high abatement costs for some polluters and relatively low abatement costs for other polluters. When they are allowed to trade emissions both polluters can gain. The former gains if buying emissions from the latter is cheaper than reducing its own emissions. The latter gains if he receives a price for those emissions which is higher than what it costs to reduce them. This is not only efficient but also effective. Like in a system of communicating vessels, the former is then allowed to emit more than the standard prescribes, but the former must emit less. The result is that the environmental target is met at lower costs.

However, in one particular section of a much broader article on sustainable development policies, Rammel and Van den Bergh (2003: 126-127) argue that the economic superiority of emissions trading is not evident from an evolutionary perspective when factors like diversity, risk and path dependence are taken into account. They stress that this is currently most relevant for climate policy. Whether this claim is modest or not is a value judgement, but in any case it is challenging a large body of literature on market-based instruments. They basically contend that (what they call partial or short-term) economically inferior policies have the advantage of increasing the evolutionary potential (systemic or long-term efficiency). This would create a reservoir of adaptive responses to unlock potentially locked-in (technological) systems that emerge over time. Maintaining (institutional) diversity is regarded upon as a risk-minimising strategy. Moreover, they call the focus on efficiency 'short term and feeble' and stress the temporary nature of optimality. As a consequence, Rammel and Van den Berg cast evolutionary doubt on the long-term efficiency of emissions trading. In this chapter, on the contrary, we will provide an evolutionary defence of emissions trading. The interesting thing is that we come to the opposite conclusion based on some of the same concepts that Rammel and Van den Bergh (2003: 122) use in their analysis, namely '(...) *elementary issues like diversity, risk-minimising, path-dependency and lock-in (...)*'.

Our research setup is as follows. Because the aforementioned authors assert that long-term efficiency and risk-minimisation require diversity, also regarding institutions, we will analyse the evolutionary consequences of creating a minimum level of institutional diversity in the form of creating *permit* trading alongside *credit* trading. Both are alternative formats of emissions trading schemes (*e.g.* Nentjes, 1998; Tietenberg *et al.*, 1999; Stavins, 2003; Woerdman, 2005). Permit trading is also referred to as allowance trading or as cap-and-trade. Credit trading is sometimes also called performance standard rate trading. We will explain in the next section why credit trading, based on relative targets, is less efficient and less effective than permit trading, which is based on emission ceilings. Basically, credit trading is inferior because the environmental scarcity is not reflected in a price for each unit of emission and because the government runs the risk of failing to reach its absolute emission target.

Although we only focus on a small set of institutional arrangements, instead of comparing a larger set of instruments (including, say, standards and taxes), we are still able to provide a limited test of Rammel and Van den Bergh's supposition. The reason for this is that most of the environmental economics literature favours an elimination of institutional diversity by adopting permit trading and rejecting credit trading, in particular when polluters face absolute targets, while Rammel and Van den Bergh (2003: 128, 130) favour '(...) *a diversity of co-existing alternatives, at any level and in every subsystem of the economy*', where diversity also relates to '(...) *institutions, legislation and informal rules (...)*'. Introducing credit trading alongside permit trading, as two co-existing legal instruments used for different target groups, is an example of such a diversity.

To falsify Rammel and Van den Bergh's conjectures, we will first consider the long-term efficiency consequences of creating institutional diversity in the form of credit trading and permit trading for different polluters with and without absolute emission targets. Second, we will study the actual evolution of these emissions trading formats in the past. Both the future and the past are analysed from the perspective of diversity, risk-minimalisation, path dependence and lock-in. Our analysis allows us to elaborate three evolutionary counterarguments which, in fact, stress the economic superiority of emissions trading.

The article is structured as follows. In section 2, we will study the relative efficiency of permit trading and credit trading in a dynamic setting for the short-term and long-term. In section 3, we will analyse the risk of an institutional lock-in when (so-called short-term) sub-optimal trading schemes are introduced as part of a reservoir of adaptive responses. In section 4, we will take a look at some landmarks in the historical evolution of emissions trading, such as the established SO_2 emissions trading scheme in the United States (US) and the emerging CO_2 emissions trading market in the European Union (EU). In section 5 we draw conclusions.

2. Short-term and long-term efficiency of emissions trading

Rammel and Van den Bergh (2003: 128, 130) interpret 'institutional diversity' as different social and economic arrangements that maintain diversity not just passively, but also actively, for instance by means of policies. Moreover, they contend that *'(...) maintained diversity represents a reservoir of alternative options and increases the possibility that altered conditions can be successfully met (...)'* (Rammel and Van den Bergh, 2003: 127). Although their interesting article stays on a theoretical level for several pages, at some point (in section 3.1 of their article) they discuss the practical implications of their evolutionary approach for environmental policy instruments, after which they move up to the conceptual level again. In this chapter, we focus on this practical example as a first attempt to falsify their more general theory on evolutionary policies for sustainable development. With regard to these policy instruments, they write:

'Economists have for long argued that market-based incentives are more efficient than the traditional approach based on direct policy regulations or command-and-control. (...) It is certainly not evident that the same insight will be obtained when using theories and models that reflect a more complex, evolutionary systems approach (...). Various instruments like Pigouvian taxes, tradeable permits and depository refund systems are practicable applications of this [traditional] approach. [However], it is not focused at all on (...) uncertainty, adaptations and path-dependence. (...) [Therefore,] environmental policies aiming at market-based incentives and stable equilibrium ignore evolutionary characteristics (...). [These] bear the risk of (...) sacrificing long-term stability for short term "optimums" and gains of efficiency. This is currently most relevant for climate policy (...)' (Rammel and Van den Bergh, 2003: 126).

Given our assumption of absolute emission targets on the national level, suppose that we abandon the 'traditional' economic preference for permit trading and introduce a minimum level of institutional diversity in the form of permit trading and credit trading for different groups of polluters. Is the latter institutional design with two co-existing instruments more efficient in the long run than a scheme with just permit trading? The answer is no. If adaptations need to be made to the emission target in the long run as new information unfolds on the environmental damage function, permit trading is more efficient than credit trading in reaching the adjusted target, because only the former is based on absolute emission ceilings and attaches a price to each unit of emission. We will explain this both from a static and dynamic point of view.

Under permit trading a government allocates emission ceilings to private parties, allowing them to trade emissions with each other. However, under credit trading one private party can sell credits to another by reducing its own emissions below some environmental standard, such as an energy-efficiency requirement. The distinction between these two basic types of legal instruments is a crucial one, because permit trading is 'superior' according to neoclassical economic theory (Tietenberg *et al.*, 1999: 106).

Permit trading, which takes place under emission ceilings, is both efficient and effective (*e.g.* Woerdman, 2005). Newcomers and growing firms have to buy permits from other firms (or from a government reserve) to cover the additional pollution. Firms that decide to leave the industry may keep their permits, so that they can sell them. The system is efficient because every permit that is used to cover the emissions has a price: either the purchase price of new permits or the (opportunity costs that consist of the) revenues that the polluter foregoes by not selling the permits it uses. In addition, when the economy grows the demand for permits increases, but the supply remains constant as a result of the overall emission ceiling. The consequences are, first, that the emission target will be achieved and, second, that the emission (or 'environmental') scarcity is reflected in a higher price for pollution or energy intensive products. This creates incentives for an efficient restructuring of the economy in the direction of sustainable energy use.

Credit trading, however, does not incorporate emission ceilings for firms, making it less efficient and making its effectiveness uncertain. A firm can create credits voluntarily by reducing its emissions below the emission level required by the applicable voluntary or regulatory policies. Under credit trading, firms can increase absolute emissions so long as they comply with the relative standard. Suppose that the policy is a relative performance standard that requires a certain maximum amount of CO_2 emissions per unit of output or energy. A firm should then multiply this standard with its production volume to obtain its total emission figure. If this firm emits less CO_2 than this baseline or benchmark figure by initiating certain abatement activities, it can sell this abundant number of credits to another firm.

Although companies can achieve cost savings by selling credits, the emission scarcity under credit trading is not reflected in a price for each unit of emission. If the economy grows, the supply of credits increases as well, since firms do not have an emission ceiling but have to comply with the relative standard. This means that if a firm wants to expand production, or if a newcomer enters the industry, it has a right to new emissions. The polluter *de facto* receives its emission credits above and beyond the existing quantity. The consequence is that the social costs of the extra emissions are not fully reflected in the costs per unit of output and therefore not in the output price. This means that carbon-intensive products are priced too low, which will lead to an inefficient restructuring of production.

This has important dynamic implications for the conjectures expressed by Rammel and Van den Bergh. First, it means that permit trading stays efficient, also in the long term when adaptations need to be made to the absolute emission target. In the future, the emission ceiling may turn out to be inefficient when the costs and benefits of reducing environmental pollution are reconsidered. New information on the damages of environmental pollution could necessitate a strengthening (or weakening) of this target. Although one may debate about whether this is more mechanistic rather than evolutionary dynamics (*e.g.* Winder *et al.*, 2005), we emphasise that permit trading will be a more efficient instrument than credit trading to implement the adjusted target. The reason for this, as outlined above, is that only the former allocates absolute emission caps to individual polluters and reflects the environmental scarcity in a price for each unit of emission. Permit trading then ensures that the adjusted ceiling is effectively met at the lowest costs possible. Second, it means that maintaining diversity is not always a risk-minimising strategy. Under a credit trading system the government would have to adjust the underlying relative standard in an uncertain attempt to achieve the renewed absolute emission target. In the long term, this means that implementing credit trading alongside permit trading rather introduces a risk, namely the risk that the government fails to reach its emission target.

Importantly, the long-term efficiency of tradable permits also holds when the assumption is dropped that countries have absolute emission targets. With regard to the climate regime, for instance, one could imagine a future evolution in which some countries adopt relative targets. This could be a carbon-intensity target, as proposed by the US government in 2002, fixing greenhouse gas emissions per unit of GDP. Because credit trading would 'institutionally' fit such a relative target, one might be tempted to believe that implementing credit trading now, next to permit trading for other target groups, has long-term efficiency advantages when a carbon-intensity regime would emerge in the future. However, the opposite is true. Even if countries comply with the relative target, total emissions may still rise, which means that the environmental scarcity is 'blown up'. These countries *de facto* receive a right to this additional pollution, which means that the externality of those extra emissions will not be fully reflected in the costs per unit of output. Moreover, several studies confirm that creating credit trading for one target group together with permit trading for another is inefficient, both in the short and long term. An example is Fischer (2003) who found in a partial equilibrium model that under a hybrid permit and credit trading scheme, when transferring emission entitlements across both schemes is allowed, combined emissions are higher than under a permit trading scheme for all target groups.

3. The risk of an institutional lock-in of inefficient regulation

According to Rammel and Van den Bergh (2003: 126), it is 'certainly not evident' that market-based instruments like 'tradable permits' are more efficient than command-and-control regulation when factors like path dependence, lock-in and uncertainty are taken into account. Instead, we argue that evolutionary thinking based on path dependence rather provides an additional argument in favour of reducing institutional diversity to the single instrument of permit trading. The reason for this is that increasing diversity by including credit trading involves the risk that this sub-optimal instrument itself becomes locked-in via path dependence. Not just inefficient technologies, but also inefficient policies like credit trading might get stuck due to institutional rigidities (Woerdman, 2004a). The political decision to implement such a sub-optimal policy instrument now can result in an institutional lock-in from which it may be difficult to escape later on.

Path dependence generally refers to situations in which decision making processes (partly) depend on earlier choices and events (*e.g.* Arthur, 1994). This is more than just a recognition that 'history matters'. The path dependence approach also shows that a decision making process can exhibit self-reinforcing dynamics, so that an evolution over time to the most efficient alternative not necessarily occurs. An institutional lock-in then refers to the dominance of regulation in the presence of one or more alternative(s). Dominance means that the regulation is formally adopted and effectively implemented, whereas the alternative form of regulation is not. The policy arrangement that has become locked-in could be sub-optimal. In that case, the institutional lock-in refers to the dominance of sub-optimal regulation in the presence of a superior alternative.

The next question is why inefficient regulation might become locked-in once it is actively pursued in co-existence with other alternatives. Essential is the distinction between the setup costs of establishing a formal institution and the running costs of continuing it (Woerdman, 2004a). Setup costs can be subdivided into the sunk costs of the existing institutional arrangement and the switching costs of a new arrangement. The former are not relevant for the decision whether or not to continue and extend the existing arrangement because they were made in the past, that is, 'bygones are forever bygones'. However, switching costs are relevant in case of establishing a new arrangement, since these type of costs still have to be made. At least four factors can then be identified that may contribute to an institutional lock-in of credit trading (*e.g.* Woerdman, 2005).

First, credit trading benefits from the experience and learning effects of existing environmental regulation because the former can be built upon the latter. A firm can create credits by reducing its emissions below the emission level as required by the imposed policy measure. Extending current policy with credit trading ensures that learning advantages lower the average costs of running the system. Moreover, it is possible that policymakers expand the existing institutional arrangements with credit trading since they are unfamiliar or insufficiently acquainted with permit trading.

Second, credit trading builds upon the sunk costs of existing environmental regulation. These setup costs have already been incurred and thus play no role in the decision to continue an environmental policy without emission ceilings, whether or not modified to include credit trading. Although permit trading reduces running costs, it also involves relatively high setup costs as it implies a transition to a new institutional arrangement. Moral opposition against the idea of 'pollution rights', but also the resistance by vested interests contributes to these switching costs. The energy-intensive industry, for instance, would not want to switch to permit trading. When they expand their production, they receive free emission entitlements under a credit trading regime, whereas they would have to buy entitlements from other emitters under permit trading (Dijkstra, 1999).

Third, regulators will be more inclined to opt for credit trading if there is a dominant perception that the problem-solving capacity of existing environmental policy is more or less stable and manageable. In particular if we acknowledge that bounded-rational policymakers exhibit satisfying rather than optimising behaviour, one might expect that they will be less receptive to theoretically superior alternatives such as permit trading, especially because credit trading, albeit inefficient, also allows for cost reductions.

Fourth, credit trading can be said to benefit from network or coordination advantages by building upon extant policy. These advantages are primarily driven by increasing returns to scope, to use Chandler's (1990) term. If regulation is what the government produces, administrative costs can be seen as the associated production costs. The advantage for the government of building upon existing institutional arrangements is that differential administrative costs (the extra costs of adding another collection of units) decline as the institutional scope increases. This scope can be widened horizontally by expanding an existing policy instrument to cover extra target groups or vertically by expanding the instrument to add another institutional element to it, such as credit trading.

The conditions for an institutional break-out are basically the opposite of those set out above for an institutional lock-in. In general terms, the chances for permit trading ameliorate, for instance, as the information on this instrument improves, as the costs of switching to a permit trading system decline, and as the problem-solving capacity of existing environmental regulation deteriorates.

'From the perspective of path-dependence and lock-in, risk minimising emphasises an adaptive design of environmental policies, (...) by stimulating and fostering diversity', Rammel and Van den Bergh (2003: 130) write. We do not agree that this is always evolutionary efficient. Adapting relative performance standards to include credit trading, for instance, rather introduces the risk that governments do not reach their absolute emission targets. Moreover,

the 'perspective of path-dependence and lock-in' does not prescribe the use of an 'adaptive design', as they claim, but instead warns against the risk that an inefficient design in a 'diversity of co-existing alternatives' might become locked-in via path dependence.

4. Some landmarks in the historical evolution of emissions trading

Evolution is not just a theoretical artefact: evolution occurs for real. Therefore, as another answer to Rammel and Van den Bergh's (2003: 128) evolutionary doubt of the long-term efficiency of emissions trading and their subsequent plea for institutional diversity, we will demonstrate that permit trading is, in fact, the *outcome* of an evolutionary process. This not so much restricts but rather reinforces the economic superiority of emissions trading. This becomes clear when we examine why emissions trading was introduced and how this system evolved historically over the last decades, both in the US and in the EU, in a path-dependent process of adaptation and selection.

To qualify as evolutionary, a historical development must satisfy three conditions (Winder *et al.*, 2005: 353). The first is ontology: there must be a recognisable type or species capable of continued existence, like institutions. The second is diversity: there must be a mechanism for creating diversity spontaneously, like the adoption of diverse policies by more or less similar entities. The third is stress: there must be a process of selection by punishing failure. We will argue that all of these elements can be found in the history of emissions trading, either partly or completely, and that we have witnessed an evolution over the last century towards the use of tradable permits in environmental policy.

After the theoretical invention of emissions trading in the literature (Dales, 1968), the first emissions trading schemes implemented in practice can be found in the US. In the 1970s (say at $t = 0$, where t denotes time) no choice was made between a diversity of standards, credits and permits, but there has rather been an 'emergent evolution', to use the terminology of Matutinović (2001: 240), from standards (at $t = 0$) via credit trading (at $t = 1$) to permit trading (at $t = 2$). The Environmental Protection Agency (EPA) started to use credit trading in 1975 to control air pollution. In an evolutionary process of 'trial-and-error' (*e.g.* Sartorius, 2006), credit trading was introduced in the US as an adaptive devise to lift the inflexibility of the environmental standards, so that firms could reduce compliance costs. However, in spite of the cost savings that were reached, these early credit trading schemes not only had an uncertain environmental impact but also suffered from relatively high transaction costs, for instance because they required advance approval of every entitlement transfer (Tietenberg *et al.*, 1999). This partial failure posed an element of stress on this adaptive institutional design. To reduce uncertainty and to lower transaction costs, the US government then decided to select permit trading under the 1990 Clean Air Act Amendments (CAAA) to abate SO_2 emissions. This scheme proved to be highly successful, since the absolute emission targets were reached and transaction costs turned out to be relatively low.

Outside the US some experience was gained with tradable quota systems, such as tradable ammonia quota in the Netherlands. However, the definitive breakthrough of emissions trading outside the US occurred in the context of the 1997 Kyoto Protocol. Article 17 of the Kyoto Protocol, that entered into force early 2005, allows international emissions trading between 2008 and 2012. Moreover, the annex on emissions trading in the 2001 Marrakech Accords allows governments to authorise legal entities to transfer and/or acquire emissions under Article 17.

In 2003, when entry into force of the Kyoto Protocol was still uncertain, the EU had already approved a Directive that enables CO_2 permit trading for power generators, steelmakers as well as cement, paper and glass manufacturers to start in 2005. This permit trading scheme is now up and running. Also outside the EU, various countries, such as Norway, Japan and Canada, intend to build some kind of national tradable permit system, which could eventually be linked to the European scheme provided that they mutually recognise their transferable units. Permit trading has not only moved from theory to practice, but the instrument is clearly expanding around the globe, particularly in climate policy. In a recent overview, Stavins (2003) counts more permit trading than credit trading schemes. Tradable permits are more efficient than standards and, compared to credit trading, they are better able to minimise the risk that the government does not reach its emission target.

However, the evolution towards permit trading in the EU shows a somewhat different path than in the US. Basically, there was a similar development from standards via credit trading to permit trading, but there are (at least) two essential differences with the emergent evolution as witnessed in the US. First, the experiences with credit trading in Europe were not so much gathered in domestic schemes, but rather in the international context of Activities Implemented Jointly (AIJ) that later evolved into Joint Implementation (JI) for project-based credit trading with transition countries and the Clean Development Mechanism (CDM) for project-based credit trading with developing countries, where the CDM has more stringent rules on environmental integrity because of the absence of emission targets for developing countries. Although these projects lowered the costs to reduce emissions, they were criticised for their relatively high transaction costs and for the questionable additionality of the emission reductions. Second, a marked difference with the evolution in the US is that European policymakers could actually learn from the experiences gained in America, where credit trading schemes had largely evolved into permit trading systems. This lead some of them to propose to implement permit trading in Europe, although several, at least initially, opposed to the idea of allocating 'pollution rights' for ethical reasons. As these perceived switching costs to permit trading were steadily declining, also when it became clear that calculating the tradable emissions under credit trading is relatively complex, the internal pressure within the EU grew to implement permit trading (Woerdman, 2004b). The EU finally adopted a permit trading scheme in 2003.

This does not mean that there has been an overall 'evolution of the fitter' in environmental policy. As a result of path dependence, for instance due to learning effects and sunk costs, some credit trading schemes persist that have been built upon earlier performance standards. For example, in the US, credit trading is applied in the State of Connecticut to reduce NO_x emissions or in the State of Indiana to facilitate the transfer of emissions of volatile organic compounds. In the EU, credit trading is used as an adaptation of existing covenants on acidification policy in the Netherlands to cut back NO_x emissions. Time will tell whether these ineffective and inefficient systems will break-out from their locked-in position. This may happen, for instance, if the costs of switching to a cap-and-trade regime are lowered or if failure becomes obvious, thus posing stress on those sub-optimal systems.

According to Rammel and Van den Bergh (2003: 124), stimulating a diversity of environmental technologies enhances long-term efficiency since these technologies have to prove themselves through ex post competition. However, we emphasise that this is different from stimulating a diversity of institutions and legislation in the form of environmental policy instruments, because permit trading has already proved its merits as an efficient and risk-minimising institutional arrangement. Although a more detailed historical analysis of the emergence of emissions trading falls beyond the scope of this chapter, we do find that the general development of adaptation and selection in environmental policy shows an evolution towards efficiency in the form of permit trading, not just in the US, but also along a somewhat different path in Europe.

5. Conclusions

As one practical implication of their much broader theoretical framework, Rammel and Van den Bergh (2003) contend that the well-known static efficiency of emissions trading is not evident from an evolutionary perspective when factors like diversity, risk and path dependence are taken into account. They argue that optimality is temporary so that long-term efficiency and risk-minimisation require diversity, also regarding institutions and legislation. However, contrary to their conjecture, we come to the conclusion that tradable permits are also efficient from a long-term, evolutionary perspective. It appears that path dependence and lock-in rather provide additional, dynamic arguments in favour of emissions trading.

In this chapter, we have taken the use of credit trading alongside permit trading as a minimal version of the institutional diversity that Rammel and Van den Bergh desire. Credit trading is inefficient and its effectiveness is uncertain. Because it is based on relative standards, polluters *de facto* receive a right to new emissions when the economy grows. This means that the social costs of the extra emissions are not fully reflected in the output price. In case of an absolute emission target on the national level, credit trading also puts the government at risk of failing to reach this target. Permit trading, on the other hand, is based on emission ceilings, which is both efficient and effective. When the economy grows, the demand for emissions increases. The environmental scarcity will then be reflected in a higher price for energy intensive products and the emission target will still be reached. However, the question posed by Rammel and Van den Bergh is whether emissions trading can also be defended from an evolutionary perspective. Our answer is yes, based on three arguments.

First, if an absolute emission target has to be adapted in the long run as new information unfolds on the environmental damage function, permit trading stays a more efficient instrument than credit trading. The reason for this is that only the former is based on emission ceilings and reflects the environmental scarcity in a price for each unit of emission. This also means that maintaining diversity by implementing credit trading alongside permit trading rather introduces a risk, namely the risk that the government fails to reach its emission target.

Second, path dependence learns that increasing diversity by implementing credit trading involves the risk that this sub-optimal instrument itself becomes locked-in. Sunk costs, switching costs, learning effects and increasing returns to scope help to explain such an institutional lock-in, for instance when the energy-intensive industry lobbies against a transition to permit trading.

Third, we find that the historical development of adaptation and selection in environmental policy largely shows an emergent evolution towards efficiency in the form of permit trading, not just in the US, but also along a somewhat different path in the EU. Permit trading is, in fact, the outcome of an evolutionary process.

These three evolutionary observations lead us to conclude that the efficiency of emissions trading, based on an institutional design of cap-and-trade, is also evident from an evolutionary perspective when factors like diversity, risk and path dependence are taken into account. Such an evolutionary perspective does not undermine, but rather underlines the economic superiority of tradable emission permits. However, the emission target itself may still be inefficient due to imperfect information on the environmental damage function. As a consequence, policymakers cannot determine the optimal emission ceiling in practice. Given this basic uncertainty, we have shown that by taking account of evolutionary mechanisms, permit trading is superior in terms of efficiency compared to credit trading.

Acknowledgements

We want to thank Andries Nentjes as well as the participants at the Eighth International Conference of the International Society for Intercommunication of New Ideas (Wageningen University, The Netherlands) and the participants of the Second International Conference on Rational Choice and Social Institutions (University of Groningen, The Netherlands) for their useful remarks. We also appreciate the constructive comments by Jeroen van den Bergh. Any remaining errors are our own.

References

Arthur, W.B., 1994. Increasing Returns and Path Dependence in the Economy. University of Michigan Press, Ann Arbor.

Chandler, A., 1990. Scale and Scope: The Dynamics of Industrial Capitalism. Harvard University Press, Cambridge.

Dales, J.H., 1968. Pollution, Property and Prices: An Essay in Policy-Making and Economics. Toronto University Press, Toronto.

Dijkstra, B.R., 1999. The Political Economy of Environmental Policy: A Public Choice Approach to Market Instruments. Edward Elgar, Cheltenham.

Fischer, C., 2003. Combining Rate-based and Cap-and-Trade Emissions Policies. Climate Policy 3: 89-103.

Matutinović, I., 2001. The Aspects and the Role of Diversity in Socioeconomic Systems: An Evolutionary Perspective. Ecological Economics 39: 239-256.

Nentjes, A., 1998. Two Views of Emissions Trading. Change: Research and Policy Newsletter on Global Change from the Netherlands 44: 4-7.

Rammel, C. and J.C.J.M. Van den Bergh, 2003. Evolutionary Policies for Sustainable Development: Adaptive Flexibility and Risk Minimising. Ecological Economics 47: 121-133.

Sartorius, C., 2006. Second-order Sustainability - Conditions for the Development of Sustainable Innovations in a Dynamic Context. Ecological Economics 58: 268-286.

Stavins, R.N., 2003. Experience with Market-Based Environmental Policy Instruments. In: K.G. Mäler and J.R. Vincent (Eds.), Handbook of Environmental Economics, Volume 1. Elsevier, Amsterdam, pp. 355-435.

Tietenberg, T., M. Grubb, A. Michaelowa, B. Swift and Z.X. Zhang, 1999. International Rules for Greenhouse Gas Emissions Trading: Defining the Principles, Modalities, Rules and Guidelines for Verification, Reporting and Accountability, UNCTAD/GDS/GFSB/Misc.6. United Nations Conference on Trade and Development (UNCTAD), Geneva.

Winder, N., B.S. McIntosh and P. Jeffrey, 2005. The Origin, Diagnostic Attributes and Practical Application of Co-evolutionary Theory. Ecological Economics 54, 347-361.

Woerdman, E., 2005. Tradable Emission Rights. In: J.G. Backhaus (Ed.), Elgar Companion to Law and Economics. Edward Elgar, Cheltenham, pp. 364-380.

Woerdman, E., 2004a. The Institutional Economics of Market-Based Climate Policy. Elsevier, Amsterdam.

Woerdman, E., 2004b. Path-Dependent Climate Policy: The History and Future of Emissions Trading in Europe. European Environment 14: 261-275.

Projecting costs of emission reduction

Yoram Krozer
Cartesius Institute, Institute for Sustainable Innovations of the Netherlands Technical Universities, Druifstreek 72, 8911 LH Leeuwarden, The Netherlands. krozer@xs4all.nl

Abstract

This paper discusses how to estimate costs of stricter environmental regulations with limited empirical data. Cost data on 28 categories of abatement options, each category with 4 to 256 options, are used to assess accuracy and reliability of the cost estimates with empirical data for only two options. The costs of emission reduction functions are exponential. The exponential interpolations between the combinations with engineering characteristics that cause high and low unit costs are accurate, but the score for reliability is less good. Statistical theory explains the accuracy.

JEL classification: Q55

Keywords: environmental regulations, abatement, control cost

1. Introduction

Policymakers forecast costs of stricter regulations to avoid excessive burden of the regulations on specific groups and companies. In European environmental policy, the forecasting is even mandated to avoid high costs at emission sources, which is stated by the principle "As Low As Reasonably Achievable" (ALARA) due to implementation of the "Best Available Technologies" (BAT) at emission sources (IPPC Directive, 1996). A major problem that the policymakers encounter is that any stricter regulation aiming to achieve additional emission reduction requires the implementation of new, more effective technologies, or by use of available technologies from the past at emission sources that have not been regulated before. Hence, there are no empirical data about costs and effects of the implementation at emission sources. The question that is discussed in this paper is how the environmental policymakers can estimate costs of additional emission reduction in this context where little empirical information is available.

The problem of lack of information on the costs and effects of stricter regulations is usually tackled by involving experts and demonstrating technologies at a few emission sources, to establish the cost of reducing kilogram emission (unit costs) in an inventory of emission sources such as polluting companies in an industry branch, or sources in a company. Based on the unit costs of the source-specific abatement options, the average unit cost for all sources in the inventory is estimated. The selected technologies below the average cost are considered BAT and can be mandated for every emission source (Sørup, 2000). It is, however, a misconception that the BAT option is the most effective and low-cost in an inventory. Firstly, the experts' opinions are biased because they can use abundant data about technologies of the past but possess little data about the new ones. In addition, the only empirical data about the newly to be regulated sources stem from a few demonstration projects, whilst the costs and effects of a technology can differ among emission sources. Furthermore, the selected sources for the demonstrations need not to be representative for other situations. A subsidy for providing the environmental authority with information about the costs and effects, as has been proposed by Carraro and Sinicalco (1992), can reinforce the disputes because companies have an interest in exaggerating the costs and playing down the effects in terms of size of emission reduction, because it can impede stricter regulations, whereas the policymakers cannot verify the companies' data.

Ideally, the policymakers would use information about costs of additional emissions at every single emission source, but in reality they must make a decision about regulation of many emission sources in an inventory based on the information about a few source-specific studies and demonstrations. The problem of how to regulate many emission sources with the information only about a few cannot be solved without a theory on how to estimate costs of emission reduction functions. The question is how to construct the costs of emission reduction functions with little data, taking into consideration different emission sources and pollution control technologies. To answer the question we shall proceed as follows (Krozer, 2002). The empirical data to underpin the answer are presented in section 2. Then, we postulate a equation in section 3 to construct costs of emission reduction functions on the basis of only two abatement options: one with low cost and one with high cost. The equation is applied to calculate the cost functions and compare the results of calculations with empirical data. Section 4 provides conclusions.

2. The data on abatement options

An abatement option for a pollutant is a control technology applied at an emission source, or a group of similar sources. A cost of emission reduction function relates costs of several abatement options with emission reduction percentage in an inventory. For abating fluoride emission, for example, applications of absorption and filtering in the aluminium industry or alkaline flue gas cleaning in the glass fibre industry are abatement options. An illustrative example is the cost of reduction of fluoride emission to air in the Netherlands with eight abatement options, as shown in Figure 1 with basic data presented in Table 1. The unit costs in Euro per kilogram of fluoride emission reduction on the vertical axis are function of emission reduction as a percentage of the untreated emission in the inventory on the horizontal axis on the graph. The unit costs increase from about € 1.4 per kg fluoride emission at the bottom of the cost function to almost €700 per kg fluoride emission at the top. A maximum of 32% reduction of the uncontrolled emission can be attained. A higher emission reduction percentage is either technically not possible, or there are not enough

Table 1. Inventory of source-technology combinations for fluoride emission reduction, Slooff et al., 1989 (all major sources 2,539,000 kg).

nr	Branches	Emission sources	Untreated emission (kg/year)	Technology	Emission reduction kg/year	Residual emission kg/year	Reduction % at each source	Reduction percent at the sources	Total costs (Cr) in € per year	Unit costs (cr) €/kg
1	Household	Old bottles	56,000	Higher recycling old glass	18,000	38,000	32.1	0.07	24,885	1.4
2	Fine ceramics	Flue gas	35,000	Dry treatment and CaO	33,000	2,000	94.3	2.0	230,415	6.9
3	Brick	Flue gas	600,000	Dry treatment and CaO	570,000	30,000	95.0	24.4	4,068,295	8.3
4	Aluminium industry	Anode preparation	298,000	Absorption at alien earth processing	12,000	286,000	4.0	24.9	230,415	19.3
5	Glass fibre industry	Flue gas	30,000	Alkaline flue gas treatment	26,000	4,000	86.0	26.0	1,152,074	44.2
6	Aluminium industry	Evaporation in halls	286,000	Flue gas washing	120,000	166,000	42.0	30.7	9,216,590	77.0
7	Phosphate production	Phosphoric acid process	20,000	P-acid various measures	1,000	19,000	5.0	30.7	207,373	207.4
8	Iron and steel	Cindering	39,000	Electro-filter SO_2 washing	30,000	9,000	76.9	31.9	20,737,327	691.2
	Netherlands	Used data	1,364,000		810,000	554,000	59.4		36,403,737	45.2 average

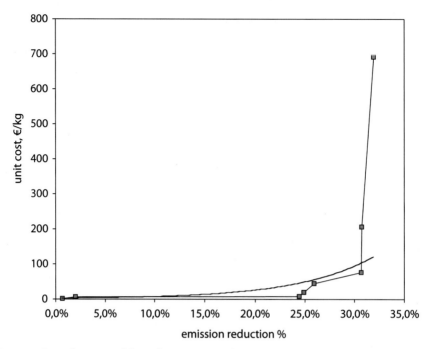

Figure 1. Costs function of fluoride emission reduction to air in the Netherlands.

data. An emission reduction of up to 25% can be achieved at unit costs below €20 per kg fluoride. A higher percentage creates much higher units costs.

The estimates based on two sets of empirical data with interpolation by an exponent k, as shown in the figure by a 'streamlined' cost function, are compared with the costs of emission reduction function that are constructed by experts with solely empirical data. The empirical costs of emission reduction functions to be used in the next section cover 28 emission-specific inventories. The number of abatement options varies from 4 to 256 per inventory. The data sets are 'best guess', which is a mix of calculations and measurements collected in the eighties and the nineties of the last century, based on information of technology suppliers and engineers, then checked and adapted by experts from industry and authorities. The databases have been used for the environmental policies of The Netherlands, the EU, and by the World Bank. Some relevant basic data about the inventories are shown in Table 2.

The data cover 19 branch-wise inventories in which a branch or a large company is considered an emission source. The branch-wise inventories address:
• Benzene, Cadmium, Phenol, Fluoride, Fine Dust, Copper, Polycyclic Aromatic Hydrocarbons (PAH), Propylene oxide, Styrene, Toluene, Zinc, based on the Basis- and Criteria Documents of the National Institute for Public Health and Environment (RIVM) (Van Apeldoorn, 1986; Van Koten-Vermeulen *et al.*, 1986; Van der Meulen,

Table 2. Some data of inventories and the exponents by interpolation between the highest and the lowest cost options.

Name inventory	n	Scale of emission reduction		Unit costs		Exponent (*)
		Smallest source	Largest source	cr_1	cr_n	k
Sector-wise inventories						
Benzene	13	3,000	144,000	0.86	987	0.59
Cadmium	4	40	400	150	57,600	1.98
CO_2	79	4,724,496	1,264,917,176	0.0003	1,4	0.10
Copper	4	3,300	27,200	76	1,260	0.94
Fine dust	13	42,000	3,114,000	0.52	9,0	0.24
Fluoride	8	1,000	570,000	1.4	690	0.89
Phosphate	10	200,000	32,160,000	1.9	68	0.40
Metals air	13	2,400	1,138,000	82	1,198	0.22
Metals water	14	750	570,000	11	614	0.27
NH_3	12	500,000	30,095,167	1.7	14	0.19
NOx	99	23,333	125,970,000	0.07	23	0.06
PAH's	6	1,000	256,000	84	822	0.46
Phenol	7	2,000	12,000	0.92	53	0.68
Propylene	7	8,600	21,500	0.87	27	0.57
SO_2	35	60,000	613,850,000	0.22	3	0.08
Styrene	15	6,000	567,000	0.98	35	0.26
Toluene	20	2,000	796,860	0.03	461	0.51
VOC	47	200,000	18,000,000	0.3	7	0.07
Zinc	6	650	17,100	46	3,383	0.86
Company-wise inventories						
Cl-metals	23	25	26,000	1.7	656	0.27
NOx chemical	253	12	4,368,320	0.02	1,005	0.04
NOx electric power	97	20,292	7,030,171	0.14	99	0.07
NOx basic metal	70	3	1,373,445	0.10	16,109	0.17
NOx refineries	39	90	4,211,100	0.43	878	0.19
SO_2 chemical	53	150	4,099,000	0.59	2,166	0.15
SO_2 electric power	17	568,958	28,224,342	0.35	5	0.15
SO_2 basic metal	43	881	4,199,630	1.2	188	0.12
SO_2 refineries	17	39,600	18,726,300	1.2	31	0.19

1987; Slooff, 1987a, b; Slooff *et al.*, 1987, 1989a, b; Slooff and Blokzijl, 1987; Ros and Slooff, 1988; Cleven *et al.*, 1993);
- CO_2 reduction, based on ICARUS-model of Ecofys (Blok *et al.*, 1990);
- NOx, SO_2, Volatile Organic Compounds (VOC), Ammonia (NH_3), Heavy Metals and Phosphate, based on Model on Sustainable Environmental Strategies (Moses) of the Institute for Applied Environmental Economics (TME) (Jantzen, 1992).

In addition, there are 9 company-specific inventories in which every single emission source in a company is included separately (a few extreme values in a few inventories are extracted to avoid erroneous data). The company-specific inventories cover SO_2 emissions and NO_x emissions in the Netherlands chemical industry, electric power, basic metal and refineries (Heijnes *et al.*, 1997), as well as VOC emissions in the metal products industry (Heslinga, 1995).

Far-reaching emission reduction can be achieved, generally up to 70%. In 7 inventories more than 90% of untreated emission can be reduced. So the issue in environmental policymaking is not primarily to invoke development and implementation of technologies that can reduce emission even further, but it is to keep unit costs low. In most cases the unit costs increase steeply. In 13 inventories the highest unit costs are more than 100 times higher than the lowest unit costs. The increase is more than 50,000 times for NO_x emission reduction in the chemical industry and even 161,000 times for NO_x reduction in the basic metal. The spread between the highest and the lowest unit costs is less in the inventories with a limited number of abatement options than in the inventories with many options, but no significant correlation (R < 0.9) between the spread and the number of abatement options is found, for example the spread is 384 times for cadmium emission with only 4 options. Nor is there a significant correlation between the number of options and the emission reduction percentage. For example 85% reduction of PAH emission can be attained by only 6 options and 77% reduction of NOx in basic metal by 73 options. The average costs are usually many times higher, or lower than the lowest respectively the highest unit costs and unrelated with the scale of the source, *e.g.* the average unit cost in the fluoride inventory is €45 per kg versus €8 per kg at largest emission source (570,000 kg) and €77 per kg at the second largest source (120,000 kg). The data suggest that the costs function of emission reduction is exponentially increasing and that the spread of the highest and lowest unit costs is usually so large that presenting only the average costs obscures the spread of the unit costs in inventories.

3. A method for estimating emission control costs

In neoclassic theory the cost of output function can be derived if the production function, which relates inputs to outputs and the prices of inputs, are known. The conventional neoclassical assumption is that all inputs are perfectly divisible at any level of output. The result of the exercise is a marginal and average cost of output function that is continuous and increasing. In analogy, emission reduction can be considered the lowest cost output of the perfectly divisible inputs. Such a neoclassical approach may be elegant but, due to lack of information, it is useless when it comes to constructing empirical pollution control cost functions. In practice, the number of abatement options is discrete, which implies indivisibility of essential inputs as illustrated by the stepwise increasing empirical cost function in Figure 1. The usual approach is to make an inventory of the abatement options, then to rank the abatement options in ascending order of cost per unit emission reduction, which means to start with the lowest unit costs and end with the highest unit costs. This approach is an adaptation of cost-engineering functions that relate manufacturing technologies with products (Lassman, 1958; Gold, 1975; Porter, 1996). The information for such costs of emission reduction functions is often only partially available at the moment when it is needed to assess the economic feasibility of more stringent emission requirements. So what can be done if the costs of only two abatement options are known in an inventory with many options? To answer this question it is postulated that the costs of emission reduction functions can be defined by the equation:

$$cr_{i+m} = cr_i * e^{m*k} \qquad \text{(Eq. 1)}$$

where:

cr_i and cr_{i+m} are the unit costs of abatement option i respectively i+m,
e is the Euler number
kcr the exponent defining the steepness of the cost curve.

The cost exponent, k, that determines the relation between the options, hence the steepness of a cost function, can be calculated when all abatement options can be ranked in an ascending order of their unit costs and information is available on the unit costs of the option i and the option i+m. Equation 1 postulates a logarithmic cost relation between successive abatement options. If indeed such a relation exists, costs of emission reduction functions can be derived by exponential interpolation between the combinations with the high and the low unit cost. From Equation 1 follows:

$$cr_{i+m} / cr_i = e^{m*k} \qquad \text{(Eq. 2)}$$

$$\ln (cr_{i+m} / cr_i) = m*k \qquad \text{(Eq. 3)}$$

$$k = (\ln (cr_{i+m} / cr_i))/m \qquad \text{(Eq. 4)}$$

Thus, for the lowest cost abatement option 1 and highest cost abatement option m the cost exponent is:

$$k = (\ln (cr_n / cr_1)) / (n - 1) \text{ for the cost exponent} \qquad \text{(Eq. 5)}$$

Three scenarios for streamlined cost functions by interpolation of the Equation 4 will be presented: (1) only the cost data of the highest and lowest unit costs are known, (2) only the cost data of two at random combinations are known, (3) all cost data are known.

For illustration, the calculations for the fluoride emission reduction are shown below in Table 3.

In Table 3, columns 1 to 4 contain the empirical data. Suppose we only know the ranking and the empirical costs on the lowest cost abatement option (nr. 1) and the highest cost option (nr. 8). The cost exponent is $k1 = \ln (cr_8/cr_1)/(8-1) = \ln (691/1,4)/7 = 0.89$. As a next step the cost of the option 2 to 7 can be calculated: $cr_2 = cr_1 * e^k = 1.42 * 2.718^{0.89} = 73.2$, and so on. The costs calculated in this way are presented in column 5 and 6. Following this, one needs empirical information on total unabated emission and emission reduction per option to relate the cost of the successive abatement options with the emission reduction percentage, which is given in column 2 (emission reduction by all abatement options is 810,000 tonne). The streamlined cost function, calculated on basis of the lowest and highest cost option and the emission reduction percentage per combination, is shown in Figure 1.

How well do the streamlined cost functions, based on incomplete cost information, predict the empirical cost? Rank correlation of calculated costs (in columns 5, 7, and 9) with the

Table 3. Empirical and constructed fluoride data about abatement options, with accuracy (R) and reliability (C).

Rank	Empirical data			Highest-lowest unit cost		Ad random n 3 and 4		All data known	
	Er (total emission)	Cr (total cost)	cr (Cr/Er)	cr_1 k1=0.89	Cr_1/Cr	cr_2 k2=0.86	Cr_2/Cr	cr_3 k3=0.90	Cr_3/Cr
1	1,8000	19,800	1.4	1.4	100	1.4	104	1.4	100
2	33,000	230,415	6.9	3.2	48	3.2	49	3.7	50
3	570,000	4,608,295	8.3	8.3	101	8.3	100	8.3	105
4	12,000	230,415	19.4	19.8	103	19.4	100	21	108
5	26,000	1,152,074	44	48.3	109	45.6	103	50	113
6	120,000	9,216,590	77	117	152	108.3	141	118	159
7	1,000	207,373	207	284	137	257	124	297	143
8	30,000	20,737,327	691	691	100	611	88	721	104
Tot.	810,000	36,407,373		$R_{k1}=$ 0.99	$C_{k1}=$ 114	$R_{k2}=$ 0.99	$C_{k2}=$ 104	$R_{k3}=$ 0.99	$C_{k3}=$ 118

empirical costs (in column 3) should have a value R > 0.9, which is our criterion for accuracy. Next to that we define a criterion for reliability: it requires that the streamlined total costs calculated over all combinations deviate less than 30% from the empirical total costs (in column 6, 8, and 10). In case of the calculation with the data about the highest and lowest unit costs for fluoride emission that provides the cost exponent k1, the correlation is R_{k1} = 0.99, which means that the streamlined cost function accurately indicates the costs of emission reduction function. The total calculated costs C_{k1} are 14 percent above empirical costs, which means that the outcome is reliable. In this example reliability and accuracy are fine, but would the criteria also be met if the abatement options would have been available at random?

With a randomizer we have selected two abatement options with the cost rank number 3 (cr = 8.3) and number 4 (cr = 19.4). Hence k2 is calculated: $k2 = \ln (cr_{i+m}/cr_i)/(m-1)$, so numerically $k2=(19.3/8.3)/(4-3)=0.86$. Based on the k2 other costs can be calculated: $cr_5=cr_4*2.718^{0,86}$ and $cr_2 = cr_3\, 2.718^{-0,86}$, and so on. The result is shown in columns 7 and 8. Reliability is equal and accuracy is even better.

The streamlined cost using the information on all abatement options have also been calculated. It can be considered as a benchmark for the others two scenarios. The calculation is for k3 = $[\ln (cr_{i+1}/cr_1)+\ln (cr_{i+2}/cr_{i+1})...\ln (cr_n/cr_{n-1})]/(n-1)$. For example, if we have only information about cost rank number 1, 2 and 3, the calculation is: n=3, it is $cr_1=1.4$, $cr_2=6.9$, $cr_3 = 8.3$, so $k1 = [\ln (6.9/1.4)+\ln (8.3/6.9)]/2=0,90$ that is $cr_4 = cr_3*2.718^{0,90}$. The results show that reliability and accuracy are very similar in the other two cost calculations.

The question researched in this paper is whether the fit obtained in the scenarios with restrictions on available cost information is a lucky coincidence, or whether it is more general. Therefore the three scenarios have been calculated for all 19 branch-wise inventories and for the 9 company-wise inventories. The accuracy and reliability of the streamlined cost functions are assessed. The streamlined cost functions are regarded accurate for the significant correlation (R > 0.9) between the empirical unit costs and the streamlined ones. The streamlined cost functions are regarded reliable if the total costs deviate less than 30% from the empirical total cost ($130\% > Cr_{emp} / Cr_{kcr} > 70\%$). The results of the estimates are summarised in Table 4.

The streamlined cost functions are generally accurately estimated with the exponents. Almost all cost functions are accurately estimated by using the exponent derived from the highest and lowest costs abatement options (96% of all cost functions). All but one sector-wise cost functions and all company-wise cost functions are accurately estimated. The results are somewhat less positive with the exponent derived from two randomly selected abatement options (86% of all cost functions) and with the exponent derived from all abatement options (89% of all cost functions). The number of reliable estimates is lower. Nevertheless, most cost functions are reliably estimated with the exponent derived from the

Table 4. Accuracy and reliability of streamlined cost functions for the 19 sector-wise (S) and 9 company-specific inventories (C).

	Accuracy: correlation between estimates and empirical unit costs R > 0.9	Reliability: deviation from estimated total inventory costs below 30%
k1 highest-lowest unit cost	Total 27 of 28: 18 S; 9 C	Total 21 of 28: 16 S; 5 C
k2 two at random	Total 24 of 28: 17 S; 7 C	Total 14 of 28: 10 S; 4 C
k3 all data known	Total 25 of 28: 18 S; 7 C	Total 25 of 28: 18 S; 7 C

highest and lowest costs options (75% of all cost functions). The use of at random data often does not provide reliable results (50% are reliable). Contrary to that, most cost functions are reliably estimated with the exponent derived from all data about abatement options (89% of all cost functions).

Linear interpolations and exponential interpolations between the smallest and the largest scale are usually inaccurate and unreliable even if all abatement options are used for the calculations. The results confirm the postulate that the streamlined cost functions can be constructed by logarithmic interpolation between the high-cost and the low-cost sources.

Why is the postulate that the cost of emission reduction function is increasing exponentially so successful in predicting empirical costs? The conventional economist explanation of the exponentially increasing cost functions is economy of scale (Rosseger, 1980), which argues that production costs increase exponentially as a function of decreasing scale of output. In analogy it means increasing costs to reduce an additional unit of emission as a function of the scale of emission sources (Remer *et al.*, 1994). This position, however, does not hold for the inventories that we have studied because escalating unit cost based on scale of emission reduction does not provide sufficiently accurate and reliable results. The cost escalation does not explain the cost increase between the highest and lowest cost abatement options, which is not necessarily the smallest emission source respectively the largest emission source. On contrary, the correlation between the scale of emission sources and the costs is generally low. Therefore a different, non-conventional, explanation of the issue is used.

The results can be explained with the statistical theory that is used for sampling of product quality. The question is: what is the probability of deficiency from a quality standard in the inventory based on the deficiency in a sample. The answer is provided by the Poisson distribution, which shows the probability of deficiency with a random variable (x), which is the number of samples, and a positive number (m), which is the average number of the deficiencies in the sample. The probability is formally: $P_{(x)} = e^{-m} m^x / x!$

For a single variable x, the probability is accounted consecutively. The probability of deficiency in the inventory is an exponential function of the average number of deficiencies in a sample (Mood and Graybill, 1963): $P_{(x)} = e^{-m}$.

The abatement options can be considered as a sample of many possible combinations in an inventory. The probability of finding additional options decreases exponentially as a function of emission reduction percentage. So, more efforts are needed to find a new option, which implies exponentially increasing unit costs. The streamlined cost reflects the probability to find options for the targeted percentage emission reduction. The cost exponent of the Euler number k represents the difficulty in finding a new option to attain the target: larger k means lower probability to find the required abatement option.

4. Conclusion

The question of how to estimate the costs of stricter environmental regulations aiming at additional emission reduction has been examined. Policymakers rely on the estimates of average cost of emission reduction in an inventory based on experts' opinions about available technologies from the past and little empirical data derived from demonstrations of new technologies at a few emission sources. In our view it is an unreliable method because it is biased in favour of the technologies from the past. In addition, the empirical costs data indicate that average costs obscure the spread of the costs that, as we have shown, increase exponentially as a function of emission reduction.

We have shown that even in those cases where little information on control cost is available, cost functions can be constructed with sufficient accuracy in 86 to 96 percent of cases and reliability in 50 to 89 percent of cases. For the construction of the streamlined cost functions the following data are needed: (1) the data on a high-cost and a low-cost abatement option based on two demonstration projects of a new technology, (2) total technically viable emission reduction in the inventory and (3) number of abatement options with the available technology, which are usually known by experts. This information is sufficient to derive cost exponent k as in Equation 5 and consecutive calculation can be made, starting from the lowest unit cost combination as in Equation 1. The streamlined cost functions are accurately estimated (R > 0.9) for 27 out of 28 inventories, although the estimates of the total costs are less reliable. The accuracy of the estimate is explained by the statistical theory. The streamlined cost functions indicate the probability to find an additional technology for the demanded emission reduction: the stricter the demand, the more difficult and costly to find a new, suitable technology.

Acknowledgements

I am grateful to prof. dr. A. Nentjes of the University of Groningen for co-operation and to unknown referees for comments.

References

Blok, K., E. Worrell, R.A.W. Albers and R.F.A. Cuelenaere, 1990. Data on energy conservation techniques for the Netherlands (en het ICARUS 2 model op diskette). Vakgroep Wetenschap en Samenleving, Universiteit Utrecht.

Carrao C. and D. Sinicalco, 1992. Environmental Innovation Policy and International Competition. Environmental and Resource Economics 2: 193-200.

Cleven, R.F.M.J., J.A. Janus, J.A. Annema and W. Slooff, 1993. Integrated Criteria Document Zinc. Report No. 710401028, Bilthoven.

Gold, B., 1975. Technology, Productivity and Economic Analysis. In: B. Gold (Ed.), Technological Change: Economics, Management and Environment, Pergamon International Library, Pergamon Press, Oxford, pp.1-42.

Heslinga, D.C., 1995. Reinigen en ontvetten met gehalogeneerde oplosmiddelen en waterige systemen - een vergelijkende studie. KWS 2000 rapporten nr. O10, Apeldoorn.

Heijnes, H.A.M., H.J. Jantzen, C.A.J.C. Sedee, F. Schelleman, K. van den Berg, A.W. Dilweg, F. van Woerden, J. Okkema and A. Nentjes, 1997. Milieu-emissies: kiezen voor winst!, Marktwerking in het milieubeleid: de potentiële kostenvoordelen van een systeem van verhandelbare emissierechten. Interprovinciaal Overleg (IPO), Den Haag.

IPPC Directive, 1996. European Council Directive 96/61/EC concerning integrated Pollution Prevention and Control, Brussels.

Jantzen, J., 1992. Model on Sustainable Environmental Strategies (Moses). Institute for Applied Environmental Economics, The Hague.

Krozer Y., 2002. Milieu en Innovatie. Rijksuniversiteit Groningen, dissertation.

Lassman, G., 1958. Die Produktionsfunktion und ihre Bedeutung für die betriebswirtschaftliche Kostentheorie. Westdeutscher Verlag, Köln/Opladen.

Mood, A.M. and F.A. Graybill, 1963. Introduction to the Theory of Statistics. MacGraw-Hill New York.

Porter, M.E., 1996. Concurrentievoordeel. Uitgeverij Contact, Amsterdam/Antwerpen.

Remer, D.S., B.L.Low, G.T. Heaps-Nelson, 1994. Air Pollution Control: Estimate the Cost of Scaleup. Chemical Engineering, November, EE10-EE16.

Ros, J.P.M. and W. Slooff, 1988. Integrated Criteria Document Cadmium. RIVM, Report No. 75847600, Bilthoven.

Rosseger, G., 1980. The Economics of Production and Innovation. Pergamon Press, Oxford.

Slooff, W., 1987a. Basisdocument benzeen. RIVM rapportnr. 758476001, Bilthoven.

Slooff, W. (red.), 1987b. Ontwerp basisdocument propyleenoxide. RIVM, rapportnr. 758473001, Bilthoven.

Slooff, W. and P.J. Blokzijl (red.), 1987. Ontwerp basisdocument tolueen. RIVM, rapportnr. 758473005, Bilthoven.

Slooff, W., R.F.M.J. Cleven, J.A. Janus and J.P.M. Ros, 1987. Ontwerp basisdocument koper. RIVM, rapportnr. 758474003, Bilthoven.

Slooff, W., H.C. Eerens, J.A. Janus and J.P.M. Ros, 1989a. Integrated Criteria Document Fluorides. RIVM, Report No. 758474010 (a), Bilthoven.

Slooff, W., J.A. Janus, A.J.C.M. Matthijsen, G.K. Montizaan and J.P.M. Ros (eds), 1989b. Integrated Criteria Document PAHs. RIVM, Report No. 758474011 (b), Bilthoven.

Sørup, P., 2000. Technology, Innovation and environment; Integrated Pollution Prevention and Control. The European IPPC Bureau at Work, paper at Euro Environment, Alborg.

Van Apeldoorn, M.E., C.A. van der Heijden and F.X.R. van Leeuwen, 1986. Criteriadocument styrene. RIVM, rapportnr. 738513003, Bilthoven.

Van der Meulen, A., P.J. Rombout and C.J. Prins, 1987. Criteriadocument Fijn Stof. RIVM, rapportnr. 738513006, Bilthoven.

Van Koten-Vermeulen, J.E.M., C.A. van der Heijden and F.X.R. van Leeuwen, 1986. Criteriadocument Fenol. RIVM, rapportnr. 738513002, Bilthoven.

Environmental issues in APEC: the case of the Latin American economies

Antonina Ivanova, Manuel Angeles and Antonio Martinez
Universidad Autónoma de Baja California Sur, Departamento de Economía, 23000 La Paz,
B.C.S., México. aivanova@uabcs.mx

Abstract

Beyond working to expand market access, APEC (Asia Pacific Economic Cooperation Mechanism) countries must cooperate to create conditions which provide incentives for sustainable resource and ecosystem use. The central argument of this paper is that regional economic integration must be complemented by the creation of regional frameworks for environmental management. In this way, trade and environmental policies can mutually reinforce each other. The crucial issue is how deep and broad will be the integration of trade and environmental concerns. This chapter analyses the policies adopted by APEC regarding the trade-environment interface, stressing on the three Latin American members, Mexico, Chile and Peru, and suggests some guiding principles and strategies.

JEL Classification: F15, F18

Key words: trade, integration, environment, APEC, Latin America

1. Introduction

The Asia Pacific Economic Cooperation Mechanism (APEC)[1] is a unique inter-governmental process. The composition of APEC's membership is seen as a novel arrangement as it has brought together developing, newly industrialising, and advanced industrial economies into a process of regional consultation and cooperation. As a process of cooperation and as a forum for consultations APEC definitely has undergone a significant evolution since the first historic meeting in Canberra, Australia, 1989.

The commitment of the APEC Community to promote a sustainable development is expressed in the Leaders' Declaration Bogor, Indonesia, 1994, p.2: *"We set our vision for the community of Asia-Pacific economies based on recognition of the growing interdependence of our*

---

[1] APEC includes 21 members, which are ASEAN countries (Brunei, Indonesia, Malaysia, the Philippines, Singapore, Thailand and Vietnam), the United States, Canada, Australia, New Zealand, Republic of Korea, Japan, People's Republic of China, Hong Kong, Republic of China (Taipei), Russia, Papua New Guinea, Mexico, Peru and Chile. APEC members represent about 40% of the world's population, about 50% of world total GDP and about 40% of world total trade (the intra-regional trade being about 30%.). Its intra-regional trade in monetary terms is larger than that of the EU's intra-regional trade.

economically diverse region, which comprises developed, newly industrialising and developing economies. The approach will be coherent and comprehensive, embracing the three pillars of sustainable growth, equitable development and national stability."

One of the purposes of this chapter is to show that the institutional frame of APEC for a sustainable free trade agenda is behind the advances in economic cooperation, even though compatibility between free trade and environment protection is recognised in the organisation. From the point of view of economics to make compatible economic efficiency with environmental care it is necessary that all member economies internalise the environmental externalities fulfilling at least three requirements: (1) Efficiency of the market to rationalise use of natural resources by changes in supply and demand of final goods as a result of corresponding changes of costs and prices (Coase, 1960); (2) Sufficiently low transaction costs of internalisation to have net social profit (Coase, 1960); (3) Global agreement on the world sustainable development agenda to internalise, especially agreement between the main large economies. It seems obvious that the APEC agenda to internalise is very dependant on the world agenda. It is important to surpass a situation similar to that described in the "Tragedy of Commons" (Hardin, 1968), but now the prairie where the peasants grass their cattle is substituted by the international trade system where exporters and importers make transactions, namely "The Global Commons". In this situation, for example a strong economy like the US would not accept to impose certain ecological taxes that affect exportable goods if the EU does not do it and vice versa, because nobody wants to affect negatively the competitiveness of the national firms.

As a consequence of the global commons an economy could gain international competitiveness by imposing relatively lax environmental policies on the production of a set of goods, engaging in 'ecological-dumping', or 'eco-dumping', a policy which does not internalise all environmental externalities. (Rauscher, 1994). In this regard, to avoid a *"tragedy of global commons"*, there has been a resurgence of calls for a 'harmonisation of environmental standards' and 'fair trade' (Xu, 1998).

On the other hand, besides the primordial moral and aesthetic reasons to "green" development and international trade, there are economic advantages of a global and APEC agreement on internalisation. By this means a homogeneous system of national regulations concerning trade and environment could be possible. This in turn could favour a diminishing of the transaction costs currently paid by exporters and importers to cope with a heterogeneous system of regulations.

Despite some first steps to "green" APEC, free trade diplomacy has to date taken little consideration of the environment. And if in the past years priority was given to the trade liberalisation and facilitation goals of APEC, it is time to reinforce the goals of sustainability and environmental protection. This chapter will address these basic questions by examining the process and progress in the area of APEC's environmental cooperation, and suggest some guiding principles and innovative strategies. Special attention is given to the Latin American economies.

2. Trade liberalisation, economic integration and the environment

The relationship between trade liberalisation, economic growth and the environment in Asia-Pacific has not yet been charted. Conceptual frameworks and evidence from other regions suggest first, that trade openness has both positive and negative impacts on the environment; and second, that economic integration constrains national environmental policymaking. When regions are highly integrated economically, they must develop common frameworks to govern the trade-environment interface.

According to Ivanova (1998: 30) the positive impacts of the openness to trade and foreign investment can include: transfer of more efficient, cleaner production technologies and consumer goods via foreign direct investment and imports; norm-building that occurs through cross-border exchange of goods, services, capital and ideas; transmission of higher environmental standards via import requirements by "large market" countries. If the goal of good environmental management is not simply ecosystem and resource conservation but sustainable human development, then the benefits of growth-inducing trade openness would also include rises in per capita income and consumption (Zarsky, 1999).

On the negative side, trade openness subjects national economies to rising market demand and the pressures of international market prices, which rarely include any, let alone full, calculation of environmental damage. With environmental degradation simply outside the market equation, market signals do not give information about the true costs of production (Grossman and Krueger, 1992). As a result, global production and consumption patterns could be grossly inefficient, in both narrowly economic and ecological terms.

Moreover, trade openness subjects national policymaking to competitive pressures. A country which attempts to internalise its own environmental costs will be priced out of markets. In this way, trade openness can be a transmission belt not for high and rising but for low and immovable environmental standards. For example, the U.S. will not enact a tax on the carbon content of energy until the EC does - and vice versa. Indeed, the failure of studies to find any significant impact of environmental standards on competitiveness is most likely due to the fact that market pressures influence heavily domestic standards. Experience and empirical data increasingly show that the costs of environment-blind economic growth are likely to be higher than development paths that build in environmental protection (Zarsky, 1999: 35).

The point is that without explicit environmental disciplines and constraints, trade and investment liberalisation will not promote sustainable use of resources and ecosystems. A host of rules and disciplines has been erected to frame the architecture of the world's trading system (Wee and Heyzer, 1995).

Some analysts consider environmental degradation to be the "cost of development" and suggest that "grow now, pay later" is the only way to overcome poverty and achieve industrialisation. Attention to environmental concerns, they posit, will come at the cost of GNP growth, which will itself generate the resources for future clean up and restoration.[2]

The way to calculate potential trade-offs between environment and development is not the absolute, additional cost of environmental investment but the net cost, that is, the additional cost minus the benefit (Lucas *et al.*, 1992).

The rapid industrialisation of the Asia-Pacific region has produced an environmental situation that can only be described as a situation bordering on crisis. High rates of environmental degradation are also evident throughout Southeast and Northeast Asia, as well as Mexico, Chile and Peru.

As Ban (2000: 281) notes, over the last three decades, APEC economies have been the major source of world pollution. In fact, the world's top three emitters of greenhouse gases are in the region. Carbon dioxide emissions from the region are expected to rise 1.7 to 3.2 times in the next few decades, from the current 25 per cent of the world total today to 36 percent by 2025.

3. Latin American economies in APEC

Latin America has a very rich base of natural resources. With abundant minerals, from Mexico's silver to Chile's copper; it has plentiful oil deposits (second largest reserves after the Middle East), has the largest forested surface of any continent, and the greatest proportion of arable land per person outside of North America, including some very good quality soils. Both the Pacific Coast and the South Atlantic are very rich in seafood.

Yet Latin America also has some of the most serious environmental problems in the world: air pollution in several Latin American cities is the worst anywhere; rivers flowing through industrial centres are tremendously contaminated by industrial wastes; the rate of deforestation is alarming; soil erosion is severely degrading some of the best agricultural land of the world.

---

[2] According to the 'Environmental Kuznetz Curve' hypothesis (EKC), countries develop according to a two-stage development path. Due to scale effects and the composition effects economic growth is associated with higher levels of environmental pollution in the first stage of development. As services become more important and the overall population becomes increasingly aware of the risks associated with pollution, the second stage of development is characterised by decreasing emissions levels (Kuznetz, 1963).

Throughout Latin America, environmental problems reflect the clash between the use of nature as a private good with the concept of nature as a public good providing certain functions without which human life is not possible.

Nowhere is the clash between these two views more in evidence than in the debate over deforestation in the Amazon basin. While inhabitants of temperate industrialised countries (as well as sizable minorities in many tropical countries) rally to the slogan of "save the forests", colonisation of the Amazonian forest is encouraged by several South American countries and financed (at least in the past) by international agencies such as the World Bank.

Two issues dominate the debate: (1) securing food security and the kind of agriculture to adopt, and (2) reducing deforestation and landscape transformation. The first of these is of primary concern in Latin America; deforestation dominates the debate in the industrialised countries.

The use of the land as a private good is in conflict with the broader view held by the international community that see the tropical forest - and to a lesser extent other lands - as a public good. The dilemma and the challenge is to find ways of meeting, if not completely at least partially, both needs.

3.1. Food security

With the proper land use practices, Latin American agriculture could become an important source of wealth in the next century; with inadequate practices, Latin America has the potential of destroying much of its fragile soils.

In the next fifty to a hundred years the world's population - from about 6 billion - will increase to about 10 billion. Much of that growth will be concentrated in the tropics and subtropics, including Mexico, Central America and much of South America. Food and fibre production will have to be doubled worldwide just to keep up with population growth. Although reports in the news emphasise mostly surpluses in the United States and Europe, in the last few years these surpluses have shrunk significantly with subsequently volatile grain prices. This is a formidable challenge, particularly if it is to be done without massive land degradation and soil erosion. Latin America has the largest reserves of potentially arable land, but this is largely marginal land, with soil and humidity limitations, easily degraded if used incorrectly.

The problem of the proper use of natural resources and agricultural land use include not only physical, biological, and ecological questions, but involves also issues of trade, national credit policies, the cost of capital, and international relations between nations. Consequently the development of solutions demands a truly interdisciplinary effort.

Economic policy makers often feel that transfer of foreign technology is cheaper than maintaining a national research establishment. This view is bolstered by the successful privatisation of other government enterprises. Although some technology can be and should be transferred, given that the physical and climatic conditions that affect agricultural yields vary from site to site, some local research capacity is always necessary.

3.2. Deforestation

Tropical forests are the greatest reservoir of prokaryote, fungal, plant, and animal species diversity in the world and hold the largest stocks of sequestered carbon, whose release into the atmosphere in the form of CO_2 could significantly affect world climate. As such they probably constitute the worlds largest public good. The preserving the biodiversity of tropical forests and reducing greenhouse gas emissions is of general concern to society at large (Solbrig, 1998: 13).

Tropical forests occupy a large portion of the surface in eleven Latin American countries with significant population pressures and low to medium incomes: Mexico, Guatemala, Costa Rica, Panama, Honduras, Colombia, Venezuela, Ecuador, Peru, Bolivia, and Paraguay. The use of these forest lands as timber resources, for growing tropical products, or for crop agriculture or cattle grazing, can help alleviate poverty and fulfil the local countries need for more foreign exchange and food.

The only viable option is to encourage increased agricultural productivity through modernisation of the agrarian sector in areas already deforested. The development of rural industries to increase agrarian production can both satisfy the local and national needs for food and fibre and produce necessary savings for development and non-rural employment, thus reducing pressure on the forest. These were the successful strategies pursued by Europe and the United States and later by countries such as Argentina and Australia, and more recently Chile and Thailand among others.

3.3. Other policy issues

Because industrial activities, especially those of large corporations, are often the source of pollutants, the tendency world-wide has been to develop prescriptive rules to force polluters to internalise environmental costs, under the generally accepted rule that who pollutes should pay rather than have downstream users pay. In many instances these rules are necessary and welcomed by industry because they equalise the costs and reward responsible behaviour. The attempt to prescribe behavioural rules to individual citizens, rules that conflict with their own self-interest is ineffective. Instead we need to develop environmentally friendly techniques that are also economically attractive so that it eventually be in our self-interest not to degrade (Solbrig, 1998: 15).

For citizens to adopt environmentally friendly behaviour, reliable and fair legal mechanisms must be created to enforce long-term property rights and other legal obligations. Unfortunately too often the judicial system in Latin America responds to political pressures when it is not downright corrupt. Legal reforms are also needed to ensure the adoption of environmentally friendly policies by both governments and individuals. Many countries possess adequate environmental legislation; almost all Latin American countries have a cabinet level environmental official. Yet these officials are usually without enforcement power (Solbrig, 1998).

It is important to present some specific environmental issues for the three Latin American APEC members:

3.4. Chile

The primary environmental threats to Chile are air pollution from vehicle and industrial emissions, water pollution from untreated industrial sewage, deforestation and soil erosion. Air pollution in Santiago is the most obvious and severe environmental problem in Chile.

Mitigating threats to the environment, however, is the increasing use of alternative fuels in Chile's industrial and energy sectors. Reliance on natural gas and hydroelectric generation to power the country has kept total carbon emissions in check over the past decade.

The Joint Commission for Environmental Cooperation, set up under the Export Credit Agency (ECA), is responsible for establishing and developing programs of work in accordance with the provisions of Article III.

Under the recent U.S.-Chile Free Trade Agreement (USCFTA), the U.S. and Chile made a precedent setting commitment to cooperate on environmental enforcement and to promote civil society participation in these cooperative activities (US-Chile Joint Commission on Environmental Cooperation, 2005).

3.5. Mexico

Rapid increases in Mexico's economy and population are putting massive pressure on the environment, increasing pollution and depleting natural resources. Mexico now has a solid environmental legal and institutional framework which is starting to bear positive results. To encourage further implementation, the OECD recommends that Mexico better enforces and funds these environmental policies, and integrates environmental concerns into sectoral policies. The OECD Environmental Performance Review of Mexico recognises Mexico's major environmental achievements, but also makes 61 concrete recommendations to help improve the country's environment. Mexico has adopted an ambitious approach to environmental governance, increasingly mainstreaming sustainable development into sectoral policy-making.

Since the signing of the La Paz Agreement in 1983, the United States and Mexico have worked together to realise their shared commitment to environmental quality along their common border. In recent years, these collaborative efforts have been expanded from the border to embrace new areas of bilateral cooperation, in partnership with State governments and with active civil society participation.

The U.S.-Mexico Binational Commission Environment Working Group reports the following accomplishments in this area. (US - Mexico Binational Commission, 2004). The ten Border States finalised the U.S.-Mexico Environmental Program, Border 2012, in December 2002. Both sides are taking steps toward implementing the Border Environment Cooperation Commission (BECC) and North American Development Bank (NADBank) reforms agreed upon by Presidents Bush and Fox, amplifying the geographic coverage of both institutions to 300 kilometres within Mexico and thereby improving the financing options through low-interest loans and grant funds.

3.6. Peru

Peru subscribed together with Bolivia, Colombia, Venezuela and Ecuador the Paracas Declaration, the Andean Environmental Agenda (1st Meeting Andean Community Council, 2005).

This declaration stresses the importance of the environment for the Andean integration process and takes due note of the progress made toward implementing the Regional Biodiversity Strategy - RBS and of the Andean Plan to follow-up on the Johannesburg Summit on Sustainable Development 2003-2005, which includes the issues of Climatic Change, Water and Sanitation.

Some of the important agreements were: to request the CANGS (Andean Community General Secretariat) to study possibilities for appropriate mechanisms to finance the Andean Environmental Agenda, placing special importance on the financial mechanism of the Regional Biodiversity Strategy, the creation of the Andean Institute for Biodiversity (AIB), the Andean negotiation strategy on the International Regime on Access to Genetic Resources, Regional Strategy on Climate Change and Integrated Water Resource Management. It is important to stress the decision to take steps toward the preparation of the sui generis Andean regime for the protection of traditional knowledge, in compliance with Decision 391 and Directive 36 of the Quito Presidential Act and to create strategic alliances.

The Sustainable Environment Natural Resources Management (SENREM) Project seeks to improve the conservation and use of natural resources in Peru. This project, financed by the

US Agency for International Development (USAID), has as its institutional counterpart Peru National Environmental Council (CONAM). The project's objective is to increase the capacity of public and private institutions to identify and resolve environmental and natural resource problems.

4. Towards common principles in APEC's environmental agenda

Most APEC countries have taken steps in the last decade to improve environmental management and reduce the ecological costs of rapid growth. At a regional level, however, joint environmental discussion and action is in its development stage and the political will to discuss environmental issues at APEC is just emerging. The key common principles to guide the governance of the trade-environment interface must be:

4.1. Integration of trade and environment

The very first principle is the recognition that trade and environment impacts and policies are interlinked, both at the national and regional levels. Trade and investment policies should maintain the environmental integrity of ecosystems.

4.2. Cooperation

Common rules, guidelines and frameworks for environmental management should be developed through processes of regional discussion and consensus-building. The more powerful countries should eschew the use of unilateral trade sanctions to impose environmental conditionality, except in the context of international or regional agreements. Ample opportunities must be created for environmental concerns to be articulated by all members of APEC.

4.3. Mutual responsibility

No APEC country can claim the moral high ground as the guardian of ecologically sound development. The embrace of regional mechanisms which promote environmentally sound trade patterns will require all APEC countries to make changes in their existing domestic policies and to enact new policies.

4.4. Efficiency, eco-efficiency, and cost internalisation

One of the central aims of regional trade-environment cooperation is to generate market prices which take ecological costs into account. The reverse is also important: environment policies should promote economic efficiency and aim to ensure that scarce financial resources are well-spent. It is evident that cost internalisation based on the polluter pays principle must play a central role in efforts to improve efficiency, improve the management of natural resources and promote worldwide sustainable development.

There are formidable problems in identifying and valuing the costs of using environmental resources and allocating costs to particular goods. But that only underscores how urgently those problems need to be addressed. Broadly speaking, the problems can be divided into three groups. First, consensus is only beginning to emerge on essential concepts, definitions, measurement techniques, data needs and methods of analysis, and further research is urgently needed. Even where the theory is fairly clear, there is often disagreement as to how internalisation should be put into practice. Frequently the process is further complicated by poorly-defined property rights to environmental resources. Second, in the course of internalising costs, producers fear there will be inadequate offsetting gains in efficiency, and that they will lose business to competitors facing less onerous requirements. It is not yet clear to what extent these fears are in fact valid, as evidence on this issue remains inconclusive. Third, cost internalisation is not an adequate approach to dealing with environmental costs stemming from irreplaceable losses, such as species extinction or lasting damage to the regenerative capacity of renewable resources.

4.5. Scientist and stakeholder participation

The creation of sound approaches to regional environmental management requires APEC to open its doors to scientists, especially ecological scientists, citizen groups and other stakeholders. Scientists and stakeholders should receive ongoing opportunities to participate in the design and implementation of regional trade, investment and environment policies. Stakeholders include community, consumer, environment and development groups, labour unions, farmers, businesses and others.

4.6. Diversity and commonality

The general approach of APEC should be to promote common guidelines and frameworks while leaving micro-management to national and sub-national governments. Rather than the same standards, for example, APEC could aim to standardise information gathering and testing procedures, as well as standard-setting methodologies such as environmental and health impact and risk assessment. Harmonisation of standards should be pursued where appropriate (Ivanova and Angeles, 2005).

A broad environmental agenda aims to embed an environmental rationality into APEC's fundamental goals and institutions, and to do so in a way which does not create a low ceiling on mutual environmental commitments (Zarsky, 1999).

5. Conclusions

More than ten years after APEC's founding, the not very attractive reality of the status of the environment in it is summed up by a report by the Nautilus Institute for Security and Sustainable Development, to the effect that the seeds of environmental cooperation at APEC are still germinating, that significant areas of sustainable resource management are not yet on the agenda, there is resistance to discuss policy change, and institutional mechanisms to coordinate environmental work and to interface with environmental NGOs are lacking.

First, the US, APEC's prime actor, has not been sympathetic to any effort within APEC that might detract from the primacy of free trade: the use of APEC to advance the global free trade agenda remains uppermost in the US agenda for APEC and the environmental agenda within APEC is in many ways like the aid agenda.

Second, investors in the Western Pacific are not sympathetic to a serious environmental program that would add to their costs of doing business in the region, and this would be the same for other Asia-Pacific corporate elites.

Third, the Latin American countries elites have pursued the NIC development model, which sees no need to invest in pollution control and externalises environmental costs. They would be loath to sacrifice their immediate economic gains to trans-national environmental controls.

Fourth, Chile, Mexico and Peru are parts of different regional and bilateral free trade agreements (FTA), which include environmental resolutions, so they must coordinate these policies with the multilateral process within APEC.

Finally, there is the question of the future direction of APEC's institutional evolution. The above examination helps identify a number of issues that should be examined by APEC. The APEC Leaders Meetings should be re-engineered, to return to free-wheeling format without a preset agenda, as, indeed, they were originally conceived. And concrete actions as emission permit trading and voluntary agreements must be instrumented.

References

Ban, K., 2000. Application of CGE modeling to analysis of environmental measures in APEC. Asia Pacific Economic Cooperation (APEC).

Coase, R.H., 1960. The Problem of Social Cost. Journal of Law and Economics 3: 1-44

First Meeting of the Andean Community Council of Ministers of the Environment and Sustainable Development. Paracas, Peru, 31 March - 1 April, 2005.

Grossman, G. and A. Krueger, 1992. Income Increase and Rates of Contamination, National Bureau of Economic Research Study.

Hardin, G., 1968. The Tragedy of Commons. Science 162: 1243-1248.

Ivanova Boncheva A., 1998. Free Trade and Environment. In Journal: Paradigmas, April-June, Tijuana, B.C., pp. 37-47.

Ivanova, A. and M. Angeles, 2005. Trade and Environment Issues in APEC. In: F. Khosrow (Ed.), Opportunities and Challenges for East Asia The Haworth Press, Binghampton, N.Y.

Kuznetz, S., 1963. Quantitative Aspects of the Economic Growth of Nations, Economic Development and Cultural Change 11: January.

Lucas, G., N. Wheeler and R. Hettige, 1992. The inflexion point of manufacture industries. International Trade and Environment, World Bank Discussion Papers, # 148, pp. 98-112.

Mitchell, S.K., 1997. Enforcing APEC. Policy 13: 35-36.

Rauscher, M., 1994. On ecological dumping. Oxford Economic Papers 46: 822-840.

Solbrig, O., 1998. The Environmental Agenda in Latin America. The Issue of 21st Century, DRCLAS News, Fall 1998.

US-Chile Joint Commission for Environmental Cooperation, Environmental Cooperation Agreement, 2005-2006. Washington D.C., February 16, 2005.

US-Mexico Binational Commission, Environmental Working Group. Bureau of Western Hemisphere Affairs, Washington, D.C., November 12, 2004.

Wee, V. and N. Heyzer, 1995. Gender, Poverty and Sustainable Development, Centre for Environment, Gender and Development, Singapore.

Xu, X., 1998. International Trade and Environmental Policy: How Effective is 'Eco-Dumping'? Trade and Environment Workshop, Beijing, China, 22-24 July 1998, Papers and Proceedings, Economic Committee Asia-Pacific Economic Cooperation, pp. 21-40.

Zarsky, L., 1999. APEC, Citizen Groups and the Environment. Working Paper #167, Nautilus Institute for Security and Sustainable Development, San Francisco, USA.

Adaptation to environmental standards in foreign trade of the Central and Eastern European Countries

Zofia Wysokińska
University of Lodz, Economic and Social Faculty, ul. Narutowicza 65, 90-131 Lodz, Poland.
zofwys@uni.lodz.pl

Abstract

This paper first reviews the literature related to the theory of the relationship between foreign trade and environmental issues with special reference to the impact of Multilateral Environmental Agreements on foreign trade in environmental products, in transition economies. Secondly, it presents the results of a survey of 286 enterprises in Poland concerning the relationship between the application of European and international environmental norms and standards and the enterprises' competitiveness in both the domestic and foreign markets prior to Poland's accession to the European Union. The countries analysed in the paper undertook significant steps in the 1990's to improve their natural environments, increasing their imports of goods designed to aid in environmental protection and technologies to implement "clean production" of export goods. These steps improved recently the competitiveness of Polish, Czech, and Hungarian environmental goods in both the domestic and European markets. Research results confirm the pro-ecological emphasis of transition economies' restructuring efforts, particularly when read together with the significant increase in their foreign trade in environmental goods and services.

JEL classification: F15, F18

Keywords: environmental goods, foreign trade, transition economies

1. Theoretical framework: Foreign trade and the environment

International trade becomes a significant contributing factor in effecting strategies of stable development among participating countries when raw material resources are effectively utilised in production and when the cross-border movement of environment-friendly products and technology is encouraged. Trade and free trade policies regarding the movement of goods have a significant impact on the environment and should be closely connected with the basic standards of environmental protection policies. In countries with high environmental protection standards, losses resulting from environmental destruction have been assessed at 1-2% of the GNP, while in countries with much lower standards of protection, these losses have been known to reach 3-5% of the GNP (Repetto, 1993).

Applicable regulations regarding environmental protection standards may encompass both the protection of indigenous natural resources as well as bans on the import of goods that may be harmful to the environment (such as large vehicles with excessive emissions that pollute the air, products containing heavy metal compounds such as lead, very noisy vehicles or machines and devices or fuels that may be harmful to the environment (Lucas, 1992).

The effects of raising environmental protection standards in a country's foreign trade practice become especially visible in the following sectors of the economy: agriculture, forestry, fishing, transport, as well as in heavy industry sectors such as mining, metallurgy and heavy chemical production. These effects are usually two-sided; on the one hand the trade of goods harmful to the environment is limited (these goods usually belong to the above-mentioned industrial sectors and are known as raw material absorbent - they have a negative impact on the flow of imports and exports taking place between a country and its foreign trade partners), while on the other hand the raising of standards can cause a trend towards cleaner technological production through the reallocation of production resources, which will be closer to meeting international standards (which in turn will translate into more effective competition on foreign markets and an improvement in competition among enterprises in foreign as well as domestic markets, and will in the long run stimulate a rise in exports). Goods which may also have a significant impact on the changing face of foreign trade are those which encourage the improvement of the state of the environment, mainly goods and services related to the measurement, prevention and/or moderation of water and air pollution, as well as those that aid in the resolution of problems regarding waste, noise pollution and ecosystems. These encompass cleaning technologies, goods and services that limit environmental risk and lessen the pollution and exhaustion of natural resources, recycling, as well as waste disposal plant, tools and technology (OECD, 1999).

From a review of studies published concerning the relationship between trade and environmental protection, it can be concluded that the effects of this relationship may be either positive and negative. Some authors (Ekins *et al.*, 1994) believe that the accelerated deregulation and liberalisation of trade is a factor of major importance in this regard. Generally speaking, two distinct opinions can be portrayed. The traditional approach is that environmental standards limit the competitiveness of companies, which are forced to adopt these standards and as a result limit their export potential. The more contemporary opinion is that the implementation of appropriate environmental standards has long-term benefits which should improve the competitive position of complying companies in the long run (Alpay, 1999).

In examining the relationship between foreign trade and the transfer of pollutants, it is useful to distinguish between overt and covert transfers. Overt transfer occurs when pollutants are emitted across borders through the air, water or land as a result of natural causes (wind, oceanic or river currents) as well as human transport of pollutants (waste and other harmful products) onto other countries' territories. Covert transfer occurs through the import of goods and services which degrade the environment in the country of origin - the importing country, while usually avoiding the direct effects, nevertheless is a covert contributor thereto.

Empirical studies on the impact of foreign trade on the environment are scarce in the existing scientific literature. Nevertheless, an interesting analysis of this issue was presented by Antweiler, who created an index (the Pollution Terms of Trade Index - PTTI) that represents the quantity of pollutants emitted as a result of the production of exportable goods worth one US Dollar, as compared to imported goods of the same value (the index is multiplied by 100). This is a terms of trade index, which means that the prices are replaced by the amount of pollutants. If the index is higher than 100 and if a given country conducts zero-balance foreign trade, then this exchange results in an increase in pollutants on this country's territory (Antweiler *et al.*, 1988).

A number of publications analysing foreign trade with respect to environmental protection factors are available (Xu and Song, 2000). One of the most complex of these analyses regarding the interdependence of competitiveness and environmental protection standards is that of the World Bank, in which Sorsa develops determinants in the trade of environmentally-sensitive materials, as categorised in level 3 SITC, whereby changes in the structure of trade volume were analysed during the period 1970-1990 (Sorsa, 1994).

One can conclude from the European Commission's analysis that even though it may be very expensive to achieve positive results within the scope of environmental protection, there are also benefits related to the improvement of the productivity of utilised resources, increased competitiveness, and a positive effect on employment levels (EC, 1996). These studies also show that although there is no direct correlation between economic growth and environmental protection, it would be very difficult to achieve a continuous improvement in the state of the environment without economic growth (EC, 1994). Economic growth is capable of generating additional resources that may be utilised in limiting pollution and protecting the environment. Positive effects can be strengthened even more by appropriate economic policies, including trade policy.

The relationship between trade policy and environmental protection raises two main issues. The first is based on answering the following question, "what type of trade policy should be adopted from the environmental protection point of view?" - in other words, what trade restrictions should be enforced if we are dealing with cross-border environmental protection issues as well as with common global resources? The second problem is related to the variation of environmental protection standards among nations and how these standards relate to competitiveness. Here, the question posed is, "do lower environmental protection standards have an effect on "unfair" trade advantages?. This includes the problem of using these lower standards as non-tariff barriers.

2. Market access and multilateral regulations in international trade of environmental products

The elimination of trade barriers also increases the efficiency of the world economic system by enabling countries to specialise in those sectors in which they possess economic advantages, which includes those sectors in which they possess favourable natural environmental conditions. In the latter half of the 1990's one can observe a rapid and dynamic increase in the environmental protection industry's share in the world economy. The overall global value of production in the environmental protection industry was estimated at 453 billion USD in 1996, 483 billion USD in 1997, 518 billion USD in 2000 (OECD, 2001: 12) and 550 billion USD in the year 2001 (UN, 2004). It is estimated that the OECD countries possess 90% of the environmental protection industry. This industry grew by over 14 per cent between 1996-2000. Over-capacity slowed annual growth in the developed countries to 1.6 per cent in 2000 and 2001. During the same period annual growth in developing countries was at 7 to 8 per cent. Analysts expect that the industry will continue to expand, reaching over US$ 600 billion by 2010. Most of the growth will continue to take place in developing countries and economies in transition, at an annual rate of 8 to 12 per cent (Trade and Environment, 2003). In relative terms, this environmental market is not as big as the steel or agriculture markets, but roughly the same size as the pharmaceuticals and information technology markets (UN, 2004).

Markets in developed countries are mature: they are highly competitive, with a sophisticated customer base, and experience slow or negative growth in many segments. Environmental regulations are by far the most important factor. However, in spite of regulatory drivers, environmental markets are very sensitive to economic cycles. Capacity in environmental goods and services is growing in certain developing countries, mostly from involvement in partnerships with established foreign firms but also from the increased demand in the domestic market. However, there are few data to indicate that any of this capacity is translating into exports (Vikhlyaev, 2003).

Currently barriers to trade understood as bound tariffs on many capital goods used to provide pollution-management services are low in developed countries-generally under three per cent for products on the OECD list (OECD, 2001). In most developing countries these tariffs remain relatively high, with the bound tariffs ranging from 20 to 40 per cent, and applied rates mostly ranging from 10 to 20 per cent. In some cases the rates are considerably higher. In practice, imports of environmental goods may sometimes benefit from incentives. Technical regulations affect the type of environmental goods used to meet environmental requirements. The lack of uniformity of environmental requirements in different national markets has been an important non-tariff barrier.

In particular, standards and certification requirements affect trade in environmental protection products (EPPs). On the other hand, trade in niche products seeking to enter new markets may be hindered by the lack of appropriate standards for such products. Also, imported environmental technologies need to be tested and certified by local authorities in individual markets (Vikhlyaev, 2003).

3. Multinational environmental agreements

Trade-related measures permitted for environmental purposes include those carried out within the framework of multilateral environmental agreements (MEA). Although most MEA-s do not contain such environmental measures, the few that do, also contain provisions relating to non-discrimination and transparency. WTO notes that MEA-s provide an effective alternative to trade obstruction in order to achieve multilateral solutions to trans-boundary environmental problems.

The gradual removal of other trade restrictions, specifically tariffs, non-tariff barriers, as well as export and import restrictions, has fostered hope among both developed and developing countries that a more open multilateral trade system will facilitate the protection of the environment and accelerate the progress of sustainable development efforts. However, the effectiveness of trade measures and their efficiency in meeting the stated environmental objective of the MEA-s will significantly depend on the flexibility mechanism and the provision of effective supportive measures for developing countries (Trade and Environment Review, 2003).

The integration of trade and environment concerns in developing countries has emerged as one of the priority areas in moving towards sustainable development. Intensive debate and dialogue as well as pilot projects at the national and regional levels have led to the evolution of possible strategies, elements of which are slowly becoming visible. It is now becoming clear that integrating trade and environment in a development-friendly manner needs concrete mechanism that span several aspects of national and international economic activity.

ISO 14001 (the international environmental management systems requirements standard) is heavily discussed and debated by developing countries and countries in transition. While it is clear that product-related eco-related eco-labels and related standards are covered by the TBT (Technical Barriers to Trade) Agreement, the position is less clear for environmental management systems. The question as to whether management standards (such as ISO 9000 and 14000) or only those standards directly related to products should be covered by the Agreement remains subject to internal discussion at WTO. There is as yet no empirical evidence of trade implications arising from the use of the ISO 14000 series of standards.

According to the Report to the 5th Session of the WTO Ministerial Conference in Cancun covering the work undertaken by the regular session of the Committee on Trade and Environment (CTE) between the Fourth (Doha) and Fifth (Cancun) Ministerial

Conferences of the WTO, it was recognised that improved market access for developing countries' products was key to the goal of achieving sustainable development. It was recalled that, in line with Rio Principle 11 (4th), environmental standards and priorities needed to reflect the particular environmental and development context to which they applied and that standards applied by some countries could be inappropriate and of unwarranted economic and social cost to others, particularly developing countries. Small and medium sized enterprises (SMEs) were especially vulnerable in this regard (WTO, 2003: 2).

Several Members stressed that the protection of the environment and health were legitimate policy objectives and that Members had the right to set their own appropriate level of environmental protection so as to address such objectives. However, it was also acknowledged that environmental requirements could affect exports adversely. The answer to concerns about reduced market access was not to weaken such standards, but rather to enable exporters to meet them. The key role of technical assistance, capacity building and technology transfer to help developing countries' exporters to meet environmental requirements and to adjust production methods as appropriate should be mentioned in this respect. In discussing ways forward, several WTO Members felt that more weight had to be given to the identification of trade opportunities for sustainable growth. The CTE could look at incentives and means to assist developing countries to identify products, and develop export markets for environmentally friendly products in areas where these countries enjoyed comparative advantage. Several Members agreed on the need for more analysis, and the identification of concrete cases regarding the effects of environmental measures on market access, particularly on exports of products of importance of developing countries.

Such analysis, particularly if sector specific and based on real situations, could further the understanding of the issues and could serve to target taxation and subsidy schemes in OECD countries were generally biased and discriminatory vis-à-vis petroleum products. There were negligible taxes on coal and gas, and, in addition, coal products in many OECD countries were subsidised. Such policies should be corrected. It was suggested that subsidies should be removed and that fuel taxation be restructured to reflect carbon content-this would ensure that polluting sources (with higher carbon content) be penalised, not favoured. It was stressed that the issue was not climate change mitigation *per se,* but the impact on environmental policies on market access on the one hand, and their consistency with WTO rules on the other -as above).

4. Empirical aspects of the relationship between foreign trade and the environment in the CEE countries

In this part of the paper, changes in the structure of foreign trade of Poland, the Czech Republic, and Hungary will be discussed with special regard to goods and products deemed environmentally harmful as well as to goods and products designed to aid in environmental protection. The analysis will be based on the classification system proposed by supranational organisations in the 1990's.

The analysis covers two types of goods and products: (1) those deemed environmentally harmful; and (2) those designed to aid in environmental protection. Both groups of goods were classified based on the HS (Harmonised System) nomenclature and were analysed with regard to the dynamics of import and export thereof during 1992-2000.

The definition of goods and products designed to aid in environmental protection is given by the OECD/Eurostat Informal Group as follows: *"Goods, products and services protecting the environment, including activities which create such goods and products or offer services concerning the measurement, prevention, limitation, minimisation, or correction of air, water, or sunshine pollution, or address problems of waste management, noise pollution, and eco-system management."*

The above definition encompasses waste treatment and prevention technologies and goods, products, and services aimed at reducing risks to the natural environment or minimising pollution and the depletion of natural resources.

I. OECD/EUROSTAT lists three groups of goods and products designed to aid in environmental protection (OECD, 1999).[1]

a. goods and products designed to aid in environmental management: includes goods and services created exclusively with the aim of environmental protection and having a significant impact on pollution reduction and the identification and collection of statistical data;

b. cleaning products and technologies: includes goods and services which reduce or eliminate environmental harm. These are sometimes used for other purposes as well, and their identification and classification in relevant statistical data is difficult, expensive, and open to controversy.

c. management and avoidance: this group includes goods, products, and services which may have significant positive environmental effects but which are designed and implemented for other purposes (such as energy saving technologies, creation of alternative energy sources, *etc.*). This category may be considered optionally and its classification and analysis depends to a great extent on existing environmental policies as well as access to statistical data.

---

[1] Based on the definition of the environmental protection industry set forth in the OECD/Eurostat Informal Group: *"Goods and services protecting the environment include the manufacturing of products and the development of services regarding the measurement, prevention, minimalisation, elimination, or correction of water and air pollution and solar system pollution, as well as addressing the problems of waste disposal, noise pollution, and eco-system maintenance"*.

II. Goods and products harmful to the environment include mainly those produced by the following industries: mining, metallurgy, chemical, paper and cellulose, energy, construction materials, and means of transportation.

The analysis which follows is based on the author's own research, taking into consideration the earlier-presented analyses in the theoretical part of this paper.

An empirical analysis of import and export of the above goods in Poland, The Czech Republic, and Hungary, based on the aggregate reports presented in Figures 1-8, leads to the following general conclusions:

1. In all three of the analysed countries one can observe significant increases during 1992-2000 in the import of goods designed to aid in environmental protection. This trend is particularly observable in absolute terms based on values expressed in USD. In the case of Hungary, a period of relatively low investment in the first half of the 1990's was followed by a dynamic increase in the second half of the decade, spurred by a particularly intensive import of goods and products relating to waste-water management and solid-waste management. In Poland a period of significant growth in imports was observable between 1994-1996, followed by a declining trend between 1997-2000, particularly in goods and products relating to solid waste management (in the second half of 1996 and 1997), followed in 1998 by a decline in imports of goods and services relating to waste-water management. A similar trend of initial increases in imports followed by a decline is observable in the Czech Republic, although the changes there are less intense than in the case of Poland. The most stable and gradually increasing trend in the import of the three groups of goods and products relating to environmental protection, that is air pollution control, waste-water management, and solid waste management, took place in Hungary throughout the period in question (See Figures 1, 3 and 4).

2. Exports of goods designed to aid in environmental protection in the three Central European Free Trade Agreement (CEFTA) countries examined during the time period in question rose at a significantly slower level than imports. Nevertheless one can observe that the greatest increase in exports in the 1990's took place in the Czech Republic, while in Poland a significant growth in exports collapsed in the 1998-2000 period. A stable growth trend, albeit at a lower absolute level, is observable for Hungary during this period (See Figure 2).

3. On the other hand import of goods deemed harmful to the environment was characterised by a growth trend in all three analysed countries throughout the 1990's. In absolute terms the growth trend was lowest in Hungary, and somewhat higher in the Czech Republic, particularly in the latter half of the decade. The largest increase in the import of goods deemed harmful to the environment was noted in Poland in the second half of the decade, where such imports were 2 to 2.5 times greater than in the other analysed countries (See Figure 5 and 6).

4. The export of goods deemed harmful to the environment was also characterised by a growth trend in all three analysed countries throughout the 1990's, although once

again the absolute growth trend was lowest in Hungary, while in Poland and the Czech Republic the export of goods deemed harmful to the environment increased more than two- and three-fold during the period analysed (see Figure 7 and 8).

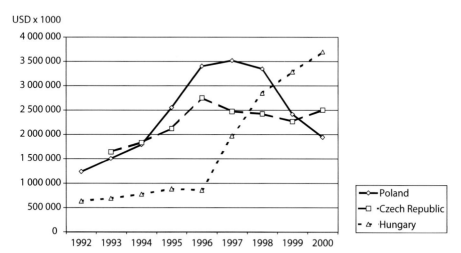

Figure 1. Import of environmentally friendly goods.

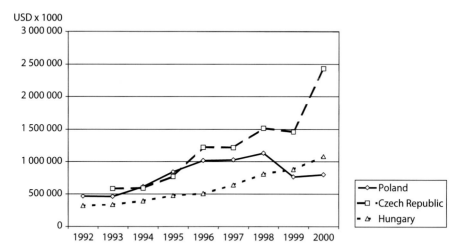

Figure 2. Export of environmentally friendly goods.

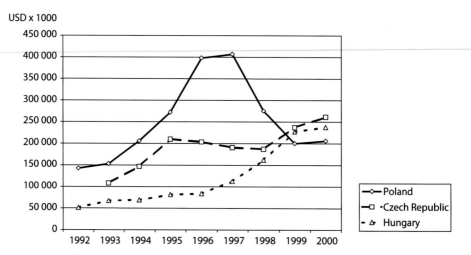

Figure 3. Import of environmentally friendly goods "solid waste management".

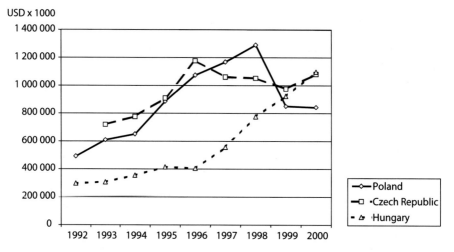

Figure 4. Import of environmentally friendly goods "waste-water management".

5. Environmental norms and standards and the activities of Polish enterprises

The aim of the research survey questionnaire was to conduct an analysis of the changes in the competitive positions of Polish enterprises as a result of applying the environmental norms and standards of the European Union, WTO, and OECD. The survey questionnaire contained 28 questions and was sent to 2138 firms. Replies were received from 286 firms,

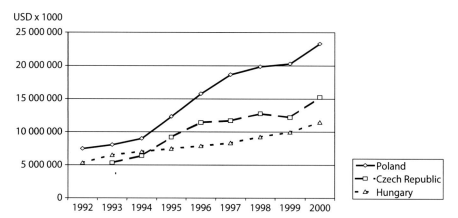

Figure 5. Import of commodities difficult for the environment.

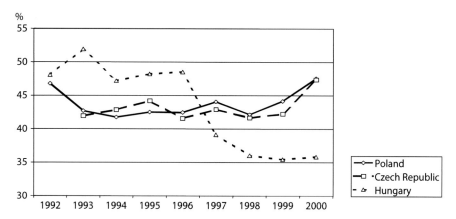

Figure 6. Share of commodities difficult for the environment in total import.

constituting about 14% of the survey sample. 57 survey questionnaires were returned without delivery owing to incorrect address information.

An analysis of the structure of the respondents, based on the European Classification of Activities (NACE) system, showed that 14% of the surveyed firms were engaged in the production of ready-made metal products, with the exception of machinery; 12% were engaged in the construction industry; 9% were engaged in the production of otherwise unclassified machinery and equipment; 8% were engaged in the production of chemical products and artificial textiles; 7% were engaged in the production of rubber-products and artificial creations as well as in producing radio, television, and communications equipment and machinery; 6% were engaged in metal production; and 5% were engaged in

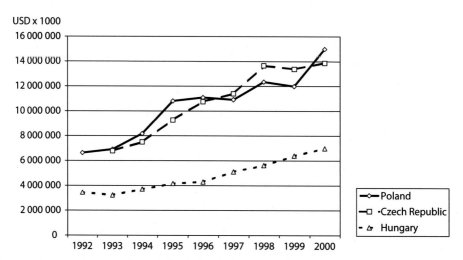

Figure 7. Export of commodities difficult for the environment.

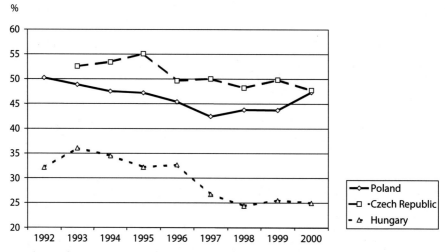

Figure 8. Share of commodities difficult for the environment in total export.

the production of products from non-metallic natural resources as well as in the productions of foodstuffs and beverages.

18.9% of the respondents were in the public sector and approximately 71% in the private sector. Polish domestic firms dominated the private sector respondents, constituting 84.2% of the surveyed firms, while approximate 7% were foreign firms and 9% contained a mixture of Polish and foreign ownership. German, French, and Swiss firms dominated among the foreign firms.

In response to questions concerning the import of clean technologies and environmental products, approximately 34% of the respondents confirmed the import of such products and technologies, while 61% stated that they did not engage in such import. Approximately 5% of the surveyed firms failed to provide a response to this question.

More positive were the responses of the surveyed firms to questions concerning the environmental strategies they employed. Almost 78% of the respondents stated that they employed a strategy of avoiding environmental harm from the beginning of the production process, while only 36% of respondents stated that they applied the "end of the pipe" strategy.

54% of the surveyed firms confirmed that they have implemented ecological norms in recent years, while only 16% stated that they have not engaged in such activities in recent years. 30% of the surveyed firms, however, failed to respond to this question. Among the firms implementing ecological norms nearly 37% confirmed that they are in compliance with the ecological norms of the European Union; 31%, on the other hand, stated that they were not in compliance therewith. Only 30% of the respondents indicating that they were complying with ecological norms confirmed compliance with international ecological norms of the type ISO 14000, while 70% confirmed that they did not apply such norms to their activities.

The most common barriers listed by the respondent firms to the implementation of ecological norms were primarily the following:
- lack of legal and financial solutions, in particular the lack of means to finance such investments;
- lack of financial aid programs and funds earmarked for ecological purposes, as well as the high costs of expertise in the area of implementing new technologies;
- frequent and inconsistent changes in the legal regulations and unclear interpretations of environmental regulations;
- instability in national environmental regulation;
- a poorly developed system of waste segregation;
- a complicated system of assessing fines and clean-up charges for environmental damage;
- organisational difficulties with implementation of a system of outside consultation within a firm;
- technical obstacles, including the lack of a network for collecting industrial wastes and a poorly organised market for waste control;
- lack of information, including information about firms engaged in utilisation of waste products;
- bureaucratic and administrative barriers.

Among the firms responding to the survey only about 12% noted a positive relationship between the implementation of ecological norms and growth in domestic sales, while 15%

confirmed the existence of such a relationship as regards sales in the foreign markets. 14% of respondent firms stated that they had more opportunities to cooperate with international firms operating in Poland as a result of their compliance with ecological norms, while 16% of respondents felt that they had more opportunities to cooperate with foreign firms abroad as a result of their compliance with ecological norms.

One quarter of the respondent firms indicated that they feel that their compliance with ecological norms and standards and their participation in Integrated Programs of Environmental Management will result in increased sales on the domestic market upon Poland's accession to the European Union, while 12% consider that the same will have no effect on their position on the domestic market and 5% consider that the effect, if any, will be minimal. About 35% of the surveyed firms failed to respond to this question.

The respondent firms' assessment was more positive however as regards increased sales on the single European market upon Poland's accession to the European Union, where 29% of respondents indicated that they feel that their compliance with ecological norms and standards will have a positive effect on export sales. 22% of respondent firms, on the other hand, feel that their compliance with ecological norms and standards will have either little effect on export sales or none at all, and 37% of respondents once again failed to respond to this question.

6. Conclusions

The market of environmentally friendly goods is one of the most expanding markets during the period 1995-2001. It achieved roughly the same size as the pharmaceuticals and information technology markets.

Barriers to trade understood as bound tariffs on many capital goods used to provide pollution-management services are low in all developed countries, but in most developing countries these tariffs remain relatively high. Technical regulations affect the type of environmental goods used to meet environmental requirements. On the other hand, trade in niche products seeking to enter new markets may be hindered by the lack of appropriate standards and certificates for such products. Imported environmental technologies need to be tested and certified by local authorities in individual markets.

Central and Eastern European countries analysed in the paper undertook significant steps in the 1990's to improve their natural environments, increasing their imports of goods designed to aid in environmental protection and technologies to implement "clean production" of export goods. These steps should improve the competitiveness of Polish, Czech, and Hungarian goods and products in the future on both the European and global markets.

Research results confirm the pro-ecological emphasis of transition economies' efforts in restructurisation, particularly when read together with the significant increase in their foreign trade in pro-ecological goods and services.

An analysis of the results shows that most foreign investors do take environmental protection issues into account in making their decisions, but they do not consider them to constitute a major investment factor. A majority of the respondents favour centralising strategies. This strategy seems advantageous for recipient countries. Firms with foreign capital frequently introduce environmental protection norms and take part in an environmental protection program.

References

Alpay S., 1999. The Trade and Environment Nexus. In: E. Ortiz and A. Cabello (eds.), Economic Issues and Globalization: Theory and Evidence, ISINI.

Antweiler, W., B. Copeland and M. Taylor, 1988. Is Free Trade Good for the Environment?, NBER Working Paper Series, 1988, No. 6707.

Ekins, P.C., C. Folke and R. Costanza, 1994. Trade, Environment and Development: The Issues in Perspective. Ecological Economics 9.

EC, 1996. Communication to the Council and the Parliament on Trade and Environment. Brussels, 28.02.96.COM (96) 54, Final.

EC, 1994. Communication on Economic Growth and Environment. COM(94)465 Final, Brussels, 1994.

Lucas, R.E.B., 1992. Economic Development, Environmental Regulation and International Mitigation of Toxic Industrial Pollution: 1960-1998. In: P. Low (ed.), International Trade and the Environment, Discussion Paper 159, Washington, DC, World Bank.

OECD, 1999. Environmental Goods and Services Industry - Manual for Data Collection and Analysis. OECD-EUROSTAT, WTO, Paris.

OECD, 2001. Environmental Goods and Services, The Benefits of Further Global Trade Liberalisation. Paris.

Repetto, R., 1993. Trade and Environment Policies: Achieving Complementarities and Avoiding Conflicts. Washington, DC: World Resources Institute.

Sorsa, P., 1994. Competitiveness and Environmental Standards, The World Bank Research Working Papers, February.

UN, 2004. Trade and Environment Review 2003. United Nations, New York, Geneva.

Vikhlyaev, A., 2003. Environmental Goods and Services: Defining Negotiations or Negotiating Definitions? In: Trade and Environment Review 2003, United Nations, New York, Geneva.

Xu, X. and L. Song, 2000. Regional Cooperation and the Environment: Do "Dirty" Industries Migrate? Weltwirtschaftliches Archiv 136: 137-157.

Modelling environmental cooperation on reciprocal emission reduction via virtual market system

Andries Nentjes and Sergey Shibayev
Groningen University, Groningen, The Netherlands. a.nentjes@wanadoo.nl

Abstract

Mainstream economic theory views international agreements on reduction of trans-boundary pollution as a Pareto-optimal outcome of negotiations among self-interested parties. This paper elaborates that notion by modelling negotiation as a multilateral trade in reciprocal emission reductions within the framework of non-cooperative games. A simulation of negotiations on joint reduction of sulphur dioxide emissions in Europe is carried out. The question is whether economic theory's postulate of Pareto-efficient international conventions on pollution reduction are adequate and do explain actual commitments of the parties. We verify by comparing the Pareto-optimal simulation with the actual emission reduction commitments made in the Second Sulphur Protocol (SSP, 1994) and find that for SSP joint benefits exceed joint costs but some countries have negative benefits.

JEL classification: H87, Q53, Q58

Keywords: non-cooperative games, international environmental policy, emission reduction exchange

1. Introduction

In the 1980s it became apparent that acid rain in Europe had grown to be a severe environmental problem. Deposition of acid substances in the emissions of sulphur dioxide (SO_2), nitrogen oxides (NO_x) and ammonium accumulate in the soil and water and cause damage to the ecosystem when the load of the pollutant exceeds a critical level. Most European countries started national control programmes. As a first step towards an international approach the First Sulphur Protocol was signed in 1985 in Helsinki. Twenty states committed themselves to reducing their sulphur emissions by at least 30 percent compared with the 1980 emission level at latest by 1993. By the end of the 1980's it had become clear to most participants and also to governments of states that did not take part in the Helsinki agreement that the acid rain problem had been severely underestimated and that more substantial emission reductions were called for. It set the stage for the negotiations on the Second Sulphur Protocol (SSP) that was signed in 1994. The parties to the protocol promised to have reduced their emissions in 2010 with percentages varying from 0 to 62 percent compared to emissions in their (unilateral) current reduction plans.

How do the commitments of parties to SSP relate to what economic theory has to say about international environmental coordination? A typical feature of SSP, which it shares with many other international environmental conventions, is the commitment of the parties to reduce emissions by varying percentages and without any side payments made. These facts make cooperative game theory unsuitable for analysing the problem at hand. Cooperative game theory assumes that parties maximise the joint net benefits and have agreed on a rule for distribution among the coalition members. It implies that a party which makes excessively high control costs to reduce pollution damage for other parties receives side payments. SSP does not contain such compensation rules and by that it makes cooperative game theory a priori inapplicable. Instead, one needs a theory which recognises that emission reductions are the crucial variables and that those commitments are made on reciprocal base.

Next to that cooperative game theory focuses on coalition formation and stability, which we consider not the most relevant problems. A party will join if it expects a higher payoff being a member of the coalition than by staying out. It will leave if unilateral payoff is higher than that of a coalition member. Contributions to that issue have been made among others by Bauer (1992), Barrett (1992), Botteon and Carraro (1995) and Chandler and Tulkens (1992, 1995). However, studying SSP coalition membership is not the most interesting part of the problem. The protocol was signed and ratified by the parties; a stable coalition evidently exists. The crux of our research is to explain the difference in emission reduction commitments among parties with an economic model. Acid rain is very much a phenomenon of multilateral, reciprocal trans-boundary air pollution among European countries. The basis of our model is the notion that in such a context a country can enhance the efficiency of its pollution control by making its emission reduction dependent on similar actions in countries, from which emissions are "imported". There is an incentive to participate in an international environmental agreement on reciprocal reduction of emissions from which all participants gain net benefits. This paper focuses on the question how this notion of Pareto-efficient international convention relates to the real world, specifically the commitments of the parties to the Second Sulphur Protocol.

Empirical work on acid rain in Europe has been done mainly by IIASA's Trans-boundary Pollution Control Group (TAP) in support of the parties negotiating on a new protocol providing them with information on the costs and environmental effects of various options. For SSP their least-cost analysis of acid deposition reduction in Europe, that is, simultaneous joint cost minimisation subject to deposition constraints (Amann and Schoepp, 1993), was particularly relevant. When such an approach is adopted, the cheaper environmentally-acceptable emission the better, regardless of environmental benefits brought about by the particular emission reduction policy. Cost-effective solutions can be found via linear (Alcamo *et al.*, 1990) or non-linear (Heyes *et al.*, 1997) optimisation. Instead of cost functions only, in cost-benefit analysis one uses net utility functions, that incorporate both costs of emission reductions and environmental benefits, derived from these reductions. Because of the trans-boundary nature of acid rain, deposition in any country results from the actions of all the parties. It is reflected in the benefit function, rather than in constraints, and facilitates analysis of countries' reciprocal dependencies using the concepts of non-cooperative and cooperative game theory. Pareto-optimal allocation of emission reductions, based on cost and benefit functions was studied by Nentjes and Shibayev (2000); it applies non-cooperative game theory and will be presented in the next sections. Although the economic model of reciprocal reduction of trans-boundary pollution can explain differentiated emission reduction commitments it remains to be seen whether the theory's postulate of Pareto-optimal international agreements on pollution reduction is correct. In this paper we set out to answer that question by comparing the net benefits of parties to the Second Sulphur Protocol with the net benefits of the same parties, assuming that they participate in a virtual Pareto-optimal scheme for reduction of SO_2, based on the same data as SSP, thus bridging the gap between theoretical and empirical research. The theoretical part in the section 2, is based on our earlier work with Kryazhimskii and Tarasyev (see Nentjes 1990, 1994; Kryazhimskii *et al.*, 1999, 2000). The empirical part in sections 3, 4 and 5. In section 3 the data used as the input in the negotiation on SSP, serve to construct marginal benefit functions for the model of Pareto-efficient reciprocal emission reduction (RER). The simulation procedure is explained in section 4. In section 5 the strength of the theoretical model is tested by comparing the net benefits of SSP with the predictions of the simulation performed with the model. The concluding section 6 provides the answer to the question of whether the Pareto-efficiency postulate fits the facts.

2. Theoretical model of unilateral and reciprocal emission reduction

Countries emit sulphur dioxide that is transported atmospherically to countries-receptors. If a country's acid pollution load does not exceed buffering properties of soils, its ecosystems sustain. If a country's acid pollution load does exceed a threshold value of buffering abilities of soils, a country becomes environmentally damaged. From reduction of environmental damage the country derives environmental benefits, marginal benefit functions of which are constructed below. As a local measure of environmental damage we use the excessive local domestic deposition. In order to compute national damage, local damage indicators are aggregated.

An emission reduction vector $z = (z_1,...,z_N)$ and country i's decrease of domestic pollution load r_i are connected by the linear source-receptor transmission function

$$r_i = \Sigma_{j=1}^{N} a_{ji}z_j = \Sigma_{j=1}^{N} r_{ji} \hspace{4cm} \text{(Eq. 1)}$$

where $a_{ji} > 0$ is a country-to-country transport coefficient for the emission originating in country j, exported to country i, $r_{ji} = a_{ji}z_j$ being country j's contribution to domestic deposition reduction in country i. A party's monetary valuation of its cost of emission reduction and benefits of having lower deposition are captured in the following equation

$$W_i(r_i(z)) = B_i(r_i(z)) - C_i(z_i) \tag{Eq. 2}$$

2.1. Unilateral reduction

Given net utilities $W_i(r_i(z))$ of the form (Equation 2) emission reduction bounds z_i^{min}, z_i^{max}, a normal form game is defined in which emission reduction vectors z_i belong to emission reduction intervals: $z_i^{min} \leq z_i \leq z_i^{max}$. The net benefit function W_i implies that national governments are interested in benefits and costs at home and not in the benefits and costs in other countries. The governments pursue the national interest by maximising the net benefit function under the constraints, imposed by the technical feasibility of emission reductions and by the relevant transmission equations. The outcome of such a behaviour depends on whether countries reduce trans-frontier emissions unilaterally, or coordinate their abatement policies in a specified way. In the absence of international coordination, each party decides unilaterally on its emission reduction taking the other parties' actions for granted. Emission reduction in the Current Reduction Plan (CRP) is pursued to the point where marginal costs of national emission control equals the national marginal benefits of emission reduction. According to Kryazhimskii *et al.* (2000, 2001) such unilateral actions result in a Nash equilibrium

$$C_i'(z_i) = a_{ii} \cdot B_i'(r_i(z)) \tag{Eq. 3}$$

Quite a number of people appear to have difficulty in accepting the idea that the marginal cost of pollution control a party is willing to make in its unilateral emission reduction plan reflects the marginal value the party attaches to reducing pollution. Such scepticism is not without reason. One has to admit that in different areas of health and safety regulations have been introduced without regard for and even without calculating their costs (see for example Table 20.4 in Viscusi *et al.*, 1992). Yet from the 1970s on for such countries as the US and the Netherlands such calculations of cost of controlling SO_2 emissions have been made before introducing new programmes and have been an argument for seizing down or delaying new regulation introducing more stringent emission standards. From the 1980s on calculations of cost was standard practice in the EU before introducing environmental directives. Therefore, the assumption that the parties' national governments have private knowledge of their marginal cost functions in the relevant planned (unilateral) emission reductions is a plausible one.

The next assumption is that parties, knowing their marginal cost, also have a (possibly fuzzy) notion of benefits and adhere to the principle that they should not make additional costs if those costs do exceed the expected additional value of improved environmental quality. We assume that in 1994 the plan each party had made for emission reduction to be achieved in 2010 by unilateral action has known marginal cost which indicate the marginal value assigned to the resulting reduction in pollution load. The view that CRP can be conceived as a Nash equilibrium has been the basis for our earlier work in the field and it is shared by the other authors. It should be noted, that parties in a Nash equilibrium are supposed to maximise a utility function and realise their optimum. In our approach it is specified as a maximisation of net benefits $W_i(r_i(z))$ from Equation 2. In short, acceptance of CRP as a Nash equilibrium implies that marginal net benefits are zero and it supports our assumption that marginal costs reflect the marginal benefits.

2.2. Reciprocal emission reduction

Countries can improve their welfare by cooperation, that is, by coordinating their actions with decisions of others. Nash equilibrium is usually Pareto-dominated. Steps towards Pareto-optimality can be made better by coordination of efforts undertaken by participants. Coordination implies that country i makes its own emission reduction in some way dependent on emission reductions of the other countries, according to some rule that has been accepted by negotiators. Following Nentjes (1994) one can interpret the country-to-itself transport coefficient $a_{ii} = r_{ii}/z_i$ as an individual rate of exchange between the country's unilateral emission reduction and reduction of internal deposition it gets in return. If countries act simultaneously they inevitably influence each other and therefore unilateral emission reductions result in multilateral domestic depositions reductions. This can be captured in form of an 'extended' exchange rate, where countries influence each other via domestic deposition reduction due to emissions reduction abroad:

$$p_i = \frac{r_i}{z_i} = \frac{\sum_{j=1}^{N} r_{ji}}{z_i} = \frac{\sum_{j=1}^{N} a_{ji} z_j}{z_i} = a_{ii} + \frac{\sum_{j \neq 1} a_{ji} z_j}{z_i} \qquad \text{(Eq. 4)}$$

The equation brings out that if other countries respond to emission reduction of country i it will get more reduction of deposition than in the case of unilateral action, thus raising its marginal benefits of emission control. Suppose that each player accepts the extended exchange rate as given. This implies maximisation of the net benefit function W_i under $r_i = p_i z_i$ constraint and technical feasibility of reductions:

$$\max_{zi} W_i = \max_{zi} \{B_i(r_i(z)) - C_i(z_i)\} \text{ subject to: } r_i = p_i z_i \text{ and } z_i^{min} \leq z_i \leq z_i^{max} \qquad \text{(Eq. 5)}$$

Maximum net benefits are realised if the following condition is fulfilled for each country i:

$$C_i'(z_i) = p_i \cdot B_i'(r_i) \qquad \text{(Eq. 6)}$$

where p_i is the rate of exchange. In case of N countries, compared with NE the 'return' of controlling emissions for country i has increased from $a_{ii} B_i'(r_i)$ to $p_i B_i'(r_i) = (a_{ii} + (\Sigma_{j \neq i} a_{ji} z_j) / z_i) B_i'(r_i)$. If a solution to Equation 6 exists, it calls for extra emission reduction, that would balance the following increment, compared to NE: $\Sigma_{j \neq i} a_{ji} z_j / z_i \cdot B_i'(r_i)$. Such an outcome may dominate NE in sense of Pareto. The reciprocal emission reduction outcome for N countries is realised when all participating countries at an exchange rate vector $p = (p_i, ..., p_N)$ are in position that Equation 6 is fulfilled. Analysis of the conditions for existence, uniqueness and Pareto-optimality of RER for N countries is carried out in Kryazhimskii *et al.* (2000). In the procedure to find RER each country has its own individual exchange rate, which is variable dependent on emission reductions offered by all parties. Assume that each party considers its exchange rate as a price signal and agrees to reveal its optimal amount of emission reduction at that exchange rate. The higher the exchange rate is the larger the emission reduction is that maximises the party's net benefits.

One might ask why parties will not behave strategically to affect the exchange multiplier p_i in such a way that it is changed in their favour. For example, a higher p_1 for party 1. The answer is that the parties have only knowledge of their own costs and benefits. Strategic behaviour requires that the party has full information on the cost and benefit functions of other parties and can predict their reactions to his own actions. In the absence of such precise information the party has no clue as to how to affect other parties' actions in his own favour, which makes efforts to behave strategically like playing a lottery. Therefore, it makes sense to take the information on exchange rates, provided by the auctioneer as a beacon, and to respond by choosing optimal emission reduction.

3. Constructing marginal benefit functions for acid rain

In the next sections 3, 4 and 5 the empirical research part will be presented. The first step is the construction of a marginal benefits of lower pollution load function for each party, which is explained in section 3. The marginal benefit functions, marginal costs of emission reduction functions, and the source-receptor transport matrix are the inputs for the simulation. The simulation algorithm is discussed in section 4. Its results is the prediction of net benefits for all parties. In section 5 the outcome of the simulation is presented and compared to the net benefits calculated for SSP.

3.1. The data

To feed parties involved in negotiating SSP with information IIASA's Transboundary Air Pollution Group built version 6 of the RAINS model. It contains the following building blocks, which we have used in our simulation of a Pareto-optimal allocation of emission reductions between the parties:

1. Source-receptor country-to-grid transport coefficients; source: Norwegian Meteorological Institute, Synthesizing Centre-West (MSC-W), Oslo, Norway.
2. Critical loads; source: Institute of Public Health and Environmental Protection (RIVM), Bilthoven, the Netherlands.
3. Cost functions of emission reductions $C_i(z_i)$; source: the RAINS model, version 6, International Institute for Applied Systems Analysis (IIASA), Laxenburg, Austria.

The RAINS model transforms emissions per country to deposition per grid (150x150km). Normally a country contains several grids and some grids are shared with other countries, or the sea. This implies that we work with transport on a country-to-grid rather than country-to-country level. Since a country's territory does not precisely fit into the existing grid frame we need grid shares μ_{ij} to calculate internal deposition reductions. Critical loads c_{ij} (the first index corresponds to a country, the second corresponds to a grid number inside the country) are defined per grid as the level of deposition where 95 percent of ecosystems is protected (Hettelingh *et al.*, 1991). The number of ecosystems varies among grids and sensitivity of ecosystems to sulphur deposition differs within and across grids.

3.2. Assumptions

The model of Pareto-efficient reciprocal emission reduction assumes that environmental effects are assessed in monetary units to make them comparable with the cost of achieving the positive environmental effects. Such monetary valuations were not included in the sixth version of the RAINS model and we have constructed piece-wise linear marginal benefit functions of domestic acid deposition reduction, based on the following assumptions (for in-depth description of construction of marginal benefits see Nentjes and Shibayev, 2004):

1. the marginal benefits are linear in reduction of internal deposition;
2. two reference points on the national marginal benefit function can be identified;
3. the first reference point is the marginal cost a party is willing to make for emission reduction in case of unilateral action;
4. the second reference point defines the saturation level in domestic deposition reduction; exceeding this level of internal deposition reduction does not result in receiving any extra environmental benefits.

3.3. Identification of reference points

The first reference point is the marginal benefits of reducing deposition, calculated at Nash equilibrium. According to Kryazhimskii *et al.* (2000, 2001), at Nash equilibrium (Equation 3) holds true. Information on planned unilateral emission reduction is available in the so called Current Reduction Plan (CRP) collected by IIASA's TAP group. Figure 3 illustrates how z_i^{CRP} allows to calculate $C_i'(z_i^{CRP})$. $r_i^{CRP} = r_i(z^{CRP})$. is calculated with the transport model from RAINS model version 6 (using source-receptor relationship (Equation 1)). This provides the information for calculating $B_i'(r_i(z^{CRP}))$ for every party. The basic idea behind Equation 3 is that each party has revealed its willingness to pay for reduction of domestic deposition by committing itself to its current reduction plan. The second reference point on the national marginal benefit curve is that where the level of deposition is so low, that marginal benefits of further reduction of deposition are zero. If r_i' is the correspondent deposition reduction the equation for the second reference point takes the form:

$$B_i'(r_i') = 0 \qquad \text{(Eq. 7)}$$

A functional form that meets assumptions 1) to 4) and Equations 3 and 7 is a piecewise-linear functional of the form:

$$B'_i(r'_i) = k_i \cdot \max\{r'_i - r_i, 0\}$$

with k_i being a country-dependent positive constant.

4. Simulation

In the simulation with 13 countries, we use a tâtonnement-like procedure where an auctioneer iteratively proposes lower and upper bounds of emission reduction. The auctioneer starts the process on both sides of feasible emission reduction interval, corresponding to non-cooperative Nash equilibrium and maximum reduction technically achievable. As the process unfolds over time, he intends to narrow down the emission reduction gap iteratively, while keeping the solution of (Equation 6) inside progressively diminishing emission reduction intervals. Let $n=0,1,...$ and $x_{in}^{\min}$, $x_{in}^{\max}$ be respectively the number of negotiations rounds and the auctioneer's offer to country i at the round n, $x_{in}^{\min} \leq x_{in}^{\max}$.

Initially $x_{i0}^{\max} = z_i^{\max}$, $x_{i0}^{\min} = e_i^{unab} - e_i^{NE}$, where $z_i^{\max}$ is the abovementioned maximal emission reduction technically feasible, e_i^{unab} is unabated emission, which cost is 0, and e_i^{NE} is Nash-equilibrium emission, discussed in the section 3. Reduction multipliers $p_{i0}^{\min}$ and $p_{i0}^{\max}$ are calculated through the transmission source-receptor relation. The 4-tuple ($x_{in}^{\min}$, $p_{in}^{\min}$, $x_{in}^{\max}$, $p_{in}^{\max}$) represents the auctioneer's offer to a country i at the stage n. Conditions

$$C'_i(x_{in}^{\max}) - p_{in}^{\max} \cdot B'_i(p_{in}^{\max} x_{in}^{\max}) > 0$$

and

$$C'_i(x_{in}^{\min}) - p_{in}^{\min} \cdot B'_i(p_{in}^{\min} x_{in}^{\min}) < 0$$

imply that the benefits from extra environmental improvement for the emission reduction offer of $x_{in}^{\min}$ are higher than the cost of such emission reduction, whereas for emission reduction $x_{in}^{\max}$ it is reversed, so that the optimal emission reduction x_i^*, such that

$$C'_i(x_i^*) - p_i(x_i^*) \cdot B'_i(p_i(x_i^*)x_i^*) = 0$$

always meets the condition $x_{in}^{\min} \leq x_i^* \leq x_{in}^{\max}$. Thus, if both of the abovementioned conditions have been met, the representative accepts the offer, otherwise he re-negotiates the part(s) corresponding to the unsatisfied condition(s) by offering his own emission reduction scheme $x'^{\min}_{in}$ and/or $x'^{\max}_{in}$ to the auctioneer.

If the auctioneer's current proposal has been approved by all countries' representatives, countries-participants commit themselves to the current emission reduction offer: $z_{i(n+1)}^{\min} = x_{in}^{\min}$, $z_{i(n+1)}^{\max} = x_{in}^{\max}$ and the negotiations progress into a next round where the procedure repeats. If the current offer has been rejected by some countries, this means, that for these countries at least one of the abovementioned conditions is not met because of the auctioneer's too optimistic beliefs. In this case the auctioneer revises respective emission reductions using $x_{in}^{\min}$ and/or $x_{in}^{\max}$, so that the updated offers call for less radical change. eduction multipliers are recalculated according to (4). The revision goes on until all representatives agree on their emission reductions. As a result acceptable lower and upper emissions reductions $z_{i(n+1)}^{\min}$ and $z_{i(n+1)}^{\max}$ would satisfy the conditions $z_{in}^{\min} < z_{i(n+1)}^{\min} \leq x_{in}^{\min}$ and $z_{in}^{\max} > z_{i(n+1)}^{\max} \geq x_{in}^{\max}$. This can be captured in the following form:

$$z_{i(n+1)}^{\min} = (1-\tau_{in}) \cdot z_{in}^{\min} + \tau_{in} \cdot x_{in}^{\min}, \quad z_{i(n+1)}^{\max} = (1-\rho_{in}) \cdot z_{in}^{\max} + \rho_{in} \cdot x_{in}^{\max}$$

where τ_{in}, ρ_{in} are positive adjustment coefficients: $0 < \min\{\tau_{in}, \rho_{in}\}, \max\{\tau_{in}, \rho_{in}\} \leq 1$.

As the process unfolds over time such tâtonnement-like emission gap closure dynamics results in successive reductions of each country's emission gap:

$$0 \leq x_{in}^{\max} - x_{in}^{\min} \leq z_{i(n+1)}^{\max} - z_{i(n+1)}^{\min} \leq z_{in}^{\max} - z_{in}^{\min}.$$

The following two conditions are valid at any iteration of the process:

$$C_i'(z_{in}^{\min}) - p_{in}^{\min} \cdot B_i'(p_{in}^{\min} z_{in}^{\min}) < 0$$

$$C_i'(z_{in}^{\max}) - p_{in}^{\max} \cdot B_i'(r_{in}^{\max} r_{in}^{\max}) > 0$$

leading eventually to $z_{in}^{\max} = z_{in}^{\min} = z_i^*$ and $C_i'(z_i^*) - p_i^* \cdot B_i'(p_i^* z_i^*) = 0$.

5. Comparison of RER with CRP and SSP

In 1994 21 European countries signed the Second Sulphur Protocol. Parties agreed to reduce their emissions compared to their Current Reduction Plans with individual percentages of reductions. In Table 1 we present the costs and benefits if parties had searched for a Pareto-optimal convention, following the procedure for detecting RER equilibrium explained in section 4. For the simulation the same data have been used that served as information for the actual negotiations on SSP. Using the benefit functions - their construction was explained in section 3 - we have computed the costs and benefits of the actual SSP. They are shown in Table 2.

For the simulation of Pareto-efficient RER-equilibrium we could use the CRP targets of 13 countries as benchmark. Table 1 shows that indeed RER dominates CRP in the sense of

Table 1. Costs and benefits of reciprocal emission reduction compare to CRP.

Country	Costs (Mio DM)	Benefits (Mio DM)	Benefits/Cost	Net benefits (Mio DM)
Austria	140.87	409.67	2.91	268.80
Belgium	107.47	110.94	1.03	3.48
Czech and Slovakia	404.88	405.02	1.00	0.15
Denmark	77.83	109.73	1.41	31.90
Finland	283.94	455.26	1.60	171.31
Germany	420.70	1244.06	2.96	823.35
Italy	70.48	90.35	1.28	19.87
Netherlands	399.77	504.78	1.26	105.01
Norway	126.94	128.84	1.01	1.90
Poland	446.47	446.51	1.00	0.04
Sweden	116.64	764.03	6.55	647.39
Switzerland	6.60	20.83	3.16	14.24
UK	180.67	182.87	1.01	2.20
Total	2783.26	4872.09	–	2089.63

Table 2. Costs and benefits of Second Sulphur Protocol relative to CRP.

Country	Costs (Mio DM)	Benefits (Mio DM)	Net benefits (Mio DM)
Austria	0.00	623.09	623.09
Belgium	-382.59	196.75	-185.84
Czech and Slovakia	-537.22	524.42	-12.80
Denmark	-229.70	131.50	-98.20
Finland	0.00	452.57	452.57
Germany	0.00	1859.61	1859.61
Italy	-765.34	253.52	-511.82
Netherlands	0.00	840.43	840.43
Norway	-204.06	248.54	44.49
Poland	-1478.03	858.38	-619.65
Sweden	0.00	1450.84	1450.84
Switzerland	0.00	21.14	21.24
UK	-1853.44	691.74	-1161.69
Total	-5450.37	8152.54	2702.17

Pareto: no participants have negative net benefits. Net benefits are unequally distributed: Sweden and Germany, both being highly sensitive to acid rain, have considerable benefits compared to their control cost while Poland is merely compensated for its extra effort. Total emission reduction in RER is 1598 kT, that is 15 percent relative to CRP. Joint net benefits are 2 billion DM (in prices of 1996) and the overall benefit-to-cost ratio is 1.75.

The ratio of SSP emission reduction to that in CRP is much higher than the ratio of the reduction in RER to the one in CRP: 4694 kT = 43 percent emission reduction versus 1598 kT = 15 percent reduction. Responsible for the difference of 3096 kT between SSP and RER are mainly the UK (1325 kT lower emissions in SSP than in RER), Poland (837 kT lower) and Italy (838 kT). On the other hand, a set of countries (Austria, Finland, Germany, the Netherlands, Sweden and Switzerland) that are willing to reduce emissions in RER by 143 kT in total relative to CRP have an emission reduction of zero in SSP compared to CRP. It is clear that the results of our RER model on directly observable variables (emissions and emission reductions) diverge considerably from the actual SSP, concluded in 1994.

As Table 2 shows a striking feature is that SSP is not Pareto-efficient. Compared with CRP there are large negative net benefits for the UK, Poland and Italy. In contrast, Germany, Sweden, the Netherlands, Austria and Finland have large positive net benefits. We also see that joint net benefits are considerably higher in SSP (2702 millions DM) than they are in RER (2089 millions DM). The overall benefit-cost ratio of SSP is 1.50; this is lower than RER's 1.75.

What causes the difference between SSP and RER? In the first place SSP has more than 20 signatories and our RER model has only 13 participants, thus reducing the scope for efficient emission reductions. Keeping this in mind we shall turn to a more fundamental source of differences. In an early stage the participants agreed on three guidelines:

1. They would focus on uniform reduction of the gap between actual deposition in 1990 and the critical loads by 60 percent, leaving the residual 40 percent for a next protocol.
2. In allocating emission reductions to achieve the target cost-effectiveness would be the criterion: reducing the emissions in the countries where this could be done at lowest cost.
3. Countries which had planned emission reduction higher than the fully cost effective solution of 60 percent gap closure in their CRP would stick to their emission targets in SSP.

Guideline 3 explains the zero cost of six parties in SSP (relative to CRP) in Table 2. Guideline 2 explains the high cost relative to RER in countries showed a low willingness to control emissions in their CRPs, therefore having scope for large emission reductions at initially low marginal abatement cost (the UK, Italy and Poland in particular). Guideline 2 implies that country A accepts that it might have to reduce emissions, because it can do so at low cost, for the benefit of countries B and C even if the quality of ecosystems is hardly improved. Table

2 shows that some countries really accepted negative net benefits for the common good. This clearly is in contradiction with our assumption of narrow self-interest, which postulates that countries would require side payments if marginal cost exceeds national marginal benefit. The cost-effective gap reduction guideline provided countries with high emission reductions in their CRPs the argument that they already had made their contribution to gap closure in their CRPs and that now it was up to other parties to follow the example. Since the joint benefits of SSP exceed its total costs relative to CRP the Protocol is potentially Pareto-dominant compared to CRP. The countries that lose could be compensated and still there would be net benefits left. Whether in the end and in terms of joint benefits and joint costs SSP provides a better deal is open to debate: SSP has a surplus in terms of net benefits bigger than RER. However, its benefit-to-cost ratio is lower, which suggests that RER provides the best investment. On the other hand, the joint cost of SSP is double the cost of RER and its lower benefit-to-cost ratio reflects the law of decreasing marginal returns rather than inefficiency in the allocation of emission reduction.

6. Conclusions

1. Parties to the SSP accepted a sixty percent closure of the gap between actual deposition of acid substances and critical loads to be achieved at least cost as their common strategy. In contrast, we identified parties' revealed willingness to pay for gap closure and used them in cost-benefit analysis to calculate a Pareto-efficient allocation of reciprocal emission reduction.
2. In order to detect Pareto-optimum, non-cooperative game theory with informational decentralisation has been applied.
3. An RER-equilibrium, which is Pareto-efficient compared to CRP, exists.
4. Emission reduction in SSP is 3 times higher than in RER, costs are twice as high, benefits are 1.7 and net benefits 1.3 times costs.
5. SSP is Pareto-inefficient compared to CRP, but potentially Pareto-efficient.
6. The distribution of net benefits in RER is much more uniform than in SSP.
7. In terms of joint benefits and costs the efficiency of RER relative to SSP remains empirically undecided.

Acknowledgments

The authors would like to thank their former colleagues M. Amann, J. Cofala and W. Schoepp from International Institute for Applied Systems Analysis (IIASA) for useful discussions. The work of second author was supported by Dutch Organisation for Scientific Research (NWO) and HIPCON project (contract No: STRP 505467-1 HIPCON), Imperial College London.

References

Alcamo J., R. Shaw and L.J. Hordijk, 1990. The RAINS model of acidification. Science and strategies for Europe, Kluwer Academic Press, Dordrecht.

Amann, M. and W. Schoepp, 1993. Reducing Excess sulphur deposition in Europe by 60 percent. Background paper prepared for UN/ECE working group on abatement strategies, Laxenburg, IIASA.

Barrett, S., 1992. International environmental agreements as games. In: R. Pethig (ed.), Conflicts and cooperation in managing environmental resources, Microeconomic studies, Springer, Berlin, pp. 11-37.

Bauer, A., 1992. International cooperation over greenhouse gas abatement, mimeo. Seminar für empirische Wirschaftsforschung, University of Munich.

Botteon, M. and C. Carraro, 1995. Burden-sharing and coalition stability in environmental negotiation with asymmetric countries. Discussion paper 78.95, Fondazione Eni Enrico Mattei.

Chandler, P. and H. Tulkens, 1992. Theoretical foundations of negotiations and cost sharing in trans-frontier pollution problem. European Economic Review 36: 288-299.

Chandler, P. and H. Tulkens, 1995. A core-theoretic solution for the design of cooperative agreements on trans-frontier pollution. International Tax and Public Finance 2: 279-293.

Hettelingh, J.P., R.J. Downing and P. de Smit, 1991. Mapping critical loads for Europe. CCE Technical Report 1, RIVM Report 259101001, RIVM, Bilthoven.

Heyes, C., W. Schoepp, M. Amann, I. Bertok, J. Cofala, F. Gyarfas, Z. Klimont, M. Makovski and S. Shibayev, 1997a. Model for optimising strategies for controlling ground-level ozone in Europe. Tech. Report IR-97-002, IIASA, A-2361 Laxenburg, Austria.

Heyes, C., W. Schoepp, M. Amann, I. Bertok, J. Cofala, F. Gyarfas, Z. Klimont, M. Makovski and S. Shibayev, 1997b. Simultaneous optimisation of abatement strategies for ground-level ozone and acidification. Tech. Report IR-97-090, IIASA, A-2361 Laxenburg, Austria.

Kryazhimskii, A., A. Nentjes, S. Shibayev and A. Tarasyev, 2000. A game model of negotiations and market equilibria. Journal of Mathematical Sciences 100: 2601-2612.

Kryazhimskii, A., A. Nentjes, S. Shibayev and A. Tarasyev, 2001. Modelling market equilibrium for trans-boundary environmental problem. Non-linear analysis 47: 991-1002.

Nentjes, A., 1990. An economic model for trans-frontier pollution abatement. In: V. Tanzi (ed), Public finance, trade and development, Wayne State University Press, pp. 243-262.

Nentjes, A., 1994. Economic instruments for air pollution control. In: G. Klaassen and F. Forsund (eds.), Control of trans-boundary air pollution and joint implementation, Kluwer Academic Publishers, Boston-London, pp. 209-231.

Nentjes, A. and S. Shibayev, 2000. Is international environmental cooperation Pareto-efficient? ECOF Research Memorandum 26, ECOF, University of Groningen.

Nentjes, A. and S. Shibayev, 2004. Constructing marginal benefit functions for trans-boundary pollution problem. ECOF Research Memorandum, ECOF, University of Groningen.

Viscusi, W.K., J.M. Vernon and J.E. Harrington, 1992. Economic of regulation and antitrust. DC Heath and Company, Lexington (Mass.)/Toronto.

International relations

Bilateral free trade agreement in the 21st Century: the case of Thailand in late 1990s

Poonsri Sakhornrad
Department of International Development (DID), Graduate School of International Development (GSID), Nagoya University, Furo-cho, Chikusa-ku, Nagoya, Japan. m040103d@mbox.nagoya-u.ac.jp

Abstract

This article investigates the justification for changes in the trade approach of Thailand after the 1997 Asian Financial Crisis, focusing on bilateral free trade agreement (FTA) with three partners, Japan, the United States and China. By investigating trade and investment structure including protection structure of these three bilateral FTA partners with respect to Thailand utilising selected international trade indices, bilateral FTA approach could be explained by both economic and political reasons. The results suggest that the Thai government should get its priorities right on the ground of economic justifications with inclusive consideration of both economic and social aspects.

JEL classification: F13, F14, O24

Keywords: bilateral free trade agreement (FTA), trade negotiations, protection

1. Introduction

As a country in the Southeast Asian region, Thailand has participated in trade agreements and economic cooperations on several levels for decades. Thailand was a member of the General Agreement on Tariffs and Trade (GATT) since 1982 and became the 59th founding member of the World Trade Organisation (WTO) as of January 1, 1995. Thailand was also one of the founding members of the Association of South East Asian Nations (ASEAN) in 1967. In 1989, Thailand joined the Asia Pacific Economic Cooperation (APEC) and in 1993 decided to initiate the formation of ASEAN Free Trade Area (AFTA) with other original members of ASEAN. Recently Thailand started to promote the formation of bilateral free trade agreements with many countries. The bilateral trade agreement approach was initiated in Thailand at the end of 1997 during the Chuan administration of the Democrat Party. Even after the election in early 2001, the Thai government under the Thaksin administration of the Thai Rak Thai Party continued its positive approach towards more bilateral FTAs. The major difference is that Prime Minister Thaksin seems to focus on larger and more developed countries in East Asia and America compared to the bilateral FTA partners during former administration.

Among potential bilateral negotiating partners, Japan, the United States and China are the three most eminent countries at the present time. One of the key questions to ask is why

Thailand has a strong intention to establish various bilateral FTAs (Nagai, 2002) while the country has already firmly committed to regional cooperation in AFTA and APEC as well as multilateral trade liberalisation under WTO.

This article attempts to identify the reasons motivating Thailand to negotiate bilateral FTAs with Japan, the United States and China. More specifically, the author (1) investigates why the Thai government currently prefers bilateral trade agreements to multilateral and broader regional trade liberalisation, and (2) examines trade and protection structures of Thailand in comparison with potential bilateral FTA partners in order to evaluate whether their trade and protection structures with respect to Thailand would allow gains from concluding bilateral trade negotiations.

This article is organised as follows: Section 2 overviews trade policy of Thailand in the past and emphasises the bilateral trade approach, Section 3 provides an analytical framework, Section 4 discusses and analyses the findings of the article and Section 5 presents conclusion and policy implications.

2. Overview of trade policy and bilateral trade agreement

2.1. Thailand trade policy prior to 1997 Asian financial crisis

Past Thai national and social development plans show that the Thai government initially adopted an inward-looking policy as a main policy to protect some infant industries as most developing countries. However, when the government became aware of the policy's unfavourable consequences in the form of inefficiency of protected industries, the government decided to adopt a dual track trade policy by imposing an export promotion policy with a focus on labour-intensive industries while still protecting some strategic manufacturing industries (Urata and Yokota, 1994).

After the mid 1990s, the government, realising the importance of export sectors as the engine of growth, promoted an outward-looking policy emphasising export promotion strategies by relaxation of tax system and investment regulations to enhance efficiency in some industries and strengthen the country's competitiveness.

Before the 1997 Asian Financial Crisis, Thailand's prospects to promote trade liberalisation prevailed not only on a unilateral basis by reducing tariffs and restrictions, but externally Thai government also took actions on a regional basis under AFTA and on a multilateral basis under WTO.

2.2. Thailand trade policy after the 1997 Asian financial crisis

2.2.1. After the 1997 Asian financial crisis

In the wake of the economic crisis, Thailand's trade and investment policy has remained liberal. Autonomous tariff reduction was imposed. Meanwhile, the authorities have prioritised domestic recovery relative to trade liberalisation by curtailing some imports of competing finished goods via increased tariffs and promoting exports.

Apart from that, the Thai government remains fully committed to trade liberalisation and has adhered to all commitments made in every forum on the conviction that greater liberalisation will assist economic recovery.

2.2.2. Emergence of the bilateral trade approach

As mentioned earlier, bilateral FTAs approach emerged in Thailand during the Chuan administration. However, the FTA partners during that period and during the Thaksin administration are quite different in terms of size of country, socio-economic background and past trade relations with Thailand. The countries Thailand appointed as bilateral FTAs partners during the Chuan administration were Chile, Croatia, the Czech Republic, Australia, South Korea and New Zealand. Though there were some government level discussions to initiate bilateral trade ties, none of these materialised.

Interestingly, the Thai government has maintained its positive approach towards the bilateral FTAs concept despite of a shift of administration in February 2001 from the Democrat Party led by the Chuan Cabinet to the Thai Rak Thai Party led by the Thaksin Cabinet. In addition, the Thaksin cabinet gradually became an ardent supporter of bilateral FTAs and even gave more emphasises than the Chuan's cabinet to the bilateral approach to trade and investment liberalisation. It can be said that the institutional legacy the Thaksin administration inherited from the previous administration paved the way for Prime Minister Thaksin to evaluate international trade situations and develop potential trade policy for the country (Nagai, 2003).

During the Thaksin era, the National Economic Policy Committee was established to be responsible for trade negotiations. Up to the present time, the lists of prospective FTA partners vary from Australia, Bahrain, China, India, Japan, New Zealand, Peru, and South Korea to the United States.

2.3. Analysis on changes in trade policy of Thailand

2.3.1. Motives behind the Emergence of Bilateral FTA Approach

Several reasons seem to account for the changes. Firstly, the slow pace of trade liberalisation under AFTA is recognised as one of the main reasons why the Thai government opted for bilateral FTA (See Nagai, 2003). Though AFTA has been established for a decade, members generally face impasses to achieving conclusions and implementation.

Secondly, the slow pace of multilateral trade liberalisation under World Trade Organisation (WTO) is another factor deviating Thailand from multilateralism. The collapse of the Seattle (WTO) meeting in December 1999 and the eventual outcomes for developing countries made many countries feel disappointed with the progress of the GATT/WTO negotiations. Thereafter the bilateral FTAs approach became a significantly more probable alternative for the Thai government and other countries. FTAs are viewed as a safety net if multilateral negotiations reach stalemate (http://www.tusbbc.org). More specifically, a recent WTO meeting in Cancun, Mexico accentuated the dysfunction of WTO. In addition, FTA provides models for rule-making in domains which are not necessarily covered by the WTO (Urata, 2003) and where single rule-making by many countries is difficult (METI, 1999).

Thirdly, Thai policy makers recognised increasingly competitive world markets in the future, especially after China's accession to WTO. From ASEAN's point of view, China is a strong competitor not only in terms of a huge cost-saving production base but also as a more attractive foreign direct investment (FDI) destination compared to ASEAN (Chirathivat, 2002). Consequently, the Thai government might adopt the bilateral FTA concept on the conviction that bilateral FTA is conducive to attracting foreign investors and stimulating the country's economy.

Fourthly, bilateral deals are more efficient than regional or multilateral negotiations with respect to flexibility. Negotiating in a smaller group of like-minded countries, especially where socio-economic situations are homogeneous could allow meaningful outcomes for FTA partners and could help negotiators reach consensus more easily with reduced transaction costs.

Finally, bilateral FTA idea is a component of the Thaksin administration's dual track policy, which stresses the importance of the East Asian economic model, foreign direct investment as well as exports, and simultaneously works on strengthening domestic policies. The Thai government's action towards the bilateral FTA approach may also be the result of a domino effect or what is so called FTA syndrome, *i.e.* the government may fear economic losses from not conducting bilateral trade negotiations.

2.3.2. Analysis on the Thai government's strategy in appointing bilateral FTA partners

Based on general information regarding Thailand's FTA partners in terms of country size, socio-economic background and past trade relations with Thailand (see Table 1), the Thai bilateral FTA strategy can be analysed as follows.

Table 1. Potential Bilateral FTA Partners' Socio-Economic Background (2001) and Trade Relations with Thailand classified by trade volumes.

Country	Geographical location	Population (Million)	Pop. Average growth in %	GDP (Million dollars)	GDP growth in % (1990-2001)	GNI (Million dollars)	GNI per capita (dollars)	PPP GNI (Million dollars)	PPP GNI per capita (dollars)	Export (Million Bahts)		Import (Million Bahts)	
										2000	2001	2000	2001
Japan	East Asia	127.1	0.3	4,245,191	1.3	4,574.2	35,990	3,487	27,430	406,442 (14.7)	439,834 (15.2)	615,659 (24.7)	616,461 (22.4)
United States	North America	284.0	1.2	10,171,400	3.5	9,900.7	34,870	9,902	34,870	591,676 (21.4)	584,497 (20.3)	293,580 (11.8)	318,733 (11.6)
China	East Asia	1271.9	1.0	1,159,017	10.0	1131	890	5,415	4,260	113,278 (4.1)	127,205 (4.4)	135,700 (5.4)	165,060 (6.0)
Australia [a]	Australia	19.4	1.2	368,571	4.0	383.3	19,770	500	25,780	65,089 (2.4)	60,370 (2.1)	46,776 (1.9)	60,201 (2.2)
South Korea [a]	East Asia	47.6	1.0	422,167	5.7	447.7	9,400	863	18,110	50,835 (1.8)	54,601 (1.9)	87,171 (3.5)	94,243 (3.4)
India	South Asia	1033.4	1.8	477,555	5.9	474.3	460	2,530	2,450	19,784 (0.7)	21,421 (0.7)	24,879 (1.0)	29,901 (1.1)
Mexico [a]	Latin America	99.4	3.1	617,817	3.1	550.5	5,540	872	8,770	15,025 (0.5)	18,965 (0.7)	4,995 (0.2)	5,633 (0.2)
South Africa [a]	South Africa	43.2	1.9	113,274	2.1	125.5	2,900	411 [b]	9,510 [b]	14,701 (0.5)	14,017 (0.5)	12,416 (0.5)	10,768 (0.4)
New Zealand [a]	Australia	3.8	1.0	48,277	2.9	47.6	12,380	74	19,130	7,323 (0.3)	8,114 (0.3)	7,858 (0.3)	9,342 (0.3)
Russia [a]	CIS	144.8	-0.2	309,951	-3.7	253.4	1,750	1,255	8,660	3,092 (0.1)	3,587 (0.1)	14,964 (0.6)	14,070 (0.5)
Bahrain	Middle East	0.000714	3.2	n.a.	n.a.	6,247	9,370	9,605	14,410	1,153 (0.0)	1,465 (0.1)	2,283 (0.1)	2,538 (0.1)
Peru	Latin America	26.1	1.7	54,047	4.3	52.1	2000	122	4,680	n.a.	n.a.	n.a.	n.a.

Note: Figures in parentheses are percentage of total values.
[a] Indicates the countries which were included in the Committee of International Economic Policy (CIEP)'s research submitted to Thaksin administration during the first CIEP annual meeting of year 2001.
[b] The estimates are based on regressions; others are extrapolated from the latest International Comparison Programme benchmark estimates.
Source: World Bank (2003) and Nagai (2003).

Firstly, the Thai authorities may promote bilateral FTA because they are putting great effort into diversifying not only export products but also export destinations in order to reduce dependency on existing commodities and a few traditional markets, for example, European Union countries, the United States and ASEAN countries. The policy of diversifying export markets corresponds to the objectives of trade-related policies in the ninth national economic and social development plan for the years 2002-2006. The proportion of Thai export values to non-traditional export markets have increased recently, and meanwhile the export growth rate also reflects a positive trend in non-traditional export destinations compared to those of traditional markets (http://www.bot.or.th).

Secondly, Thailand's FTAs approach is characterised by a geographically dispersed pattern. This reflects the government's aim to explore market access in new regions if these FTA negotiations are successful.

Thirdly, the Thaksin government prioritises bigger trade partners and more populated countries in trade negotiating. Compared to FTA partners during the Chuan government, those during the Thaksin government are bigger not only in terms of markets with more population and higher potential consumers but also bigger in terms of their economic activities in world economy. These bigger trade partners are epitomised by Japan, the United States and China.

3. Analytical Framework

This section will investigate the trade and investment structure of Thailand in general, including its protection structure, in order to lay the framework for the analysis of the Thai bilateral FTA strategy by utilising selected international trade indices.

3.1. Trade and investment structure of Thailand

3.1.1. Trade and investment pattern with potential FTA partners[1] by country

Considering trade and net flows of foreign direct investment (FDI) of Thailand with potential FTA partners, Japan and the United States have been the two most prominent partners of Thailand both in trade and investment for several years. Especially in terms of investment, Japan and the United States have been the main foreign investors in Thailand since the 1970s. Japanese investment, in particular, has been recognised as one of the main engines of the country's economic growth since the mid 1980s. In addition, these two countries' trade volumes accounted for more than 30-40 percent of total trade value of Thailand over

---

[1] Since the combination of other FTA partners than Japan, the United States and China explains only small amount of total trade of Thailand (see Table 1) and the presence of their FDI into Thailand is completely not significant, those countries will be excluded from the main analysis. Therefore, analysis hereafter will focus on the Thai bilateral FTA with the United States, Japan and China only.

the past decade. Therefore, from the economic point of view, it is a logical decision of the Thai government to conclude bilateral FTA with Japan and the United States.

As for China, although the trade volume between Thailand and China is not of great importance, around 5-6 percent of total value, and China is not one of the major sources of direct investment in Thailand, the Chinese economy itself and trade relations, both export and import, between China and Thailand have been growing remarkably in recent years. Therefore, it also makes sense for the Thai government to initiate a bilateral FTA with China.

3.1.2. Nature of bilateral trade between Thailand and potential FTA partners

This article calculates two widely used international trade indices, namely, Revealed Comparative Advantage (RCA) and Intra Industry Trade (IIT) index to examine more details of the nature of trade between Thailand and three main FTA partners, namely, Japan, the United States and China. They are calculated as follows:

$$RCA_{ij} = (X_{ij}/\sum_i X_{ij})/(\sum_j X_{ij}/\sum_i \sum_j X_{ij}) \quad\quad\quad\quad \text{(Eq. 1)}$$

where X_{ij} is country j's export of commodity i

$\sum_i X_{ij}$ is country j's total export

$\sum_j X_{ij}$ is world export of commodity i

$\sum_i \sum_j X_{ij}$ is total world export

and $IIT_{ij} = (1 - (|X_{ij} - M_{ij}|/(X_{ij} + M_{ij}))$ (Eq. 2)

where X_{ij} is country j's export value of commodity i

      M_{ij} is country j's import value of commodity i

Table 2 shows the Spearman's Rank Correlation Coefficient of the values of RCA indices of the commodities at three-digit level of Standard International Trade Classification (SITC) Revision 3 between Thailand and potential bilateral FTA partners. India and Australia are also included in the table to allow comparison.

As specified in Table 2, all countries except China possess very low Spearman's rank correlation or a rank correlation not too far from zero. Generally, countries with negative rank correlation or with a rank correlation close to zero are those which have dissimilar trade structures and do not compete directly with Thailand. In addition, their demand structure may be complementary with the structure of Thailand's export (Sussangkarn, 2003). Countries with fairly high and positive rank correlation have an export structure similar to Thailand, so they tend to be competitive with Thailand in export markets.

Table 2. Spearman Rank Correlation Coefficient of the Values of RCA Indices of Commodities at three-digit level of SITC between Thailand and Potential FTA Partners 1996-2000.

Countries	1996	1997	1998	1999	2000
1. Japan	0.113	0.115	0.126**	0.126**	0.129**
2. United States	-0.124**	-0.100	-0.108	-0.098	-0.096
3. China	0.505***	0.472***	0.458***	0.434***	0.400***
4. India	0.311***	0.293***	0.308***	0.356***	n.a.
5. Australia	-0.213***	-0.183***	-0.183***	-0.182***	-0.235***

Note: ** Correlation is statistically significant at the 0.05 level (2-tailed).*** Correlation is statistically significant at the 0.01 level (2-tailed).

The result demonstrates that the trade structure of Thailand and those of potential bilateral FTA partners are dissimilar except for the case of China. Consequently, in this sense Thailand and most potential bilateral FTA partners except China can be complementary to each other whereas China is a strong competitor to Thailand given the similarities of trade structures and China's lower cost of production. For more details about similarities of export structures between Thailand and China, see Sabhasri (2001) and Sussangkarn (2003).

However, this interpretation is obtained from examining the RCA index only, which indicates the country's international comparative advantage in inter-industry trade aspect. After incorporating the scope of intra industry trade, which plays an integral part in modern trade regimes and can be explained by intra industry trade (IIT) index, the conclusion might be different.

The idea to embrace intra-industry trade into consideration is in accordance with the notion made in Robson (1998), which discusses the inability of the orthodox theory to explain intra-industry trade in similar products which has become large part of modern trade.

Even when two countries have similar trade structures, implying that their factor endowments are quite indistinguishable, they could be complementary if they are engaged in intra-industry trade. IIT indices of SITC Revision 3 Classification at one-digit level in food and manufactured goods, which are the commodities of SITC 0 and SITC 5 to SITC 8, by potential bilateral FTA partners during 1996-2000, are demonstrated in Table 3. An IIT index close to 1 suggests intensive intra-industry trade between two countries, and the growth in one country's export could lead to a lot of demand for its trading partner's exports, for instance, through the demand for intermediate products (Sussangkarn, 2003).

The result indicates that Thailand is engaged in intra-industry trade with all three main bilateral FTA partners in various product groups with the improvement of degree of intra-industry trade intensity year by year for most cases. Thailand and Japan have a relatively high degree of intra-industry trade among other potential FTA partners in all manufactured goods.

For Thailand and the United States, both countries are extensively engaged in intra-industry trade in commodities of some manufactured commodities. The fairly high IIT indices between Thailand and Japan in overall manufactured commodities could be explained by the high degree of intra-firm trade between Japanese parent companies in the manufacturing sector and their subsidiaries in Thailand. This reflects the presence of multinational corporations in developing countries' trade structures in modern trade regimes. The same notion applies to the case of high IIT indices between Thailand and the United States.

Compared to other partners, China and Thailand have extremely high intra-industry trade in food products and some manufactured goods (Sabhasri, 2001), which are classified as

Table 3. Intra Industry Trade (IIT) Index between Thailand and Potential FTA Partners of SITC Revision 3 at one-digit level in Food and Manufactured Products during 1996-2000.

Commodity	Country	1996	1997	1998	1999	2000
IIT SITC 0	Japan	0.06989	0.10675	0.12524	0.08348	0.06732
	United States	0.27324	0.19095	0.14939	0.15113	0.14514
	China	0.09161	0.13624	0.13868	0.30683	0.42996
IIT SITC 5	Japan	0.23565	0.30961	0.34808	0.37867	0.41916
	United States	0.11098	0.11127	0.18080	0.18438	0.26066
	China	0.56975	0.50948	0.45162	0.56531	0.45142
IIT SITC 6	Japan	0.31402	0.33339	0.35860	0.35998	0.44042
	United States	0.57307	0.62067	0.58070	0.53347	0.45724
	China	0.29809	0.35565	0.40929	0.35429	0.38930
IIT SITC 7	Japan	0.31864	0.42067	0.52386	0.53493	0.52168
	United States	0.64117	0.62420	0.54114	0.59364	0.67938
	China	0.58792	0.61267	0.64206	0.68337	0.74284
IIT SITC 8	Japan	0.51635	0.55432	0.57666	0.58739	0.60921
	United States	0.37033	0.30654	0.22563	0.18279	0.14561
	China	0.31025	0.29172	0.35177	0.19126	0.30258

Note: 1. Initially, the author computed the IIT indices at the SITC two-digit level and then aggregated them into the SITC one-digit level by weighted average method. 2. See Sakhornrad (2004) for all IIT figures.

chemical products and capital commodities. In the case of China, it is to be noted carefully that the two countries could simultaneously have similar export structures inferring competitiveness in inter-industry trade with complementarities in intra-industry trade of some particular product groups. However, overall, RCA and IIT indices suggest that Thailand and China are likely to be competitive rather than complementary in world markets.

Besides, the extent of intra-industry trade between Thailand and potential bilateral FTA partners has been increasing gradually in accordance with improvement of RCA indices during 1996-2000 in all manufactured products, indicating that Thailand recently has been gaining international specialisation and competitiveness in the manufacturing sector. For more details and the results of RCA indices of Thailand and three trade partners, see Sakhornrad (2004).

3.2. Protection structure of Thailand

Table 4 illustrates the nominal rate of protection in comparison with effective rate of protection (ERP) of Thailand in year 1995 and 1999. ERP in case of multiple inputs was calculated by the simple Balassa Method as follows.

$$ERP_j = (\, t_j - \sum_i a_{ij} t_i) \, / \, (1 - \sum_i a_{ij}) \qquad\qquad \text{(Eq. 3)}$$

where t_j is nominal tariff rate on commodity j
$\quad\;\; t_i$ is nominal tariff rate on imported input i
$\quad\;\; a_{ij}$ is share of imported input i in the total value of the final product j.

From past tariff data, protection structures of Japan and the United States, which are developed countries, are similar in that they seem to place more protection on the agricultural sector than on the manufacturing sector[2]. On the contrary, China has the same protection structure as Thailand in that both countries put less emphasis on protecting the agricultural sector than the manufacturing sector. This implies the difference in protection structure between developed countries and developing countries.

More specifically, the effective rate of protection in Table 4 indicates that among manufactured goods, the Thai government heavily protected food products, beverages and tobacco, wearing apparel, excluding footwear, rubber and rubber products, and electrical machinery and transport equipment. These products are also profoundly protected in China. For nominal and effective rates of protection of China, see Osada (2003).

---

[2] The data is obtained from country's Trade Policy Review provided by the website of WTO (http://www.wto.org).

Table 4. Nominal Rate of Protection (NRP) and Effective Rate of Protection (ERP) of Thailand 1995 and 1999.

I-O Code	Commodities	1995		1999	
		NRP	ERP	NRP	ERP
001-024	agricultural and livestock production	37.80	53.929	32.90	47.110
025	logging	1.00	2.419	1.00	2.316
026-027	Forestry	21.60	25.019	19.50	22.045
028	Ocean and coastal fishing	56.60	86.751	11.60	17.885
029	Fishing n.e.s.	48.20	69.073	10.80	18.343
030	Coal mining	1.00	1.508	1.00	1.346
031	Crude petroleum and natural gas production	0.00	0.665	0.00	0.245
032	Mining of iron ores	1.00	5.706	1.00	5.579
033-036	Non-ferrous ore mining	7.00	10.075	1.00	2.111
037	Mining of fertilizer and chemical products	7.20	9.017	5.80	7.622
038	Salt mining	11.00	11.464	10.00	11.162
039	Mining of feldspar	13.70	20.444	8.70	13.658
040-041	Mining and quarrying n.e.s.	4.60	6.918	3.80	6.367
042-061	Food products	41.60	129.195	39.40	130.895
062-064	Beverages	52.60	81.173	45.70	69.872
065-066	Tobacco	51.40	67.064	60.00	77.991
067-071	Textiles	30.10	77.019	20.20	50.718
072-074	Wearing apparel, except footwear	41.30	107.366	46.90	115.442
075-077	Leather, leather products and footwear	28.00	69.611	19.40	42.656
078-079	Wood and cork	17.90	46.815	16.10	35.416
080	Furniture and fixtures	40.00	74.345	20.00	35.735
081-082	Paper and paper products	18.40	58.116	15.20	30.814
083	Printing, publishing and allied industries	20.00	49.447	17.10	38.307
084-092	Chemical products	15.90	45.032	10.10	26.281
093-094	Petroleum products	8.10	18.864	5.70	12.004
095-098	Rubber and rubber products	33.70	103.454	25.30	71.292
099-104	Non-metallic mineral products	24.40	44.474	17.20	29.459
105-107	Basic metal industries	10.80	52.473	9.00	22.236
108-111	Fabricated metal products, except machinery and equipment	22.90	63.075	18.70	45.758
112-116	Machinery	10.00	47.157	8.50	33.667
117-122	Electrical machinery	16.50	89.350	13.00	69.578
123-128	Transport equipment	26.30	100.853	25.60	72.392
129-134	Miscellaneous n.e.s.	20.10	55.612	13.90	37.229

Note: Input-Output Table of Thailand uses I-O code in classifying commodities while Trade Policy Review of Thailand where the nominal tariff rates are quoted uses ISIC 3-digit code. The author mapped the I-O code with the ISIC code in corresponding to commodity description because they are quite similar. The nominal tariff rates for commodities of which I-O code fall between 001-041 are the average rate of year 1999 while the nominal tariff rate for other commodities are the rate of September 1999. The author calculated the Effective rate of Protection from the Thai input-output table 1995 and 1998 provided by National Economic and Social Development Bureau, Thailand (NESDB). Because the 1999 Input-Output table of Thailand is not available, the author utilised 1998 Input-Output table of Thailand in calculating ERP for year 1999 by assuming that the input coefficients were constant between year 1998 and 1999. Nominal tariff rates are quoted from Trade Policy Review of Thailand (WTO, 2000), based on UNSD, Comtrade database; and WTO Secretariat estimates and data provided by the Thai authorities.

Regarding investment, the Thai government issued a Royal Decree in 1973 permitting up to 100 percent foreign ownership for such businesses as agriculture, industry and handicrafts, and commerce and services, provided that they are granted permission by the Board of Investment of Thailand (BOI). In addition, since November 1998, new projects in the manufacturing sector are allowed to be 100 percent foreign-owned including approval of foreign take-over of existing manufacturing plants with the consent of Thai partners This implies complete investment liberalisation in Thailand. However, the Thai government controls foreign activities in the service sector through the Alien Business Law (WTO, 2000), implying some protection against foreign operation.

4. Discussions on bilateral FTA of Thailand

4.1. Analysis on Thai bilateral FTA strategy

By examining trade and investment structure as well as protection structure of potential bilateral FTA partners with respect to Thailand, the past trade data and the result of selected international trade indices reveal that the Thai government's strategy to conclude bilateral FTAs with countries during the Thaksin administration could be explained by both economic and non-economic reasons such as political and foreign policy motivations (Kiyota, 2003).

Japan-Thai bilateral FTA and the United States-Thai bilateral FTA are economically justified because, first, both countries have significant trade relations and have been major foreign capital sources for Thailand for more than a decade. Second, trade structures of the United States and Japan with respect to Thailand are dissimilar, indicating that export structures of the United States and Japan are complementary to that of Thailand. This implies that there is a great scope to take advantage of inter-industry trade. Lastly, apart from complementarities with regard to international comparative advantage, Thailand is engaged in extensive intra-industry trade, which plays a prominent role in recent trade regime, with Japan and the United States. The Thai side anticipates most advantage from Japan-Thailand bilateral FTA in the agricultural sector and lower input cost in the manufacturing sector. However, agricultural liberalisation in Japan can not be easily achieved. The Thai economy would benefit from the U.S.-Thai bilateral FTA in the textile industry and the electronics sector, mainly computer parts.

Regarding China, even though the nation's presence in trade relations with Thailand is not of great significance compared to Japan and the United States, and overall trade structures of China and Thailand are fairly similar suggesting that China and Thailand are competitive in world markets, China-Thai bilateral FTA is still economically justified for four reasons. First, China and Thailand have participated in intra-industry trade in some particular products in the manufacturing sector. Second, pre-FTA tariff rates in China and Thailand are quite high. Therefore, if trade flows between two countries increase, bilateral FTA between

China and Thailand may produce trade creation effect to the Thai economy. Third, since the Chinese economy has been growing remarkably in recent years along with its GDP per capita, China could be viewed as another potential market for Thai producers. Lastly, trade relations between China and Thailand have expanded recently year by year, so that concluding China-Thai bilateral FTA may allow benefit to the Thai side. However, there would also be losers from concluding the China-Thai bilateral FTA, for example, some particular agricultural products and manufacturing sectors.

Besides, establishing bilateral FTA with Japan, the United States and China can be justified not only by economic reasons. Political and foreign policy motivations are probably also behind the Thai government's active progress towards concluding bilateral FTA with these three powerful countries.

4.2. Current situation of bilateral trade negotiations of Thailand

Table 5 lists sectors which are under bilateral trade negotiations with Japan, the United States and China and notes some difficulties in each sector.

Regarding the Japan-Thai FTA, the so called Japan and Thailand Closer Economic Partnership (JTEP), there are four commodities which are always mentioned when discussing JTEP, namely, rice, sugar, chicken and cassava. From the trade negotiation round between the Japanese and Thai governments in 2004, rice was excluded from the negotiations while other sensitive goods such as chicken, sugar and cassava remain on the process of negotiations. Most commodities in the sensitive list of Japan are agricultural products. Meanwhile, steel is the most mentioned commodity in the Thai sensitive list because Thai steel industry still has not been developed and the industry has great linkages to other main industries in the economy.

With respect to concluding the US-Thai FTA, the Thai government anticipates benefiting in agricultural products, processed food, textile and automobile. Liberalisation in the service sector, such as telecommunication, can also improve consumer's welfare as a result of greater competition. Thai consumers will get access to wider arrays of products with lower service prices.

The China-Thai FTA is expected to be completed in 2010 covering free trade in goods, services and investment. Tariff elimination was implemented in most of the product lines since October 1, 2003. As a result of the early harvest scheme, the tariff of the commodities under the Harmonisation System (HS) 01 to 08 had been eliminated. Especially the commodities under the HS 07 and HS 08 which are vegetables and fruits, respectively, have been traded much more intensively. The debate on whether Thailand will benefit or lose from concluding FTA with China becomes the contemporary topic at this moment.

Table 5. Sectors under trade negotiations with Japan, the United States and China with some remarks.

Partner	Sector	Remark
Japan	1. agricultural sector, for example, sugar, chicken, leather, and fishery product	Japan has several agricultural products filed in Japanese sensitive list but Thai side still expects the benefit from this sector.
	2. Service sector, especially movement of natural persons, for example, Thai cuisine cook, Care assistant	Japanese government has strict regulation concerning immigration and period of stay.
	3. Steel industry	This commodity is filed in Thai sensitive list.
	4. Cooperation in agricultural sector and technology	Still in the initial process of negotiation.
The United States	1. Intellectual property right products	Thai side need to improve related legal framework.
	2. agricultural products	These sectors are inclined to yield benefit to the Thai economy from the US-Thai FTA.
	3. processed food	
	4. computers and parts	
	5. automobile industry	
China	1. agricultural sector	– Thai producers in some particular commodities are negatively affected after China-Thai FTA became in effect. – Trade transactions are decelerated by Chinese custom procedure, documentation and sanitary examination process.
	2. Investment	
	3. Trade in service	n.a.

Source: the author compiled the data from various Thai sources.

For other countries, the Thai government may have taken other factors into consideration in initiating bilateral trade negotiations and expected some other merits than those from an economic aspect. In addition, the plausible benefits from bilateral FTA with other countries may not be obvious immediate gains, and may not be simply calibrated by trade statistical data. For example, those benefits can be brought about by the cooperation in some industries. Therefore, the benefits from other cases should be re-evaluated in the future in order to cover the long-run impact on the Thai economy.

4.3. Concerns over bilateral trade policy of Thailand

Bilateral trade governance adopted by the Thai government gives rise to some concerns in both economic and social aspects. From an economic point of view, firstly, concluding bilateral FTA with many countries might lead to inconsistency among bilateral FTA commitments and unsustainable trade agreements. The issue of inconsistency covers both inconsistency of commitments among several pairs of bilateral FTA and incompatibility of obligations between recent bilateral FTA negotiations and trade liberalisation in other fora such as AFTA and WTO. Secondly, forming bilateral FTA with many countries is likely to yield fairly high transaction costs to Thailand. Thirdly, some issues such as movement of natural persons, which is very complex and hard to quantify, would certainly cause social changes. The Thai government should evaluate the possible impact on the economy both in economic and social aspects. Finally, structural adjustment to meet prospective requirements set by FTA partners should also be considered as a kind of transaction cost of adopting bilateral FTA approach. Both public and private sectors inevitably have to facilitate themselves in order to prepare for upcoming consequences of bilateral FTAs.

5. Conclusion

This article concludes that the factors motivating the Thai government to adopt a policy of bilateral FTAs as the main trade governance are both external and internal. The external factors are the slow pace of trade liberalisation under AFTA and the slow progress and dysfunction of multilateral trade liberalisation under WTO. The internal factors are the Thai government's perception that bilateral trade negotiations are more efficient and flexible than regional and multilateral negotiations, and that bilateral FTAs would be conducive to attracting foreign direct investment and in effect stimulating the Thai economy. Besides, the new trade governance is part of international trade and foreign policy of the Thaksin administration and emerged partly because of a FTA syndrome.

By investigating trade and investment structure as well as protection structure of potential bilateral FTA partners with respect to Thailand utilising the international trade indices, namely, Revealed Comparative Advantage (RCA), Intra-Industry Trade (IIT) Index and the calculation of Effective Rate of Protection (ERP), the bilateral FTA approach of the Thailand could be explained by both economic and non-economic reasons, such as political and foreign policy motivations. The sectors which promise to produce most advantage to the Thai side from Japan-Thai bilateral FTA are the agricultural sector and the manufacturing sector due to the lower cost of input. For the U.S.-Thai bilateral FTA, the Thai economy can expect to benefit in the electronics sector and textile industry. Furthermore, Thailand is expected to gain most from investment creation and technological progress in establishing bilateral FTA with Japan and the United States. Regarding the China-Thai bilateral FTA, it promises to generate some gains to the Thai economy from increased competition effect and market expansion effect.

Bilateral trade governance gives rise to both economic and social concerns for Thailand, namely, inconsistency of trade commitments among sequence of trade negotiations, high transaction cost in negotiation process, and other incurred cost of social and structural adjustment to meet prospective requirements set by FTA partners. The results of this investigation suggest that the Thai government should get its priorities right on the ground of economic justifications with inclusive consideration of both economic and social aspects in order to get most benefit from bilateral FTA approach with reduced overall cost.

References

Chirathivat, S., 2002. ASEAN-China free trade area: background, implications, and future development. Journal of Asian Economics 13: 671-686.

Kiyota, K., 2003. Bilateral trade agreements in the Asia-Pacific: a case study of Thailand. Paper prepared for the Bilateral Trade Agreements in the Asia-Pacific: Origin, Evolution, and Implications, December 5-6, 2003 Honolulu, HI.

Ministry of Economy, Trade and Industry (METI), Japan, 1999. White Paper on International Trade.

Nagai, F., 2002. Thailand's trade policy: WTO plus FTA? Working paper series 01/02-No.6. Chiba, Institute of Developing Economies, APEC Study Center.

Nagai, F., 2003. Thailand's trade policy: continuity and change between the Chuan and Thaksin governments. In J. Okamoto (Ed.), Whither free trade agreements? Proliferation, evaluation and multilateralization. Chiba, Institute of Developing Economies, Japan External Trade Organization, pp.252-284

Osada, H., 2003. Short-run economic impacts of China's accession to WTO. Forum of International Development Studies, Graduate School of International Development, Nagoya University, 24, 16 (in Japanese).

Robson, P., 1998. The economics of international integration (4th ed.). New York, Routledge.

Sakhornrad, P., 2004. Bilateral Trade Agreement (FTA) in the 21st Century: The Case of Thailand. Mimeograph.

Sabhasri, C., 2001. Forging closer ASEAN-China economic relations in the twenty-first century: national report of Thailand in a report submitted by the ASEAN-China expert group on economic cooperation.

Sussangkarn, C., 2003. Thailand and the China-ASEAN FTA. Thailand Development Research Institute (TDRI) Quarterly Review 18: 13-19.

Urata, S. and K. Yokota, 1994. Trade liberalization and productivity growth in Thailand. The Developing Economies 32: 444-459.

Urata, S., 2003. Bilateral trade agreements in the Asia-Pacific: a case study of Thailand. Paper prepared for the Bilateral Trade Agreements in the Asia-Pacific: Origin, Evolution, and Implications, December 5-6, 2003 Honolulu, HI.

World Bank, 2003. World Development Report 2003. New York, Oxford University Press.

World Trade Organisation, 2000. Trade policy review: Thailand 1999. Geneva, WTO.

The effects of the free trade arrangement on social welfare and urban employment

Watcharas Leelawath
International Institute for Trade and Development, Bangkok, Thailand. watcharas.l@itd.
chula.ac.th

Abstract

A theoretical model concerning the effects of the Free Trade Arrangement (FTA) is developed in this study. The model examines how discriminatory tariff elimination influences social welfare and the urban employment rate for the Harris-Todaro type of economy in the presence of variable returns to scale in agricultural and manufacturing sectors. Assume that the home country is the net exporter of agricultural products and the net importer of manufacturing products. Agricultural products are produced in rural areas, while manufacturing products are produced in urban areas. Workers are allowed to move freely between rural and urban areas. The analysis is based upon the Social-Utility approach to welfare comparison. The results show that the formation of an FTA would cause urban employment to increase regardless of the degrees of returns to scale in both sectors and the occurrence of either trade creation or trade diversion. The findings indicate that the comparison of degrees of returns to scale play a role in determining the effects of trade creation and trade diversion on social welfare. Trade creation is welfare-improving, only if the elasticity of return to scale in the manufacturing sector is at most as much as that of the agricultural sector. Under the same condition, trade diversion is more likely to cause an increase in social welfare than otherwise would be.

JEL classification: F15, F16

Keywords: FTA, variable returns to scale, Harris-Todaro model, urban employment

1. Introduction

The main objective of this paper is to examine the effects of forming a Free Trade Arrangement (FTA) on social welfare and the urban employment rate for the Harris-Todaro economy in the presence of the degree of variable returns to scale in the rural sector which produces only agricultural goods, and the urban sector which produces only manufactured goods. The paper is developed from the work of Beladi (1989), Choi and Yu (1984), and Michael and Miller (1992), which adopted the Harris-Todaro type of economy assuming that wage rates between urban and rural sectors are not equal. It investigated the effects of a customs union on social welfare and the urban employment rate in the presence of the degree of returns to scale only in the production of manufactured goods in the urban sector. Given that the production of agricultural goods in the rural sector exhibits constant returns to scale, its finding shows that trade creation unambiguously leads to a decrease in the urban employment rate and trade diversion leads to an increase in the urban employment rate. But the effect on social welfare is unclear. It depends on the degree of returns to scale in the urban sector as well as types of trade creation and trade diversion defined in Yu (1981) and Yu and Parai (1989).

This paper is organised as follows. Section 2 presents assumptions and the structural equations of the model. The effects of forming an FTA on social welfare and urban employment rate for the Harris-Todaro economy are analysed in section 3. Finally, the paper is concluded in section 4.

2. The model and assumptions

Suppose the world consists of three countries, the home country, H, and its trading partner countries, B and C. All three countries produce two types of products, agricultural products (X_a), produced in each rural sector, and manufacturing products (X_m), produced in each urban sector, using two factors of production, capital (K) and labor (L). Domestic supplies of both factors are fixed. Free movements of capital and labor are allowed. Capital is fully utilised, but labor is fully employed only in the rural sector, where the real wage rate (w_a) is flexible. In contrast, the real wage rate (w_m) in the urban sector is relatively rigid. As a result of the relative rigidity, there exists the urban unemployment in urban area. Assume that H is the highest-cost and C is the lowest-cost producer of X_m. Countries B and C are similar, which means they produce X_m and they do not trade with each other. Moreover, H is a price-taker, and it exports X_a to B and C but imports X_m from either B or C.

The home country's demand side of the model is represented by a strictly quasi-concave utility function:

$$U = U(D_a, D_m)$$
(Eq. 1)

where D_a and D_m are the consumption demands for agricultural and manufacturing products in home country H and $U_i > 0$, $U_{ii} < 0$, $i = a, m$. For generality, both products are normal goods.

Assume that the balance of payments is always maintained, the economy's budget constraint is

$$Y = X_a + PX_m = D_a + PD_m$$
(Eq. 2)

where P is the relative price of manufacturing products in terms of agricultural products (*i.e.* $P = P_m/P_a$). From Equation 2, we obtain

$$X_a - D_a = P(D_m - X_m) \qquad \text{(Eq. 3)}$$

The left-hand side of Equation 3 is the quantity of agricultural exports (E_a) and the right-hand side is the value of manufacturing imports (E_m). Since

$$E_a = X_a - D_a \qquad \text{(Eq. 4)}$$

and

$$E_m = D_m - X_m \qquad \text{(Eq. 5)}$$

then the balance of payments condition implies

$$E_a = PE_m \qquad \text{(Eq. 6)}$$

The production side of the model is developed from the following production function:

$$X_i = g_i(X_i).F_i(K_i, L_i) \qquad i = a, m \qquad \text{Eq. 7)}$$

where X_i is the output of sector i and K_i, L_i are its total employment of capital and labour respectively. F_{Ki} and F_{Li} denote the partial derivatives of F_i with respect to capital and labour, respectively. The function g_i represents scale economies. It is non-negative and increasing in sector's output. The function is assumed to be linearly homogeneous.

Following Beladi (1989) and Choi *et al.* (2002), output elasticity of returns to scale is written as:

$$e_i = [dg/dX_i] \, F_i = [dg/dX_i].[X_i/g_i] \qquad i = a, m \qquad \text{(Eq. 8)}$$

where $-\infty < e_i < 1$. Increasing returns to scale (IRS) is represented by $e_i > 0$; constant returns to scale (CRS) and decreasing returns to scale (DRS) are represented by $e_i = 0$ and $e_i < 0$ respectively.

Totally differentiating Equation 7, we get

$$dX_i = g_i(X_i).[F_{Ki} \, dK_i + F_{Li} \, dL_i] + F_i \, (dg_i/dX_i).dX_i$$

Rewriting Equation 7,

$$F_i = X_i/g(X_i)$$

Thus

$$(1-e_i)dX_i = g_i(X_i).[F_{Ki} dK_i + F_{Li} dL_i] \tag{Eq. 9}$$

Assuming that all firms in the urban sector are identical, cost minimisation conditions are as follows.

$$P_m g(X_m) F_{Lm} = w_m \tag{Eq. 10}$$

$$P_m g(X_m) F_{Km} = r_m \tag{Eq. 11}$$

where P_m stands for the price of manufactured products and w_m and r_m are wage rate and rental rate in the urban sector, respectively.

Similarly, cost minimisation conditions in the rural sector are

$$P_a g(X_a) F_{La} = w_a \tag{Eq. 12}$$

$$P_a g(X_a) F_{Ka} = r_a \tag{Eq. 13}$$

where P_a denotes the price of the agricultural product, and w_a and r_a are wage rate and rental rate in the rural sector.

Due to the assumption of perfect mobility of capital, equilibrium in the capital market yields

$$r_a = r_m = r \tag{Eq. 14}$$

In order to simplify, we write $g(X_a)$ and $g(X_m)$ as g_a and g_m, respectively. Recall that $P = P_m/P_a$, so

$$g_a F_{Ka} = P g_m F_{Km} \tag{Eq. 15}$$

In the Harris-Todaro model, it is assumed that the expected wage rate in the urban sector is given by the fixed wage rate times the probability of employment (δ). Equilibrium in the labor market requires

$$w_m \delta = w_a$$

Define the probability of employment in urban areas as δ, which is equal to the urban employment rate. Then

$$\delta = L_m/L_u < 1 \tag{Eq. 16}$$

where L_u is the total labour force in urban areas and thereby $\delta < 1$. Rewrite (Equation 16), total labour force (L^*) in home country H can be expressed as follows.

$$L^* = L_a + L_u$$

$$= L_a + L_m/\delta \qquad \text{(Eq. 17)}$$

Since capital is assumed to be fully utilised, then

$$K^* = K_a + K_m \qquad \text{(Eq. 18)}$$

Totally differentiating (Equation 17), we obtain

$$dL^* = dL_a + [\delta dL_m - L_m d\delta]/\delta^2$$

So with a fixed total labour supply,

$$dL_m = -\delta dL_a + L_m d\delta/\delta \qquad \text{(Eq. 19)}$$

Similarly with a fixed supply of capital,

$$dK_m = -dK_a \qquad \text{(Eq. 20)}$$

Totally differentiating the economy's budget constraint (Equation 2),

$$dY = dX_a + PdX_m \qquad \text{(Eq. 21)}$$

Using Equation 9, Equation 21 can be expressed as follows:

$$dY = dX_a + [Pg_m/(1-e_m)].[F_{Km} dK_m + F_{Lm} dL_m] \qquad \text{(Eq. 22)}$$

Substituting Equation 19 and Equation 20 into Equation 22, then using the cost minimisation conditions, the factor supply and factor market equilibrium conditions (Equation 9) - (Equation 16), we obtain

$$dY = [1- (1-e_a)/(1-e_m)]dX_a + [Pg_m F_{Lm} L_m d\delta]/\delta(1-e_m) \qquad \text{(Eq. 23)}$$

The derivation of Equation 23 is shown in Appendix A. Equating Equation 21 and Equation 23, we get

$$dX_a + PdX_m = [1- (1-e_a)/(1-e_m)]dX_a + [Pg_mF_{Lm}L_md\delta]/\delta(1-e_m)$$

$$[(1-e_a)/(1-e_m)]dX_a = [Pg_mF_{Lm}L_md\delta]/\delta(1-e_m) - PdX_m$$

This implies

$$dX_a/dX_m = [P/(1-e_a)].[(g_m/\delta)F_{Lm}L_m(d\delta/dX_m) - (1-e_m)] < 0 \qquad \text{(Eq. 24)}$$

The above equation demonstrates the slope of the transformation curve which depends on the sign of $d\delta/dX_m$. The proof in Appendix B illustrates that $d\delta/dP < 0$. In addition, the price-output response is always positive, $dX_m/dP > 0$. Then

$$d\delta/dX_m = (d\delta/dP)/(dX_m/dP) < 0$$

As a consequence, it is clear that the slope of the transformation curve is negative.

3. The analysis

Following the procedure originally developed by Batra (1973) and used in several recent studies, social utility is assumed to depend only on the consumption of agricultural and manufacturing products as expressed in Equation 1. Thus, in order to examine the welfare effects of the formation of an FTA, we need to consider the change in social utility. Totally differentiating the social utility function, we obtain

$$dU = U_adD_a + U_mdD_m \qquad \text{(Eq. 25)}$$

This can be rewritten as

$$dU/U_a = dD_a + [U_m/U_a]dD_m \qquad \text{(Eq. 26)}$$

From the utility maximising conditions it follows that the marginal rate of substitution is equal to the relative prices of two products, *i.e.* $U_m/U_a = P$. Thus

$$dU/U_a = dD_a + PdD_m \qquad \text{(Eq. 27)}$$

The budget constraint in Equation 2 with exogenously determined world price P^* implies that

$$dX_a + P^*dX_m = dD_a + P^*dD_m \qquad \text{(Eq. 28)}$$

The relationship between the domestic relative price, the foreign relative price and the tariff t is:

$$P = P^*(1+t) \qquad \text{(Eq. 29)}$$

Totally differentiating Equations 4- 6, we get

$$dD_a = dX_a - dE_a \qquad \text{(Eq. 30)}$$

$$dD_m = dX_m + dE_m \qquad \text{(Eq. 31)}$$

$$dE_a = P^*dE_m + E_m dP^* \qquad \text{(Eq. 32)}$$

Substituting Equation 30-32 into Equation 27 gives

$$dU/U_a = dX_a + PdX_m + P^*tdE_m - E_m dP^* \qquad \text{(Eq. 33)}$$

Substituting Equation 24 into Equation 33,

$$dU/U_a = [Pg_m /\delta(1-e_a)].F_{Lm}L_m d\delta + [(e_m-e_a)/(1-e_a)]PdX_m + P^*tdE_m - E_m dP^* \qquad \text{(Eq. 34)}$$

The derivations of Equation 33 and Equation 34 are shown in Appendices C and D, respectively.

According to the fact that the value of imports depends on tariffs and terms of trade, $E_m = E_m(t, P^*)$, totally differentiating this function gives

$$dE_m = (\partial E_m/\partial t).dt + (\partial E_m/\partial P^*).dP^* \qquad \text{(Eq. 35)}$$

Substituting Equation 35 into Equation 34 yields

$$dU/U_a = [Pg_m /\delta(1-e_a)].F_{Lm}L_m d\delta + [(e_m-e_a)/(1-e_a)]PdX_m + P^*t(\partial E_m/\partial t)dt$$
$$+ [P^*t(\partial E_m/\partial P^*) - E_m]dP^* \qquad \text{(Eq. 36)}$$

Since X_m is a function of t and P^*, $X_m = X_m(t, P^*)$, then

$$dX_m = (\partial X_m/\partial t).dt + (\partial X_m/\partial P^*).dP^* \qquad \text{(Eq. 37)}$$

Substituting (37) into (36), we get

$$dU/U_a = [Pg_m /\delta(1-e_a)].F_{Lm}L_m d\delta + \{[(e_m-e_a)/(1-e_a)]P(\partial X_m/\partial t) + P^*t(\partial E_m/\partial t)\}dt$$
$$+ \{[(e_m-e_a)/(1-e_a)]P(\partial X_m/\partial P^*) + P^*t(\partial E_m/\partial P^*) - E_m\}dP^* \qquad \text{(Eq. 38)}$$

Again, the change in urban employment rate δ depends on changes in t and P^*. Therefore,

$$d\delta = (\partial\delta/\partial t).dt + (\partial\delta/\partial P^*).dP^* \tag{Eq. 39}$$

Substituting the above Equation into (38), then we obtain

$$dU/U_a = \{[Pg_m/\delta(1-e_a)].F_{Lm}L_m(\partial\delta/\partial t) + [(e_m-e_a)/(1-e_a)]P(\partial X_m/\partial t)$$
$$+ P^*t(\partial E_m/\partial t)\}dt + \{[Pg_m/\delta(1-e_a)].F_{Lm}L_m(\partial\delta/\partial P^*)$$
$$+ [(e_m-e_a)/(1-e_a)]P(\partial X_m/\partial P^*) + P^*t(\partial E_m/\partial P^*) - E_m\}dP^* \tag{Eq. 40}$$

Partially differentiating $P = P^*(1+t)$, the results are

$$\partial P/\partial t = P^* \tag{Eq. 41}$$

$$\partial P/\partial P^* = (1+t) \tag{Eq. 42}$$

Substituting these equations into Equation 40 gives the key expression for the social welfare effect of the formation of the Free Trade Arrangement.

$$dU/U_a = \{[Pg_m/\delta(1-e_a)].F_{Lm}L_m(\partial\delta/\partial P)P^* + [(e_m-e_a)/(1-e_a)]PP^*(\partial X_m/\partial P)$$
$$+ P^{*2}t(\partial E_m/\partial P)\}dt + (1+t).\{[Pg_m/\delta(1-e_a)].F_{Lm}L_m(\partial\delta/\partial P)$$
$$+ [(e_m-e_a)/(1-e_a)]P(\partial X_m/\partial P) + P^*t(\partial E_m/\partial P) - E_m/(1+t)\}dP^* \tag{Eq. 43}$$

Equation 43 illustrates that a discriminatory tariff elimination leads to two crucial effects on social welfare. One through a change in tariffs imposed by the home country and the other through a change in terms of trade that the home country faces. The former is represented by the first braces and the latter is represented by the second braces. The first terms in both braces reflect the change in urban employment rate caused by the change in tariffs and the change in terms of trade, respectively. In order to simplify, let

$$\Omega = [Pg_m/\delta(1-e_a)].F_{Lm}L_m(\partial\delta/\partial P) < 0 \tag{Eq. 44}$$

Thus ΩP^* and Ω become first terms in the first and second braces, respectively. Recall that $\partial\delta/\partial P$ is negative. As a consequence, ΩP^* and Ω are negative.

Again, let

$$\Psi = [P/(1-e_a)](\partial X_m/\partial P) > 0 \tag{Eq. 45}$$

Therefore, the second terms in the first and second braces are $(e_m-e_a)\Psi P^*$ and $(e_m-e_a)\Psi$, respectively. These terms capture the effects on production of importable manufacturing products, in the presence of returns to scale. Given the positive price-output response, *i.e.* $\partial X_m/\partial P > 0$, the sign of Ψ is positive. However, the signs of second terms cannot be clearly determined. This is because they depend on the values of output elasticity of returns to scale in agricultural and manufacturing sectors. The signs of these terms are negative, when e_a exceeds e_m, and vice versa.

The third terms indicate changes in the consumption of importable manufacturing products. Let ΠP^* and Π denote third terms in the first and second braces, respectively, where

$$\Pi = P^*t(\partial E_m/\partial P) < 0 \qquad \text{(Eq. 46)}$$

Since X_m is a normal good, then $\partial E_m/\partial P$ must be negative, and thereby ΠP^* as well as Π are negative.

Substituting equations (44)-(46) into (43), the social welfare effects of the formation of an FTA can alternatively be expressed as follows.

$$dU/U_a = \{\Omega P^* + (e_m\text{-}e_a)\Psi P^* + \Pi P^*\}dt + (1+t)\{\Omega + (e_m\text{-}e_a)\Psi + \Pi - E_m/(1+t)\}dP^* \qquad \text{(Eq. 47)}$$

where $\Omega < 0$, $\Psi > 0$ and $\Pi < 0$.

In order to study the effects of discriminatory tariff elimination on social welfare and the urban employment rate, it is important to understand the basic concepts of trade creation and trade diversion. Even though both terms were originated from the theory of customs union, nowadays they are widely applied to any type of preferential tariff arrangement, especially the FTA. Viner (1950) defined trade creation as the substitution in consumption of higher cost, domestically produced goods in favour of lower-cost goods produced by the FTA member country. In contrast, trade diversion represents the shift in imports by the home country from the lowest-cost producers in a country, which is excluded in the FTA formation, to relatively higher-cost producers in a member country due to a discriminatory tariff reduction issued by the home country.

First, let us consider trade creation, which is identified as H's switch of its consumption of X_m from domestic producers to lowest-cost producers from country C due to discriminatory tariff elimination in favour of country C. According to this particular scenario, dt < 0. However, the terms of trade faced by H remain unchanged, then $dP^* = 0$.

The negative change in the tariff rates causes Equation 47 to reduce to

$$dU/U_a = \Omega P^* dt + (e_m\text{-}e_a)\Psi P^* dt + \Pi P^* dt \qquad \text{(Eq. 48)}$$

Recall that $\Omega < 0$, $\Psi > 0$ and $\Pi < 0$ and dt < 0. As a result, it is clear that the first and the third terms in Equation 48 are positive. Hence the reduction in tariffs has a positive effect on the urban employment rate. The sign of the second term depends upon the sign of

$(e_m - e_a)$. If e_m is less than or equal to e_a, then the second term becomes greater than or equal to zero. As a consequence, dU/U_a is unambiguously positive. Now the following proposition is stated.

Proposition 1: If the elasticity of returns to scale of manufacturing sector is less than or equal to that of agricultural sector, trade creation leads to the improvement of welfare and an increase in the urban employment rate.

The intuition is that trade creation brings about an increase in production efficiency. Domestic production of agricultural goods increases, while the production of manufacturing goods falls. Urban areas become less attractive, so workers move to work in the agricultural sector, which is capable to absorb such movement of labour. This causes the urban unemployment to fall, which in turn, leads to a rise in the urban employment rate. In addition, since the elasticity of returns to scale of the agricultural sector exceeds that of the manufacturing sector, an increase in agricultural products would outweigh a decrease in manufacturing products. The net effect on income would be positive. At the same time, domestic consumers can consume more of manufacturing products at the lower price. For these favourable reasons, trade creation is able to improve the welfare of the home country.

However, if e_m is greater than e_a, then the welfare effect of trade creation I is ambiguous. Hence, we have

Proposition 2: If the elasticity of returns to scale of the manufacturing sector exceeds that of the agricultural sector, trade creation unambiguously leads to an increase in the urban employment rate, but the effect on social welfare is ambiguous.

In the case that the elasticity of returns to scale of the manufacturing sector is higher than that of the agricultural sector, the net change in total production of the home country would be negative. This is because a decrease in the production of manufacturing products dominates an increase in agricultural production. Despite positive changes on consumption and urban employment rate caused by the FTA, the negative change on income makes the aggregate change in welfare to be ambiguous.

Next, consider trade diversion, in which H switches its consumption of X_m from C's lowest cost producers to B's producers in response to the abolition of tariffs only on partner country, B. Hence, $dt < 0$ and $dP^* > 0$. This is because the home country engages in trade with B only, so it faces B's terms of trade, which is greater than before forming an FTA. Accordingly, the change in the urban employment rate is represented by $\Omega P^* dt + (1+t)\Omega dP^*$. Since the sign of $\Omega P^* dt$ is positive and that of $(1+t)\Omega dP^*$ is negative, the direction of the change seems unclear depending upon the relative magnitudes of both terms. Recall that $P = P^*(1+t)$, then

$$dP = P^*dt + (1+t)dP^*$$

Therefore, the change in the urban employment rate will be ΩdP. For trade diversion to occur, a discriminatory tariff elimination in favour of country B has to be large enough to lower domestic price of X_m ($dP < 0$) so as to lure domestic consumers to switch their sources of manufacturing products. Otherwise, there will be no presence of trade diversion. As a consequence, the sign of ΩdP is positive. Here comes another proposition.

Proposition 3: Regardless of the degree of returns to scale in agricultural and manufacturing sectors, trade diversion leads to an increase in the urban employment rate.

The economic interpretation is that trade diversion causes domestic consumers of manufacturing products to shift their consumption from domestic producers to more efficient, though not most efficient, producers of the partner country. This leads to an increase in agricultural production and a decrease in manufacturing production. The price of agricultural goods rises, while the price of manufacturing goods falls. Also, the payoffs in rural areas become higher. At the same time, the manufacturing sector pays less to the workers than before. Urban areas become less attractive. In turn, workers move to rural areas and work in the agricultural sector. As a result, total urban labour force goes down and thereby the urban employment rate goes up.

Now let us consider the social welfare effect from the equation below.

$$dU/U_a = \{\Omega + (e_m - e_a)\Psi + \Pi\}dP - E_m dP^* \qquad \text{(Eq. 49)}$$

The sign of Equation 49 seems ambiguous. However, if $e_m \leq e_a$, then it is more likely that trade diversion would enhance social welfare of the home country than otherwise would be the case.

Proposition 4: If the elasticity of returns to scale of manufacturing sector does not exceed that of the agricultural sector, trade diversion is likely to improve social welfare.

As mentioned earlier, the establishment of an FTA creates positive changes on urban employment rate and domestic consumption of manufacturing goods. These components yield favourable impact on the social welfare of the home country. However, there are two other factors that determine the net change in social welfare. One is the magnitude of the change in terms of trade. Such a factor has an impact only when trade diversion arises. The smaller it is, the bigger the change in social welfare. Again, the other factor is the elasticity of returns to scale. In the case that the elasticity of returns to scale of the agricultural sector is relatively large, an increase in agricultural production would dominate a decrease in manufacturing production. As a result, there would be a positive change in income and thereby it is more likely that there will also be an improvement on social welfare.

4. Conclusion

The purpose of this paper is to examine the effects of the formation of the Free Trade Arrangement (FTA) on social welfare and urban employment rate for the Harris-Todaro type of economy in the presence of variable returns to scale in both urban and rural sectors. Assuming that the urban sector produces manufacturing products and the rural sector produces agricultural products. The analysis has shown that under trade creation, the urban employment rate always increases regardless of the degree of returns to scale in both sectors. However, the change in social welfare depends on the magnitude of the degree of returns to scale of both manufacturing and agricultural sectors. If the elasticity of returns to scale of manufacturing sector does not exceed that of agricultural sector, trade creation is welfare improving. Otherwise, the results will be inconclusive.

Trade diversion would occur when the domestic price of manufacturing goods falls due to discriminatory tariff elimination in favour of the FTA partner country. Under this condition, trade diversion leads to an increase in the urban employment rate, regardless of the elasticity of returns to scale in agricultural and manufacturing sectors. As for the effect on social welfare, it seems ambiguous. However, if the elasticity of returns to scale of manufacturing sector does not exceed that of agricultural sector, then trade diversion is more likely to be welfare-improving than otherwise would be.

With regard to policy implications, safety nets should be provided by the government before engaging in the FTA with other trading partners. In endeavouring to maximise the benefits of forming an FTA, the government should promote technology progress in agricultural production and should ensure that there is no barrier to domestic movement of labour. An improvement in production efficiency in agriculture would make an increase in agricultural production to be large enough to outweigh manufacturing production. This would bring about a positive change in the net income of the country. Moreover, a free domestic movement of labour would help the agricultural sector to absorb labour spilled from the other sector more easily, which in turn, would lower the number of unemployed workforce in urban areas and eventually boost up the urban employment rate.

Apparently, this study provides solely a theoretical framework for analysing the FTA impacts. The model closely suits for developing countries, whose services sectors are relatively insignificant in comparison to agricultural and manufacturing sectors. Some extensions of this study can be done by encompassing the services sector and differentiated types of labour and capital in the model, so as to make such framework fit for other developing countries with more developed services sectors. Furthermore, it is generally known that the FTA induces both positive and negative effects to workers in partner countries. Because of the fact that FTA has recently started, the problem of insufficient data probably arises in pursuing empirical study concerning this particular issues. However, empirical investigations definitely should be conducted in future research.

References

Batra, R.N., 1973. Studies in the pure theory of international trade. St. Martin Press, New York.

Beladi, H., 1989. Urban unemployment, economies of scale and the theory of customs unions. Keio Economic Studies 26: 5-15.

Choi, T. Y., Yu, E. S. H., 1984. Customs unions under increasing returns to scale. Economica 51, 195-203.

Choi, J.Y., Yu, E.S.H., Jin, J.C., 2002. Technical progress, urban unemployment, outputs, and welfare under variable returns to scale. International Review of Economics and Finance 11: 411-425.

Michael, M.S., Miller, S.M., 1992. Customs union and the Harris-Todaro model with International capital mobility. Open Economies Review 3: 37-49.

Viner, J., 1950. The Customs Union Issues. Carnegie Endowment for International Peace, New York.

Yu, E. S. H., 1981. Trade diversion, trade creation and factor market imperfections. Weltwirtschaftliches Archiv 117: 546-561.

Yu, E.S.H., Parai, A.K., 1989. Endogenous wage differentials, imperfect labor mobility and Customs union theory. Journal of International Economic Integration 4: 15-26.

Appendix A. Derivation of Equation 23 in the main text.

Substituting Equation 19 and Equation 20 into Equation 22, then using the cost minimisation conditions, the factor supply and factor market equilibrium conditions (Equations 9 - 16), we obtain

$$
\begin{aligned}
dY &= dX_a - [Pg_m F_{Km} dK_a]/(1-e_m) + [Pg_m F_{Lm}/(1-e_m)].[-\delta dL_a + L_m d\delta/\delta] \\
&= dX_a - [g_a F_{Ka} dK_a]/(1-e_m) - [\delta Pg_m F_{Lm} dL_a]/(1-e_m) + [Pg_m F_{I,m} L_m d\delta]/\delta(1-e_m) \\
&= dX_a - [g_a F_{Ka} dK_a + g_a F_{La} dL_a]/(1-e_m) + [Pg_m F_{Lm} L_m d\delta]/\delta(1-e_m) \\
&= dX_a - dX_a(1-e_a)/(1-e_m) + [Pg_m F_{Lm} L_m d\delta]/\delta(1-e_m) \\
dY &= [1-(1-e_a)/(1-e_m)]dX_a + [Pg_m F_{Lm} L_m d\delta]/\delta(1-e_m)
\end{aligned}
\qquad \text{(Eq. 23)}
$$

Appendix B. Proof for the condition dδ/dP < 0.

The equilibrium in labour market yields the system of equations as follows:

$$
\begin{aligned}
w_m &= Pg_m F_{Lm} \\
w_a &= g_a F_{La} \\
w_a &= \delta w_m
\end{aligned}
$$

After total differentiation of the above system, we obtain the following matrix system:

$$\begin{bmatrix} 1 & 0 & 0 \\ 0 & 1 & 0 \\ -\delta & 1 & -w_m \end{bmatrix} \cdot \begin{bmatrix} dw_m \\ dw_a \\ d\delta \end{bmatrix} = \begin{bmatrix} g_m F_{Lm} dP + PF_{Lm} dg_m + Pg_m F_{Lm} d_{Lm} \\ g_a F_{La.a} dL_a + F_{La} dg_a \\ 0 \end{bmatrix}$$

where $F_{La.a}$ is the second derivative of $F(.)$ with respect to L_a.

Denote D as the determinant of this system. Then

$$D = -w_m < 0$$

Apply the Cramer's rule to solve this matrix system, we have

$$d\delta = D^{-1}.\{\delta.[g_m F_{Lm} dP + PF_{Lm} dg_m + Pg_m F_{Lm} d_{Lm}] - [g_a F_{La.a} dL_a + F_{La} dg_a]\} \qquad \text{(Eq. B.1)}$$

Equation (B.1) implies that

$$d\delta/dP = D^{-1}.(\delta g_m F_{Lm}) < 0$$

Appendix C. Derivation of Equation 33 in the main text.

Substituting Equations 30-32 into Equation 27 gives

$$\begin{aligned} dU/U_a &= dX_a - dE_a + PdX_m + PdE_m \\ &= dX_a - P^*dE_m - E_m dP^* + PdX_m + PdE_m \\ &= dX_a + PdX_m + [P- P^*]dE_m - E_m dP^* \\ &= dX_a + PdX_m + P^*tdE_m - E_m dP^* \qquad \text{(Equation 33)} \end{aligned}$$

Appendix D. Derivation of Equation 34 in the main text.

Substitute Equation 24 into Equation 33.

$$\begin{aligned} dU/U_a &= [Pg_m/\delta(1-e_a)].F_{Lm}L_m d\delta - [P(1-e_m)/(1-e_a)]dX_m + PdX_m + P^*tdE_m - E_m dP^* \\ &= [Pg_m/\delta(1-e_a)].F_{Lm}L_m d\delta + [1-(1-e_m)/(1-e_a)] PdX_m + P^*tdE_m - E_m dP^* \\ &= [Pg_m/\delta(1-e_a)].F_{Lm}L_m d\delta + [(e_m-e_a)/(1-e_a)]PdX_m + P^*tdE_m - E_m dP^* \qquad \text{(Eq. 34)} \end{aligned}$$

Outward foreign direct investment: is it a good thing?

Hans Visser
VU Amsterdam, Faculty of Economics and Business Administration, Department of Economics,
De Boelelaan 1105, 1081 HV Amsterdam, The Netherlands. hvisser@feweb.vu.nl

Abstract

In this survey, first the theoretical pros and cons of outward FDI are analysed. The empirical evidence generally suggests a positive effect of FDI, in particular of the vertical variety, on exports. Outward FDI has been negatively correlated with domestic investment generally. Furthermore, FDI leads to a shift from lower-skilled to higher-skilled jobs. The impact of FDI on technology in the home country finally is very diffuse and hard to establish. Whatever the result, without outward FDI a country would generally not be better off. What counts is an environment conducive to Schumpeterian 'new combinations'.

JEL classifcation: F 21, F23, L23.

Keywords: Foreign Direct Investment, multinational firms, international investment

1. Introduction

Much of the research on the contribution of Foreign Direct Investment (FDI) to the economic development of host countries has been motivated by fears of job losses from outward FDI[1]. In order to find out whether these fears are well-founded and whether outward FDI is a blessing or a curse for the home economy, we first turn to economic theory and distil the potential pros and cons of outward FDI. Next, we discuss the empirical literature, and finally we draw conclusions.

A caveat is in order with regard to the empirical studies. These shed light on the immediate consequences of outward FDI for a firm or an industry, but generally they are silent on the effects on longer-term growth and development. It should be realised that market economies are subject to an unrelenting dynamism that makes the structure of production change all the time. Old industries decline, new industries grow. Jobs are lost and new jobs are created. In the longer term, this dynamic process of, in Schumpeter's words, creative destruction is the driving force behind continuing growth of per capita income (Schumpeter, 1950). This process is hard to capture in empirical research, but even if it was found in empirical studies that FDI causes job losses, it would not follow that FDI is a negative force. Serious problems only arise if an economy is not sufficiently dynamic to produce new entrepreneurs who introduce Schumpeterian 'new combinations' (Schumpeter, 1969).

---

[1] See for a survey of the empirical literature on the motives for FDI: Blonigen, 2005.

2. Theory

2.1. The frictionless neoclassical world

Economic models are metaphors. We use metaphors in order to get a mental grip on the world around us (Klant, 1987). One such model is provided by neoclassical theory. The 'classic' analysis of FDI from this neoclassical point of view was provided by MacDougall (1958). Such a neoclassical model is not meant to give a true description of the world, but to probe into the mechanisms that one suspects are at work behind the myriads of events that occur every day.

The MacDougall model is represented by a diagram of a two-country world with one product and given amounts of the two factors of production, labour and capital. Capital is internationally mobile, labour is not. Capital is measured along the abscissa. The ordinates measure the marginal products of capital in the two countries. We start from a situation with an amount O_A-C of capital in country A and an amount of O_B-C in country B. The marginal productivity of capital MPC_B in B is higher than in A. After capital liberalisation, capital will migrate from A to B until MPC_A equals MPC_B. An amount of SC of capital moves from A to B. Production in A falls by SCWT, production in B increases by SCVT. World production consequently increases by TWV.

This is not the whole story, however, as capital owners in A are paid the value of the marginal productivity of the capital exported to B. This yields a capital income from country B represented by the area SCZT. A-production falls, but A-income rises by TWZ and country B sees its income increase by TZV. This means that income distribution changes. In country B it's the other way round. Labour has become relatively more scarce and receives higher wages (see on the effect of taxes: Caves, 1982).

In the MacDougall model, capital flows, whether in the guise of FDI or as portfolio capital flows, make both countries' income increase, but the production factor that becomes relatively less scarce sees its income fall, not only as a share of total income but also in an absolute sense.

In the MacDougall one-product model, FDI is required to maximise world production. Other neoclassical models yield other results. In the basic Heckscher-Ohlin two-product international trade model, for instance, trade and FDI are substitutes and trade leads to identical results for world production and national income as FDI, if we abstract from taxes.

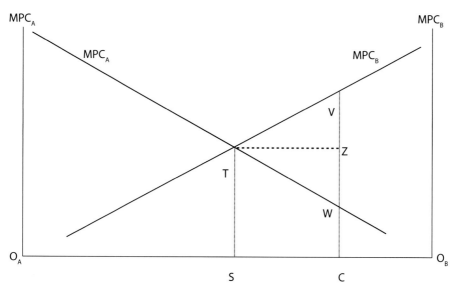

Figure 1. The MacDougall diagram: reallocation of capital in a two-country world.
Note: This is an extension of the original MacDougall diagram, which pictured the situation in one country only.

2.2. Market imperfections

FDI in the real world is done by multinational enterprises (MNEs). They can hardly find a place in the models just discussed. They are incompatible with perfect competition, but require market imperfections.

The market imperfections underlying the existence of MNEs are highlighted in Dunning's famous 'eclectic' or 'OLI' paradigm of international production (Dunning, 1993). This paradigm focuses on:
- ownership specific advantages of firms (the 'O' in OLI);
- location specific advantages of countries (the 'L' in OLI);
- internalisation advantages (the 'I' in OLI).

Ownership specific advantages mainly concern technological knowledge, including management and marketing knowledge, that creates scale economies on the level of the firm but not of the plant.

Location specific advantages are those advantages that explain the comparative advantage analysed by traditional trade theory, including artificial advantages stemming from trade restrictions, subsidies and low taxes.

A firm can often profit from its ownership specific advantages by using these not only in production for the domestic market. The costs of research and development incurred in generating these advantages can be spread over more units of production if these advantages, this knowledge, are also applied to production for foreign markets. Production for foreign markets can be organised in three ways:
1. by exporting goods and services produced in the home country;
2. by granting licenses to foreign firms;
3. by starting production abroad, that is, resorting to FDI.

If another country has location specific advantages, the choice is reduced to one between (2) and (3). FDI presents itself as an attractive solution if there are significant internalisation advantages. This is mainly the case if the granting of licenses is unattractive because of the problems of incomplete contracts. The world of MNEs and FDI is characterised not only by scale economies and imperfect competition, but also by asymmetric information. An associated benefit of FDI and thus of a presence abroad is the market knowledge that is obtained in that way. This knowledge can help to increase sales abroad and also to spot sources of supply.

Dunning (1993) also gave a useful classification of firms' motives to engage in FDI. He distinguishes between four groups:
- Resource seekers, who set up shop in other countries in order to make use of resources such as primary commodities, cheap labour and technology.
- Market seekers, who want to be near their customers in order to best fulfil their special wishes, or because the foreign government has put up trade restrictions.
- Efficiency seekers, who want to benefit from economies of scale and risk spreading or from differences in factor proportions, culture, institutional organisation and so on between countries.
- Strategic asset seekers, who resort to mergers and acquisitions in order to safeguard their long-term competitiveness.

This classification is not watertight and Dunning himself adds three other motives. These are: (1) Escape investments, made to escape restrictive legislation or macro-organisational policies (such as a controlled-investment policy) by home governments; (2) support investments, made to support the activities of the rest of the enterprise (*e.g.*, investments in marketing and distribution); (3) passive investments, with little involvement in the management of the acquired company (*e.g.*, investments in hotels, in the expectation of a rise in property values). All the motives in the four groups mentioned above concern the exploitation of location advantages, though perhaps less strictly so in the case of strategic asset seekers, who are rather out to stay ahead of their competitors.

Another useful distinction is between horizontal and vertical FDI (see, *e.g.*, Markusen and Maskus, 2001). Under horizontal FDI, similar goods are produced by an MNE in various countries. Under vertical FDI, some stages of the production process are shifted abroad. Some parts of a product may be imported from a foreign branch, or a product is shipped abroad to be processed there and sent back to the home country at a later stage to be finished.

In both variants of FDI, scale economies may figure prominently. The scale economies associated with ownership-specific advantages are largely found on the level of the firm rather than on the level of the individual plant. Often, technical knowledge can, once it has been developed, be applied at low marginal cost at different locations. Horizontal FDI will in such cases be attractive as an alternative to exports if the costs of transport or trade costs in general are high, apart from trade restrictions (Helpman *et al.*, 2004). Markets seekers, but also efficiency seekers will be involved. If scale economies are found on the level of the plant, vertical FDI will present itself as an attractive option. Under vertical FDI, parts of the production process are shifted to countries where costs are lower. Efficiency seekers and resource seekers will be active in this kind of FDI. Again, it is a classification that lacks sharp demarcation lines. Under horizontal FDI, for instance, foreign branches will often go on using the services of the head office as far as research, design, finance and marketing are concerned.

FDI may take the form of building new production facilities (greenfield investment), but also of mergers and acquisitions. In the view of Schenk (1999), mergers and acquisitions often are not motivated by the prospect of improving productivity and increasing profits, but by a strategy of managers to minimise the danger of conflicts with shareholders. In his concept of a 'minimax-regret game', managers prefer to follow the crowd once their competitors start mergers and acquisitions activities, even if the prospects of success are dim, rather than staying aloof and running the risk of seeing their competitors succeed and their own strategy proven wrong. Another strand in the literature emphasises pre-emptive actions by managers who become active as acquirers in order to increase the size of their companies and in doing so prevent being taken over themselves (Gorton *et al.*, 2005). In these two cases we have variants of the strategic asset seekers.

Still, international mergers and acquisitions activities can also be motivated by a wish to have better access to markets and resources, in particular technological knowledge.

3. Potential pros and cons for the home country

From this theoretical analysis a number of potential benefits of outward FDI can be identified:
- FDI brings in capital payments that result in a higher national income, even if domestic production may fall (as in the MacDougall case).
- FDI contributes to a better division of labour on a world scale and thus to higher productivity.

- FDI implies a presence in the host country that may be used to good advantage not only for the sales process but also for purchases.

FDI carries some potential costs with it as well:
- FDI may imply a loss of jobs and of income. To the extent that FDI takes place according to comparative advantage (non-artificial location advantages), the international division of labour improves, but there will be costs of adjustment. A higher mobility of capital and high-skilled labour, which could make it more difficult to levy taxes and social security contributions and might result in a 'race to the bottom'. So far, this danger does not yet seem to have materialised (Tanzi, 2002; Navarro *et al.*, 2004).
- Higher production and incomes abroad, plus better technology. This may lead to a fall in importance of the home country in the global political arena and a loss of political clout. Restricting FDI would, however, at best result in some delay in this process.

We now give a survey of the empirical literature, shedding light not only on the effects of FDI on jobs and income, but also on related entities, such as exports and the structure of labour demand.

4. Empirical studies

4.1. Introduction

Empirical research of the effects of FDI on the home country's economy has often been motivated by a fear of job losses. Many studies have been devoted to the relationship between employment at MNE's affiliates abroad and at the home country offices and factories. In this way, however, only first-round effects of FDI are captured. These are important for employment developments in the short term, but hardly relevant for the longer period. Nonetheless, in our roundup of the findings of empirical research the impact on employment will not be neglected. The findings on the impact of FDI on exports, investment, the structure of labour demand and investment will also be reviewed. Before we turn to these studies, a discussion of the problems associated with empirical research in this field is in order.

4.2. Problems of empirical research

There is not one universally accepted definition of FDI, and one needs a definition before setting out to measure its effects. Lipsey (2002) distinguishes between two concepts of FDI:
1. FDI as a particular form of international capital flows that gives rise to a particular form of international assets for the home countries, specifically, the value of holdings in entities, typically corporations, controlled by a home country resident or in which a home country resident holds a certain share of the voting rights.

2. FDI as a set of economic activities or operations carried out in a host country by firms controlled or partly controlled by firms in some other country (the home country). These activities are, for example, production, employment, sales, the purchase and use of intermediate goods and fixed capital, and the carrying out of research.

Balance-of-payments statistics provide information on (1), but not on (2). From the balance of payments we cannot see, for instance, whether new production facilities have been built. A takeover of a firm in country B by a firm in country A enters the balance of payments as FDI in the year of the takeover. There is only a change of ownership. If the new foreign affiliate builds new factories with the proceeds of a loan taken out in country B, no entry in the balance-of-payments statistics follows.

What balance-of-payments statistics do provide is information on the yield of FDI in the guise of primary income (capital payments, wages) and services (intellectual property). But this information is incomplete. If we try, for instance, to calculate the contribution of FDI income of Dutch firms to Dutch national income, we should subtract the capital payments of these firms to non-residents, which generally is not possible.

For the effects of FDI on home-country employment and exports, the second concept of FDI is the one to use. Here, too, it is difficult to draw conclusions on the basis of statistical evidence. A statistical relationship between FDI and employment within a firm or an industry does not say much about causality. If the location advantages of foreign production increase and a home country firm shifts part of its production abroad, there is no guarantee that home country employment would not have suffered in the absence of FDI. The question is what the counterfactual would have looked like.

4.3. The findings of empirical research

This section provides a survey of the empirical research of the effects of outward FDI on exports, employment, investment, the structure of labour demand, technology and on incoming capital payments. It should be realised that there is no guarantee that any pattern observed in the past will be repeated in the future.

4.3.1. Exports
In the Heckscher-Ohlin model, FDI and exports are full substitutes. In contrast, a 1998 OECD study found that FDI and exports are complementary, as each dollar of FDI from the member countries brought in two additional dollars from exports (OECD, 1998). In his survey, Lipsey (2002) often could find no clear relationship between exports and FDI at the industry level, but in the cases where it could, the relationship was positive most of the time. Similar results were found by others (Andersen and Hainaut, 1998; Blomström and Kokko, 1994, 2000; Kim, 1998; Pfaffermayr, 1996; Svensson, 1996; Van Beers *et al.*, 1999). There does not seem to be a fixed relationship. Possibly, vertical FDI with mainly a positive

relationship more or less balances horizontal FDI with mainly a negative relationship. This would square with the findings of Barba Navaretti *et al.* (2004), who generally found complementarity between foreign production and exports in the case of vertical FDI, but not always in the case of horizontal FDI (see also Head and Ries, 2001; Blonigen, 2001; Brainard, 1997).

Research by Jordan and Vahlne (1981) on FDI by two Swedish MNEs is worthy of special attention, as they estimated the market shares and the licence payments that would result in the cases of exporting, licence granting and minority participations in joint ventures, respectively. This means that they modelled the counterfactual. Exports, and employment for that matter, increased as a result of FDI, as those FDI led to higher market shares abroad and to exports of semi-finished products to foreign subsidiaries (see in this vein also Blomström and Kokko, 1994).

Conclusion: If there is a relationship between FDI and exports, it tends to be positive rather than negative. In so far as a negative relationship has been found, this was mainly in cases of horizontal FDI. With vertical FDI, the relationship was mainly positive.

4.3.2. Employment

Even if exports increase as a result of (vertical) FDI, employment may still suffer. This is because goods may be sent abroad at some stage in the production process and return after having been processed at a foreign subsidiary. Both exports and imports increase, but domestic value added and employment fall. The end result may well be a cheaper end product, leading to higher market shares. That in its turn may check the fall in employment.

There is research that directly focuses on the relationship between FDI and employment. Brainard and Riker (Brainard and Riker, 1997; Riker and Brainard, 1997) were able to use U.S. Department of Commerce data on individual firms (for the 1983-1992 period) and found a very low degree of substitution between employment at the parent company and employment at foreign daughters after a change in wages. The degree of substitution was much higher between daughters in different foreign countries. A similar study by Braconier and Ekholm (2000) for Sweden again found a low degree of substitution between the home country and developing countries, but a higher degree between Sweden and other rich countries (see Forfás, 2001 for Ireland; Konings and Murphy, 2001 for the European Union; Van Beers *et al.*, 1999; Haverhals *et al.*, 2004; Anonymous, 2005 for the Netherlands; Barba Navaretti and Castellani, 2004 for Italy).

Van Beers *et al.* mention Belgian research by the Federal Planning Bureau, done by means of questionnaires, revealing that ten percent of the foreign subsidiaries of Belgian MNEs were associated with production shifts from Belgium to the host country, implying an initial loss of employment (Bernard *et al.*, 1997). The authors fail, however, to provide information on the effects on employment at the Belgian headquarters. On balance, it need not decline, as is shown by the fact that in the German automobile industry three new jobs abroad are said to create one new job at home, on average (Klodt, 2004).

Research has taken place on the level of firms and industries in the first place. Macroeconomic data may give an impression of the effects of FDI on aggregate employment in an economy. For Korea, an increase in outward FDI as a percentage of GDP went hand in hand with a fall in unemployment (Kim, 1998). As those outward FDI remained below one percent of GDP, strong conclusions cannot be drawn. In the same way, the fact that employment and real incomes rose more in the United States than in Mexico after NAFTA (the North American Free Trade Agreement) started working, at the very least suggests that this FDI did not result in a serious loss of jobs in the United States (cf. Stanford, 2003).

Conclusion: Research on the level of the firm and the level of the industry so far has not shown a systematically negative effect of outward FDI on employment. A flaw in this research is the neglect of FDI on supplier firms. Macroeconomic studies do not, however, point in another direction.

4.3.3. Investment

Apart from the direct effects of FDI on employment, there are indirect effects. One such indirect effect is the impact of FDI on domestic investment. We start with two studies on the industry level. In a study of FDI by Dutch MNEs, Belderbos (1992) found a weak negative correlation between FDI (as a stock) and domestic investment. If causality runs from FDI to investment, this means that outward FDI might cost domestic jobs. Often, however, FDI takes place because of a change in location-specific advantages and the investing firm would have lost market share if it had refrained from FDI, with a higher loss of investment and jobs in the end.

Braunerhjelm *et al.* (2004) found for Swedish MNEs that in industries with horizontal FDI, domestic investment suffers, whereas vertical FDI was positively correlated with domestic investment. Industries with horizontal FDI are strongly dependent on research and development, with scale economies on the level of the firm and not the level of the plant. Industries with vertical FDI by contrast are more dependent on comparative advantages based on relative factor availability. They tend to be less knowledge-intensive. The empirical data were found to be consistent with this theoretical approach.

On the macroeconomic level, Feldstein (1994) found for OECD countries over the 1970s and 1980s that outward FDI went hand in hand with a fall in domestic investment by roughly the same amount (see also Svensson, 1993; Andersen and Hainaut, 1998 and Desai *et al.*, 2005). Feinstein's results only pertained to the share of FDI financed by the home country. The macroeconomic character of his research implies that the effects of FDI on the amount of funds available for other firms were included. Blomström and Kokko (1994) refer to the Swedish controversy over the question whether the low level of domestic investment in the early 1990s could be a result of the high level of debt with which Swedish MNEs were saddled since their FDI activities in the 1980s. Stevens and Lipsey (1992) saw a connection running from FDI by American firms through lower capital ratios and higher costs of finance to a fall in domestic investment (see also Wellink, 2004).

Conclusion: According to some research, the relationship between FDI and domestic investment is negative on a macro scale, whereas other research finds that domestic investment is not sensitive to (net) outward FDI. On the level of the firm or the industry, there are indications of complementarity in the case of vertical FDI, but there are opposing forces from the side of finance. A statistical relationship in itself says little about causality and one cannot be sure about the level in the level of domestic investment had there been no FDI.

4.3.4. The impact of FDI on the structure of labour demand
There do not seem to have been many studies on spillovers of outward FDI on other domestic firms, that is, on the consequences for, *e.g.*, suppliers and clients or the demand for infrastructure. There is, however, some empirical evidence of FDI on the structure of the demand for labour, even if this cannot always be separated from the effects of globalisation in general.

According to Lipsey (2002), outward FDI leads to a shift of low-skilled activities to host countries and high-skilled activities to the home country (see for similar results for the Netherlands Haverhals *et al.*, 2004; Anonymous, 2005). In a number of cases, employment in manufacturing plants fell whereas employment at the firm's head office rose. This points to a shift to higher-skilled jobs. Blomström *et al.* (1997) found, using American data in individual firms, that a rise in sales by \$1 million in developing countries involved a loss of 12 to 18 jobs in the United States, keeping total sales constant. This was seen by them as a shift to more capital-intensive production in the U.S.A. A relatively high cost of low-skilled labour was seen as the probable culprit. In Sweden, this effect was absent, presumably because Swedish MNEs were predominantly market seekers with branches in rich countries. American MNEs by contrast mainly were efficiency seekers producing where costs were lowest and exporting on a large scale from foreign branches.

Interestingly, in a number of cases employment in manufacturing production in the home country fell when it rose abroad, with employment at headquarters increasing. This again points to a shift to higher-skilled jobs.

In Swedish research, a shift in the home country to semi-finished products with low value added, and thus to a fall in labour productivity, has been found. Possibly, a comparative advantage for raw materials accounts for this. Research and development, however, remained concentrated at the parent companies in Sweden.

One problem in empirical research is that the effects of outward FDI on suppliers in the home country generally are neglected. This subject was studied by Mariotti *et al.* (2003). In their view, vertical FDI goes hand in hand with a shift in the home country from low-skilled labour to capital and high-skilled labour, both at the MNE itself and its suppliers.

FDI and the associated changes in the structure of trade and production may thus lead to an increase in the demand for high-skilled labour and a fall in demand for low-skilled labour (cf. Tokarick, 2002; Strauss-Kahn, 2003). This may lead to higher wage inequalities and, if wages are sticky downward, higher unemployment among the low-skilled (little effect was, however, found by Slaughter, 1995, 2000; Gorter *et al.*, 2005). It is a moot point to what degree FDI and trade are responsible. Technological developments are another important cause.

FDI makes it easier for firms to shift production abroad at short notice, in particular in the case of horizontal FDI. According to Rodrik (1997), this has perhaps not so much resulted in a lower demand for low-skilled labour but in a higher price elasticity of the demand for low-skilled labour. This has given firms a stronger position in wage negotiations and may have contributed to relatively lower wages of low-skilled labour.

Conclusion: The empirical evidence suggests that FDI provides an additional impulse to the existing shift from low-skilled to high-skilled jobs.

4.3.5. Technology

As we have seen, MNE's may resort to FDI in order to obtain foreign technology. This has often been the case for Korean firms (Kim (1998) and for Japanese firms that have invested in the U.S. (Blonigen, 1997). Irish firms in the food industry have transferred technology acquired abroad and adopted in their foreign plants back to Ireland (Forfás, 2001). For Swedish industrial MNEs, by contrast, Braconnier *et al.* (2001) were unable to detect any link between outward FDI and technological spillover, measured by changes in productivity.

According to the research surveyed by Barba Navaretti *et al.* (2004), in some cases there are spillovers of foreign technology to the home country, in other cases not. Technology acquired abroad may, however, be imported in the guise of a higher quality of imported semi-finished products, that is, through vertical FDI. This effect is hard to establish empirically (see Keller, 2004: 764). Barba Navaretti and Castellani's research on Italy reveals another effect of outward FDI on technology: firms that open their first foreign branch see their productivity increase at a fast pace (Barba Navaretti and Castellani, 2004).

Earlier research, reviewed by Blomström and Kokko (1994), revealed a positive correlation between FDI and an MNE's profits. Higher profits in their turn stimulate expenditure on research and development, which also benefits from the fact that FDI enables MNEs to grow. In so far as research and development remains concentrated in the home country, the demand for high-skilled labour is likely to grow. This may have positive externalities, such as the establishment of more and better educational institutions. More generally, it may contribute to endogenous growth.

Conclusion: Firms may resort to FDI expressly in order to get access to foreign technology. In other cases it is hard to find empirical evidence on the effects of outward FDI on technology. Still, there are clear indications that firms opening their first foreign affiliate see their productivity increase at an above-average rate.

4.3.6. The yield of FDI as a capital flow

Outward FDI should generate capital income, as emphasised in the MacDougall model. But we live in a world characterised by uncertainty in the sense of Knight and investments may turn sour. According to calculations by Boonstra (2003, 2004), the cumulative balance on the current account of the balance of payments of the Netherlands over the 1986-2002 period amounted to some €170bn, but net foreign assets deteriorated by more than €165bn, which means that roughly €335bn has disappeared into thin air. These losses cannot all be attributed to FDI, as the figures include portfolio investment, but poor results of FDI certainly played a role.

Conclusion: Outward FDI do not always fulfil their promises. Dutch MNEs have suffered a number of spectacular debacles, in particular, it seems, from mergers and acquisitions. This does, however, not detract from the positive impact of FDI in the form of real investment on growth and profits.

5. Conclusions

The research on the effects of FDI on exports generally shows a positive effect of FDI, in particular of the vertical variety. Outward FDI has been negatively correlated with domestic investment generally, especially in the case of horizontal FDI, but that does not say much about causality and the relationship does not hold for FDI financed from foreign sources.

FDI generally leads to a shift from lower-skilled to higher-skilled jobs. The impact of FDI on technology in the home country finally is very diffuse and hard to establish. There are indications of 'learning by doing'. Positive externalities are plausible but hard to measure empirically.

The results of outward FDI should be looked at with the counterfactual in mind. Many firms would not have been able to survive, or at least not have been able to maintain their market share, without FDI. Scale economies on the level of the firm and both natural and artificial trade barriers easily combine to make FDI a necessity, the more so if a firm is based in a small country. It would, then, be counterproductive to try and restrict outward FDI, even in cases where FDI in the first instance goes at the cost of domestic production and employment.

If we look at the outcomes of the empirical research on FDI in a wider context, they lose much of their significance. The research throws light on first-round effects, but these are of minor importance to economies that are dependent on Schumpeterian creative destruction and 'new combinations' for their long-term growth. In the same way as international trade, FDI contributes to the international division of labour, and with it to productivity growth and ongoing economic development.

Restrictions on outward FDI are a form of protection. They reduce the benefits a country receives from the international division of labour. These benefits not only include the effects of a reallocation of production, given technology, but also a constant improvement of technology. It is no use deploring a shift of production and jobs abroad. The receiving countries will see their production and income grow. Their import demand increases, creating new opportunities for the home countries of the MNEs involved, both directly and indirectly: those opportunities may be found in the host countries, but also in third countries that profit from the new-found growth in the FDI destination countries. The home country will in the end profit from shifting production to a cheaper place and replacing it with jobs that create higher value added. The government's first concern should be to create an attractive business climate, in order to induce sufficient entrepreneurial activity to absorb any labour set free by outward FDI.

Acknowledgements

I am indebted to Pieter Karsdorp for helpful suggestions.

References

Andersen, P.S. and P. Hainaut, 1998. Foreign Direct Investment and Employment in the Industrial Countries. Working Paper No. 61, BIS, Basel (on www.bis.org).

Anonymous, 2005. Visie op verplaatsing: Aard, omvang en effecten van verplaatsing van bedrijfsactiviteiten naar het buitenland [A vision on reallocation: The nature, scope and effects of reallocations of business activities abroad]. EZ Onderzoeksreeks, Ministerie van Economische Zaken, The Hague.

Barba Navaretti, G. and D. Castellani, 2004, Investments Abroad and Performance at Home: Evidence from Italian Multinationals. Discussion Paper 4284, CEPR, London.

Barba Navaretti, G., A.J. Venables, F. Barry, K. Ekholm, A. Falzoni, J. Haaland, K.-H. Midelfart and A. Turrini, 2004. Home Country Effects of Foreign Direct Investment. In: Multinational firms in the world economy. Princeton University Press, Princeton, N.J. Also on econ.lse.ac.uk/staff/ajv/multinationals.html.

Belderbos, R.A., 1992. Large Multinational Enterprises Based in a Small Economy: Effects on Domestic Investment. Weltwirtschaftliches Archiv 128: 543-557.

Bernard, P., H. Van Sebroek, H. Spinnewijn, P. Vandenhove and B. Van den Cruyce, 1997. Delokalisatie Mondialisering, een actualisatierapport voor België [Delocalisation Globalisation, a report on recent developments for Belgium]. Federaal Planbureau, Brussels.

Blomström, M., G. Fors and R.E. Lipsey, 1997. Foreign Direct Investment and Employment: Home Country Experience in the United States and Sweden. Economic Journal 107: 1787-1797.

Blomström, M. and A. Kokko, 1994, Home Country Effects on Foreign Direct Investment: Evidence from Sweden. Working Paper 4639, NBER, Cambridge, Mass.

Blomström, M. and A. Kokko, 2000, Outward investment, employment, and wages in Swedish multinationals. Oxford Review of Economic Policy 16: 76-88.

Blonigen, B.A., 1997. Firm-Specific Assets and the Link Between Exchange Rates and Foreign Direct Investment. American Economic Review 87: 447-465.

Blonigen, B.A., 2001. In search of substitution between foreign production and exports. Journal of International Economics 53: 81-104.

Blonigen, B.A., 2005. A Review of the Empirical Literature on FDI Determinants. Working Paper 11299, NBER, Cambridge, Mass.

Boonstra, W.W., 2003. Nederlands verdwenen vermogen [The Netherlands' disappeared wealth]. ESB 88: 535-537.

Boonstra, W.W., 2004. Extern vermogen en de gevolgen van de vergrijzing [Net foreign assets and the consequences of aging]. ESB 89: 341-343.

Braconier, H. and K. Ekholm, 2000. Swedish Multinationals and Competition from High- and Low-Wage Locations. Review of International Economics 8: 448-461.

Braconier, H., K. Ekholm and K.-H., Midelfart Knarvik, 2001. Does FDI Work as a Channel for R&D Spillovers? Evidence Based on Swedish Data. Working Paper 553, IUI, The Research Institute of Industrial Economics, Stockholm.

Brainard, S.L., 1997. An Empirical Assessment of the Proximity-Concentration Tradeoff between Multinational Sales and Trade. American Economic Review 87: 520-544.

Brainard, S.L. and D.A. Riker, 1997. Are U.S. Multinationals Exporting U.S. Jobs?, Working Paper 5958. NBER, Cambridge, Mass.

Braunerhjelm, P., L. Oxelheim and P. Thulin, 2004. The Relationship between Domestic and Outward Foreign Direct Investment: The Role of Industry-Specific Effects. Working Paper 625, IUI, The Research Institute of Industrial Economics, Stockholm. http://www.iui.se/wp/wp.htm.

Caves, R.E., 1982. Multinational enterprise and economic analysis. Cambridge University Press, Cambridge.

Desai, M.A., C.F. Foley and J.R. Hines, 2005. Foreign Direct Investment and the Domestic Capital Stock. Working Paper 11075, NBER, Cambridge, Mass.

Dunning, J.H., 1993. Multinational Enterprises and the Global Economy. Addison-Wesley, Wokingham.

Feldstein, M., 1994. The Effects of Outbound Foreign Direct Investment on the Domestic Capital Stock. Working Paper 4668, NBER, Cambridge, Mass.

Forfás, 2001. Statement on Outward Direct Investment. Dublin; www.forfás.ie.

Gorter, J., P. Tang and M. Toet, 2005. Verplaatsing vanuit Nederland: Motieven, gevolgen en beleid [Reallocation from The Netherlands: Motives, consequences and policy]. Document No. 76, CPB, Den Haag.

Gorton, G.B., M. Kahl and R.J. Rosen, 2005. Eat or Be Eaten: A Theory of Mergers and Merger Waves. Working Paper 11364, NBER, Cambridge, Mass.

Haverhals, H., R. Barendrecht, R. Jansen, S. Kappers, L. Oh and M. de Wal, 2004. Aard, omvang en effecten van verplaatsen bedrijfsactiviteiten naar het buitenland [The nature, scope and effects of reallocations of business activities abroad]. paper written for the Economics Ministry. Bureau Berenschot, Utrecht.

Head, K. and J. Ries, 2001. Overseas Investment and Firm Exports. Review of International Economics 9: 108-122.

Helpman, E., M.J. Melitz and S.R. Yeaple, 2004. Export Versus FDI With Heterogeneous Firms. American Economic Review 94: 300-316.

Jordan, J.L. and J.E. Vahlne, 1981. Domestic Employment Effects of Direct Investment Abroad by Two Swedish Multinationals. Working Paper 13, Multinational Enterprises Programme, ILO, Geneva. Cited by Blomström and Kokko, 1994.

Keller, W., 2004. International Technology Diffusion. Journal of Economic Literature 42: 752-782.

Kim, S., 1998. Effects of Outward Foreign Direct Investment on Home Country Performance: Evidence from Korea. Korea Development Institute, Seoul. http://www.kdi.re.kr/kdi_eng/main.jsp.

Klant, J.J., 1987. Filosofie van de economische wetenschappen [Philosophy of Economics]. Martinus Nijhoff, Leiden.

Klodt, H., 2004. Mehr Arbeitsplätze durch Auslandsinvestitionen [Higher Employment through Foreign Direct Investment]. Die Weltwirtschaft 3: 374-389.

Konings, J. and A. Murphy, 2001. Do Multinational Enterprises Substitute Parent Jobs For Foreign Ones? Evidence From European Firm-level Panel Data. Discussion Paper 2972, CEPR, London.

Lipsey, R.E., 2002. Home and Host Country Effects of FDI. Working Paper 9293, NBER, Cambridge, Mass.

MacDougall, G.D.A., 1958. The Benefits and Costs of Private Investment from Abroad: A Theoretical Approach. Economic Record 36: 13-53. Reprinted in: J. Bhagwati (Ed.), International trade. Penguin, Harmondsworth 1969, pp. 341-369.

Mariotti, S., M. Mutinelli and L. Piscitello, 2003. Home country employment and foreign direct investment: evidence from the Italian case. Cambridge Journal of Economics 27: 419-431.

Markusen, J.R. and K.E. Maskus, 2001. General-Equilibrium Approaches to the Multinational Firm: A Review of Theory and Evidence. Working Paper 833, NBER, Cambridge, Mass.

Navarro, V., J. Schmitt and J. Astudillo, 2004. Is globalisation undermining the welfare state?. Cambridge Journal of Economics 28: 133-152.

OECD, 1988. Open Markets Matter: The Benefits of Trade and Investment Regulation. Paris. Cited in: Forfás, 2001.

Pfaffermayr, M., 1996. Foreign Outward Direct Investment and Exports in Austrian Manufacturing: Substitutes or Complements? Weltwirtschaftliches Archiv 132: 501-522.

Riker, D.A. and S.L. Brainard, 1997. U.S. Multinationals and Competition from Lowe Wage Countries. Working Paper 5959, NBER, Cambridge, Mass.

Rodrik, D., 1997. Has Globalization Gone Too Far?. Institute for International Economics, Washington, D.C.

Schenk, H., 1999. Zijn internationale overnames meer een kwestie van strategie dan van economie? [Are international takeovers a question of strategy rather than of economics?]. Bedrijfskunde 71: 13-20. Reprinted in: Koninklijke Vereniging voor de Staathuishoudkunde, Jaarboek 1999/2000, ESB, Rotterdam 2000, pp. 53-64.

Schumpeter, J.A., 1950. Capitalism, Socialism and Democracy. Third edn. Harper & Row, New York.

Schumpeter, J.A., 1969. The theory of economic development. Oxford University Press, Oxford. Originally Harvard University Press, Cambridge, Mass. 1934 pp.

Slaughter, M.J., 1995. Multinational Corporations, Outsourcing, and American Wage Divergence. Working Paper 5253, NBER, Cambridge, Mass.

Slaughter, M.J., 2000. Production transfer within multinational enterprises and American wages. Journal of International Economics 50: 449-472.

Stanford, J., 2003. The North American Free Trade Agreement: context, structure and performance. In: J. Michie (Ed.), The Handbook of Globalisation. Edward Elgar, Cheltenham, pp. 261-282.

Stevens, G.V.G. and R.E. Lipsey, 1992. Interactions between domestic and foreign investment. Journal of International Money and Finance 11: 40-62.

Strauss-Kahn, V., 2003. The Role of Globalization in the Within-Industry Shift Away from Unskilled Workers in France. Working Paper No. W9716, NBER, Cambridge, Mass.

Svensson, R., 1993. Domestic and Foreign Investment by Swedish Multinationals. Working Paper 391, The Industrial Institute for Economic and Social Research, Stockholm. Cited by Kim, 1998.

Svensson, R., 1996. Effects of Overseas Production on Home Country Exports: Evidence Based on Swedish Multinationals. Weltwirtschaftliches Archiv 132: 304-329.

Tanzi, V., 2002. Globalization and the Future of Social Protection. Scottish Journal of Political Economy 49: 116-127.

Tokarick, S., 2002. Quantifying the Impact of Trade on Wages: The Role of Nontraded Goods. Working Paper 02.191, IMF, Washington, D.C.

Van Beers, C.P., M.C. Braber, A.R. Hoen, A.P.G. de Moor and J.A.A. Poppelaars, 1999. De gevolgen voor Nederland van Directe Buitenlandse Investeringen [The Consequences of Foreign Direct Investment for The Netherlands]. Onderzoeksreeks nr. 96, IOO bv, The Hague.

Wellink, A.H.E.M., 2004. Business cycles and foreign direct investment. Presentation given for the American Chamber of Commerce in the Netherlands, 23 September; www.dnb.nl.

Financial sector reforms and impact of monetary policy shocks in Nigeria: an implication of vector autoregressive model

Michael Adebayo Adebiyi
Department of Economics, University of Lagos, Nigeria. mikebiyi@yahoo.com

Abstract

The paper analyses the monetary policy transmission mechanism in Nigeria. A vector auto-regressive model is estimated for the pre-reform (1970-1985) and post-reform (1986-2003) periods. Forecast error variance decompositions and impulse response functions are used to see whether or not there are any observed changes in the monetary policy transmission mechanism after the reforms. Different systems are estimated in each period using alternate variables as measures of monetary policy shocks. The results from the estimated forecast error variances decompositions and impulse response analyses show that most of the variability in prices and output is explained by shocks in exchange rate and monetary aggregates after the reforms. This shows that the potency of monetary policy has increased since the reforms. Although monetary policy in Nigeria has focused almost exclusively on monetary aggregates, the study finds evidence to support exchange rates targeting as an alternative monetary policy instrument.

JEL classification: E31, E37

Keywords: financial sector reform, monetary policy shocks, vector autoregressive model

1. Introduction

Nigeria implemented financial sector reforms as a component of the structural adjustment program (SAP) in July 1986. With the switch to indirect instruments, the goals of monetary policy have been to reduce inflation and to promote economic growth, among others. For these goals to be achieved, policymakers must ascertain the effectiveness of monetary policy. The understanding of the efficacy of monetary policy and its transmission mechanism are very important to the success of monetary policy. Efficient implementation requires policy makers to understand the impact on the macro-economy and the time horizon needed for the impact. Key policy issues in the current policy framework arise. For example, do changes in reserve money actually lead to changes in money broadly defined (M_2) and inflation? If so, how long do these changes take to impact inflation? This information would then aid policy makers to know which instruments are more useful and which time horizon should be used to target inflation.

Against this background, the study attempts to investigate empirically whether or not the transmission mechanism of monetary policy to the macro-economy has changed since 1986. The rest of the paper is structured as follows. Section 2 contains the theoretical underpinnings and literature review, while Section 3 explains the sources of data and econometric framework for the study. Section 4 gives the empirical results, while the summary and conclusions are provided in the last section.

2. Theoretical underpinnings and literature review

It has been noted that monetary policy can significantly influence economic behaviour (Simatele, 2003). An interesting question then is: what is the transmission mechanism through which these effects occur? A number of empirical works on the transmission mechanism has carried out using the VAR approach. Sims (1992), using monthly data, estimates separate vector autoregressive (VARs) for Germany, France, Japan, the United Kingdom and the United States. In the study, index of industrial production, consumer price index, short-term interest rate, money supply and exchange rate are included. The findings shows that the response of output to interest rate innovations is similar in all the countries and that monetary shocks lead to an output response that is hump-shaped in pattern (Walsh, 1998).

Bernanke and Blinder (1992) do a study on the credit channel in the US, using the federal funds rate, unemployment rate, log of consumer price index, deposits, loans and securities. The identifying assumption is similar to that of Sims (1992) so that monetary policy is predetermined. They find that both the conventional money demand and the credit mechanisms operate. A positive shock to the federal funds rate reduces the volume of deposits held by institutions immediately after the shock and peaks after nine months. After a period of two years, the entire long run impact of the decline in deposits is reflected in loans. They conclude that their findings support the operation of a credit channel. On the other hand, Rossiter (1995) and Miron *et al.* (1995) suggest that the interest rate spreads are alternative focuses on monetary aggregates under the credit view.

Christiano *et al.* (1994) use US quarterly data to test the effect of monetary policy shocks. They make similar identifying assumptions as Sims (1992) and explicitly include commodity prices to avoid the price puzzle. Their variables include real GDP, the GDP deflator, commodity prices, federal fund rate, non-borrowed reserves, total reserves and net funds raised through financial markets. The policy variables used alternately are the federal funds rate and non-borrowed reserves. Their results show that the initial effect of a positive shock to the federal funds rate is to increase net funds raised by the business sector for almost a year, which declines thereafter.

Dale and Haldan (1995) and Carpenter (1996) extend Bernanke and Blinder's (1992) work, using similar methods. Dale and Haldan (1995) examine a small sectoral (household and corporate) VAR model of the UK economy. Consistent with Gertler and Gilchrist (1993), the authors show that there are significant sectoral differences among the channels of monetary transmission.

Another interesting approach for testing the credit channel is provided by Kashyap *et al.* (1993). The authors establish a simple model with two necessary conditions, which must be satisfied for monetary policy to impact on aggregate demand. The first condition is that loans and commercial papers must be imperfect substitutes to bank assets. Therefore, banks cannot just reduce commercial papers in order to keep the supply of loans unchanged. The second condition is that loans and commercial papers must be imperfect substitutes to corporate liabilities. Hence, firms must not be able to offset a decline in loan supply by issuing more paper without a cost. Their empirical evidence suggests that both conditions are satisfied.

Giovanni (1993) finds results that monetary tightening broadens the spread between marginal lending rates and corporate commercial paper rates for most of the banks. This is similar to the findings of Kashyap *et al.* (1993). In addition, banks suffering from larger negative capital shocks also experience a more marked slow-down in the expansion of loans and disproportionately raise their lending rates. Second, the central bank must be able to constrain the banks' ability to lend (Cecchetti, 1995). Third, there exist bank-dependent borrowers, for example, small or low net-worth firms, who have limited opportunities to substitute credit from other financial intermediaries but banks (Gertler and Gilchrist, 1993, 1994; Christiano *et al.*, 1996). Finally, there must be imperfect price adjustments in order to allow the monetary policy to affect real activity.

Eichenbaum (1992) presents a comparison of the estimated effects of monetary policy in the United States using alternative measures of policy shocks, discussing how different choices can produce puzzling results. He anchors his discussion on the results obtained from a VAR containing four variables: the price level, the output, narrow money supply (M_1) and the federal funds rate. He considers interpreting shocks to M_1 as policy shocks versus the alternative of interpreting fund rate shocks. He finds that a positive innovation to M_1 is followed by an increase in the federal funds rate and a decline in the output (Walsh, 1998). This result is puzzling if the M_1 shocks are interpreted as measuring the impact of monetary policy. An expansionary monetary policy shock would be expected to lead to increases in both M_1 and output. Interest rate is also found to rise after a positive M_1 shock. The results are also potentially puzzling (Walsh, 1998).

Gordon and Leeper (1994) show that a similar puzzle emerges using total reserve to measure monetary policy shocks. Their findings show that a rise in reserves raises market interest rates. In this respect, scholars have generated a large literature in an attempt to search for a liquidity effect of changes in the reserves or money supply (Gordon and Leeper, 1994; Strongin, 1995; Walsh, 1998).

In another study, Nannyonjo (2001) examines credit channel in Uganda using the VAR methodology. The macro variables used in the study are the index of industrial production and the consumer price index. The policy variable used is base money. By performing Granger causality tests and variance decompositions, she concludes that there is no significant role for either bank loans or the lending rate in the transmission of monetary policy shocks to output. She finds that output explains 37% of variations in bank loans after two years, indicating demand driven lending in Uganda. The impulse responses estimated, however, indicate a positive, though delayed, effect of bank lending on output.

Uchendu (1996) examines the channels of monetary policy transmission mechanism in Nigeria. According to him, when economic controls are relaxed as part of the Structural Adjustment Programme (SAP) launched in mid-1986, the inter-bank market and the emerging rates become important means for the transmission of monetary policy in Nigeria. The credit channel of monetary transmission works through the banks and the informal credit markets. Evidence on the credit channel of monetary policy shocks is found (Uchendu, 1996).

The summary of the review above shows that the channels of monetary policy transmission mechanism vary from country to country and the impact of these channels, on real sector, varies from mechanism to mechanism and from periods to periods.

3. Sources of data and econometric framework

3.1. Sources of data

The variables used are classified into two: policy variables, which include Treasury Bill rate, exchange rate, commercial banks' credit to the private sector and monetary aggregates. The other variables are the macroeconomic indicators, which include consumer price index and real gross domestic product. In using a VAR model, all the variables are assumed endogenous. However, our interest is to examine the impact of policy variables on macroeconomic indicators as discussed in Tables 1 and 2. The variables for the study are obtained from IMF: *International Financial Statistics* (various years) and Central Bank of Nigeria: *Statistical Bulletin* (various years). The period of study spans 1970:1 to 2003:4.

3.2. Econometric framework

VAR models are the best method for investigating shock transmission among variables because they provide information on impulse responses (Adrangi and Allender (1998). Zellner and Palm (1974), Zellner (1979), and Palm (1983) show that any linear structural model can be written as a VAR model. Therefore, a VAR model serves as a flexible approximation to the reduced form of any wide variety of simultaneous structural models.

Let us consider a bivariate AR (1) model. Let y_t be a measure of real economic activity or macroeconomic indicators such as GDP or inflation. Let z_t be the monetary policy variable such as the interest rate or exchange rate. A VAR system can be written as follows

$$\begin{bmatrix} y_t \\ z_t \end{bmatrix} = A_0 + A[L] \begin{bmatrix} y_{t-1} \\ z_{t-1} \end{bmatrix} + \begin{bmatrix} u_{yt} \\ u_{zt} \end{bmatrix}$$

A_0 is a vector of constants, A (L) is a 2x2 matrix polynomial in the lag operator L, and u_{it} serially independent errors for i. Suppose the structural equations can be represented as follows

$$y_t = b_{10} - b_{12}z_t + b_{11}y_{t-1} + b_{13}z_{t-1} + u_{yt} \qquad \text{(Eq. 1)}$$
$$z_t = b_{20} - b_{21}y_t + b_{22}y_{t-1} + b_{23}z_{t-1} + u_{zt} \qquad \text{(Eq. 2)}$$

which can be rewritten as

$$y_t + b_{12}z_t = b_{10} + b_{11}y_{t-1} + b_{13}z_{t-1} + u_{yt} \qquad \text{(Eq. 3)}$$
$$z_t + b_{21}y_t = b_{20} + b_{22}y_{t-1} + b_{23}z_{t-1} + u_{zt} \qquad \text{(Eq. 4)}$$

and in matrix form

$$\begin{bmatrix} 1 & b_{12} \\ b_{21} & 1 \end{bmatrix} \begin{bmatrix} y_t \\ z_t \end{bmatrix} = \begin{bmatrix} b_{10} \\ b_{20} \end{bmatrix} + \begin{bmatrix} b_{11} & b_{13} \\ b_{22} & b_{23} \end{bmatrix} \begin{bmatrix} y_{t-1} \\ z_{t-1} \end{bmatrix} + \begin{bmatrix} u_{yt} \\ u_{zt} \end{bmatrix}$$

let

$$B = \begin{bmatrix} 1 & b_{12} \\ b_{21} & 1 \end{bmatrix}$$

$$Z = \begin{bmatrix} y_t \\ z_t \end{bmatrix}$$

$$V_0 = \begin{bmatrix} b_{10} \\ b_{20} \end{bmatrix}$$

$$V_1 = \begin{bmatrix} b_{11} & b_{13} \\ b_{22} & b_{23} \end{bmatrix}$$

which allows us to write a more compact form of the structural equation as

$$BZ_t = V_0 + V_1 Z_{t-1} + u_{it}$$

Assuming that B is invertible, we pre-multiply the equation by B^{-1} to obtain

$$Z_t = A_0 + A_1 Z_{t-1} + \varepsilon_{it} \qquad \text{(Eq. 5)}$$

Where $A_0 = B^{-1} V_0$
$A_1 = B^{-1} V_1$
and $\varepsilon_t = B^{-1} u_{it}$

Given the a_{ij} is the element of the ith row and j^{th} column, we can now write our VAR in standard form.

$$y_t = a_{10} + a_{11} y_{t-1} + a_{12} z_{t-1} + \varepsilon_{yt} \qquad \text{(Eq. 6)}$$
$$z_t = a_{20} + a_{21} y_{t-1} + a_{22} z_{t-1} + \varepsilon_{zt} \qquad \text{(Eq. 7)}$$

and the matrix form,

$$\begin{bmatrix} y_t \\ z_t \end{bmatrix} = \begin{bmatrix} a_{10} \\ a_{20} \end{bmatrix} + \begin{bmatrix} a_{11} & a_{12} \\ a_{21} & a_{22} \end{bmatrix} + \begin{bmatrix} \varepsilon_{yt} \\ \varepsilon_{zt} \end{bmatrix} \qquad \text{(Eq. 8)}$$

Note that the errors are a composite of two errors u_{yt} and u_{zt} since $\varepsilon_t = B^{-1} u_{it}$ *i.e.*

$$\begin{bmatrix} \varepsilon_{yt} \\ \varepsilon_{zt} \end{bmatrix} = \begin{bmatrix} 1 & b_{12} \\ b_{21} & 1 \end{bmatrix}^{-1} \begin{bmatrix} u_{yt} \\ u_{zt} \end{bmatrix}$$

so that

$$\varepsilon_{yt} = \frac{u_{yt} - b_{12} u_{zt}}{1 - b_{12} b_{21}} \qquad \text{(Eq. 9)}$$

$$\varepsilon_{zt} = \frac{u_{zt} - b_{21} u_{yt}}{1 - b_{12} b_{21}} \qquad \text{(Eq. 10)}$$

Since the u_{it}s are white noise, so are the ε_ts.

From Equations 9 and 10, we can see that policy errors can be caused by exogenous y and policy disturbances. Let Σ_u be the 2X2 variance-covariance matrix of u_{it} and Σ_ε that of ε_{it}. Then $\Sigma_\varepsilon = B\Sigma_u B^1$. To determine the impact of policy on output, we need to look at the effect of u_{zt} but unless $b_{21} = 0$, ε_{zt} is not equal to u_{zt} and therefore does not provide a measure of the policy shock. If we estimate our VAR in Equations 6 and 7 as it is, B and Σ_u will not be identified without further restrictions since estimation of the reduced form in Equations 6 and 7 will yield less parameters than the structural form in Equations 1 and 2. One of the most common restrictions is to assume that the structural shocks are uncorrelated so that the off diagonal elements in the covariance matrix are zero (Simatele, 2003; Bernanke and Blinder, 1992).

Two results obtained from VARs that are useful for analysing transmission mechanisms are impulse response functions and forecast error variance decompositions. The impulse responses tell us how macro variables respond to shocks in the policy variables, while the variance decompositions show the magnitude of the variations in the macro variables due to the policy variables.

If we assume a stable system (like Simatele, 2003), we can iterate Equation 5 backwards and let n approach infinity, then we obtain as solution:

$$Z_t = \lambda + \sum_{i=0}^{\infty} A_1^i \varepsilon_{t-i}$$

Where the λs are the means of y_t and z_t and use Equation 8 to get

$$\begin{bmatrix} y_t \\ z_t \end{bmatrix} = \begin{bmatrix} \mu_y \\ \mu_z \end{bmatrix} + \frac{1}{1-b_{12}b_{21}} \sum_{i=0}^{\infty} \begin{bmatrix} a_{11} & a_{12} \\ a_{21} & a_{22} \end{bmatrix} \begin{bmatrix} 1 & -b_{12} \\ -b_{21} & 1 \end{bmatrix} \begin{bmatrix} u_{yt} \\ u_{zt} \end{bmatrix} \qquad \text{(Eq. 11)}$$

We define the 2X2 matrix as F (i) with elements F_{jk} (i) such that

$$F(i) = \frac{A_1^i}{1-b_{12}b_{21}} \begin{bmatrix} 1 & b_{12} \\ b_{21} & 1 \end{bmatrix}$$

and we write in moving average form as

$$\begin{bmatrix} y_t \\ z_t \end{bmatrix} = \begin{bmatrix} \mu_y \\ \mu_z \end{bmatrix} + \sum_{i=0}^{\infty} \begin{bmatrix} F_{11}(i) & F_{12}(i) \\ F_{21}(i) & F_{22}(i) \end{bmatrix} \begin{bmatrix} u_{yt-1} \\ u_{zt-1} \end{bmatrix}$$

or in a more compact form

$$Z_t = \mu + \sum_{i=0}^{\infty} F(i)u_{t-i} \qquad \text{(Eq. 12)}$$

$F_{jk}(i)$ are the impulse response functions. As we vary (i), we get a function describing the response of variable j to an impulse in variable k (Simatele, 2003). In using a VAR model, the selection of lag order is very essential. Without a formal method, the selection of lag order in a VAR model will be arbitrary and could lead to specification error (see Fair and Schiller, 1990; Funke, 1990). Several criteria, similar to those used in the distributed lag models, are suggested to determine the model dimension (see Judge *et al.*, 1985; Lutkepohl, 1985).

In selecting the number of lags, the paper relies on Akaike Information (AIC) and Schwarz criteria (SC). The lags that report the minimum AIC and SC give the best VAR model. With this in mind, the study discovers that the model performs better with four lags. This may be due to quarterly time series data employed in the study.

4. Empirical results and analysis

In discussing the results, we conjecture that different transmission mechanisms are at play. Since the different policy variables are changed sometimes simultaneously, it would be interesting to see the responses in a VAR with all variables included. However, due to the small sample size, we are unable to estimate such a VAR. We estimate mechanisms that test both the money and credit views of monetary transmission. Considering the monetary view, we estimate the interest rate and exchange rate mechanisms. We also estimate a mechanism that looks at the propagation of policy changes when money supply is controlled by the use of reserve requirement, which affects the currency ratio.

The interest rate channel is based on using reserve or base money as the policy instrument. From the open market operations, we know that the Central Bank of Nigeria (CBN) auctions short term debts to commercial banks which then offer rates at which they will either deposit (for tightening policy) or borrow (for expansionary policy) funds. The changes are then expected to translate into changes in money supply given the money multiplier. This should then cause movements in prices and output. This model is considered as the base model because it portrays the mechanism which best describes basic monetary policy as conducted by the CBN. Hence, we have our first mechanism, which states that reduction in monetary base (Mb) reduces money supply (M_2). This increases interest rate (i), which invariably reduces output (y) and price (p).

$$\downarrow Mb \rightarrow \downarrow M_2 \rightarrow \uparrow i \rightarrow \downarrow y \rightarrow \downarrow p \qquad \text{(Eq. 13)}$$

The second mechanism we estimate is based on the use of liquidity ratios to control growth in money supply. The mechanism shows that reduction in liquidity ratio (L_2) reduces money supply (M_2), output (y) and price (p).

$$\downarrow Lr \rightarrow \downarrow M_2 \rightarrow \downarrow y \rightarrow \downarrow p \qquad \text{(Eq. 14)}$$

The exchange rate mechanism is based on the Central Bank of Nigeria (CBN)'s activities in the foreign exchange market. Through the sale and purchase of foreign exchange on the open market, CBN affects movements in money supply and prices. Using the nominal exchange rate as the instrument, the third mechanism is schematised as:

$$\uparrow M_2 \rightarrow \uparrow E \rightarrow \uparrow y \rightarrow \uparrow p \qquad \text{(Eq. 15)}$$

This shows that increase in money supply (M_2) increases nominal exchange rate (E), which increases output (y) and price (p).

We also estimate a mechanism to evaluate the credit view. We estimate a system to see whether monetary policy affects lending rates and total bank lending. The mechanism is schematised as:

$$\downarrow M_2 \rightarrow \uparrow i \rightarrow \downarrow L \rightarrow \downarrow y \rightarrow \downarrow p \qquad \text{(Eq. 16)}$$

This shows that reduction in M_2 increases interest rate (i). This reduces bank lending rate (L), output (y) and price (p).

Based on these four mechanisms, the paper estimates forecast error variance decompositions (FEVD). These decompositions tell us the proportional contribution of policy shocks to variations in a given macro variable. The larger the proportion of variation that is attributable to a given policy variable, the more important is that variable in the transmission mechanism of monetary policy. Although the forecast error variance decomposition (FEVD) shows the importance of a policy variable to movements in a macro variable, the direction of these movements can only be observed from the impulse responses. We will be able to see whether an impulse in a policy variable leads to a fall or a rise in the macro variable. Again this gives us a good idea of the transmission mechanism because we can see whether a given policy action has a negative or positive impact on target variables.

4.1. Forecast error variance decompositions (FEVD)

We show in Tables 1 and 2 the results for the contributions of policy variable innovations to price and output decompositions for the four mechanisms estimated in Equations 12 to 14. The value in each cell is the forecast error variance decomposition contribution of the innovations in the policy variable in that column to the variations in the macro variable in the corresponding row. For example, reading the first cell in Table 1, broad money (M_2) contributes 2% to variations in output in the first quarter while narrow money (M_1) and the Treasury Bill rate contribute 0% and 3% respectively.

From Table 1, we notice that the contributions of innovations in most policy variables to changes in prices and output during the pre-reform period are quite small. During the first quarter, movements in prices are explained by own shocks.

Thereafter, the currency ratio (CC/M_2) and the credit to the private sector (CPS) become important. Currency ratio innovations explain just over 14% of price variations after the first quarter of the first year and 30% after second quarter of the third year while credit to the private sector explains 6% in the first quarter of the first year and 23% in the second quarter of the third years.

Table 1. Output and price variance decompositions - pre-reform period.

Horizon	Mech[1] 1 M_2	Mech[1] 1 M_1	Mech[1] 1 TBR	Mech[2] 2 CCr	Mech[2] 2 M_2	Mech[2] 2 TBR	Mech[3] 3 M_2	Mech[3] 3 ER	Mech[4] 4 M_2	Mech[4] 4 LR	Mech[4] 4 CPS
Rgdp 1	2	0	3	6	0	3	0	1	0	1	8
2	5	4	9	7	1	9	1	0	1	1	8
3	5	5	12	8	2	14	2	1	2	1	7
4	5	6	13	8	2	17	2	1	2	1	6
5	5	6	13	8	3	19	2	2	1	1	5
6	5	6	13	8	3	19	2	3	1	2	5
7	5	6	13	8	3	20	2	4	1	2	4
8	5	6	12	8	4	19	1	5	1	2	4
9	5	9	12	8	3	19	1	6	1	2	4
10	5	6	12	7	3	18	1	7	1	2	4
CPI 1	2	10	0	14	1	0	2	0	2	1	6
2	3	6	0	11	3	1	2	1	2	3	7
3	2	4	0	10	3	1	3	1	2	4	12
4	2	3	0	11	3	1	4	1	2	5	16
5	2	3	0	15	3	1	4	1	1	5	20
6	2	2	0	19	3	1	4	2	1	4	22
7	2	2	0	22	3	1	4	3	1	4	23
8	2	2	0	25	4	1	4	4	1	4	23
9	2	2	0	28	4	1	4	5	1	5	23
10	2	2	0	30	4	2	4	5	1	5	23

Since the data is quarterly, each step is equivalent to one quarter. In the pre-reform period, the exchange rate Is ordered before money supply since during this period the exchange rate was fixed and money supply adjusted to maintain the level of the exchange rate.

The figure in each cell is the variance decomposition of output (rGDP) and price (CPI) attributed to innovations in the policy variable in each column.

[1] Mechanism 1 (output (rGDP), price (CPI), broad money supply (M2), narrow money supply (M1), Treasury Bill rate (TBR)).

[2] Mechanism 2 (output (rGDP), price (CPI), broad money supply (M2), liquidity ratio (ccr), Treasury bill rate (TBR)).

[3] Mechanism 3 (output (rGDP), price (CPI), broad money supply (M2), exchange rate (er)).

[4] Mechanism 4 (output (rGDP), price (CPI), broad money supply (M2), lending rate (LR), credit to private sector (cps)).

Table 2. Output and price variance decompositions - post reform period.

Horizon	Mech[1] 1 M_2	Mech[1] 1 M_1	Mech[1] 1 TBR	Mech[2] 2 CCr	Mech[2] 2 M_2	Mech[2] 2 TBR	Mech[3] 3 M_2	Mech[3] 3 ER	Mech[4] 4 M_2	Mech[4] 4 LR	Mech[4] 4 CPS
Rgdp1	1	2	1	4	3	3	0	0	0	1	0
2	9	10	0	16	13	2	13	4	6	1	7
3	23	18	1	19	26	3	19	7	8	1	9
4	31	25	1	20	33	5	27	9	11	2	12
5	37	33	1	19	42	8	33	12	14	3	15
6	41	39	1	19	47	12	37	15	17	5	18
7	46	45	1	19	52	15	40	17	21	7	21
8	49	50	1	21	55	18	43	20	24	8	23
9	52	52	1	24	58	20	45	23	26	10	26
10	53	54	2	27	61	22	46	25	2 9	11	27
CPI 1	0	1	2	0	0	2	1	1	0	8	3
2	4	1	13	15	1	7	1	1	1	18	11
3	3	2	13	15	3	9	3	1	3	22	14
4	5	2	12	14	6	10	5	2	6	24	16
5	6	2	12	15	8	11	8	2	8	25	18
6	7	2	12	15	9	11	11	2	11	25	18
7	6	2	13	15	10	11	12	3	13	25	18
8	6	3	13	15	11	11	15	3	15	26	18
9	7	4	13	14	11	11	16	4	16	26	17
10	8	6	13	13	11	11	17	4	18	27	17

The figure in each cell is the variance decomposition of output (rGDP) and price (CPI) attributed to innovations in the policy variable in each column.

[1] Mechanism 1 (output (rGDP), price (CPI), broad money supply (M2), narrow money supply (M1), Treasury Bill rate (TBR)).

[2] Mechanisms 2 (output (rGDP), price (CPI), broad money supply (M2), liquidity ratio (CCr), Treasury bill rate (TBR)).

[3] Mechanisms 3(output (rGDP), price (CPI), broad money supply (M2), and exchange rate (er)).

4 Mechanisms 4 (output (rGDP), price (CPI), broad money supply (M2), lending rate (LR), and credit to private sector (cps)).

Monetary aggregates (M_1 and M_2), exchange rate and Treasury Bill rate (TBR) shocks were not important for price changes during the pre-reform period. In fact, TBR contributed 0% (mechanism 1) to price variations throughout the periods.

Innovations to Treasury Bill rate explain relatively large amounts of the variations in output in mechanism 1 and 2. Before the reforms, Treasury Bill rates were important for movements in output but this changes after the reforms. Treasury Bill rates explain large amounts of variations in output in the pre-reform period. Total bank lending becomes more important in output changes after the reforms, although the changes are not as marked as in the other variables. The explanation to this is found in government's withdrawal of her involvement in economic activity and the removal of various controls, which has motivated private sector participation in economic activities. This has increased the importance of credit in output growths.

Table 2 shows price and output decompositions for the post-reform period. During this period, innovations to most policy variables make large contributions to movements in prices and output. The two monetary variables, M_1 and M_2 become more important after the reforms, contributing more to output developments than to price. In mechanism 1 (the base channel), M_2 explains 8% of price variations in quarter 2 of year three and when liquidity ratio is included, M_2 explains only 11% of movements in prices in the same period.

In mechanism 3, Table 2, the exchange rate explains between 1% and 4% of price variations in the whole period. In this mechanism, we notice that while the exchange rate explains small variations in prices, M_2 explains more variations than the exchange rate. Innovations to the exchange rate explain relatively large amounts of the variations in output in mechanism 3 after the reforms. This reveals the significance of exchange rate in an economy, particularly when it is deregulated.

During the post-reform period, output variations are due to innovations in most of the variables except TBR and the lending rate. Monetary aggregates together account for 56% of the developments in output in the fourth quarter of the first year in mechanism 1 (the interest rate channel). The exchange rate becomes important for long run output developments during this period explaining 25% of the variations in the 2nd quarter of the 3rd year. In mechanism 4 (the credit channel), lending becomes important for long-run output developments during this period explaining between 0% in the first quarter of the first year and 27% in the second quarter of the third year.

4.2. Impulse response functions

Impulse response analysis is a device to display the dynamics of the variables tracing out the reaction of each variable to a particular shock at time t. According to Figure 1 (in the pre-reform period), a positive monetary aggregate (M_2) shock affects real gross domestic product (rGDP) only in the short run as real GDP increases significantly within the first two periods. These results of the impulse responses of M_2 shock are consistent with findings in other African countries (Simatele, 2003). The impulse responses show that there is no long-run impact of M_2 shocks on real GDP. In the post reform period, we find that monetary aggregate (M_1 and M_2) have no effect on real GDP in the long run. This result is puzzled since an increase in money supply is expected to increase output.

In the short run, Treasury Bill rate shock has no effect on real GDP in the pre-reform period. It is not surprising to have this result since the Federal government, through the Central Bank of Nigeria, influences the economy directly by varying interest rates. The Treasury Bill rate then was not attractiveness to the investors and this has negative impact on economic growth.

In Figure 1 and 2, M_2 shock apparently raises inflation in the long run significantly in the pre and post reform periods, which is consistent with economic expectations. It appears that monetary aggregate (M_2) shocks are crucial factors in explaining inflation in the long run, as inflation rises consistently.

Apparently, increased money supply translates into higher transaction and precautionary demand for money and goods and services, which cannot be met due to the decrease in productivity in the short/long run. The consequence, therefore, is inflation. According to Appendix 1, a positive exchange rate shock affects inflation in the long run as inflation rises significantly. This it to be expected since prices like exchange rates affect demand faster than supply, a positive shock to the exchange rate would lead to an increase in output whose effect may then wane as supply is later affected by increased production costs (Simatele, 2003).

4.3. Impulse response

It is also discovered that exchange rate shocks have no effect (in the pre-reform period) and negative effect (in the post reform period) on output (real GDP) in the short run. The behaviour in output can be explained by the nature of the Nigerian economy and the way it has changed since the reforms. The country was quite dependent on the external sector's revenue to finance both consumption and production. Crude oil exports were the main source of revenues for government expenditure. Since a lot of socio-economic goods and services were supplied by the government, shocks to the exchange rate affected revenue and hence consumption significantly. The exchange rate also affected production through the cost of imported inputs. An increase in the exchange rate would, therefore, increase the cost of production and hence have a negative effect on output.

The findings in this study differ from other studies in Africa by Mwansa (1998) and Anti-Ego (2000). Mwansa and Anti-Ego's results, on the role of exchange rates for prices, are similar. While they found that the exchange rate was more important for price movements than money supply, this study shows that none was important in the post-reform period

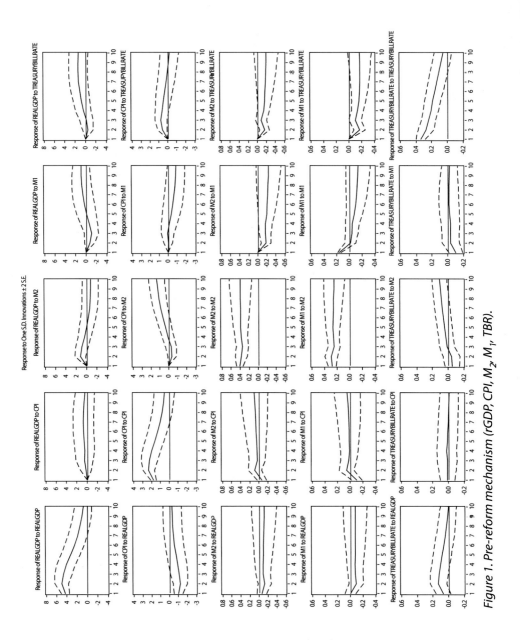

Figure 1. Pre-reform mechanism (rGDP, CPI, M_2, M_1, TBR).

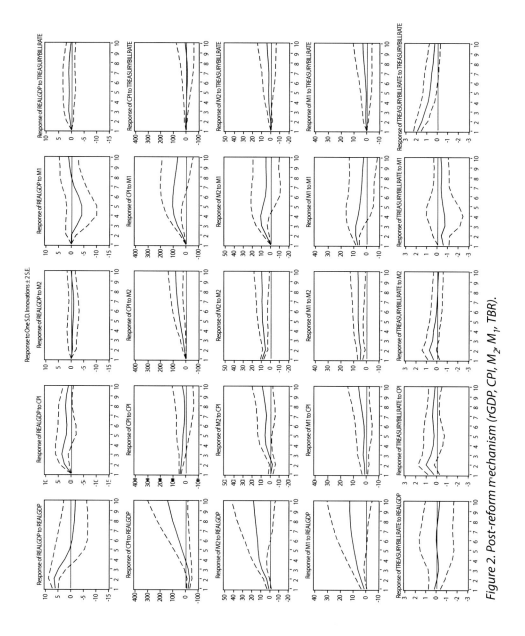

Figure 2. Post-reform mechanism (rGDP, CPI, M₂ M₁, TBR).

in Nigeria. Anti-Ego found an important role for the Treasury Bill rate in both price and output movements and discovered that base money impact lags to prices were significantly longer than those of the Treasury Bill rate. In line with his results, we find that the Treasury Bill rate was important for output variations in the pre-and post reforms period. Our results on the price movements are identical. Like Anti-Ego (2000), we find significant importance of the Treasury Bill rate for prices in the post reform period.

5. Summary and conclusions

The paper analyses monetary policy transmission mechanism in Nigeria. Vector auto-regressive model is estimated for the pre-reform and post-reform periods. Forecast error variance decompositions and impulse response functions are examined to see whether or not there are any observed changes in the monetary transmission mechanism after the reforms. Four systems are estimated in each period using alternate variables as measures of monetary policy shocks. When we compare the results of the two estimation periods, we observe that both the responsiveness of prices and output to policy shocks and the magnitude of their forecast error variance decompositions, explained by these variables, have increased since the reforms.

The forecast error variances decompositions show that more of the variability in prices and output are explained by shocks to money aggregates and the exchange rate after the reforms than before. When both M_2 and the exchange rate are put in the system, M_2 explains more of the movements in both prices and output (more at shorter horizons for prices). The study gives evidence for bank-lending channel both before and after the reforms. Of the mechanisms estimated, the exchange rate and lending mechanisms seem to be the most important mechanisms for transmission of policy shocks to both prices and output during the post-reform period.

The overall conclusions are as follows. Firstly, the potency of monetary policy in Nigeria has increased since the reforms. Secondly, the exchange rate seems to be a better indicator of the Central Bank's policy stance than the Treasury Bill rate in the post reform period. The importance of the exchange rate suggests a good policy option for monetary targeting. Lastly, though monetary aggregates are important for price movement in Nigeria, the exchange rate seems to be more significant in explaining movements in price. This underscores the importance of a stable exchange rate. However, foreign exchange intervention does not seem to provide the complete solution. A possible option or complement is exchange rate targeting.

Acknowledgements

I am grateful to Professor Siyanbola Tomori of the Department of Economics, University of Lagos, Nigeria, for his useful comments.

References

Adrangi, B. and M. Allender, 1998. Budget deficits and stock prices: international evidence. Journal of Economics 22: 57- 66.

Anti-Ego, 2000. Setting monetary policy instruments in Uganda. In: Monetary policy frameworks in a global context. L. Mahadeva and G. Sterne (eds.).

Bernanke, B.S. and A.S. Blinder, 1992. The federal funds rate and the channels of monetary transmission. American Economic Review 82: 901-921.

Carpenter, S.B., 1996. Informal credit markets and the transmission of monetary policy: evidence from South Korea. Princeton University working paper, November 1996.

Cecchetti, S.G., 1995. Distinguishing theories of the monetary transmission mechanism. Federal Reserve Bank of St. Louis Review 77: 83-97.

Christiano, L.J., M. Eichenbaum and C. Evans, 1994. Identification and effects of monetary policy shocks. Federal Reserve Bank of Chicago, working paper (94-7).

Christiano, L.J., M. Eichenbaum and C. Evans, 1996. The effects of monetary policy shocks: evidence from the flow of funds. The Review of Economics an Statistics 78: 16-34.

Dale, S. and A.G. Haldan, 1995. Interest rates and the channels of monetary transmission: some sectoral estimates. European Economic Review 39: 1611-1626.

Eichenbaum, M., 1992. Comments: interpreting the macroeconomic time series facts: the effects of monetary policy by Christopher Sims. European Economic Review 36: 1001-1011.

Fair R.C. and R.J. Schiller, 1990. Comparing information in forecasts from econometric models. The American Economic Review 80: 375-389.

Funke, M., 1990. Assessing the forecasting accuracy of monthly vector autoregressive models: the case of five OECD countries. International Journal of Forecasting 6: 363-378.

Gertler, M. and S. Gilchrist, 1994. Monetary policy, business cycles, and the behavior of small manufacturing firms. Quarterly Journal of Economics: 309-340.

Gertler, M. and S. Gilchrist, 1993. The role of credit market imperfections in the monetary transmission mechanism: arguments and evidence. Scandinavian Journal of Economics 95: 43-64.

Giovanni, A., 1993. Financial and development: issues and experience. New York: Cambridge University Press.

Gordon, D.B. and E.M. Leeper, 1994. The dynamic impacts of monetary policy: an exercise in tentative identification. Journal of Political Economy 102, 1228-1247.

Judge, G.G., et al., 1985. The theory and practice of econometrics. New York: John Wiley, 2nd ed.

Kashyap, A.K., J.C. Stein and D.W. Wilcox, 1993. Monetary policy and credit conditions: evidence from the composition of external finance. American Economic Review 83: 78-98.

Lutkepohl, H., 1985. Comparison of criteria for estimating the order of a vector autoregressive process. Journal of Time Series Analysis 6, 35-52.

Miron, J.A., C.D. Romer and D.N. Weil, 1995. Historical perspectives on the monetary transmission mechanism. National Bureau of Economic Research Working Paper No. 4326.

Mwansa, L., 1998. Determinants of inflation in Zambia. Ph.D. thesis, University of Gothenburg, Gothenburg.

Nannyonjo, J., 2001. Monetary policy and credit under market imperfections. Ph.D. Thesis, University of Gothenburg, Gothenburg.

Palm, F., 1983. Structural econometric modelling and time series analysis. In: A. Zellner (ed.), Applied time series analysis of economic data, Economic Research Report ER-5 (US Department of Commerce, Washington, DC), pp. 199-233.

Rossiter, R.D., 1995. Monetary policy indicators after deregulation. The Quarterly Review of Economics and Finance 35: 207-223.

Simatele, M.C.H., 2003. Financial sector reforms and monetary policy in Zambia. Unpublished PhD Dissertation, Economic Studies, Department Of Economics School of Economics and Commercial Law, Göteborg University.

Sims, C., 1992. Interpreting the time series facts: the effects of monetary policy financial repression and economic growth. European Economic Review 36.

Strongin, S., 1995. The identification of monetary policy disturbance: explaining the liquidity puzzle. Journal of Monetary Economics 35: 463-497.

Uchendu, O.A., 1996. The transmission of monetary policy in Nigeria. Central Bank of Nigeria: Economic and Financial Review 34: 606-625.

Walsh, E., 1998. Monetary theory and policy. Massachusetts Institute of Technology, Chapter 1, pp. 9-39.

Zellner A., 1979. Statistical analysis of econometric models. Journal of the American Statistical Association 74: 628-643.

Zellner A. and F. Palm, 1974. Time series analysis and simultaneous equation econometric models. Journal of Econometrics 2: 17-54.

Index of subjects

Index of persons

Printed in the United States
by Baker & Taylor Publisher Services